T0215729

Apple macOS and iOS System Administration

Integrating and Supporting iPhones, iPads, and MacBooks

Drew Smith

Apress®

Apple macOS and iOS System Administration: Integrating and Supporting iPhones, iPads, and MacBooks

Drew Smith
Cincinnati, OH, USA

ISBN-13 (pbk): 978-1-4842-5819-4   ISBN-13 (electronic): 978-1-4842-5820-0
https://doi.org/10.1007/978-1-4842-5820-0

Managing Director, Apress Media LLC: Welmoed Spahr
Acquisitions Editor: Aaron Black
Development Editor: James Markham
Coordinating Editor: Jessica Vakili

Distributed to the book trade worldwide by Springer Science+Business Media New York, 233 Spring Street, 6th Floor, New York, NY 10013. Phone 1-800-SPRINGER, fax (201) 348-4505, e-mail orders-ny@springer-sbm.com, or visit www.springeronline.com. Apress Media, LLC is a California LLC and the sole member (owner) is Springer Science + Business Media Finance Inc (SSBM Finance Inc). SSBM Finance Inc is a **Delaware** corporation.

For information on translations, please e-mail rights@apress.com, or visit http://www.apress.com/rights-permissions.

Apress titles may be purchased in bulk for academic, corporate, or promotional use. eBook versions and licenses are also available for most titles. For more information, reference our Print and eBook Bulk Sales web page at http://www.apress.com/bulk-sales.

Any source code or other supplementary material referenced by the author in this book is available to readers on GitHub via the book's product page, located at www.apress.com/978-1-4842-5819-4. For more detailed information, please visit http://www.apress.com/source-code.

Printed on acid-free paper

*This book is dedicated to my mother, Betty,
who has always encouraged me to pursue
my interest in technology and bought our family's
first computer—an Apple.*

Table of Contents

About the Author

Drew Smith has been providing technology support and designing solutions for higher education for over 20 years. He has supported thousands of Macs and tens of thousands of iPads in multisite deployments across the continental United States. In 2012, his team deployed and supported a 1:1 iPad initiative that put over 30,000 devices in the hands of students and educators across 15 states, the largest at the time.

Drew has a passion for Apple products and services. He enjoys sharing best practices with others to help them simplify and streamline the management of devices in multi-platform environments. When he is not busy writing technical documentation, he enjoys watching films, playing video games, writing code, and spending time with his wife, Lindsey, and children, Christian and Alyssa.

About the Technical Reviewer

Charles Cruz is a mobile application developer for iOS and Android platforms. He graduated from Stanford University with BS and MS degrees in engineering. He lives in Southern California and runs an antique mall business with his wife. Charles enjoys music, photography, and backpacking. He can be reached at codingandpicking@gmail.com.

CHAPTER 1

Introduction to Apple Platforms

Introduction and Overview

Back in the mid- to late 1990s, Apple Computer's products and the Macintosh platform specifically were in the low single digits of personal computer market share. These systems were typically found only in small graphic design departments, creative firms, or schools. Driven by the excitement of the Internet, Information Technology departments were tasked with building and maintaining large homogeneous network computing environments that invariably used solutions developed by Microsoft. If you were a Mac technician, your skills were not in high demand, and I used to joke that being able to repair an Apple-branded PC was becoming a *dark art*.

Today, Apple's platforms have seen a major resurgence, thanks to the iPhone's "halo effect" of driving more customers to iPads and Apple Watches and back to the Mac. Due to the rise of cloud computing, web applications, mobile devices, and "bring your own device" (BYOD) policies, it is not uncommon to find many companies allowing Apple products onto corporate networks. Users expect that their Macs and iPads will integrate seamlessly with others that use Microsoft or Google platforms. This has presented some unique challenges for corporate

© Drew Smith 2020
D. Smith, *Apple macOS and iOS System Administration*,
https://doi.org/10.1007/978-1-4842-5820-0_1

Information Technology departments that must still keep their networks secure and costs in line with budget expectations while also supporting cross-platform computing environments.

If you are reading this book, then you are likely one of the many technology professionals who have been tasked with supporting some number of Apple devices and need a crash course in Mac and/or iOS system administration. In this book, you will find a comprehensive overview of both *iOS* (including iPadOS) and *Macintosh Operating System* (*macOS*), strategies for managing Apple devices using Mobile Device Management (MDM), useful how-to guides for integrating with popular Microsoft solutions, and helpful tips for automating some of the more rigorous tasks of staging, deploying, or upgrading Apple hardware and software.

A Brief History of Apple Platforms

It is important to understand some of the history surrounding Apple's current hardware and OS platforms as you may come into contact with some of these older products in your day-to-day interactions within the Apple ecosystem.

The *Macintosh* is Apple's brand of desktop and laptop personal computers. The first Mac was shipped in 1984 and has been an iconic product for nearly 40 years. The Mac product line includes desktops like the *iMac, Mac mini,* and the *Mac Pro* as well as laptops like the *MacBook Pro* and *MacBook Air.*

The Mac's internal hardware has changed significantly over the years. Initially based on the *Motorola 68k* processor architecture in the 1980s, it moved to the *IBM PowerPC* architecture in the 1990s and finally moved to the *Intel* architecture in the early 2000s. Today, all Macintosh systems are based on the same Intel processor specification as Windows-based PCs. Using *Boot Camp* or virtualization solutions, you can run *Microsoft's Windows 10* alongside *macOS* on any of Apple's current Mac hardware.

The *Macintosh Operating System* (*macOS*) has also evolved since the 1980s. Mac OS versions **1.0–9.2** are now called Mac OS "Classic" and were originally written for Motorola and IBM architectures. Apple phased out support for this operating system and associated software in the early 2000s. In 1996, Apple purchased a small software company called *NeXT*, bringing business legend and Apple co-founder **Steve Jobs** back to the company. NeXT had an operating system based on Unix, called *NeXTSTEP*, that became the foundation for all of Apple's future software platforms from *macOS* to *iOS* and beyond.

The next phase of Apple's Mac operating system was called *Mac OS X* (**10**). Each version of Mac OS X from **10.0** to **10.8** was named after a species of cats: *Snow Leopard* (**10.6**), *Lion* (**10.7**), *Mountain Lion* (**10.8**), and so on. Eventually, Apple ran out of cats and began naming their operating systems after parts of California including *Mavericks* (**10.9**), *Yosemite* (**10.10**), *El Capitan* (**10.11**), *Sierra* (**10.12**), *High Sierra* (**10.13**), *Mojave* (**10.14**), and most recently *Catalina* (**10.15**).

Around the same time that Apple was changing from cats to California code names, they announced at *WWDC 2014* that they were going to be bringing more features from iOS to the Mac. This became a larger paradigm shift as Apple encouraged system administrators to use *Mobile Device Management* (MDM) tools to manage macOS-based computers in a similar way that they managed mobile devices running *iOS*. The majority of this book will focus on these newer versions of *macOS* and the modern management concepts that Apple is asking administrators to embrace for the Mac platform.

While the Macintosh was the most iconic brand from Apple for many years, its most popular product (based on market share) is undoubtedly the *iPhone*. Released in 2007, the iPhone was a completely reimagined cell phone that used a *multi-touch* touchscreen and a graphical user interface that was based on the same technology used in Mac OS X. In 2010, Apple released the *iPad* tablet, which also featured a touchscreen display and ran the same operating system as the *iPhone*. Renamed *iOS*, the mobile operating system that started on the iPhone was now Apple's second major consumer operating system and its most popular.

With the release of the newest *iPhone* product line in the summer of 2019, Apple is now on version **13** of the *iOS*. Apple has also designated a special version of iOS 13 for the iPad, now called *iPadOS*. I will explain the differences and optimizations found in *iPadOS* over standard *iOS* throughout the book.

Introduction to macOS

This book focuses on the technologies found in the most recent versions of *macOS*, specifically those in *Sierra* (10.12), *High Sierra* (10.13), *Mojave* (10.14), and *Catalina* (10.15). These are the versions that most technicians will encounter because at least one of these will support Mac hardware manufactured as early as 2009. Figure 1-1 provides a quick overview of the differences between these operating systems.

macOS	Version	Key Features
macOS Sierra	10.12	• Enhanced the *Continuity* feature between iOS and macOS so you can copy and paste between devices. • Added Siri support to macOS. • Integrated iCloud Drive to sync and store Documents and Desktop folders in iCloud.
macOS High Sierra	10.13	• Introduced the APFS file system to macOS as an option. • Includes performance enhancements and provided compatibility all the way back to 2009 MacBooks. This is likely the newest macOS most of the older Macs still in use today should be running. • Added new privacy and security features including Safari privacy protection and Gatekeeper options for drivers.
macOS Mojave	10.14	• System-wide Dark Mode. • UI enhancements like stackable desktop folders and new Finder views. • *Continuity* camera that allows your iOS device camera to act as a camera for your Mac. • Additional privacy and security features like blocking your mic and camera unless a user specifically allows it.
macOS Catalina	10.15	• Integrates *Project Catalyst* which allows iPad apps to be modified to run as native macOS apps by developers. • Replacement of *bash* with *zsh* as the default shell in Terminal. • Enables an iPad to function as a second display in *Sidecar* mode. • Adds *ScreenTime* to macOS to help users manage their web browsing, social media, etc while on their Mac.

Figure 1-1. *The four most recent versions of macOS as of this publication*

Hardware Compatibility

It is very important to understand which of Apple's hardware can support these operating systems. Many system administrators will want to standardize on a common OS version across their entire Mac fleet. Please note that while this is a worthy goal, depending on the mix of hardware you are supporting, you may need to manage across a couple of different versions of *macOS*. To make things a little more difficult, as Apple releases new hardware, they do not typically allow older versions of *macOS* to run on the newest Macs. For example, a brand-new 2019 *Mac Pro* will **not** run *macOS High Sierra*. In this case, you would need to also support *Catalina*, even if every other Mac in your organization is still on *High Sierra*.

Apple makes available a Knowledge Base (KB) article that you can use to check *macOS* compatibility against their various hardware models (https://support.apple.com/en-us/HT201686).

Apple will reference the various Macintosh hardware models by their official name, year of manufacture, and/or model identifier. Since they routinely name their products as simply *Mac Pro* or *iMac*, it can often be difficult to identify an exact model based on the name or looks alone. This is where **About This Mac** and **System Report** can be helpful, as shown in Figures 1-2 and 1-3.

Figure 1-2. *Selecting About This Mac from the Apple menu*

Figure 1-3. *The About This Mac dialog box and System Report button*

You can access **About This Mac** by selecting the option under the **Apple** menu. This will display the most basic information about your Mac's hardware including which version of macOS you are running, the official name of the hardware model, the amount of RAM, the processor speed, the graphics card, and the serial number. If you need more in-depth information, you can click the **System Report** button to view more extensive hardware information.

The **System Report** is featured in Figure 1-4. In older versions of macOS, this is called the *System Profiler,* and it can be extremely handy when diagnosing peripheral and connectivity issues. **Model Identifier** is the most specific way to identify a Mac as it includes the major version number and revision number separated by a comma.

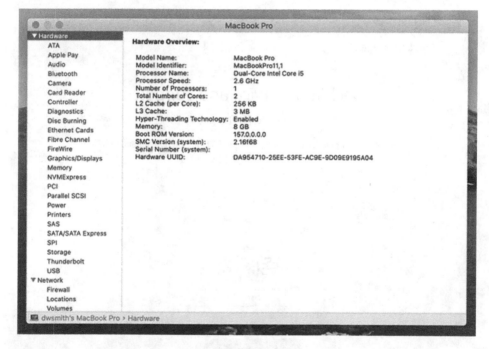

Figure 1-4. *System Report details all of the hardware components*

Windows Administrator Pro Tip   If you are an experienced *Windows* system administrator, then you are familiar with **Device Manager**. *System Report* is very similar in that it shows all of the connected peripherals, onboard components, network information, and more.

In some cases, you may be working with a Mac that cannot boot an operating system or whose hardware has failed, and you are trying to determine if it is worth repairing or not. In both of these cases, it may be difficult to ascertain what specific model you are working with. Apple provides a web site where you can look up the specific model information if you know the serial number. This site also provides you with the warranty and AppleCare coverage status for a given computer, as shown in Figures 1-5 and 1-6 (`https://checkcoverage.apple.com/us/en/`).

Figure 1-5. *Enter your serial number and CAPTCHA code*

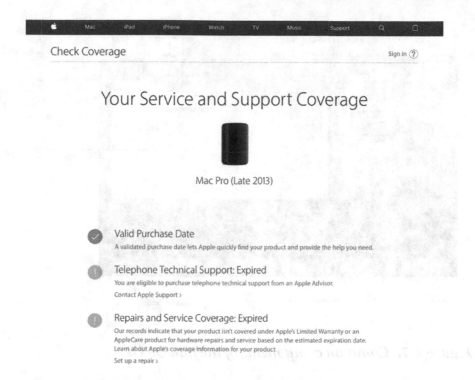

Figure 1-6. *Model and warranty information*

Pro Tip This site will also work with other Apple hardware including iPhones, iPads, and more.

---

macOS User Interface

If you are completely new to macOS, Figures 1-7 and 1-8 and their accompanying descriptions will aid you in quickly navigating the operating system to perform many of the common tasks used throughout this book.

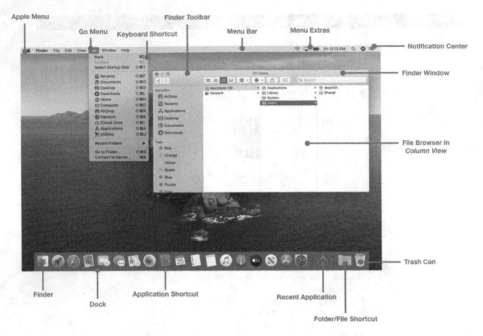

Figure 1-7. *Common components of the macOS UI*

- **Apple Menu:** This is the catch-all menu for things like logging out, restarting, accessing *System Preferences*, and recent items.

- **Menu Bar:** The menu bar in macOS sits above all applications and dynamically changes depending on which application is in the foreground. The foreground application will have its name displayed in a **bold typeface** to the right of the *Apple menu*.

- **Finder:** The *macOS* GUI shell enabling common operating system functions and the file browser.

- **Go Menu:** One of the more useful menus in the *Finder*. It includes shortcuts to many common local and network resources. Holding down the **option** key will provide access to the hidden user **Library** directory which is often used in client administration and troubleshooting.

- **Keyboard Shortcut:** Whenever available, keyboard shortcuts are displayed next to the menu item.

- **Finder Toolbar:** Every *Finder* window includes the name of the current directory, customizable shortcut buttons, and the traffic light–inspired *close, minimize,* and *maximize* buttons. The green button puts the foreground application into full-screen mode in more recent versions of the OS.

- **Menu Extras:** Various applications and system utilities provide these icons for quick access to common features such as *VPN, Wi-Fi,* and *volume control.* Some of these can be rearranged or removed by holding down the **command** key and clicking and dragging the icon to move it or drag it off the menu.

- **Notification Center:** Clicking this icon will slide out a shelf of various *widgets* that can be pinned here for quick access. Common widgets include Calculator, Weather, and *Apple Music.* Notifications from other applications such as Mail or Messages will also appear here. You can also toggle *Do Not Disturb* on/off, and *Night Shift* controls are also available to help limit exposure to blue light on Macs that support this feature.

- **Dock:** The Dock contains all of the running applications, application shortcuts, minimized windows, and the *Trash Can.* It provides quick and easy access to switch between applications and files when multitasking. The Dock can be relocated, auto-hidden, or resized using the *Dock System Preference*.

- **Application Shortcut:** A symbolic link to the actual application that resides in the /**Applications** folder. These shortcuts provide quick access to applications that are used most often. Drag an icon on or off the Dock to add or remove it.

- **Recent Applications:** On by default in *macOS Catalina*, the Dock has a section devoted to storing the most recently used applications.

- **Folder/File Shortcut:** Like application shortcuts, these are symbolic links to files or folders that are stored elsewhere on your hard drive. Use this when you need quick access to commonly used documents. Folders can be viewed as a stack, a grid, or a menu.

- **Trash Can:** Dragging files or folders into the *Trash Can* will prepare them for deletion. You can empty the trash using the command under the Apple menu or ***control-clicking (holding the control key and clicking)*** or ***right-clicking*** the Trash Can and selecting **Empty Trash**.

- **File Browser:** The *Finder* has three views—**Icon**, **List**, and **Column** views. These views help you navigate folders and files on your hard disk or other connected media.

Windows Administrator Pro Tip   Windows system administrators who are just becoming familiar with macOS may benefit from some of these interchangeable concepts.

- **Control Panel:** In *macOS,* this is called *System Preferences* and is found under the *Apple menu.*

- **Right-Click:** You can use the *mouse* and/or *Trackpad System Preference* to enable *secondary-click.* If you are using a one-button mouse, you can also hold the **control** key on the keyboard and click to mimic the right-click functionality. Figure 1-8 provides more information on the contextual menu options in the *Finder.*

- **Control Key:** In macOS, the common **control** key commands like *Ctrl+V* for paste and *Ctrl+C* for copy will work but you must use the ***command*** key, which is the one to the left of the spacebar on the keyboard. Less often used but also interchangeable between Mac and Windows are the **option** and **alt** keys.

- **Task Manager:** If you have a misbehaving application and need to *end this task*—in *macOS* this is called **Force Quit**. You can find this in the **Apple menu** or by pressing the keyboard combination of **command+option+escape**. This will bring up a list of currently running applications, and you can select one and force it to quit.

- **Windows Explorer:** In macOS this would be the *Finder.* I personally prefer *Column view* or *List view* if you are used to *Windows Explorer* as those are also a hierarchical way to drill down into the directory structure.

- **Taskbar:** In *macOS* the Taskbar is probably most similar to the Dock. One trick that I have used in the past is to make a folder shortcut to the ***/Applications***

folder in the Dock and choose to display it as a **List**.
That does a nice job of mimicking the *Start menu* for
quickly browsing all of your applications.

- **Properties:** In *macOS*, this is called *Get Info*. Nearly
everything that you would find in the *Properties* dialog
box in Windows is displayed when you select any file or
folder and choose **Get Info** from the **File** menu or the
contextual menu.

- **Recycle Bin:** The *Trash Can* in *macOS*. It functions
nearly identically.

- **Shortcut:** Symbolic links to files and applications in
macOS are typically referred to as an *alias*.

- **Map Network Drive:** Found under the **Go** menu, you
can select ***Connect to Server,*** and that will allow you to
browse the network for shared resources or enter a path
to a specific resource. One thing to note in *macOS* is
the *back-slash* (\) should be substituted with a *forward-
slash* (/) when entering a full path.

- **Run:** Use the *Spotlight button* in the **Menu Extras**
area of the *macOS* menu bar and start typing to search
files as well as applications to launch based on a few
keystrokes.

- **Command Prompt:** To open the command line
interface on *macOS*, click the **Go** menu in the *Finder*
and choose **Utilities** and then launch the Terminal
application.

- **Print Screen:** Creating a quick screenshot in *macOS*
can be done by using the following keyboard
combination: **command+shift+3**.

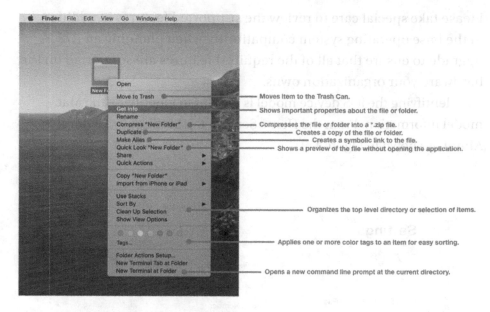

Figure 1-8. *The macOS fully supports right-click functionality*

Introduction to iOS

Like macOS, there are many versions of *iOS*, and a new one is released every year. This book is going to focus primarily on iOS 13. Apple also maintains an *iOS* compatibility guide for iPhone and iPad for the two most recent operating systems.

These can be found here:

iPhone:

https://support.apple.com/guide/iphone/supported-models-iphe3fa5df43/ios

iPad:

https://support.apple.com/guide/ipad/supported-models-ipad213a25b2/ipados

To prolong the usable life of an iOS device, Apple will often make some features available to only the most recent hardware models.

Please take special care to review the supported features in addition to the base operating system compatibility when planning an *iOS* upgrade to ensure that all of the required features are supported on the hardware your organization owns.

Identifying the iOS device model is similar to identifying the Mac model information. From the Home Screen, tap **Settings ➤ General ➤ About** as shown in Figure 1-9.

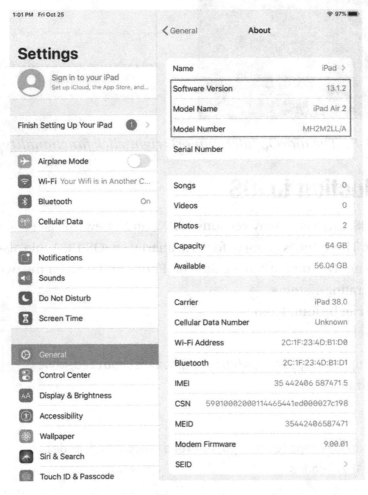

Figure 1-9. *The About screen on an iOS device*

iOS User Interface

If you are completely new to *iOS*, Figures 1-10 and 1-11 will aid you in quickly navigating the operating system to perform many of the common tasks used in this book.

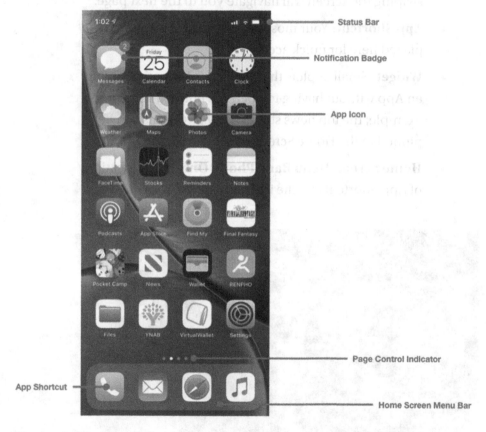

Figure 1-10. The iPhone Home Screen

- **Status Bar:** The area at the top of the iOS device that includes the clock and network indicator.

- **Notification Badge:** The badge is a red circle with a number indicating that the App needs attention.

- **App Icon:** Tapping the App icon will launch that application or wake it from background mode.

- **Page Control Indicator:** This indicates which navigation page you are on as you swipe from one screen to another. If you have multiple pages of icons, swiping the screen will navigate you to the next page.

- **App Shortcut:** Your most commonly used Apps can be placed here for quick access.

- **Widget:** Small applets that provide information about an App without having to open the entire thing, for example, the top news stories. In *iPadOS* this can be pinned to the Home Screen as seen in Figure 1-11.

- **Home Screen Menu Bar (iPhone Only):** The location of App Shortcuts on the iPhone.

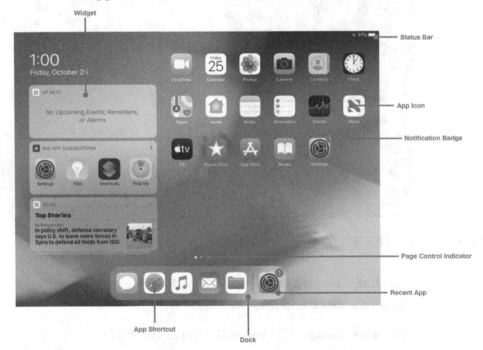

Figure 1-11. The iPadOS Home Screen

- **Dock (*iPadOS* Only):** The location of App Shortcuts as well as recent applications and files; it provides more of a *macOS* look and feel on the *iPad*.

- **Recent Applications (*iPadOS* Only):** Like in *macOS*, the *iPad* can now display the most recently used applications in the Dock.

Summary

Apple's platforms have continued to change and evolve over the past several decades. Major changes in hardware architecture, operating system software, and device form factors have challenged our notion of what a computer should be. This book focuses primarily on the more recent *macOS* and *iOS* including *macOS Catalina*, *iOS 13*, and *iPadOS*.

Navigating these operating systems could be familiar but also intimidating to users of other systems. If you are new to Apple's platforms, I recommend spending some time exploring both *iOS* and *macOS* before going onto the next chapter so that you gain a working knowledge of how to interact with these platforms from an end-user perspective.

CHAPTER 2

macOS Client Administration

In this chapter, we will explore the administration of a single Mac. Topics will include managing local user accounts, exploring the file structure of *macOS*, learning about the command line interface, and performing some basic hardware troubleshooting.

Mac Hardware Troubleshooting

Unlike most PC hardware manufacturers, Apple has always been quite particular about who they *allow* to repair their hardware. They enforce a comprehensive *Authorized Repair Center* process for third-party companies wishing to do repairs in addition to offering hardware repair services through their own *Apple Retail Stores*. That being said, there are limitations to how many hardware repairs most technicians can safely do themselves without voiding their warranties. As a Mac technician, it is important to know a few basic hardware troubleshooting techniques to try before setting up a *Genius Bar* appointment and hauling your Mac into the local *Apple Retail Store*.

© Drew Smith 2020
D. Smith, *Apple macOS and iOS System Administration*,
https://doi.org/10.1007/978-1-4842-5820-0_2

Nonvolatile Random-Access Memory (NVRAM)

Nonvolatile Random-Access Memory (NVRAM), or *Parameter RAM*
(PRAM) as it is sometimes referred to by long-time Mac users, is basically
a small amount of memory on the logic board that stores information that
doesn't get erased when the computer powers down. It stores settings for
volume levels, time zone, the display resolution, and your startup disk.
While it does not happen very often, sometimes this memory can become
corrupt; and by *zapping it* by using a keyboard combination found in
Figure 2-1, it will reset these settings to factory default. This is often the first
step in troubleshooting a misbehaving Mac. It will typically solve issues
related to time zones, slow boot times where it takes a long time before the
Apple logo appears after powering on the Mac, or issues related to audio or
the internal speakers.

Pro Tip   If you are using an *extensible firmware interface (EFI)
password,* as detailed in Chapter 3, it is important to note that
you will not be able to zap the NVRAM until after you remove the
password. Once you have finished clearing the NVRAM, don't forget
to re-enable your password.

The System Management Controller (SMC)

The System Management Controller (SMC) is a component of the
Macintosh Intel hardware architecture. This is unique to Mac hardware,
and besides enforcing the *macOS* end-user license agreement (one
reason that you cannot *easily* run *macOS* on an Intel-based PC from a
manufacturer other than Apple), it also works as a catchall for managing
many of the integrated hardware components. Apple publishes an
exhaustive list on their support web site, but in general, the SMC has some

level of involvement in things ranging from turning the fans on/off to the function of LED lights on the logic board, sound, Bluetooth, sleep/wake, and more.

In the course of troubleshooting a Mac hardware problem, you may need to reset the SMC. Apple recommends waiting to do so unless you have exhausted all other options including a standard restart and zapping the NVRAM. Some of the most common reasons to reset the SMC include having a Mac where the fans are constantly running even when under light processor loads or if your MacBook battery is refusing to charge. It won't solve every problem, but it is definitely worth a try before taking your Mac to a repair center for a potentially expensive diagnostic visit.

In general, the process for resetting the SMC on your Mac is going to be determined by which model you have. There is a different procedure for desktop vs. laptop Macs and laptops with removable batteries vs. those that do not have a removable battery. Most recently with the advent of the *Apple T2 Security chip*, there is yet another different method to reset the SMC of Macs that feature that co-processor onboard. It is recommended that you refer to Apple's support page for instructions on how to reset the SMC of the particular Mac you are troubleshooting.

Apple's KB article about the SMC can be found here:

```
https://support.apple.com/en-us/HT201295
```

Pre-boot Keyboard Combinations

There are a number of keyboard combinations that you should be familiar with when troubleshooting a Mac. Figure 2-1 shows the various pre-boot keyboard shortcuts, many of which can be used to select a startup disk other than the internal hard drive. You can boot into *safe mode*, turn on verbose logging during bootup, enter *recovery mode*, or even turn your Mac into a giant external Thunderbolt hard disk using *Target Disk mode*.

Pro Tip   *Target Disk mode* can be an effective way to troubleshoot a
Mac that refuses to boot from the internal hard disk. By using Target
Disk mode, you can attempt to mount the internal drive to another
Mac and make it appear like a Thunderbolt- or Firewire-connected
external hard drive. If the drive refuses to mount, it may be indicative
of a hardware malfunction. If the drive does mount, but the Mac will
still not boot up from it, you may be able to retrieve data or create
a backup of the drive before erasing it and installing a fresh copy of
macOS.

Keyboard Shortcut	Description	When To Use
option	Invokes **Startup Manager** to select a startup disk and/or login to Wifi before the OS loads.	As soon as you press the power key from a cold boot, hold this down and keep holding until you see the **Startup Manager**.
C or **N**	Skips **Startup Manager** and selects the startup disk. **C** = CD/DVD/USB. **N** = Network/NetBoot.	As soon as you press the power key from a cold boot, hold this down and keep holding until you see the Apple logo.
T	Invokes **Target Disk Mode**. In this mode the Mac doesn't boot from the internal hard disk, but makes the internal disk available via Thunderbolt or Firewire cable to another Mac.	As soon as you press the power key from a cold boot, hold this down and keep holding until you see the **Target Disk Mode** screen. Then connect your Mac to another Mac to mount the disk.
D	Launches **Apple Diagnostics** or **Apple Hardware Test** (depending on model) and will test your hardware and provide you with any information or issues found.	As soon as you press the power key from a cold boot, hold this down and keep holding until you see the **Apple Diagnostics** screen.
shift	Places your Mac into **Safe Mode** which disables 3rd party extensions, fonts, etc.	As soon as you press the power key from a cold boot, hold this down and keep holding until you see the Apple logo.
command + **S**	Places the Mac into **Single User Mode** and into the Unix shell with a command line interface only.	As soon as you press the power key from a cold boot, hold this down and keep holding until you are at the command line.
command + **V**	This will boot your Mac in **Verbose Mode**. Instead of seeing the Apple logo during boot you will get a detailed read-out of the startup process.	As soon as you press the power key from a cold boot, hold this down and keep holding until you start seeing the verbose statements.
command + **R** (+ **option**)	This will boot your Mac into **Recovery Mode** if a local recovery partition exists. Add the *option/alt* key to boot into **Internet Recovery** if connected to a network with Internet access.	As soon as you press the power key from a cold boot, hold this down and keep holding until you see the Apple logo (local recovery) or the spinning globe (Internet recovery).
command + **option** + **P** + **R**	This will **reset** the NVRAM on the **SMC**. In the past this was called "zapping the P RAM".	As soon as you press the power key from a cold boot, hold this down and keep holding through two power-up cycles (you should hear 2 chimes on an older Mac, two faint SMC "buzzes" on a newer Mac). Release.

Figure 2-1. *Keyboard combinations for pre-boot options*

macOS Recovery

On standard installations of *macOS,* Apple provides a hidden partition that holds a limited copy of the operating system and a few applications like *Disk Utility, Terminal,* and a *macOS Installer* package. This area is effectively called *macOS Recovery,* and just like you guessed, it is used to try to revive your Mac if there is an issue with the operating system.

If for some reason your Mac does not have a local Recovery partition, you can also take advantage of the *Internet Recovery* service. Internet Recovery is a cloud-based bootable network volume that Apple hosts. Booting from Internet Recovery requires an active Internet connection and may take quite a bit longer to boot depending on the speed of your connection.

Once you are booted into recovery mode, there are a handful of things you will be able to do including the following:

- Restore from a Time Machine Backup.

- Reinstall or install a fresh copy of *macOS.*

- Browse Apple's support web site via Safari (if you have an active Internet connection).

- Use Disk Utility to perform Disk First Aid or other drive-related tasks.

- Access the Terminal.

- Interact with hardware security settings (covered in detail in Chapter 3).

Disk Utility

While most of these options are self-explanatory, *Disk Utility* includes a number of tools that are particularly useful when in *macOS Recovery* mode. Because we are booted from the Recovery partition and not the

same partition with the full macOS System folder (often referred to as
the *startup disk*), we can run utilities and commands against the startup
volume. While you can access many of these same options from the Disk
Utility application inside **/Applications/Utilities** when you are booted
into your Mac's startup disk, you may run into issues executing them on
the same volume the system is currently running from. This makes *macOS
Recovery*, and in particular Internet Recovery, the best option for working
directly with your Mac's internal hard disk. Figure 2-2 shows the default
view of Disk Utility with some important options identified.

Pro Tip   Be careful when using Disk Utility in *macOS Recovery*
mode. It is very easy to accidentally delete your boot partition or even
the entire internal hard disk. Make sure you have a backup of any
important data before experimenting with Disk Utility on your Mac.

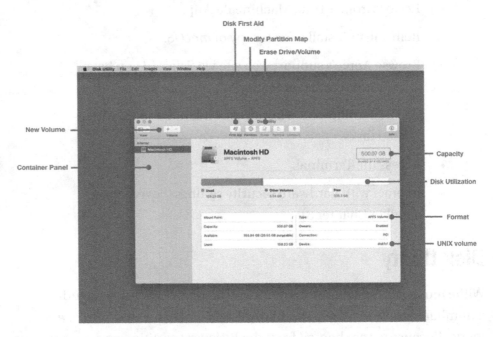

Figure 2-2. *The Disk Utility interface*

- **Container Panel:** A list of volumes, drives, partitions, containers, and mounted disks.

- **New Volume:** Add or remove volumes to or from the selected disk.

- **Disk First Aid:** Opens the *Disk First Aid* sub-utility to check and repair or optimize the hard drive, similar to disk defragmentation in Windows.

- **Modify Partition Map:** Allows you to add or remove partitions to or from a specific disk.

- **Erase Drive/Volume/Partition:** Erases the selected container, drive, partition, or volume.

- **Capacity:** Shows the overall capacity of the selected drive and how many volumes are contained.

- **Disk Utilization:** The composition of the drive including partitions or volumes and how much space is used by each.

- **Format:** The drive's file system format such as **Apple File System** (APFS) or **Hierarchical File System Plus** (HFS+).

- **Unix Volume Descriptor:** The volume description in Unix. Used to reference the drive location when running bash or zsh scripts.

Pro Tip   As Apple has continued to abstract away the various removable disks in the *macOS* GUI, you may not see mounted volumes appearing on the Desktop or in the Favorites pane in the Finder. To find a mounted drive via the GUI, the fastest thing to do is to use the **Go** menu and choose **Computer**. That will display all mounted volumes including hard disks, mapped network drives, and any other available attached storage.

Time Machine Backup

As a system administrator, you should have some kind of backup mechanism in place to store copies of critical data in the case of a catastrophic system failure. *Time Machine* is a simple and effective way to back up a personal Mac or a Mac server in a secure data center. In an office or a classroom environment, it may not be the best solution as external drives can easily go missing. While Time Machine drives can be encrypted, external drives for every user may not be feasible from a cost perspective. Consider using some kind of cloud-based file backup solution such as *iCloud Drive* or *Microsoft OneDrive for Business* in these instances.

Pro Tip   If you are using Time Machine to back up your Mac, if it is formatted for HFS+, **do not** let *macOS* convert it to APFS as it can destroy the existing backup data in the process. It is best to start with a newly formatted drive if you are planning to change to an APFS-formatted disk and archive your HFS+-formatted drive.

File Systems and macOS

Every operating system has its own preferred file system(s). If you have a background in *Microsoft Windows* system administration, you have certainly heard of **NTFS** or **FAT32,** but you may only know of the file system that Apple uses as *Mac format* or *Apple format*. There are actually a few common file systems for the Mac. **Hierarchical File System** (HFS) and its newer cousin **HFS+**, an enhancement to the old HFS format, are now the legacy Apple file systems. The relatively new **Apple File System** (APFS) was released with *macOS High Sierra* and sports a modern set of features and enhanced security. In addition to *macOS*, APFS is also the file system for iOS devices like the *iPhone* and *iPad*.

Hierarchical File System Plus (HFS+)

The legacy file system for the Mac has its roots in Mac OS Classic and is referred to as **Mac OS Extended** in the more recent versions of the operating system. It lacks many of the modern features like checksumming, snapshotting, and simultaneous multiprocess access found in ZFS, NTFS, and APFS. You can still format drives for HFS+, but APFS is now considered the standard for *macOS*, particularly in the case of solid-state drives (SSDs) configured as the startup volume.

Apple File System (APFS)

APFS is the modern standard for *macOS* and *iOS* file systems. It provides a number of modern features including space-sharing containers, snapshotting, stronger encryption, and faster performance over HFS+. The concept of containers is new to *macOS* and is used heavily in APFS. *Containers* hold one or more individual volumes that appear like separate partitions but share the same space and can dynamically grow or shrink depending on need. That means that as more space is required on a particular volume, that data can be allocated to that volume without user interaction or knowledge.

This space allocation scheme is particularly useful with the new *macOS Catalina* where the System files are on a separate read-only volume from the user data. If you look at a drive that has *macOS Catalina* installed on it via Disk Utility, as shown in Figure 2-3, you will see the two distinct volumes. **Macintosh HD** provides the base operating system and applications on one volume, while **Macintosh HD – Data** stores the user directories and user-installed applications. These are all in a single container (appearing as Macintosh HD), and the volumes will grow as needed.

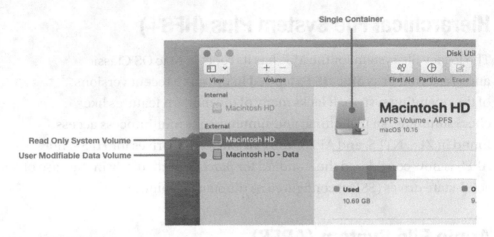

Figure 2-3. *A container comprised of multiple volumes makes up Catalina's startup disk*

Partition Map and Drive Security Options

One thing you will notice when choosing to format a drive in *macOS* is there are a lot of options including various combinations of *case-sensitive, encrypted, journaled,* and so on. Apple makes available a Knowledge Base article to define what each of these options is.

The Knowledge Base article can be found here:

https://support.apple.com/guide/disk-utility/file-system-formats-available-in-disk-utility-dsku19ed921c/mac

In addition to various formatting options, you may also be prompted to select a **drive partition map** scheme. There are three options:

- **GUID:** This is the standard partition map option for Intel-based macOS startup volumes.

- **Apple Partition Map:** This is rarely used any longer, and it is the old partition map for Mac OS Classic and very early versions of Mac OS X that ran on the PowerPC architecture.

- **Master Boot Record:** This is the Windows partition scheme to use with FAT and ExFAT formats.

Finally, you may also have noticed the **Security Options...** button when you are erasing a volume and selecting a format. These security options are there so you can choose how thoroughly the data on the disk is erased. Some organizations require a completely secure sanitization of any disks that are to be decommissioned. By default, *macOS* uses the least secure (but fastest) single-pass erase option. If you need something more secure, for example, something that complies with the *Department of Defense 5220.22-M* protocol, you can select that option by moving the secure erase **slider** all the way to the **right**.

APFS Snapshots

We will discuss APFS in more detail in the next section, but it is worth mentioning that in terms of system recovery, one of the features of Apple's new file system is the ability to take file-level snapshots of the computer's state. If a drive is formatted for APFS, when a major *macOS* update is about to be installed, an APFS snapshot is taken and saved as a recovery point. In general, the operating system determines when it is appropriate for a snapshot be taken and it is automatic, so no user interaction is required.

There may be times when you want to force a snapshot. Apple does provide this capability through a command line utility in the *Terminal*. We will go into greater detail with the Terminal later in this chapter, but to follow along here, simply browse with the Finder to */Applications/ Utilities* and launch the Terminal application. You will be presented with a command prompt. To create a snapshot, we will use the tmutil command. Enter the following command at the Terminal's command prompt and press enter to create a snapshot:

```
tmutil snapshot
```

If all went well, Terminal will give you a message letting you know that it created a snapshot with a date/time stamp of today's date. You can also use the tmutil command to list all available snapshots if you are curious if any exist. Snapshots are stored at the file system level and are only mounted when needed by the OS (e.g., when using Time Machine). Input the following command and press enter on your keyboard:

```
tmutil listlocalsnapshots /
```

If you ever need to restore your Mac from a snapshot, simply boot into *macOS Recovery*, and select the **Restore from Time Machine Backup** option. Select the drive that holds your snapshots (most likely this will be your internal startup disk). You will be presented with a list of available snapshots (if any exist). Simply select the one you want to restore and click **Continue**. Once the restore process is completed, your Mac will restart, and it should be restored to the state it was in at the selected snapshot.

Pro Tip   APFS snapshots are more of a recovery tool than a backup. I would recommend to use snapshots as a way to recover back to a point in time before a major change and instead continue to back up the entire disk to another drive or to the cloud. Snapshots are deleted 24 hours after they are created, so they are not a reliable long-term backup method.

Installing and Upgrading macOS

The default method for upgrading from one version of *macOS* to the next is by using the *Mac App Store* or the *Software Update System Preference* to download and install the next major release. This is helpful if you already have a healthy Mac that just needs the newest OS, but if you need to do a clean install of *macOS* on a newly formatted drive, we need to do a little more legwork.

Install from Internet Recovery

A common option, if you have Internet access, is to boot into *macOS Recovery* via the Internet Recovery option. From here, you can erase and format your internal hard disk and then install a new copy of *macOS* from Apple over the Internet. While effective, this can take some time and may not be feasible for large numbers of Macs that share a single Internet connection in a school or large corporation.

Creating a Bootable USB Install Disk

In the case where you may not have an active Internet connection or you have many Macs that need to have their internal drives erased and a clean copy of *macOS* installed, you will want to create one or more bootable install USB disks. To do this, you need a **USB flash drive with at least 8 GB of space**, a copy of a **macOS Installer** application, and access to the **Terminal** app.

CREATE A BOOTABLE USB INSTALL DISK

The first step is to download the **macOS Installer** from the *Mac App Store* or via the *Software Update System Preference*. When it finishes downloading, the installer will likely automatically launch and prompt you to begin installation. When it does this, **cancel** the installer and **quit** the installation application. Use the *Finder* to browse to the */Applications* folder and verify that the **Install macOS Catalina** application is present.

If you haven't already done so, now insert the **USB flash drive** and open *Disk Utility*. Format the drive for **APFS** and name it. Make note of the name. In the script I'm using, the disk is named **Untitled**. Next, browse to */Applications/Utilities* and then open the *Terminal* app. At the prompt, enter the following command:

```
sudo /Applications/Install\ macOS\ Catalina.app/Contents/
Resources/createinstallmedia --volume /Volumes/Untitled
--nointeraction
```

If you entered the script correctly, it will prompt you for your administrative password. This is the same password that you use to log in to the Mac, assuming you have local administrative rights. It may also ask you to grant the Terminal application permission to access the attached USB disk, and if it does, you can allow this. After authenticating, you will see the output of the Terminal as it formats and creates the bootable USB disk as shown in Figure 2-4.

Figure 2-4. *Using the Terminal to create a bootable USB disk*

Pro Tip   The script in this example assumes you are using *macOS Catalina*. If you are using one of the other versions, simply substitute the name of the installer application. For example, use *macOS High Sierra* instead of *macOS Catalina*, and the script will still work. The script is simply referencing the installer application we specify in the ***/Applications*** path.

Creating a Bootable Technician Drive

A bootable USB installer is useful, but it is also still as limited as using *macOS Recovery* in that you are limited to just a few utilities and the Terminal app. Wouldn't it be nice to have a full Mac interface with a Desktop, many applications, and *Finder* access? Yes! Every good Mac tech should have a bootable external hard disk that has a full copy of *macOS* for troubleshooting purposes. I recommend one of the new external solid-state drives as they are more portable and less prone to wear and tear as they get jostled around in your laptop bag.

The purpose of one of these drives is to have all of your *macOS* troubleshooting tools in one place. I usually keep copies of various software installers, Disk First Aid tools, and things of that nature on mine. It can be really helpful to diagnose issues involving the internal startup volume, retrieve user data if a recent backup doesn't exist, or make any other alteration to the startup volume without having to resort to doing everything via the command line interface.

Pro Tip   When booting a Mac from one of these external drives, particularly if you don't have a way to log in due to a technical issue, use the **option** key modifier at boot so you can select the drive as the *startup disk* without having to boot into the OS and set it via *System Preferences*.

It is very simple and straightforward to create one of these drives. Simply connect it to your Mac, format it as an **APFS** volume using the **GUID** partition map, and then run the **macOS Installer** from the */Applications* folder but specify the **external drive** when stepping through the install screen. Note that you may need to click the button that says **show all disks** to see the external drive. Once *macOS* is installed on the drive, you just step through the *Setup Assistant* and create the local user account just as if you were installing it on the internal disk.

Pro Tip   As part of the installation process, your Mac will likely set the external drive as its new preferred startup volume. Be sure to change this back to the internal drive by using the *Startup Disk System Preference*, or else it may create an unnecessary pause in the boot time of your Mac as it looks for the external drive before booting from the internal startup disk.

Introduction to the Terminal

You got a Mac because they were *easy to use* and didn't require those command line interfaces like *Windows* or *Linux*, right? So why are we talking about command line interfaces already in the second chapter of this book?! The answer is simple—because you will run into situations where powerful utilities are *only* available via the Terminal, as evidenced by the command we just had to use to create a bootable USB install disk. Beyond that, using scripts can be an effective tool for automating various mundane tasks across many Mac clients at once using tools like Apple Remote Desktop (ARD). This section introduces many of the common commands and concepts that you will use on a regular basis when using the Terminal or writing your own scripts.

NAVIGATING WITH THE COMMAND LINE INTERFACE

When you open the Terminal, you will see something like the following:

```
dwsmith@dwsmiths-MBP ~ %
```

This is the command prompt, and it is showing you which user you are signed in as and where you currently are on the computer. The ~ (tilde) represents the absolute path in relation to my home directory. In my case, it is the home directory of my user account on my MacBook Pro. Technically, we are in **/Users/dwsmith** if I were to browse to the same location in the *Finder* as shown in Figure 2-5.

Figure 2-5. *Viewing the same directory via the Terminal and the Finder*

I may want to see what else is in this directory, and if I want to do that, I would use the command `ls`. Go ahead and enter the following at the command prompt:

`ls`

When I type `ls`, I get the output as shown in Figure 2-6. As you can see, these are the subfolders of my home directory. If you are familiar with DOS/Windows, this is similar to the `dir` command.

Figure 2-6. *The output of the ls command and the contents of my home directory in the Finder*

Now that I know what the other files and folders are in this location, I want to change my directory to explore further. Let's say I want to get to the Desktop, which is a folder in my **/Users/dwsmith** directory. I can use the cd command along with specifying the folder I want to move to as shown in Figure 2-7. Enter the following command at the prompt:

cd Desktop

You will see that now the command prompt has changed to specify that we are now in the **Desktop** folder of the home directory. See how **Desktop** is listed after my user account info instead of the tilde?

dwsmith@dwsmiths-MBP Desktop %

Figure 2-7. *I am at the Desktop folder in my Users/dwsmith directory*

Let's try something a little more interesting. Let's create a folder on our Desktop. We do this using the `mkdir` command, which is short for *make directory*. We use this command by specifying the name of the directory after we enter this command as an *argument*. At the command line, enter

`mkdir MyFolder`

You should see a new folder appear on the Desktop called ***MyFolder*** as shown in Figure 2-8.

Figure 2-8. *A folder called MyFolder is created on the Desktop*

Notice how there is no space in the folder name? Let's make a new folder, but this time let's put a space in between. At the command line, we cannot just make a space in the filename without being *explicit*. That means we either have to write "My Folder" using double quotation marks or we have to use a special character combination of a \ (back-slash) and a space after to create a single space.

Let's try this by making two more folders.

To create the first folder, we will use quotations marks. Use the same mkdir command and name the folder *Important Stuff* like this:

mkdir "Important Stuff"

Next, use mkdir and create a folder using the *back-slash space* method called *More Stuff* like this:

mkdir More\ Stuff

Your screen should look similar to the one in Figure 2-9.

Figure 2-9. *Terminal commands and the resulting folders*

COMMAND MANUALS

Before we continue, let's clean up our Desktop by removing all of these bogus folders we created in the previous exercise. The rm command is short for *remove.* Let's use it to specify the folders we want to delete. Go ahead and enter this command like so:

rm "More Stuff"

What happens? You probably thought that this would delete the folder, but instead we get a cryptic message that says rm: More Stuff: is a directory. Clearly, we did something wrong. How do we find out what we did wrong or how to do it correctly?

We read the freaking manual, of course!

This is a good opportunity to introduce you to man pages. Most commands
have a *manual*, and you can view it right in the Terminal by typing man before
the command. Let's open the man page for the rm command. Enter the
following command:

```
man rm
```

You can see in Figure 2-10 that if we want to remove a directory, we must
specify an argument of -d before the name of our directory. We are going to
try this again, but first press the **q** key on the keyboard to exit the man page
and go back to the command prompt.

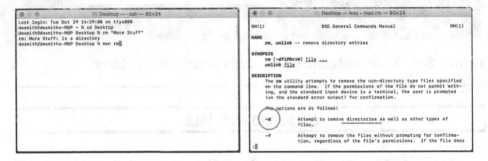

Figure 2-10. *The man page shows the command options we need to
know*

Now let's try entering this:

```
rm -d "More Stuff"
```

Success! This will delete the folder as shown in Figure 2-11.

Figure 2-11. *Removing directories using Terminal commands*

Go ahead and delete the other two folders using the same methodology, and when completed, you should have a clean Desktop again.

Now that you are armed with the power of man pages, you will be unstoppable with the command line!

Elevated Privileges

If you have had some previous exposure to the Terminal, you have probably entered a command or two that started with sudo. This is a special command that invokes *elevated privileges*. Even if you are in the **admin** group on your Mac, you are still not the most privileged user on the system. That power belongs to the *root* user or *super* user.

Some commands can only be run as the super user; and when that is the case, we need to use the sudo command, which is short for *super user do*.

When you use a command that begins with sudo, you will be prompted to enter a password before the command will run. If you are the local admin on the Mac, the password will be the same one you use with your local user account. For example, in my case, the password for my *dwsmith* account is the same password for the super user.

Shells

There are several different kinds of Unix shells that you can use with the Terminal app including **zsh**, **bash**, **tcsh**, and more. Until *macOS Catalina*, the default login shell for the Mac was **bash**. However, starting with *Catalina*, Apple has promoted **zsh** to the default login shell. You can still change it to bash using the **Advanced Options** page in the *Users & Groups System Preference*, which we will explore later in this chapter.

Common Commands

There are many common commands that can be used in various shell scripts. The diagram in Figure 2-12 shows a few more that you should familiarize yourself with. Take a look at the description for each and use the man page for each command and experiment with some test files and folders to master the use of each of them.

Command	Description
pwd	This command outputs the current directory path.
touch	This command will change the modification or file access times for any file specified. If the specified file doesn't exist, it will create one.
cp	Use this command to copy files.
mv	Use this command to move files.
chown	Use this command to change file owner and group permissions.

Figure 2-12. *A few common commands to familiarize yourself with*

System Preferences

System Preferences are the *Control Panel* or *Settings* for macOS. There are controls for user settings like the size, location, and look of the Dock, where each user can change it based on their preference. There are other controls that affect the system as a whole and typically feature a little **padlock icon** that requires authentication from a user in the **admin** group before changes can be made. Let's explore a few of the more important admin-level System Preferences in Figure 2-13.

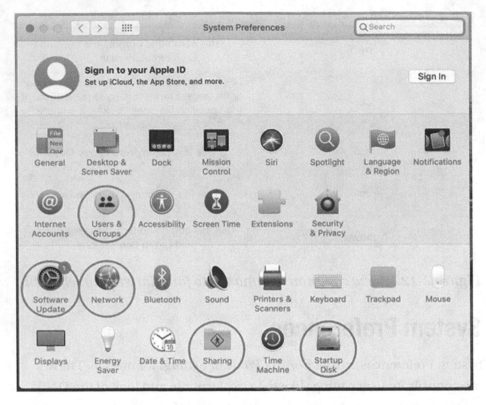

Figure 2-13. *System Preferences covered in this chapter*

Startup Disk

As shown in Figure 2-14, the *Startup Disk System Preference* is relatively
straightforward. It will scan all available connected media, including network
media on systems that support *NetBoot*, and will return any volume that has a
valid System folder. Simply select the volume you wish to boot from and restart.

This information will be saved to NVRAM, so if the media disconnects
at some point in the future, you may not have a bootable Mac. It will
display either a flashing folder with a question mark **[?]** indicating that
the system cannot boot from the selected volume since it cannot find the
System folder, or it will take a long time to boot as it scans for any other
available volume with a valid System folder.

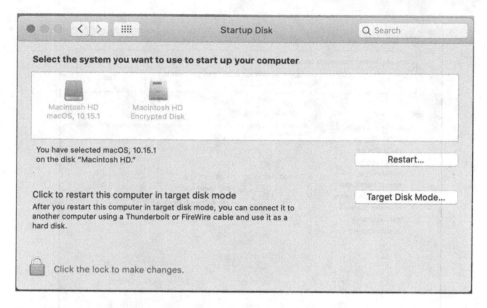

Figure 2-14. *The Startup Disk System Preference pane*

Pro Tip   If you are trying to set an encrypted volume as the startup disk, you must have the disk password to unlock the drive before the *Startup Disk System Preference* can identify if there is a valid bootable System on the disk.

Sharing

The *Sharing System Preference* will be explored in greater detail in Chapter 7, which covers *macOS Server*. Because *macOS Server* is an application that runs on top of *macOS*, many of the services in the *Sharing System Preference* apply to Macs being used as a server. There is one key item to cover as it relates to *macOS* clients specifically, and that is the **Computer Name**. Figure 2-15 shows the area where you can name your Mac and what kind of name it broadcasts to other computers on a network, also known as the *hostname*.

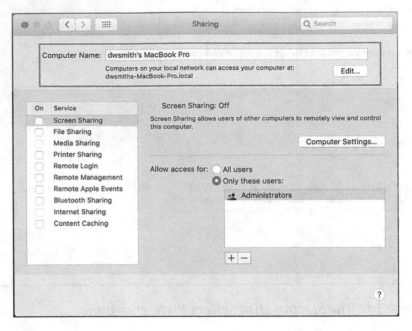

Figure 2-15. *The location to set the friendly name as the Computer Name*

You can think of the **Computer Name** as a friendlier name, allowing for things like spaces and special characters. The *hostname*, because it broadcasts on the network, cannot have special characters and spaces. Figure 2-16 shows the hostname, and you can see how it changed the name of my Mac slightly by using dashes instead of spaces and eliminating special characters.

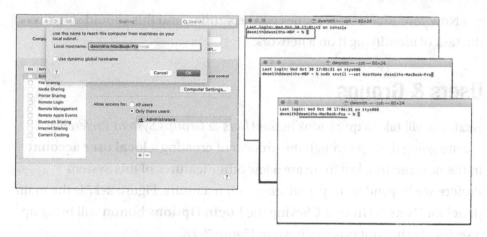

Figure 2-16. *Comparing the hostnames between the GUI and command line*

We have another potential problem as it relates to the Computer Name. Take a close look at the Terminal window in Figure 2-16. Do you see how the Unix hostname at the command prompt is **dwsmith-MBP**? Why do I have two different hostnames? Because macOS has *three* different computer names—the **Computer Name**, the **Local Hostname**, and the **Unix hostname**. I would recommend as a best practice to set the Unix hostname and Local Hostname to match. It may not be a big deal in some cases, but it can definitely save you from some potential issues later on when running scripts on remote systems. I have seen horror story cases where every single Mac on a network is named *differently* with the Computer Name and all of them are named with the *same* Unix hostname.

Fortunately, it is very simple to change the Unix hostname. Using the `scutil` command as shown in Figure 2-16, you can change the Computer Name to match the Local Hostname. Enter the following command, substituting **dwsmith-MacBook-Pro** with your chosen hostname, and authenticate with the `sudo` command:

```
sudo scutil --set HostName dwsmiths-MacBook-Pro
```

Now your Mac's three names will be similar, and this should simplify the task of identifying it on a network.

Users & Groups

Next, we will take a quick look at the *Users & Groups System Preference*. We are going to step through the process of creating a **local user account** in the next section, but there are a few other features of this System Preference beyond simply managing user accounts. Figure 2-17 is the main panel for Users & Groups. Clicking the **Login Options** button will bring up a series of other options as shown in Figure 2-18.

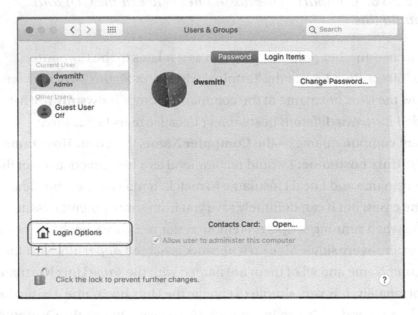

Figure 2-17. *The Login Options button in the Users & Groups pane*

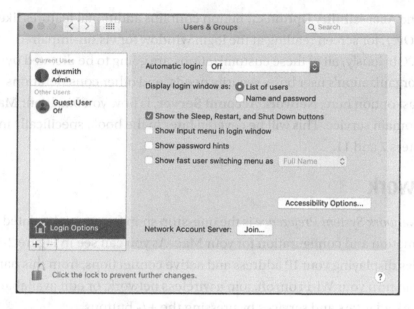

Figure 2-18. The Login Options pane

The **login window** is actually its *own application* of sorts, and this is where you configure it. You can turn **automatic login** on/off and select a user to sign in automatically. If you are choosing to use a login window instead of automatic login, you can display a **list of all users** or a **name and password field**. You can also show or hide the **power control** buttons, which may be important if you are administrating a server and you want someone to authenticate before they can power down or restart the computer.

Fast user switching can be a useful solution if you want to allow multiple users to sign in on the same Mac and then switch between them without one user signing out first. This allows administrators to sign in and fix something and then give the system back to the user without interrupting their work. It can also be useful in service industries like a print shop, where multiple users are sharing the same computer and alternating in real time.

The **Accessibility Options...** button contains additional features like *VoiceOver*, for screen reading at the login window for vision-impaired users. Obviously, all of these customizations are going to be dictated by your organization's user base, security needs, and other considerations. The last option here, **Network Account Server**, is how you *bind* your Mac to a domain service. This will be covered later in the book, specifically in Chapters 7 and 11.

Network

The *Network System Preference* is the one-stop shop for network-related information and configuration for your Mac. As you can see in Figure 2-19, besides displaying your IP address and active connections, from this pane you can turn your Wi-Fi on/off, join a wireless network, or edit available network adapters and services by pressing the +/- buttons.

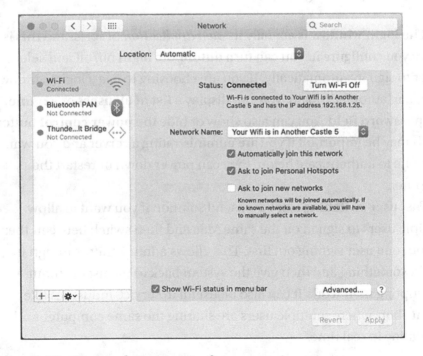

Figure 2-19. *Network System Preference main pane*

Pressing the + button will prompt you to add a number of new adapter options including a built-in VPN. Figure 2-20 shows the various network adapters you can add, and Figure 2-21 shows the specific VPNs you can choose from including **Cisco IPSec**.

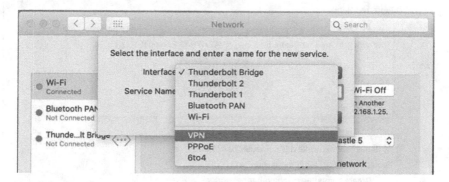

Figure 2-20. *Additional network interface options*

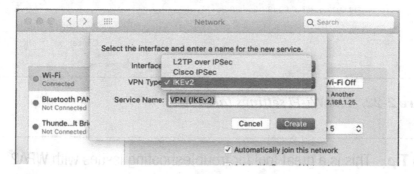

Figure 2-21. *Built-in VPN protocols*

Clicking the **Advanced…** button will allow you to modify specific network adapter settings. There are several tabs in the Advanced dialog box with the first being **Wi-Fi**. As shown in Figure 2-22, this is where you will see all of the wireless networks that your Mac has connected to and you can arrange them in order of preference. Clicking the +/- buttons will allow you to forget a wireless network (-) or manually add (+) a wireless network.

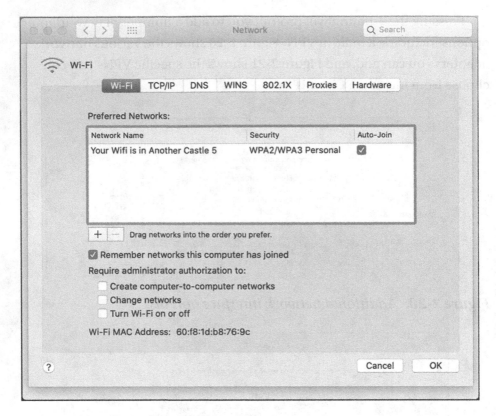

Figure 2-22. *The Wi-Fi settings tab*

Pro Tip   This is a great tool for troubleshooting issues with WPA2 Enterprise wireless networks that have embedded user credentials and certificates. You can delete an existing network to easily remove cached credentials and certificates. You can also manually add a network and specify the required wireless security settings.

The next tab is **TCP/IP,** and this is where you can configure your IP address settings as shown in Figure 2-23. In this pane, you can specify dynamic or static addressing as well as see your current IP address, subnet mask, and gateway (labeled Router). The **Renew DHCP Lease** button can be used with dynamic addressing to either refresh the existing DHCP-provided IP address or receive a new one.

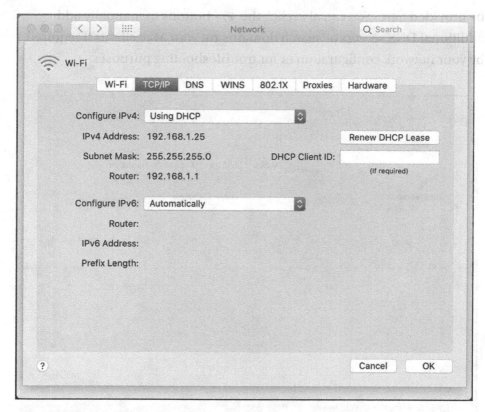

Figure 2-23. *TCP/IP settings tab*

Windows Administrator Pro Tip   Windows sysadmins can think of this tab as a place to easily get **the ipconfig** information as well as perform the **ipconfig /release** or **ipconfig /renew** task graphically on a Mac. It also functions the same as the TCP/IP v4 or TCP/IP v6 **Properties** dialog box on Windows.

Finally, the **DNS** tab as shown in Figure 2-24 provides the DNS servers and search domains for your network. If you have your DHCP server options set to hand out DNS information to your clients, that info will be provided here. You can also click the +/- buttons to manually add additional DNS servers or search domains on your Mac clients if required by your network configuration or for troubleshooting purposes.

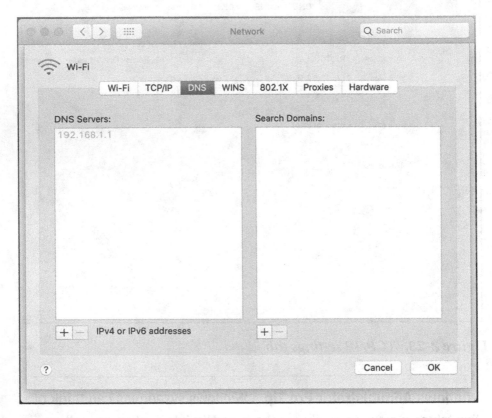

Figure 2-24. *DNS settings tab*

Pro Tip   *macOS* also provides a comprehensive set of network configuration and troubleshooting commands through the Terminal app. The `ifconfig` command can be used to do any number of things including flushing the DNS resolver cache, disabling network interfaces, adding network interfaces, and manipulating TCP/IP settings. If you plan to script any network configuration changes, definitely spend some time reading through the `ifconfig` man pages and trying out some of the commands as shown in Figure 2-25.

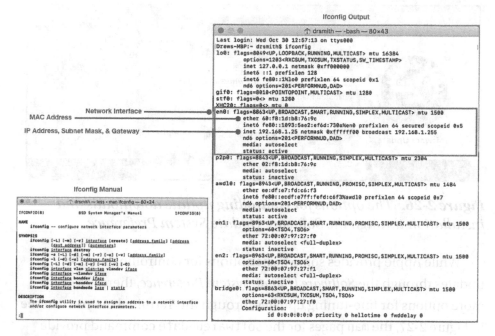

Figure 2-25. *Example output of the ifconfig command and the ifconfig manual*

Software Update

Similar to other operating systems, it is important to keep your *macOS* clients up-to-date with the latest security patches. The *Software Update System Preference* gives you the ability to control the updates your Macs receive and when to update them. Figure 2-26 shows the basic categories and options for configuring your Mac to receive important updates and security patches. In addition to controlling updates for *macOS*, you can also use *Software Update* to install upgrades and patches for any applications that were installed from the *Mac App Store*.

Figure 2-26. *The options for controlling update downloads and installation through the Software Update System Preference*

While Apple provides some basic options for controlling macOS updates through the *Software Update System Preference*, there are even more options for fine-tuning updates through the Terminal. As you can see in Figure 2-27, the man pages for the softwareupdate command provide some very interesting scripting options.

```
● ○ ○              ⊙ drsmith — less ◂ man softwareupdate — 80×57

    -l | --list
               List all available updates.

    -i | --install
               Each update specified by args is downloaded and installed.
               args can be one of the following:

               -r | --recommended
                          All updates that are recommended for your system.
                          These are prefixed with a ★ character in the
                          --list output.

               -R | --restart
                          Automatically restart (or shut down) if required
                          to complete installation. If the user invoking
                          this tool is logged in then macOS will attempt to
                          quit all applications, logout, and restart. If
                          the user is not logged in, macOS will trigger a
                          forced reboot if necessary. If you wish to always
                          perform a forced reboot, pass --force.

               -a | --all All updates that are applicable to your system,
                          including those non-recommended ones, which are
                          prefixed with a _ character in the --list output.
                          (Non-recommended updates are uncommon in any
                          case.)

               item ...   One or more specified updates. The --list output
                          shows the item names you can specify here, pre-
                          fixed by the ★ or _ characters. See EXAMPLES.

    -d | --download
               Each update specified by args is downloaded but not
               installed. The values of args are the same as for the
               --install command. Updates downloaded with --download can be
               subsequently installed with --install, or through the App
               Store (as long as they remain applicable to your system).
               Updates are downloaded to /Library/Updates, but are not
               designed to be installed by double-clicking the packages in
               that directory: always use --install or the App Store to
               actually perform the install.

    --ignore identifier ...
               Manages the per-machine list of ignored updates. The
               identifier is the first part of the item name (before the
               dash and version number) that is shown by --list.  See
               EXAMPLES.

    --reset-ignored
               Clears the per-machine list of ignored updates.

    --schedule on | off
               Manages the per-machine automatic (background) check prefer-
               ence.

:▮
```

Figure 2-27. *The softwareupdate command manual via the Terminal*

CONFIGURE SOFTWARE UPDATE VIA THE TERMINAL

Let's try something fun. Open the Terminal and run the following command:

softwareupdate -l

Notice how your Mac will take a few minutes of checking for the latest updates, and if it is like mine, it will come back with a list of available updates. Figure 2-28 shows that I have two pending updates available for my system.

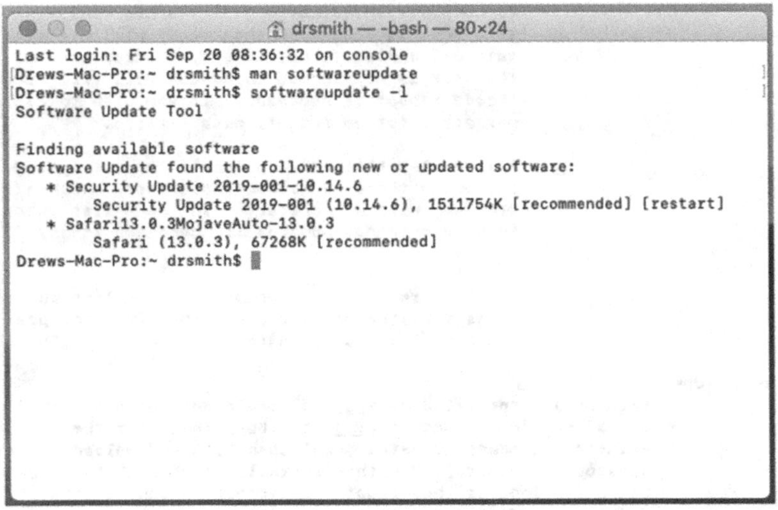

```
● ● ●                        ⓘ drsmith — -bash — 80×24
Last login: Fri Sep 20 08:36:32 on console
[Drews-Mac-Pro:~ drsmith$ man softwareupdate
[Drews-Mac-Pro:~ drsmith$ softwareupdate -l
Software Update Tool

Finding available software
Software Update found the following new or updated software:
   * Security Update 2019-001-10.14.6
        Security Update 2019-001 (10.14.6), 1511754K [recommended] [restart]
   * Safari13.0.3MojaveAuto-13.0.3
        Safari (13.0.3), 67268K [recommended]
Drews-Mac-Pro:~ drsmith$ ▊
```

Figure 2-28. *Available update output via the Terminal*

One of the more powerful options that we have at our disposal when scripting with the softwareupdate command is the ability to *exclude* updates we don't want users to see. For example, a favorite one of mine is the advertisement banner that Apple displays in System Preferences when a new full version of *macOS* is released. An example of this is the top image in Figure 2-29 where it is prompting my users to download and install *macOS Catalina* on their Macs running *Mojave*. I don't want my users asking me about installing the new OS, and I don't want them attempting to install a new operating system on their computers themselves.

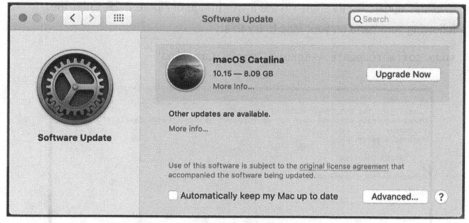

Software Update before running script.

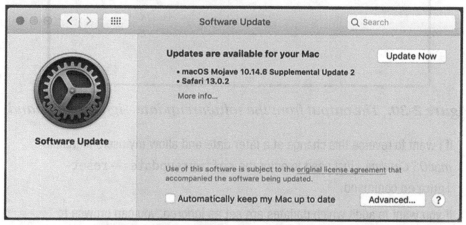

Software Update after running script.

Figure 2-29. *Software Update window before and after excluding the update*

Using the `softwareupdate --ignore` command along with the name of the update that it is prompting me to install, in this case *macOS Catalina*, I can hide this banner. As you can see in Figure 2-30, when you run this command with `sudo`, it will set the *Catalina* update to **ignored;** and when I restart my Mac, if I go back to *Software Update*, the *Catalina* prompt is gone from my available update list as shown in the lower image of Figure 2-29. Enter the following command on your Mac to try this:

```
sudo softwareupdate --ignore "macOS Catalina"
```

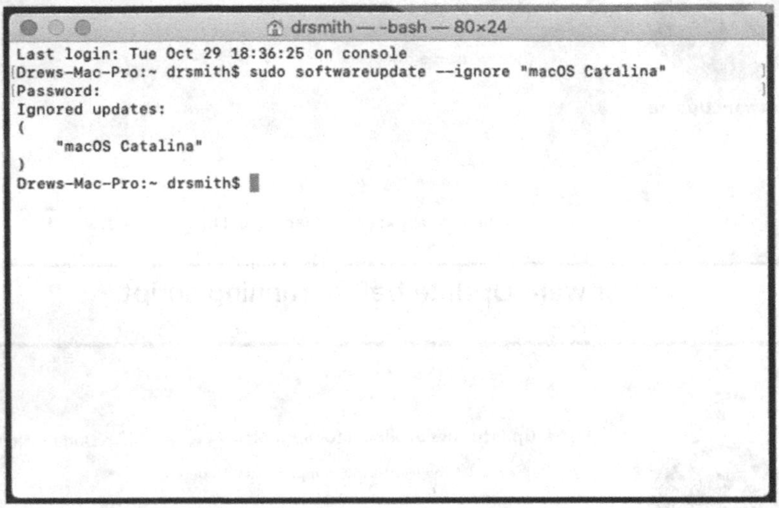

Figure 2-30. *The output from the softwareupdate --ignore command*

If I want to reverse this change at a later date and allow my users to install *macOS Catalina*, I just need to enter the `softwareupdate --reset-ignored` command.

If you want to audit which updates are set as ignored, you can browse to **/Library/Preferences** and find the **com.apple.SoftwareUpdate.plist**. Open this file in *Xcode* or another application that can open xml files of the **∗.plist** file type, also known as **Property Lists**.

When you open the ∗.**plist** file, you will see there is an *array* for **InactiveUpdates** with keys set for each ignored update nested inside the array. Close out of the ∗.**plist** file. Enter this command to reverse the ignored updates:

```
softwareupdate -reset-ignored
```

Pro Tip   Unless you are developer, Xcode is probably a bit of an overkill for opening and editing Property Lists. There are a number of free or low-cost Property List editors out there. **Prefs Editor** by *Thomas Tempelmann* is one that I find quick and easy to use.

Managing Local Users & Groups

Before exiting out of System Preferences, let's go back to *Users & Groups*. In this section, we are going to create a new local user account and explore some advanced settings.

Create a New User

To get started, click the + button on the *Users & Groups System Preference* to add a new account. You will see in the drop-down menu next to **New Account** that we have a few options for the account type. We can select **Administrator**, **Sharing Only**, **Standard** user, or a new **Group**. We'll discuss Sharing Only and Group options in Chapter 7. For this illustration, we will select **Standard** as shown in Figure 2-31.

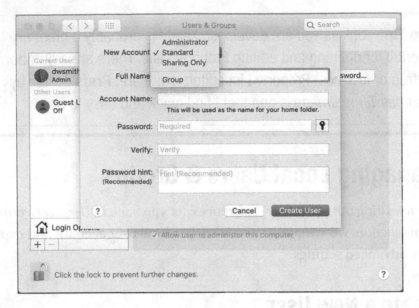

Figure 2-31. *Creating a new Standard local user account*

Fill in the required fields with whatever data you want. Note that the
Full Name is the *friendly name* and the **Account Name** is the actual user
account in Unix and it will also be the name of the user's **home folder by
default**. There cannot be any spaces or special characters in the account
name. When you are finished filling out the information, click the **Create
User** button to continue. See Figure 2-32.

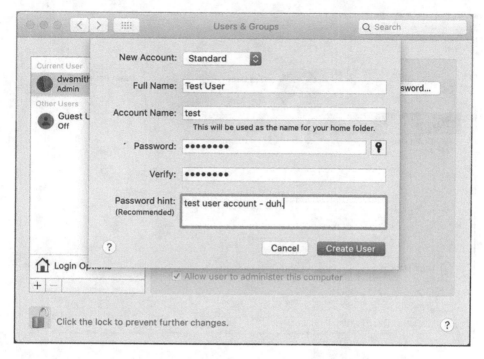

Figure 2-32. *Our new account's username and password information*

Once it has finished creating the user account, you will see the friendly name and a randomly assigned photo in the *Other Users* list on the left side of the *Users & Groups* pane. If you click it to **select** it, you can modify a few things on the right side. You can reset the password using the **Reset Password** button. Finally, you can upgrade it to a *local administrator account* by clicking the checkbox for **Allow user to administer this computer**.

Advanced Options

Next, let's explore some of the *advanced options* for this new user account. **Right-click** the user account in the *Other Users* list and choose **Advanced Options...** from the contextual menu that appears as shown in Figure 2-33.

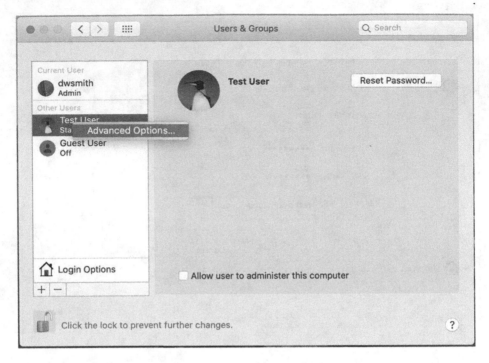

Figure 2-33. *Finding the hidden Advanced Options... menu via right-click*

When the Advanced Options sheet appears, you will be presented with a warning about making changes to these settings. I don't typically interact with many of these on a regular basis, but since this is a test, feel free to play around to understand the cause-and-effect relationship without fear of damaging a production user account.

There are a few items to point out that are quite useful here as shown in Figure 2-34. You can see the default group is **staff** in this case because they are a Standard user. The login shell is defaulted to **zsh** because I'm using *Catalina*. I can modify this and select **bash** if I want to instead so that it's consistent with previous versions of *macOS*. It shows my **home directory path** here, and I can change it to another location or volume if I need to. I can set an **Apple ID** to tie to this particular user account for *iCloud* or the *Mac App Store* so they don't need to do so when they first sign in. This could be useful for assigning *institutional Apple IDs* that we will cover later in this book.

Finally, we can add **aliases** to this user account. Aliases let us add other usernames that can be entered instead of the official account name. For example, if my account name is very long or complex, I can add a shorter username as an alias. Some organizations may do this to maintain some kind of standardization of network user home directories but then give the user a friendly username to sign in with. I personally have not used aliases all that often, but your mileage may vary.

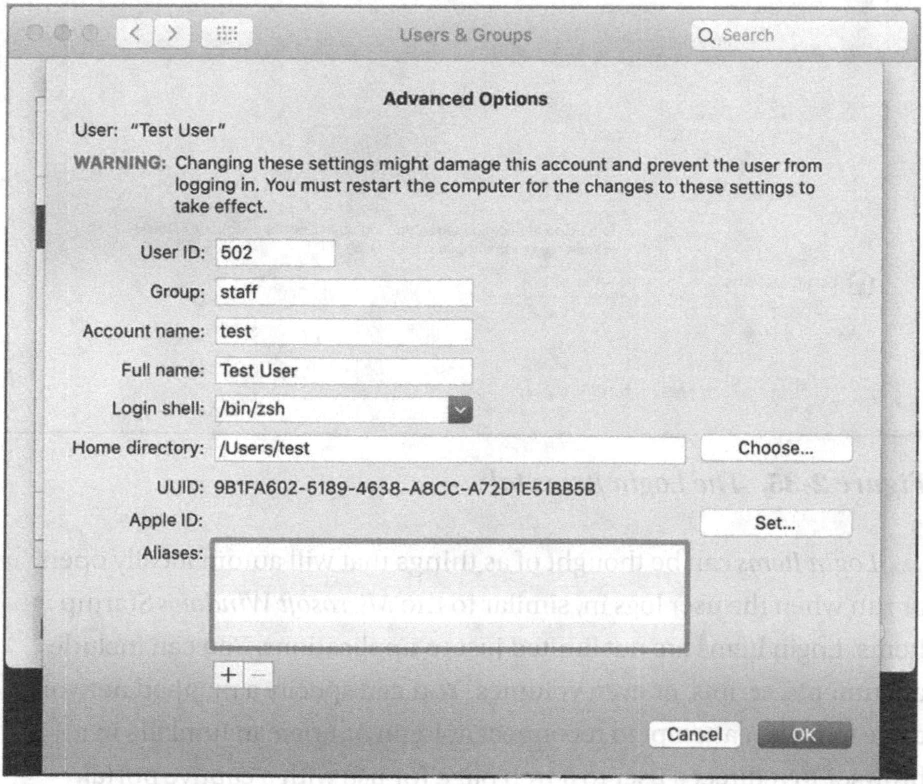

Figure 2-34. *Advanced user options*

Login Items

Next, we are going to explore the concept of *Login Items*. Go ahead and cancel out of the *Advanced Options* sheet and click your user account listed under *Current User*. Click the **Login Items** tab as shown in Figure 2-35.

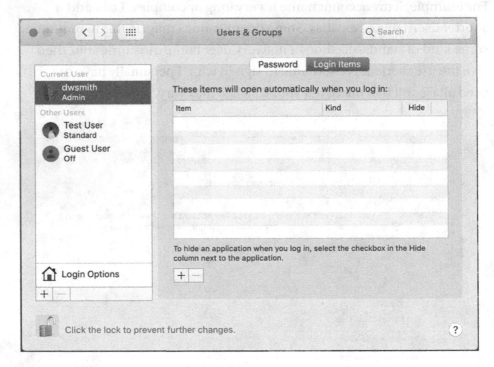

Figure 2-35. *The Login Items tab*

Login Items can be thought of as things that will automatically open or run when the user logs in, similar to the *Microsoft Windows* Startup Items. Login Items are not limited just to applications. You can include documents, scripts, or even volumes. You can specify a mapped network drive to have it attempt to reconnect at login or open an html file in a browser to redirect a user to a web page for use with a captive portal.

Sometimes applications will add things to the Login Items list as part of the installation process. If you do not want these helper applications launching automatically, this is where you can disable that functionality. You can use the +/- buttons to add or remove Login Items. You can also use **drag and drop** to add items from the *Finder* directly to the list.

User Template

Close out of the System Preferences and go back to the *Finder*. Using the **Go** menu, select **Computer** to get a Finder window up that we can use to browse the directory of the **Macintosh HD**. Browse to the */Users* directory as shown in Figure 2-36. You should see your home directory and a folder for your other user. When you try to drill down into the new user's home folder, while you can see the folders Desktop, Documents, and so on, you cannot view their contents.

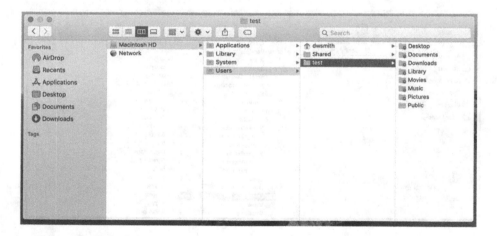

Figure 2-36. *Attempting to browse another local user's home directory*

While we could change file permissions on these folders and drill down to view the contents, we are not going to do so at this time. I wanted you to browse to this directory to illustrate that there is a standard folder structure that gets built when the new user account is created. To understand how this works, we are going to browse to another area of the startup disk, the system's **Library** directory. Go back to the root of Macintosh HD and then drill down to */Library/User Template/* as shown in Figure 2-37.

Pro Tip   Please note that I'm using *macOS Catalina*. Older versions of *macOS* place the User Template folder in the **/System/Library/** directory, while *Catalina* places it in **/Library**. If you did browse to **/System/Library/** in *Catalina*, Apple has been kind enough to place an **alias** to the new location for the User Template.

Figure 2-37. *The User Template directory in macOS Catalina*

The **User Template** folder is basically what it sounds like—a template of default user settings and a directory structure that is used to build a new user's home folder. There are also various folders for the language and keyboard settings for geographic locations around the globe.

Prior to *macOS Mojave*, many Mac system administrators utilized the User Template folder for preloading various preferences and settings that modified the default look and feel for new users. Most recently, Apple has made changes to the way that *macOS* works with regard to the User Template that break this capability. The use of configuration profiles is now the recommended means for customizing the look and feel of user accounts. Configuration profiles are covered in later chapters of the book involving Profile Manager and MDM solutions.

Advanced Finder Techniques

Option Key Modifier

One secret that Apple uses across many *macOS* applications, including the *Finder*, is the **option key** as a modifier for showing *advanced menu options*. As shown in Figure 2-38, pressing and holding the **option key** changes or adds additional functions to the various menus.

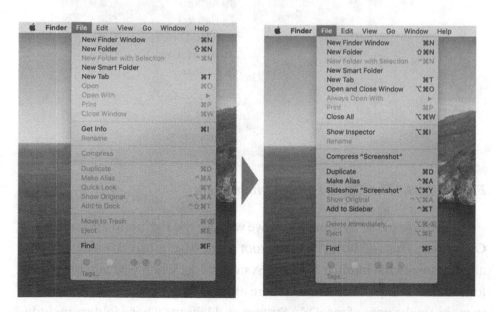

Figure 2-38. *Using the option key to change or add hidden menu items*

Directory Structure

To best understand how to manage and troubleshoot *macOS*, it is important
to be familiar with three key areas of the operating system's directory
structure. In this section, we are going to explore the **System folder**, the **User
folder**, and the **hidden Unix private directory**. We are going to use the **Go**
menu and the **Go to Folder...** option as seen in Figure 2-39.

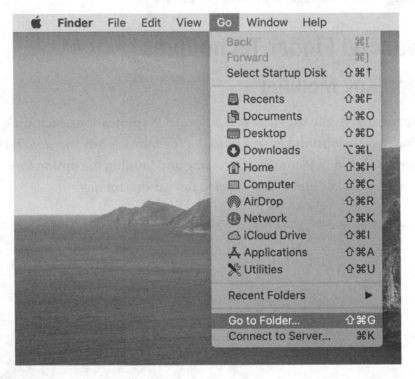

Figure 2-39.   *The Go To Folder... menu item*

To browse to the **System** folder, we will use the **Go** menu and select
Computer. This will bring us to the root of the Macintosh HD. You are
already somewhat familiar with the System folder when we were browsing
for the User Template directory. There are two folders that work together
to make up the core of macOS—System and Library. These folders include

system-wide settings, drivers, system files, and any third-party extensions that are installed along with various applications.

As part of Apple's *System Integrity Protection* (SIP) initiative, most of these directories are read-only. Starting with *macOS Catalina*, Apple also stores the base set of applications that are included by default with the operating system in a symbolically linked Applications folder in */System/ Applications*. These folders are all on a separate read-only volume and included in the overall **Macintosh HD** container, which, along with the user-modifiable **Macintosh HD – Data** volume, appears like a single drive to the end user as illustrated in Figure 2-40.

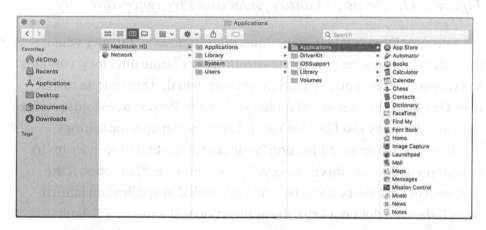

Figure 2-40. *The System folder now contains the stock applications that ship with the operating system in macOS Catalina*

Next, we can use the **Go** menu with the **option** key modifier to make the *Library* folder appear as an option on the list. Select **Library,** and a new Finder window will appear and take you to the */Users/username/ Library* directory as shown in Figure 2-41. Please note that this Library folder is different from the system-wide Library folder in that it is unique to the *currently signed-in user* and hidden by default.

Figure 2-41. *The user's Library folder and Preferences directory*

This user Library folder, sometimes referred to as ~/***Library*** where the tilde represents the path to the current user's home directory, contains the various settings and application support data that are unique to that user. One key subfolder to be familiar with is the **Preferences** folder, which contains **Property List** files that control application-specific settings.

Typically, when an application launches for the first time, it writes its default preferences to this directory. Upon subsequent launches, if the preferences data exists, it will be read and loaded at application launch time. If the data does not exist, the application will write new default preferences again. Therefore, a common first step to troubleshooting an application that is having an issue is to try to remove a support folder or Property List file to see if resetting the preferences to default results in a fix.

Next, let's use the **Go** menu's **Go to Folder…** option to browse the hidden Unix **private** directory at the root of the Macintosh HD as shown in Figure 2-42. This is essentially the Unix core of *macOS* and includes various directories like */etc*, */var*, and */tmp*. It is usually for the best to leave these directories alone, but if you browse through /tmp (temp folder), there are caches here that various applications dump data into that get deleted on a regular basis through the reboot process. We will use the /tmp directory later when scripting mass application installations.

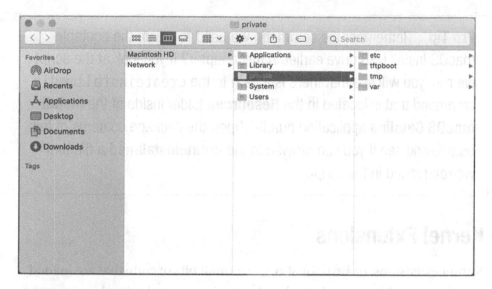

Figure 2-42. *The hidden Unix private folder and its contents*

Finally, let's open the Terminal again and at the command prompt type
cd / to move to the root of our startup disk. Next, use ls to list the contents
of the directory. In addition to the folders we would expect to see like
System, Library, and **Applications,** we also see a number of other folders
like **bin, sbin, usr, dev, cores**, and **opt**. These are additional hidden folders
that are used by the operating system, similar to the /**private** folder. You
can explore these folders on your own, but be aware that these are best left
alone for the OS to function as expected.

Application Bundles

Application bundles, or *application packages* as they are sometimes
referred to, are really a type of folder or container that looks like a single file
to the end user but is actually a self-contained executable with supporting
data in one package. We can **right-click** the application icon and choose
to **Open Package Contents** to drill down into the support files included
in this bundle. This is rarely used on a day-to-day basis, but it is worth
knowing that there is more to an application than meets the eye.

Pro Tip   Remember the command we used to create the bootable macOS Install USB drive earlier in this chapter? If you look at the script we ran, you will see that there is a path to the `createinstallmedia` command that is located in the **Resources** folder inside of the **Install macOS Catalina** application bundle. Open the package contents of this bundle and see if you can browse to the **createinstallmedia** file that we referenced in the script.

Kernel Extensions

Kernel extensions, or *kexts* for short, are small bits of code that are loaded into the operating system kernel and provide support for hardware or other components. You will typically see third-party kexts used with external hardware like pro audio mixers that connect via Thunderbolt or USB. You can view these kext files by browsing to */System/Library/Extensions* or by running the `kextstat` command via the Terminal as shown in Figure 2-43.

Starting with macOS High Sierra, Apple introduced a new security feature that requires users to *approve* kexts the first time they need to load. The user is prompted to approve them with a dialog box and then redirected to the *Security & Privacy System Preference* to click the **Approve** button under the **General** tab. Apple has continued to increase the security around kexts in *Mojave* and *Catalina*, both of which require kexts to be *code-signed* by developers. It is also important to note that if you zap the NVRAM, all authorized kexts must be reauthorized again.

Pro Tip   If you are using applications or workflows that involve kexts, it is a best practice to make sure you are using the latest application releases to avoid issues due to security requirements that Apple continues to tweak. You should also consult with the developers of applications that use kexts extensively to ensure compatibility before approving an OS update on your client systems. Even small updates like a move from 10.15.0 to 10.15.1 run the risk of breaking software compatibility.

Figure 2-43. *Output from the kextstat command showing all running kernel extensions*

Extra System Utilities

As long as we are exploring the various System and Library folders, it makes sense to talk about a couple of additional utilities that are hidden inside of *macOS* that can be of great use to network and system administrators. Browse to */System/Library/CoreServices/Applications/;* and in this folder you will see a number of applications like **Archive Utility**, **DVD Player**, **Network Utility**, and **Wireless Diagnostics**.

Some of these applications are accessible via other means in *macOS*, like the **Archive Utility**, **Wireless Diagnostics**, and **About This Mac**. Others are utilities from hardware that are no longer included as standard, like the **DVD Player** (my *MacBook* has no optical media). One utility in particular, **Network Utility**, is very useful and probably deserves to be promoted back into the ***/Applications/Utilities*** directory where it used to live in earlier versions.

As seen in Figure 2-44, the Network Utility features common tools such as **ping**, **nslookup**, **trace route**, and more. You may want to save this to your Dock, make an alias to it from the Utilities folder, or remember that you can use the **magnifying glass** in the top-right corner of the menu bar and search for the Network Utility by name when you need it.

Figure 2-44. *Using the Network Utility to ping* `www.apple.com`

Keychain Access

No chapter on *macOS* client management would be complete without a discussion around the dreaded **keychain**! If you have done Mac support for any length of time, you have likely come across cryptic messages about the **login** keychain or other annoying keychain-related errors. What is the keychain, and why is it causing my users so much grief?

The keychain can be managed through the **Keychain Access** utility found in */Applications/Utilities;* and it stores all of the various username and password combinations used on your Mac to access various web sites, secure applications, services, and wireless networks. It can also store certificates and encryption keys. There are several keychains on your Mac including **System**, **Local Items**, and **login**, and if you are signed in and have it activated, the **iCloud Keychain** can also play a role by synchronizing items across multiple Apple devices. Figure 2-45 illustrates the Keychain Access application and the various keychains, passwords, certificates, and keys on my Mac.

Figure 2-45. *Keychain Access data found in the login keychain*

While this seems pretty straightforward and innocuous, the problem with the keychain usually begins when a user has their password reset or changes it. After the password change, the next time the user logs in, they may be greeted with a dialog box prompting them to update their login keychain with the new password or create a new login keychain. Users being users, they will probably select the wrong option, skip this step, or won't know their old password to be able to effectively update it, and now we have the notorious login keychain issue.

If the user knows their old password, this is relatively easy to fix. Simply open *Keychain Access*, select the **login** keychain, then choose **Change Password for Keychain 'login'** from the **Edit** menu. It will prompt for the old password and the new password, and then it will update the keychain accordingly.

But what if the user doesn't know the old password? In that case we must create a new login keychain. To do this, open *Keychain Access* and select **Preferences...** from the **Keychain Access** menu. In the Preferences dialog box, click the **Reset My Default Keychains** button as shown in Figure 2-46. Please note that this will erase the **login** and **Local Items** keychains and replace them with new *default* ones. This means any passwords or entries stored in those keychains will be erased and the user will need to sign in again on various web sites and services to reestablish these keys.

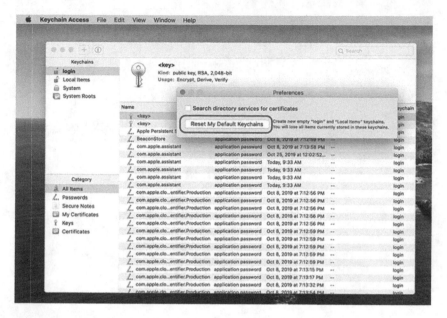

Figure 2-46. *Resetting the login and Local Items keychains*

Summary

In this chapter, we covered a lot of ground. You should now be familiar with the basic file system and directory structure of *macOS*. You should be relatively comfortable using the Terminal. You have been able to create and manage a new local user account. Finally, you learned how to find and use powerful hidden applications and features.

Apple's *macOS* is a very powerful and feature-rich operating system that continues to grow and change with each new version. The focus on security and privacy has been the driving force behind many of the enhancements found in the latest releases. Because this is such an important and ever-changing topic, our next chapter is solely devoted to the latest security and privacy features found in *macOS*.

CHAPTER 3

macOS Security

It is debatable if *macOS* is really more secure than *Windows*, but Apple has gained a reputation that a Mac is less susceptible to malware and privacy breaches than other platforms. Much of Apple's security and privacy services have continued to evolve over the last several iterations of *macOS*, with *Mojave* and *Catalina* placing an even greater emphasis on **sandboxing** and **user acknowledgement**. This chapter explores both hardware and software security and privacy controls that Mac system administrators must be familiar with.

Mac Hardware Security

Basic EFI Boot Security

Every modern Mac features *extensible firmware interface* (EFI) boot security through the use of a **pre-boot password**. Using the *Firmware Password Utility* or the *Startup Security Utility* (depending on the version of *macOS* being used), system administrators can lock down the ability for users to boot their Mac into a pre-boot environment without first entering a password. When you set an EFI password, you won't normally see the password prompt through the normal use of the system. When a user attempts to boot the Mac into **recovery mode**, **network boot**, or **removable media boot**, the EFI will prompt for the password before proceeding. This locks the Mac into booting only from the internal hard disk's operating system.

© Drew Smith 2020
D. Smith, *Apple macOS and iOS System Administration*,
https://doi.org/10.1007/978-1-4842-5820-0_3

To access the Firmware Password Utility or Startup Security Utility, you must first boot the Mac into *recovery mode* as outlined in Chapter 2 of this book. Once you are booted into the *macOS Recovery* environment, choose **Firmware Password Utility** or **Startup Security Utility** from the **Utilities** menu as shown in Figure 3-1. Follow the prompts on screen to set the firmware password and then restart. Make sure that the password you set is something you will remember or is documented somewhere within your IT organization.

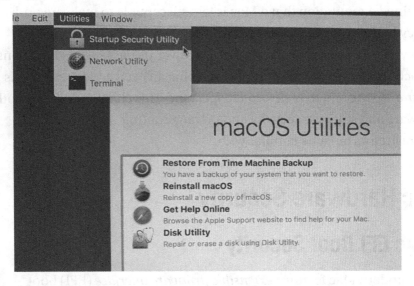

Figure 3-1. *Find the Startup Security Utility in macOS Recovery mode*

Pro Tip   Be aware that setting the EFI password saves it to a persistent memory space on the Mac's logic board. It is not easily reset, and according to Apple's official documentation, the only authorized way to reset this password is to bring the computer to an Apple Retail Store or another Authorized Apple Repair facility to have the password reset.

Apple T2 Security Chip

Beginning with the release of the *iMac Pro* in late 2017, Apple began shipping most new Macs with a next-generation custom chip called **T2**. The T2 integrates a number of different hardware controllers into a single chip with an eye toward hardware-enabled security. For example, it integrates the *SSD controller* along with a new *Secure Enclave* co-processor that manages boot security and storage encryption at the hardware level.

The following models have the T2 chip as of this writing:

- 2017 iMac Pro *(and later)*

- 2018 Mac mini *(and later)*

- 2018 MacBook Air *(and later)*

- 2018 MacBook Pro *(and later)*

To determine if your Mac has the T2 Security chip, you can find this by looking at the *System Report* for your Mac through the **About This Mac** dialog box and clicking the **System Report** button. In the System Information screen, drill down to **Hardware ➤ Controller (or iBridge);** and if the *Controller Model Name* is **Apple T2 chip,** then your computer has it. The T2 Security chip enables/impacts the following features:

- Touch ID (stores the Touch ID data in the Secure Enclave)

- Signal Image Processing with the front-facing FaceTime HD camera for facial recognition

- Enables Secure Boot

- Enhanced Encrypted Storage

- Secure System Management Controller (SMC)

- Secure Audio Controller for microphone security

Secure Boot is one of the T2 features that should be of particular interest to Mac system administrators. This function is only available on Macs that have the T2 chip, and it is found when you boot into *macOS Recovery* mode. To configure the Secure Boot feature as shown in Figure 3-2, once you boot into recovery mode, select the **Startup Security Utility** from the **Utilities** menu.

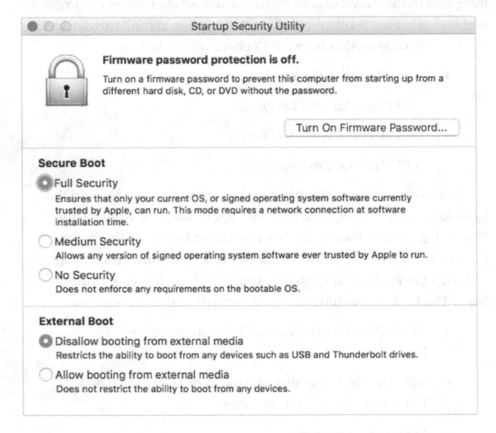

Figure 3-2. *The configuration options of the Secure Boot feature*

Secure Boot features three options—*Full Security, Medium Security,* and *None.* **Full Security** is on by default with any T2 machine as it ships from the factory. This option requires an Internet connection and checks to see if the OS you are attempting to install is currently trusted by Apple.

Medium Security checks to see if the OS you are attempting to install was ever trusted by Apple and does not require an Internet connection. **None** does not enforce OS signing or trusting at all.

Please note that on T2-enabled systems, this utility replaces the **Firmware Password Utility**. It features the ability to control external booting, and you can either disallow or allow booting from external media like USB flash drives, Thunderbolt hard drives, and the like. It is also worth mentioning for long-time Mac system administrators, network booting or **NetBoot** is *not possible* with the T2. The only supported network-enabled boot option for T2 Macs is by using Apple's Internet Recovery service. If you are using a NetBoot-based imaging workflow to stage your hardware, be aware that you will not be able to do so with T2-enabled Macs.

File Permissions

Like other Unix-based operating systems, *macOS* uses **POSIX** file permissions. There are four standard permissions that can be assigned by user or group for any file, folder, or volume.

POSIX

Read Only: Users can browse a file directory and open/copy files from the directory, but they cannot write to the directory or save changes to the files.

Read & Execute: Users can read files in the directory and execute applications in the directory.

Write Only: Users can only write to a folder with these permissions. They cannot open the folder or browse the contents. They can only drop a file into a directory with write-only permissions.

No Access: The user has no access to the file or folders.

In addition to the file permissions options, every file or directory in *macOS* features an **owner** (a specific user), a (specific) **group**, and an **Everyone** group. The Everyone group is a catchall for anyone who may be accessing the file or directory that isn't the specific owner or group. You should think of this as *everyone else*. The owner is the specific user who created the file or copied it into the current directory. The group is typically inherited from the folder that the file or folder exists within.

The default file permissions groups in *macOS* include

> **staff:** This is the group that all of the local user accounts belong to, including the Standard user.
>
> **admin:** This is the group that all of the local user accounts with admin rights belong to and has some elevated privileges such as the ability to write to the */Applications* folder.
>
> **wheel:** This is reserved for the *super user*, or **root** account. The root account is the only member of this group and should remain that way. Many system files and directories are protected by this group.

Modifying File Permissions

Unless you are setting up some specific file sharing over the local area network or the Internet with your Macs, leaving the default permissions to files and folders is recommended and preferable. If you are sharing files locally between multiple users on the same Mac, Apple provides a **Public** folder in each user's home directory for placing files meant to be shared across multiple users on the same machine.

If you do need to modify file permissions, you can do so by selecting the file or folder in the Finder and choosing **Get Info** from the **File** menu or via **right-click**. Figure 3-3 outlines how to make these changes.

- **Padlock:** If locked, click it to authenticate as a user with permissions to unlock it and make changes to the sharing and security settings of the file or folder.

- **+/- Buttons:** Use these to add or remove users or groups and set additional permissions.

- **Gear Button:** Use this option to copy permissions on a folder to enclosed files and folders. This allows you to change the permissions on a top-level directory and copy those permissions down.

- **Privileges Drop-Down Menu:** Use this to set permissions for a given user or group.

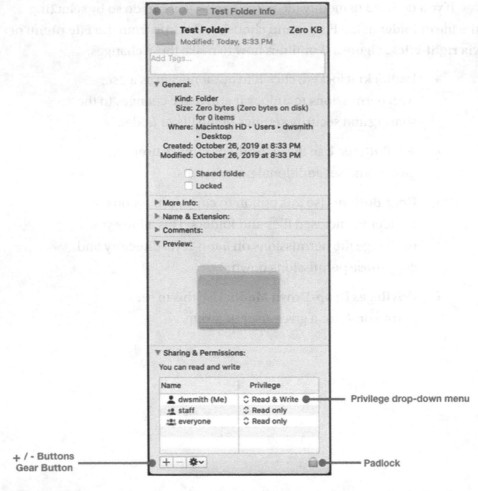

Figure 3-3. *The Sharing & Permissions pane of the Get Info dialog box*

Parental Controls and Screen Time

Versions of *macOS* prior to *Catalina* feature a *Parental Controls System Preference* that allows a local administrator to create a Standard user account with additional configurable limitations. You can create a user governed by Parental Controls when you create a new user and choosing

Managed by Parental Controls as the user type. Alternately, when you open the Parental Controls System Preference, it will prompt you to create a managed user account as shown in Figure 3-4.

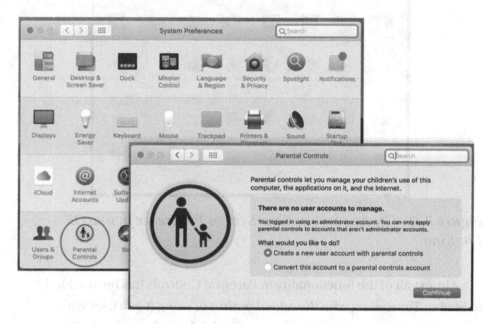

Figure 3-4. *The Parental Controls System Preference as seen in macOS versions prior to Catalina*

Apple decided to remove *Parental Controls* in *macOS Catalina* and instead port a feature that first appeared in iOS 12 over to *macOS* called *Screen Time*. Configuring Screen Time is done through the new System Preference shown in Figure 3-5.

Figure 3-5. *The new Screen Time System Preference in macOS Catalina*

Almost all of the functionality in Parental Controls has been added to Screen Time along with the added option of using it as a user with local administrative rights. The reason for this is to allow people to police their own computing and social media habits while still having full administrative control over their system. Screen Time is relatively self-explanatory, but there are a few very cool new features to highlight here.

One of those features is the ability to manage all of your child's devices from your own Mac and not having to interactively set it up on their devices. As long as you have *Family Sharing* enabled on your iCloud account and your child's iCloud account is part of the Family Sharing plan, you can manage all of the Screen Time features over the air. If you are going to manage your child's devices, you will want to set a Screen Time passcode so they are unable to override your settings. To do this, click the **Options** button in the *Screen Time System Preference* and set the code as shown in Figure 3-6.

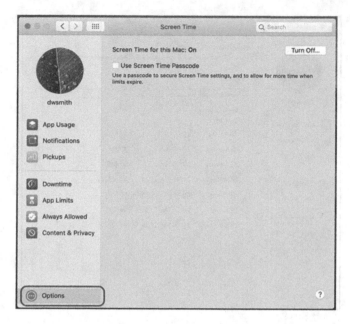

Figure 3-6. *The Screen Time Options button and passcode option*

Another feature of Screen Time on the Mac is the ability to control your *iOS* and *macOS* **Content & Privacy Restrictions** independently. For example, as long as you are sharing your Screen Time data between *iOS* and *macOS*, you can restrict inappropriate content on your Mac but not on your iOS device. Beyond these features, much of what makes up Screen Time is similar to what you will find on older versions of *macOS* as far as *Parental Controls* go. There are **time limits** for policing device use during school hours or at bedtime, now called *Down Time* as shown in Figure 3-7, and **content and privacy** settings that can be defined as shown in Figure 3-8.

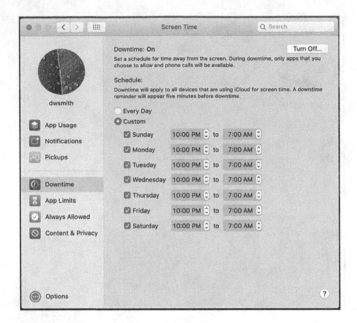

Figure 3-7. *Down Time schedule settings*

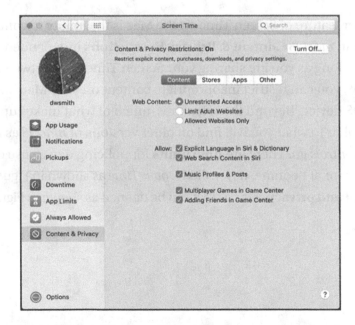

Figure 3-8. *Content & Privacy Restrictions in Screen Time*

App Limits provide a new level of granular control over which applications are able to be used, when they can be used, and for how long. You can choose categories of applications or specify specific applications as being *restricted* or *whitelisted*. Use the **Always Allowed** configuration option to specify applications to be whitelisted, that is, to be able to be used regardless of the time of day or duration of use as shown in Figure 3-9. If you are managing your child's devices, they can also request more time after an application limit is reached, and you can approve that request through the *Screen Time System Preference* on your Mac.

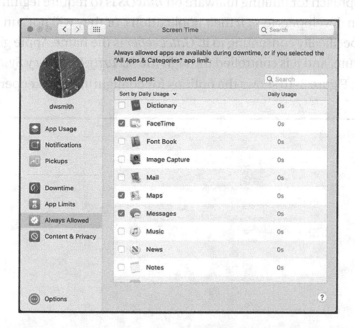

Figure 3-9. *App Limits allow you to specify which applications are available and how long they can be used each day*

Pro Tip   Screen Time offers some basic functions for controlling computer usage and filtering content, but it is important to note that this was developed for consumer use and is not a bulletproof security solution for large-scale 1:1 deployments. There are other commercial security applications that may be a better fit, depending on your organization's specific needs. **Mobile Device Management** (MDM), which we will discuss in Chapter 8, enables a more granular and effective approach to restricting a large number of Macs than Screen Time alone.

Gatekeeper

Apple's approach for limiting malware on *macOS* is to require legitimate application developers to *sign* their applications, or they will not run without the user specifically consenting to it. *Gatekeeper* is the name Apple gives to this feature, and it is controlled through the *Security & Privacy System Preference*. Figure 3-10 shows the options for configuring Gatekeeper.

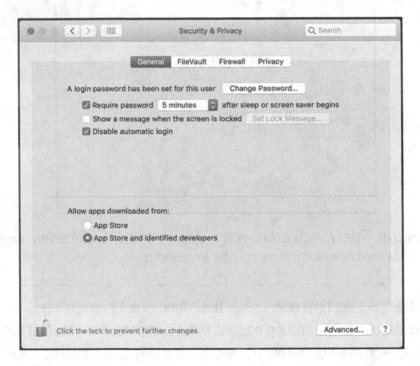

Figure 3-10. *Gatekeeper options in the General tab of the Security & Privacy System Preference*

Gatekeeper provides system administrators with two options for allowing Macs to run applications from third-party developers. **App Store and identified developers** is the default option which prevents applications that are not code-signed or downloaded from the *Mac App Store* from running. **App Store** is the more secure option, which limits users from running any application downloaded from the Internet and only allows applications that are downloaded from the *Mac App Store.*

As an administrator, you may still need to run an application for some reason that isn't code-signed or downloaded from the Mac App Store. In versions of macOS that are older than *Sierra*, there was a third option of **Anywhere** that allowed you to run applications without Gatekeeper getting in the way. Despite the fact that this option has now been removed in more recent releases, administrators can still override Gatekeeper by **right-clicking** an application that Gatekeeper blocks, choosing to **Open,** and then consenting to the warning dialog box to allow the application to run even though it may not be safe to do so.

FileVault

FileVault is Apple's build-in disk encryption technology, and it is currently at version 2.0. To enable FileVault, you use the *Security & Privacy System Preference* and click the **Turn on FileVault**... button in the FileVault tab as shown in Figure 3-11.

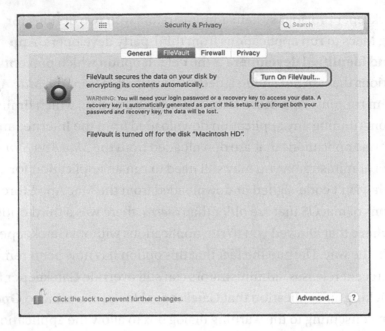

Figure 3-11. *Turn on FileVault encryption in the Security & Privacy System Preference*

When you are enabling FileVault, you need to configure a recovery key option in the event that you want to decrypt the drive or mount it on another Mac. For personal use, you may want to configure your iCloud account to decrypt the drive. For small businesses or companies that only need to support FileVault encryption on a couple of Macs, it is recommended to create a recovery key for each system and save the key strings somewhere secure that you can reference if you ever need to decrypt the drive. This option is shown in Figure 3-12.

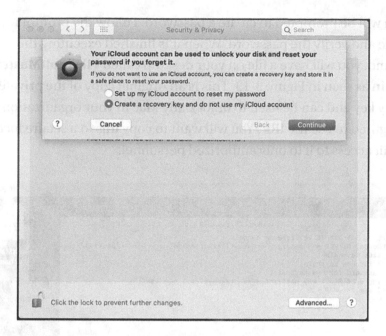

Figure 3-12. *Selecting a FileVault recovery key*

FileVault Institutional Recovery Key

What if you have hundreds or *thousands* of Macs that need to be encrypted and you don't want to manage individual recovery key strings for every individual user or machine? Fortunately, Apple provides the option to create and deploy an **Institutional Recovery Key** (IRK) for use on every Mac in your organization. Deploying an IRK involves three steps: creating the **master keychain** on one Mac, editing a copy of the master keychain to **remove the private key**, and then **deploying** the configuration to all the other Macs.

Creating the FileVault key involves using the command line interface. Open the Terminal and enter the following command at the prompt to create the master keychain:

```
security create-filevaultmaster-keychain ~/Desktop/
FileVaultMaster.keychain
```

You will be prompted to create a password. Follow the prompts to create and verify the password. When it is finished executing the command, you will have a file on your desktop called **FileVaultMaster. keychain** as seen in Figure 3-13. This is an original copy of the private recovery key and can be used to unlock any Mac in your organization that is configured to use the IRK. You will want to copy this to a secure location and limit access to it to only authorized personnel.

Figure 3-13. *The command has generated a FileVaultMaster keychain on the desktop*

Next, we need to prepare a copy for deployment to other Macs:

1. Open the **FileVaultMaster.keychain** file with the *Keychain Access* application.

2. In the *Keychain Access* application, click **FileVaultMaster** on the left side to select it. If required, click the **padlock** icon and authenticate to unlock it.

The password will be the same one you used when you created the **FileVaultMaster** file in the Terminal.

3. Locate the *private key* file on the right called **FileVault Master Password Key** shown in Figure 3-14. Click it to select it and then choose **Delete** from the **Edit** menu to delete it. You now have a keychain file that is missing the private key.

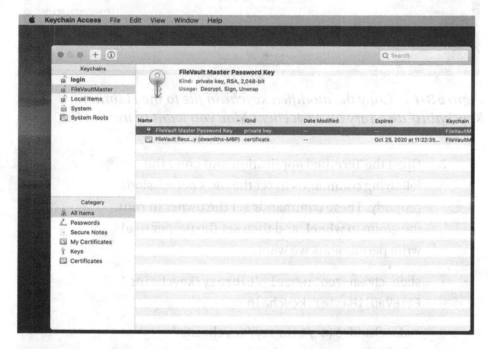

Figure 3-14. *Delete the FileVault Master Password Key*

We are now ready to deploy the IRK to other Macs. Follow these steps on each Mac you want to configure to use the IRK.

4. Copy the FileVaultMaster.keychain file that we modified to the */Library/Keychains/* folder as shown in Figure 3-15.

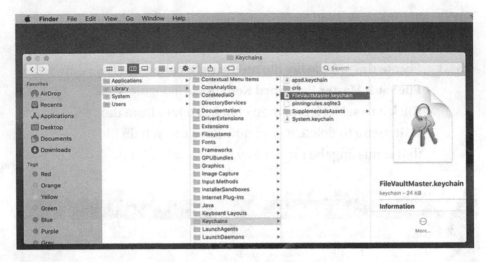

Figure 3-15. *Copy the modified keychain file to the /Library/ Keychains/ directory on each client Mac you want to use the IRK*

5. Open the Terminal application and enter the following commands to set the file's permissions properly. These commands set the owner to **root**, the group to **wheel,** and then set the proper read/ write permissions we want:

    ```
    sudo chown root:wheel /Library/Keychains/
    FileVaultMaster.keychain
    ```

    ```
    sudo chmod 644 /Library/Keychains/
    FileVaultMaster.keychain
    ```

6. Open the *Security & Privacy System Preference* and browse to the FileVault tab. Click the button to turn FileVault on. If you did this correctly, instead of being prompted to create a recovery key, you will get a message like the one in Figure 3-16.

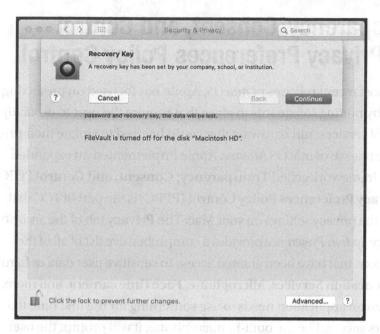

Figure 3-16. *FileVault doesn't prompt for a recovery key option; it uses the IRK automatically instead*

Pro Tip   You may have a situation where FileVault is already turned on for some of the machines in your organization that you will want to convert to the IRK. If this is the case, after copying the keychain file and setting the proper file permissions, you can enter a command into the Terminal to convert the existing FileVault recovery key to your Institutional Recovery Key.

The command to convert existing FileVault instances to the Institutional Recovery Key:

```
sudo fdesetup changerecovery -institutional -keychain /Library/
Keychains/FileVaultMaster.keychain
```

Transparency, Consent, and Control and Privacy Preferences Policy Control

In the most recent releases of *macOS*, Apple has focused on protecting users' privacy by putting safeguards in place that require the user to *explicitly allow* the use of services and hardware that could be used to violate their privacy. With the release of macOS *Mojave*, Apple implemented an expanded security framework called **Transparency, Consent, and Control** (TCC).

Privacy Preferences Policy Control (PPPC) is the part of TCC that governs the privacy settings on your Mac. The **Privacy** tab of the *Security & Privacy System Preference* provides a comprehensive list of all of the applications that have been granted access to sensitive user data or hardware such as **Location Services**, **Microphone**, **FaceTime camera**, and more.

When an application needs to use something for the first time that Apple considers secure, like the built-in microphone, it will prompt the user with a *privacy permission alert*. They can then either **grant** or **deny** permission for that application to use that resource. When granted, it is added to the Privacy pane as shown in Figure 3-17. This works on a per-user basis, so be advised that if you are administering a multi-user Mac, each user that uses that application must respond to the privacy permission alert.

There are a number of services that will prompt a privacy permission alert including

- Address Book (access Contacts)

- Calendar (access Events)

- Reminders

- Photos (access Photo Library)

- Camera

- Microphone

- Accessibility

Figure 3-17. *Privacy settings for the various restricted hardware or services in macOS Catalina*

Please note that *macOS Catalina* expands upon this to include storage locations like the user's **Desktop** or **Documents** folder and **Screen Sharing services**. In Chapter 8, we will discuss ways to whitelist some of these privacy settings, but be advised that some are deemed so secure (e.g., *Camera* and *Microphone*) that they cannot be whitelisted and will always prompt users to allow access.

Firewall

Apple provides a built-in software Firewall for *macOS* that is disabled by default. To configure it, open the *Security & Privacy System Preference* and choose the **Firewall** tab. Here you can turn the Firewall on/off. Once the Firewall is enabled, you can configure the various options. Figure 3-18 shows the available options and how to add applications to the exception list.

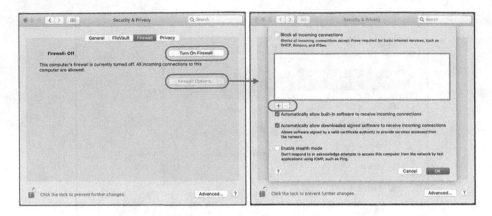

Figure 3-18. *Firewall exceptions and configurable options*

Advanced Security Options

You may have noticed the **Advanced** button on the *Security & Privacy System Preference*. When you click that button, you will have a couple of additional options that you can configure, and both are really geared toward shared computing environments like computer labs or public areas. Figure 3-19 shows these options.

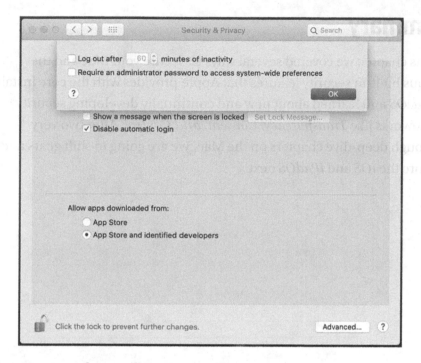

Figure 3-19. *Advanced Security & Privacy options*

- **Log out after x minutes of inactivity:** This can be configured to automatically return the Mac to the login window after a specified amount of time with no user interaction. This is helpful for protecting user data if someone walks away and leaves a computer signed in with a unique user account in a public place.

- **Require an administrator password to access system-wide preferences:** You may notice that many—but not all—System Preferences feature a padlock that can lock down changes by non-admin users. Checking the box for this option places a padlock on **all** System Preference panes. This allows system administrators to set specific user settings that would normally be modifiable by Standard users and keep them that way.

Summary

In this chapter, we covered several ways to secure your Mac and the various built-in security features that Apple provides with the core install of *macOS* and learned about new and continually developing security frameworks like *Transparency, Consent, and Control*. After two very thorough deep-dive chapters on the Mac, we are going to shift gears and explore the *iOS* and *iPadOS* next.

CHAPTER 4

iOS Client Administration

iOS and *iPadOS,* by extension, are relatively young operating systems when compared to *macOS*. Having launched with the first *iPhone* in 2007, it is only a little over 12 years old and now on its thirteenth release. *iOS* is much simpler and more straightforward to manage than a desktop operating system. Originally envisioned as an OS for a telephone handset, it didn't have the requirements of a traditional computer operating system, like the ability to install software downloaded from anywhere on the Internet or robust peripheral support. While *iOS* is less complicated than a true desktop-class system, there are a number of key features that system administrators should be familiar with when supporting fleets of *iPhones* and *iPads*. This chapter provides the foundation for understanding the capabilities that Apple provides for configuring, securing, and troubleshooting iOS devices running *iOS* 13 and *iPadOS* (13).

© Drew Smith 2020
D. Smith, *Apple macOS and iOS System Administration,*
https://doi.org/10.1007/978-1-4842-5820-0_4

iOS Hardware Support

The *iPhone* and *iPad* feature very little in the way of physical buttons or switches. For the most part, iOS devices are not considered to be user serviceable, meaning that only an ***Apple Authorized Repair Center*** or ***Apple Retail Store*** can repair them. Beyond a standard restart, one of the techniques that you can try in an attempt to fix common issues with *iPad* or the *iPhone* is a **forced restart** using special button combinations.

Forced Restart

When a simple restart is not an option because the device is completely frozen or locked up, you may need to force a restart of the device. When executed correctly, the **forced restart** will cause all Apps to close and completely shut down and restart the device. Figures 4-1 to 4-5 provide instructions for a forced restart on each of the major iOS device families available as of this writing.

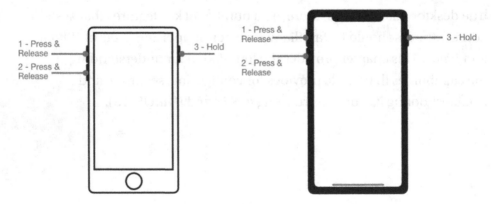

Figure 4-1. *Forced restart combinations for the iPhone 8 series, iPhone X series, and iPhone 11 series devices*

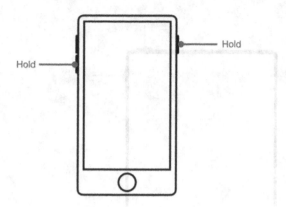

Figure 4-2. *Forced restart combination for the iPhone 7 series*

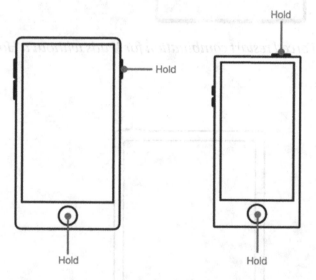

Figure 4-3. *Forced restart combinations for the iPhone 6 and iPhone SE*

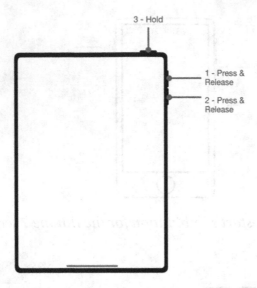

Figure 4-4. *Forced restart combination for iPads without a Home button*

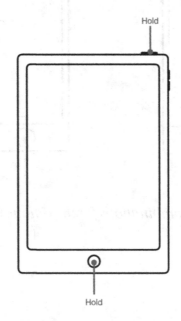

Figure 4-5. *Forced restart combination for iPads with a Home button*

Pro Tip   In some cases, an iOS device will lock up when the display is asleep, appearing as though the device is completely dead. Assuming that the battery is charged enough to power the device, using the **forced restart** method can also work in reviving a device that appears dead, but is simply appearing to not power on because it is locked up with the display off.

Battery Health

The lithium-ion battery in every iOS device will not last forever. With repeated use, eventually the battery will not be able to hold its maximum charge, thus shortening the length of the time the device will run off each subsequent charge. Apple got into some hot water in 2017 when it confirmed that it had been throttling the performance of iOS devices when the batteries were past the end of their useful life. After the subsequent consumer backlash, they added a new *Battery* Setting that provided users with information on how their batteries were impacted by the Apps they were using, how healthy their battery was, and what kind of performance impact (if any) the battery had on their device. Figure 4-6 provides a few screenshots of the Battery Setting in action.

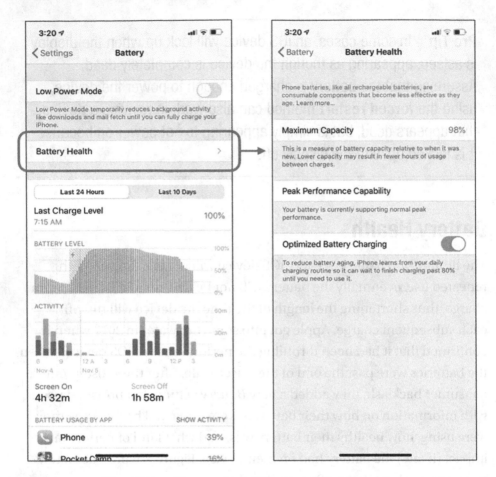

Figure 4-6. *The iOS 13 Battery and Battery Health settings*

Access the *Battery* Setting by going to **Settings** *app* ➤ **Battery**. You can view battery health information by going to **Settings** *app* ➤ **Battery** ➤ **Battery Health**.

Low Power Mode allows your iPhone to last longer on a single charge by disabling some background functions to reduce battery drain. This is recommended as a temporary setting in situations where you need to have your phone but your battery is running very low. Note that it can interfere with the performance or functionality of some Apps or services.

Checking the status of your battery's health can help to determine if it's time to get it replaced before it becomes a problem. **Maximum Capacity** and **Performance Ratings** will help you determine if your battery is in good condition or not. The device will also provide a warning and a recommendation to replace the battery when needed. Replacing the battery in an iOS device starts at $79 and can be performed at *Apple Authorized Repair* locations and the *Apple Retail Store* locations.

iOS Support

Similar to the basic hardware troubleshooting steps, there are just a handful of software support options with iOS devices. If you have access to the Home Screen and the Settings app, you can use the various built-in **iOS Reset** functions. If you do not have that access, the only other way to troubleshoot software-related issues or to potentially restore the device is through *iOS Recovery mode*.

iOS Reset

As shown in Figure 4-7, there are six different options when troubleshooting software-related issues with iOS devices. As detailed in the following, there are specific reasons to use each of these reset modes. Many of them can have some impact on the user's experience and/or data, so please use caution when attempting these and have a backup available if possible. All of these options can be found in the **Settings** app under *General ➤ Reset*.

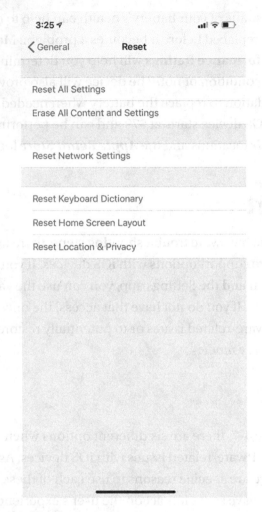

Figure 4-7. *iOS 13 Reset options*

- **Reset All Settings:** This option resets all of the
  operating system settings including the network
  settings and personal settings back to default. It does
  not touch your Apps or personal data.

- **Erase All Content and Settings:** This option resets the entire device back to a default installation of *iOS*. It erases the internal flash memory and reinstalls the operating system, and all user data and settings are deleted.

- **Reset Network Settings:** This option is similar to *Reset All Settings* in that it resets the network settings back to default, but nothing else.

- **Reset Keyboard Dictionary:** This option resets any special shortcuts or learned words that have been added to the dictionary.

- **Reset Home Screen Layout:** This option doesn't delete any data, but it does remove any customizations to the Dock and removes any folders.

- **Reset Location & Privacy:** As you use various Apps, they will prompt you to allow things like Location Services or access to the camera. By choosing this option, you remove all of the privacy allowances you have made for all Apps on the device, forcing them to prompt again the next time they are used.

iOS Recovery Mode

Recovery mode on an *iOS* device is similar to *macOS Recovery mode* (Local Recovery) in that it is a limited pre-boot environment that requires a button combination to invoke before the operating system starts to fully load. This limited environment is sometimes called **iBoot**, a boot-loader that allows the device to connect to a computer so that the user can erase and restore.

There are a few reasons why you may need to use iOS Recovery mode. A very common example is when you need to restore the OS to factory settings and the device is passcode locked and you don't have the passcode. Another very common case is if the OS is experiencing an issue booting and it's stuck at the white Apple logo during startup. Recovery mode is also useful to upgrade a new iOS device to the latest version without having to do so interactively on the unit, thus leaving it at the *Setup Assistant* screen when it is being deployed to an end user.

When you place an iOS device into recovery mode, the only thing you can really do with it is connect it to a computer running *iTunes* and follow the onscreen prompts to restore or upgrade the operating system software as seen in Figure 4-8. In this mode, when you restore the OS, it will completely erase the data on the device. Be sure to have a recent backup handy so you can reinstall all the Apps and user data after the restore completes successfully.

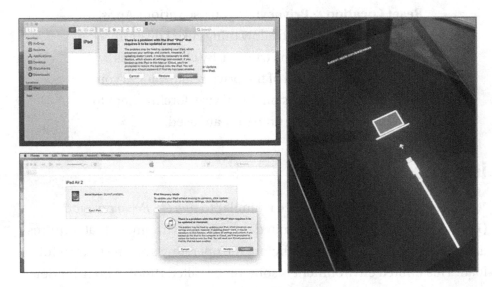

Figure 4-8. *Using iOS Recovery with iTunes or Finder (macOS Catalina)*

Pro Tip   *iTunes for Windows* and *iTunes* for *macOS* versions prior to *Catalina* can be used for downloading the latest operating system release that is compatible with a given device and restoring that version of *iOS*. Starting with *macOS Catalina*, Apple has eliminated *iTunes,* and you now see the iOS device appear in the *Finder* when connected to the Mac via USB. All of the same device management features from *iTunes* are now found directly in the *Finder.*

Similar to the forced restart mode, the button combinations required to place an iPhone or iPad into recovery mode have changed over time and by model. Here are the instructions by device family for reference:

- **iPhone 8 Series, iPhone X Series, iPhone 11 Series:** Plug the USB Lightning cable into the computer and iPhone. Press and release the **Volume Up** button, then press and release the **Volume Down** button, and then press and hold the **Side** button until you see the recovery mode screen.

- **iPhone 7 Series:** Power off the device. Press and hold the **Volume Down** button and plug your iPhone into a computer with your Lightning cable. Keep holding the button until you see the recovery mode screen.

- **iPhone 6 or iPhone SE:** Power off the device. Press and hold the **Home** button and plug your iPhone into a computer with your Lightning cable. Keep holding the button until you see the recovery mode screen.

- **iPad Without a Physical Home Button:** Power off the device. Press and hold the **Sleep/Wake** button and plug the iPad into a computer with a USB-C or Lightning cable and keep holding the button until you see the recovery mode screen.

- **iPad with a Physical Home Button:** Power off the device. Press and hold the **Home** button and plug your iPhone into a computer with your Lightning cable. Keep holding the button until you see the recovery mode screen.

Device Firmware Update Mode

Device Firmware Update (DFU) mode is not something many technicians will commonly need to use. It actually loads prior to the **iBoot** boot-loader and is an even lower-level environment than *iOS Recovery mode*. Please be aware that it can be difficult to place a unit into this mode as it requires precise timing and there is no feedback from the device when it is done correctly.

DFU mode is typically only used for a couple of reasons. The main one is to downgrade the firmware of a newer release of *iOS* to an older release. For example, you may need to downgrade from iOS 13 to iOS 12 due to a compatibility concern or something similar. The other reason to use it is to attempt to repair a corrupted firmware or *iOS* install that a restore via recovery mode did not fix. While no longer as common as it used to be, if you have users who have jailbroken their devices, you would also use DFU mode to reverse the jailbreaking procedure.

To place your device into DFU mode, you should follow these instructions for your specific device family:

- **iPhone 8 Series, iPhone X Series, iPhone 11 Series:** Plug the USB Lightning cable into the computer and iPhone. Press the **Volume Up** button, then press the **Volume Down** button, and then press and hold the **Side** and **Volume Down** buttons together for 5 seconds and then let go of the **Side** button but continue to hold the **Volume Down** button. You will get a message on the computer that the device is in recovery mode, but nothing will be shown on the iPhone's display.

- **iPhone 7 Series:** Power off the device. Hold down the **Side** button and **Volume Down** button together for 8 seconds and then let go of the **Side** button but continue to hold the **Volume Down** button as you plug the device into the computer via USB cable. You will get a message on the computer that the device is in recovery mode, but nothing will be shown on the iPhone's display.

- **iPhone 6 or iPhone SE:** Power off the device. Hold down the **Power** button and **Home** button together for 10 seconds and then let go of the **Power** button but continue to hold the **Home** button as you plug the device into the computer via USB cable. You will get a message on the computer that the device is in recovery mode, but nothing will be shown on the iPhone's display.

- **Force Restart an iPad Without a Physical Home Button:** Plug the USB Lightning cable into the computer and iPhone. Press the **Volume Up** button, then press the **Volume Down** button, and then press and hold the **Sleep/Wake** and **Volume Down** buttons together for 5 seconds and then let go of the **Sleep/ Wake** button but continue to hold the **Volume Down**. You will get a message on the computer that the device is in recovery mode, but nothing will be shown on the iPad's display.

- **Force Restart an iPad with a Physical Home Button:**
  Power off the device. Hold down the **Sleep/Wake**
  button and **Home** button together for 10 seconds and
  then let go of the **Sleep/Wake** button but continue to
  hold the **Home** button as you plug the device into the
  computer via USB cable. You will get a message on
  the computer that the device is in recovery mode, but
  nothing will be shown on the iPad's display.

iOS Backup

While we are on the subject of restoring *iOS*, we should probably review
the process for creating **backups**. Apple provides two ways to back up your
iOS device. You can back it up to a computer via *iTunes* (or the *Finder* in
macOS Catalina as mentioned earlier), or you can back it up to *iCloud*.
Which method you choose depends on your specific needs and the
available storage space in your iCloud account.

Computer Backup

Connect your iOS device directly to the computer using a Lightning to
USB cable. Next, using *iTunes* or *Finder* (in *macOS Catalina*), you can
select the device and click the **Back Up Now** button in the **General** tab as
shown in Figure 4-9. You have the option to encrypt your backup, which
is recommended especially if you have *Health* or *Activity* data on your
iPhone. If you choose to back up all of your data on your iOS device to this
computer, make sure that you also have a backup mechanism in place for
the computer too. The last thing you want is to lose your computer's data
and your iOS backups at the same time!

Figure 4-9. *iOS backup options built into the Finder in macOS Catalina*

iCloud Backup

If you have the available space in your iCloud storage, this is by far the preferable method. Not only is your device going to back up more often because it will attempt to do incremental backups when on Wi-Fi and connected to a power source, but it will be easier to restore on a new device once you sign in with your iCloud credentials through the Setup Assistant. iCloud backups are always encrypted, and because they are stored in the cloud, you don't have to worry about making a backup of your backups like you do when using the computer method.

To enable iCloud backup, simply browse to your **iCloud** settings through ***Settings** app* ➤ *yourappleid* ➤ *iCloud* ➤ *iCloud Backup* as shown in Figure 4-10. Flip the **iCloud Backup** switch to the **on** position, and the next time you are connected to the Internet via Wi-Fi and connected to a power source, it will do a backup. If you want to force a manual backup, make sure you are connected to a Wi-Fi network and then tap the **Back Up Now** button.

Figure 4-10. *The steps to configure iCloud backup in iOS 13*

Pro Tip   Regardless of which method you choose, Apple will never back up the following data: *Apple Pay* data; *Face ID* or *Touch ID* settings*; iCloud* data like *Contacts, Calendars*, and so on; or Apps, books, music, movies, and other similar content that is already hosted in the App Store or on one of Apple's various services.

Restoring from Backup

Restoring your iOS device data is pretty simple. If you used the computer method, you just connect your device to the same computer your recent backup is on and click the **Restore** button and follow the prompts to choose the backup that you wish to restore from. If you are restoring from an iCloud backup, after you reset your iOS device and you are stepping through the *Setup Assistant* (welcome sequence) when it prompts you to restore from an iCloud backup or set up as a new device, choose the **iCloud Backup** option and select the most recent backup you want to restore from. Figure 4-11 shows examples of both restore options.

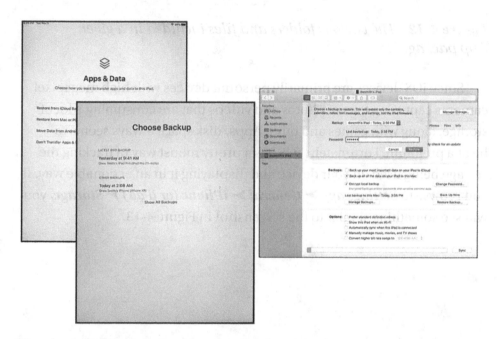

Figure 4-11. *Restore options from iCloud and via iTunes or Finder*

iOS Device Storage

Similar to the packaged applications in *macOS*, *iOS* also features *App packages* in the form of a single App icon. These are sandboxed application environments where the executable, preferences, and a unique *Documents* folder are self-contained inside each App. Figure 4-12 provides a diagram of the general layout of an iOS App bundle.

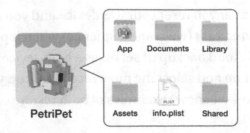

Figure 4-12. *The various folders and files included in a given App package*

Since iOS devices are primarily personal devices with high megapixel cameras capturing tons of photos and videos that are consuming a lot of storage, along with games and other Apps, disk space always seems to be at a premium. Fortunately, *iOS* has a pretty robust way of tracking the storage being used on your device and displaying it in an actionable way. If you browse to ***Settings*** *app* ➤ ***General*** ➤ ***iPhone*** *(or iPad)* ➤ ***Storage,*** you will see something similar to the screenshot in Figure 4-13.

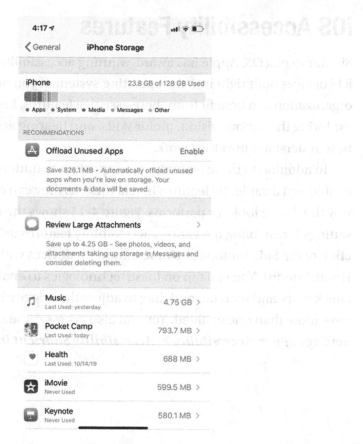

Figure 4-13. *iPhone storage information and actionable options to free up space in iOS 13*

Apple provides useful recommendations for short-term and long-term storage savings. You can enable the **Offload Unused Apps** option to temporarily delete the Apps that you don't use regularly. Then later on when you need to use them again, it will re-download them. Typically, when you delete an App manually on a device, it will remove any documents or settings associated with the App as well. When using Offload Unused Apps, it will retain that data instead.

iOS Accessibility Features

Similar to *macOS*, Apple has award-winning accessibility features for iOS devices built right into the operating system. If you or users in your organization can benefit from these assistive features, I recommend exploring the various vision, motor skills, and hearing accommodations to best understand how they work.

In addition to these features, it is important to understand how to enable and disable the features in real time, as they can often change the way the device looks or performs. Figure 4-14 shows the configuration settings for enabling the various accessibility features using a **triple-click** of the **Side** button (or **Home** button on devices with a physical Home button). You can tap on these technologies to enable them with a check mark and then tap and drag to adjust the priority in the list if you have more than one enabled. You can also access these settings through *Settings app* ➤ *Accessibility* ➤ *Accessibility Shortcut* in *iOS 13*.

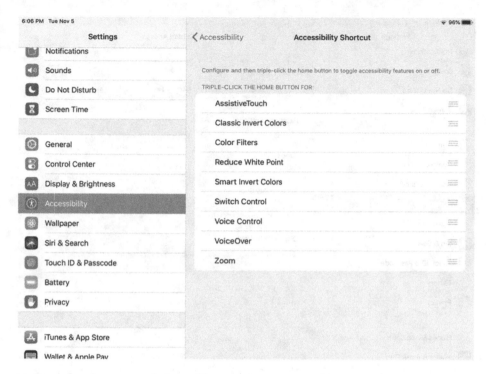

Figure 4-14. *Accessibility Shortcut options in iOS 13*

Guided Access

The other feature tucked under the *Accessibility* settings that can be helpful in cases where you are using an iOS device as a kiosk or something similar is *Guided Access*. The Guided Access feature can be enabled in iOS 13 under **Settings ➤ Accessibility ➤ Guided Access**. When this is enabled, you can **triple-click** the **Home** (or **Side**) button in any App and lock the device into only using that App. You can also disable any auto-lock features after the device has been idle for some period of time. Figure 4-15 shows an example of the Guided Access configuration settings on an iPad being used as a mobile ordering kiosk.

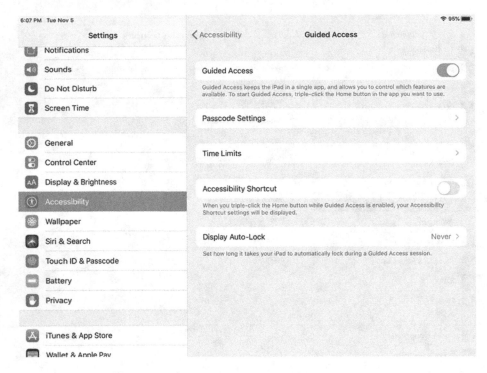

Figure 4-15. *Guided Access options in iOS 13*

Pro Tip   One additional feature of Guided Access is the ability to disable interaction with parts of the display when using a single App. For example, let's say you want to use Guided Access with a web page in Safari. You may also want to disable the ability for the user to access the address bar or the ability to create new tabs, thus locking the user to a single web page. To do this, enable Guided Access on the web page you want to lock down, **triple-click** the Home button to access Guided Access options, and then **draw a circle** around the areas of the screen that you want to disable.

Network Settings

While there is not a specific network settings pane in *iOS*, the root of the *Settings* app provides access to Wi-Fi, Bluetooth, and cellular data (if the device supports it).

Wi-Fi

To configure wireless settings, you can tap the **Wi-Fi** button from the list near the top of the *Settings* app as shown in Figure 4-16. The Wi-Fi settings will poll the network around you and display a list of available wireless networks. Tapping the button labeled **Other...** allows you to configure a hidden wireless network or preconfigure a wireless network that you want devices to automatically join after it's deployed to an end user.

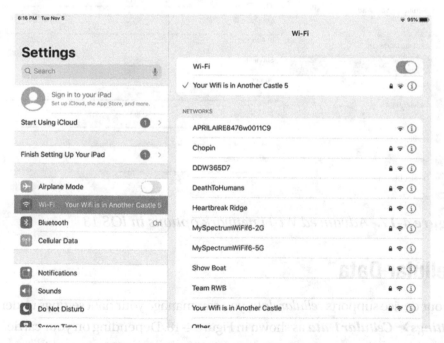

Figure 4-16. The Wi-Fi settings in iOS 13

Tapping the little blue **"i"** button to the right of the wireless network allows you to configure specific wireless settings as shown in Figure 4-17. You can configure your **TCP/IP** settings, **DNS** settings, and **HTTP Proxy** settings here. If you have already connected to a wireless network, you can tap the **Renew Lease** button to force a release and renew of the DHCP IP address lease or tap **Forget This Network** to disconnect from the network and not attempt to auto-join it again in the future.

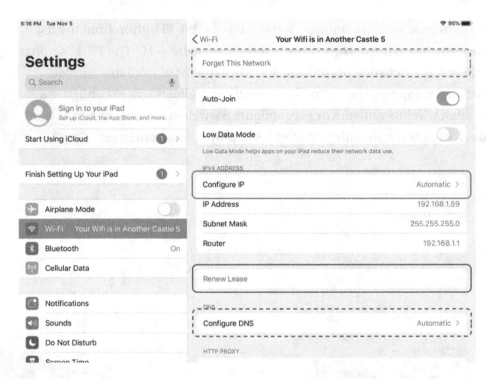

Figure 4-17. *Advanced Wi-Fi network options in iOS 13*

Cellular Data

If your device supports *cellular data*, you can manage your data settings under *Settings ➤ Cellular Data* as shown in Figure 4-18. Depending on your carrier and plan, you may have options here to enable a **Personal Hotspot**, where your iOS device shares your cellular data connection to other devices via Wi-Fi. You can toggle **Cellular Data on/off** to restrict data use to Wi-Fi only and conserve your plan's data allowance when near wireless networks. Some carriers have various roaming options, Wi-Fi calling features, or other carrier services that can be accessed from this page. You can also scroll through the list of installed Apps and toggle their ability to use cellular data. This can be especially beneficial for users with limited data plans.

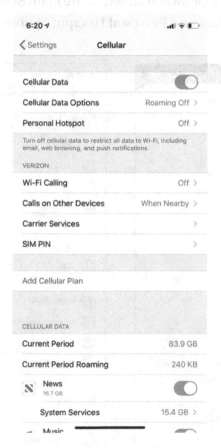

Figure 4-18. *Cellular data options for a Verizon wireless device running iOS 13*

VPN

Like *macOS*, you can also configure the built-in *VPN* for *iOS*. To configure the optional VPN settings, browse to **Settings** *app* ➤ **General** ➤ **VPN** and tap the **Add VPN Configuration...** button. You will be presented with a screen similar to the one shown in Figure 4-19. Like *macOS*, you have the option of configuring several of the most popular VPN protocols including *Cisco IPSec*. Once you have added a VPN configuration, you will see a simple **VPN on/off** toggle switch added to the main **Settings** pane just below the **Cellular Data and Personal Hotspot** options.

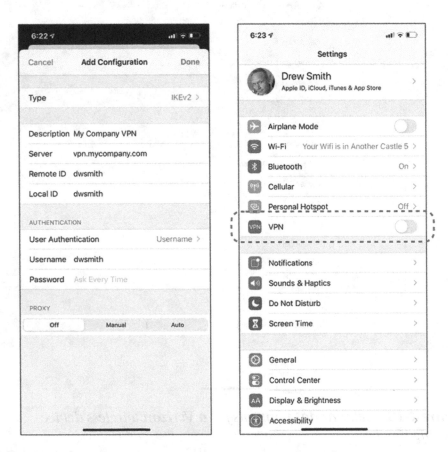

Figure 4-19. *VPN configuration settings and resulting activation switch in iOS 13*

iOS Device Security

When Apple designed *iOS*, they developed it from the ground up with modern security features. Disk encryption is enabled by default, and it's not an option in standard *iOS* installs. Apple has continued to beef up the security and privacy features in *iOS* as part of their *Transparency, Consent, and Control initiative*. *Touch ID*, *Face ID*, and *Activation Lock* are all next-generation features that help protect user data and privacy and deter device theft.

Passcode Lock/Touch ID/Face ID

Every iOS device features the *passcode* lock option. This enables a user to set a code that is required to unlock the device and access the Home Screen, user data, and Apps. This can be as simple as a four-digit number or as complex as a full phrase or password. Apple debuted the biometric fingerprint sensor, *Touch ID*, some time ago; and it is a standard feature on devices with a physical Home button. The next-generation facial recognition system, *Face ID*, is a standard feature on iOS devices without a physical Home button. Both of these technologies work in conjunction with the passcode settings to secure your devices. These features can be configured in **Settings ➤ Face ID & Passcode** in iOS 13 on devices that use Face ID and in **Settings ➤ Touch ID & Passcode** in iOS 13 on devices that use Touch ID.

Pro Tip   For added data security, particularly in government or corporate environments, you may want to set the device to reset/restore to factory default after some number of invalid password attempts. This can protect against brute-force attacks being used on a lost or stolen device.

Privacy

Similar to the *Privacy* tab in the *Security & Privacy System Preference* in *macOS*, the *Privacy Setting* in *iOS* can be found by browsing to **Settings** *app* ➤ **Privacy** and includes a list of the Apps or services that have requested to use any number of hardware or software features that Apple deems sensitive to a user's privacy. As you can see in Figure 4-20, the typical **Location Services**, **Microphone**, and **Camera** are joined by *iOS*-specific options like **Health**, **HomeKit**, and **Motion & Fitness**. You can browse these categories and manage which applications are able to use these specific features.

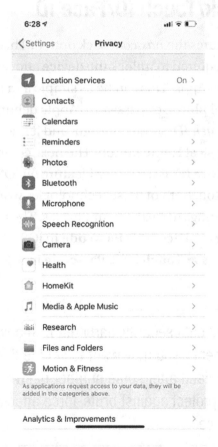

Figure 4-20. Privacy settings for iOS 13

Screen Time Restrictions

Starting with iOS 12, Apple introduced the *Screen Time* feature, which allowed users to measure the time they were spending on their devices and take action to self-impose time limits on things like games or social media. Like Screen Time for *macOS*, there are specific settings for **Down Time**, **App Limits**, and other features that we covered in Chapter 2. To access the Screen Time settings in *iOS*, browse to ***Settings*** *app* ➤ ***Screen Time***.

There is one specific set of **privacy and content** settings that are somewhat unique to *iOS*. These *Restrictions* used to be found under ***Settings*** *app* ➤ ***General*** ➤ ***Restrictions*** but have been moved into the Screen Time settings in iOS 12 and later. These settings can include restricting access to specific Apps, disabling *App Store* downloads, disabling in-app purchases, or disabling the use of specific hardware like the camera. Figure 4-21 shows a more comprehensive list of settings found under ***Settings*** ➤ ***Screen Time*** ➤ ***Content & Privacy Restrictions***.

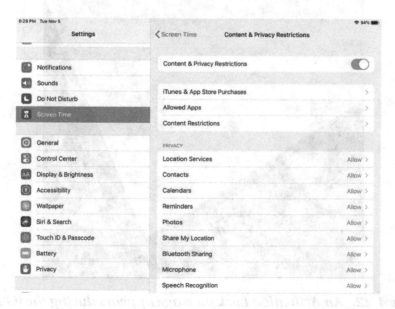

Figure 4-21. *The list of specific iOS device Restrictions in iOS 13*

Activation Lock

Activation Lock is an anti-theft feature that Apple implemented several years ago to provide another level of device security to *iOS* users. Activation Lock works in conjunction with your *Apple ID* and *iCloud* account to ensure that the only person who can reactivate an iOS device after a reset or restore is the user that owns the *iCloud* account that was signed in on that unit. If a device is placed into iOS Recovery mode, erased, and then restored with a fresh copy of iOS 13 without having the existing *iCloud* account signed out first, you will be greeted with the message shown in Figure 4-22 when attempting to use the Setup Assistant to activate the device.

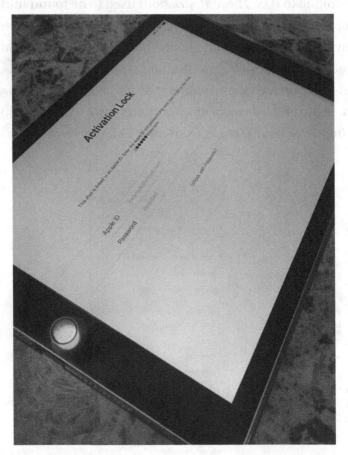

Figure 4-22. *An Activation Lock message appears during the iOS Setup Assistant*

To continue with the activation process, you must have the *Apple ID* or *iCloud* password for the account that was previously signed into the device. Without that password, you will never finish setting up the device, so it will not result in a usable system. To guard against Activation Lock headaches, you should always have the last user **sign out** of *iCloud* before resetting or restoring the operating system. In cases where a restore is required due to an inoperable device, be sure to have the iCloud password available so you can quickly authenticate through Activation Lock and finish configuring the system for use.

If you have had to restore the device for some reason and do not have the iCloud account to bypass Activation Lock, you must contact Apple Support via ***AppleCare*** or through an ***Apple Retail Store***. By providing proof of purchase, an Apple employee can reset the Activation Lock status of a device once ownership has been proven.

Pro Tip   Schools and businesses that use MDM tools or Apple's Device Enrollment Program (DEP) can disable Activation Lock on institution-owned devices. This is covered in Chapter 8.

User Accounts

All iOS devices are designed for a personal, single-user experience. There is only one local user account per device; and all of the other accounts are used to access various services like the *App Store or iCloud* or third-party email services like *Gmail* or *Microsoft Exchange*. While it is recommended that you use the same account for all of Apple's services, it is possible to use separate accounts for the *App Store* and *iCloud*, respectively.

Apple ID

The *Apple ID* is the main account you will need to use an iOS device. Apple IDs are free and can be configured using any email address, even one from competitors like Microsoft or Google. To create an *Apple ID*, your users simply need to go to http://appleid.apple.com and register for one. You can also register for an *Apple ID* in many areas of *iOS* that require a sign-in to enable a service, like the *App Store*. Education or business customers can also have *institutional Apple IDs* created, and we will cover those in greater detail in Chapter 8. Apple IDs are used for enabling any number of Apple services including *iMessage*, *FaceTime*, and the *App Store*.

iCloud Account

The *iCloud* account is often confused with the *Apple ID* because you can, and typically do, sign up for *iCloud* services using your *Apple ID* username. However, these are actually separate accounts. *iCloud* services generally involve synchronizing data between various Apple devices including *Documents*, *Messages*, *Contacts*, *Calendar*, *Safari* bookmarks, and more. *iCloud* also enables services like *Find My iPhone*, *Activity Sharing* (when paired with an *Apple Watch*), and *iCloud Keychain*.

App Store Account

The third account is the *App Store* account, which is an *Apple ID* that has been registered with a **payment method** and can be used to purchase and install Apps from the *App Store*. While the *iCloud* account is a personal account, the *Apple ID* used with the *App Store* could be shared with others in your family or organization. You can sign into the *App Store* with an *Apple ID* manually through ***Settings** app* ➤ ***iTunes & App Store*** and then click the **Sign In** button to log in as shown in Figure 4-23.

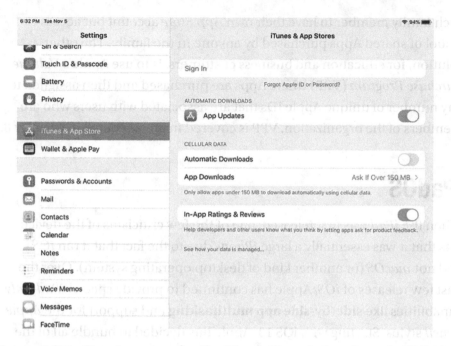

Figure 4-23. *Sign-in screen for the iTunes Store & App Store in iOS 13*

Please be aware that unless you plan to share the account credentials with all of your organization's users, a shared *App Store* account may not be a good idea. When you purchase and install an App on the iOS device using a shared *App Store* account, the next time that the app needs to update, it will prompt your user to enter the password for the shared account. If they do not know the password, they can lock the App Store account or request a password reset, which may cause problems for other devices that are also configured using the shared account. If you disclose the password to the end users, then they could potentially make unauthorized purchases and bill your account.

Fortunately, Apple has implemented two solutions to get around these issues with the *App Store* while allowing organizations to purchase Apps centrally and manage them across many devices. The first solution is for consumers, and that is called *Family Sharing*. Family Sharing allows each family member to have their own *App Store* account but access a pool of shared Apps purchased by anyone in the family. The other solution, for education and business customers, is to use Apple's *Volume Purchase Program* (VPP) where Apps are purchased and then assigned to any number of unique Apple IDs that are associated with users who are members of the organization. VPP is covered in greater detail in Chapter 8.

iPadOS

When the *iPad* was first released, one of the few criticisms of the device was that it was essentially a large *iPhone* due to the fact that it ran *iOS* and not *macOS* (or another kind of desktop operating system). Over the past few releases of *iOS*, Apple has continued to provide special *iPad-only* capabilities like **side-by-side app multitasking** and support for the *Apple Pencil* stylus. Starting with iOS 13, Apple has decided to bundle all of the iPad-only features under one moniker—*iPadOS*.

While the underlying operating system is still *iOS*, the following features are unique to the *iPad* and are only found in the *iPadOS* subset of iOS 13:

- **Removable Media Support**: The **Files** App not only allows you to browse in the macOS-like **Column** view, but it provides access to create and organize your data into folders; and if you insert a USB disk via a Lightning or USB-C adapter, you can also move data to/from removable media.

- Enhanced support for Apple Pencil.

- Desktop-class Safari browser.

- Enhanced multitasking including **Slide Over** windows and multiple **Split View** windows from the same App on screen at once.

- Smaller App icons to make room for more Apps per page and a customizable **Widget** area on the Home Screen.

- **Support for a Bluetooth Mouse**: This feature is hidden in the ***Accessibility*** ➤ ***Touch*** area of *iPadOS* as shown in Figure 4-24. You do not get a pointer as you would expect when you hear *mouse support* because what it enables is Apple's Bluetooth **pointer tool** which looks like a blob on the screen. The movement is less than smooth, and it is best used as more of an **accessibility** feature than a way to make your iPad work like a desktop computer.

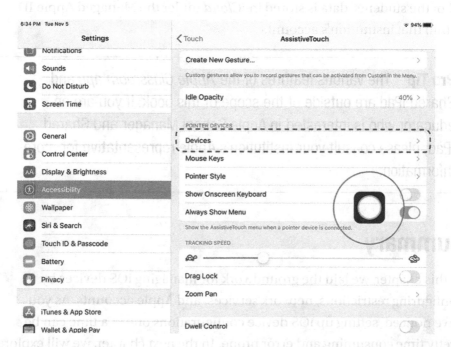

Figure 4-24. *Device's accessibility feature to enable mouse support in iPadOS*

Shared iPad

Finally, no discussion of *iPadOS* would be complete without mentioning the **Shared iPad** feature, which allows multiple users to have unique logins on a shared device. This is very similar to having multiple user accounts on *macOS*, but with one huge exception—this feature is limited to Apple's *education customers only*. If you are supporting carts full of shared *iPads* in an academic environment, enabling Shared iPad could be a big win.

To use Shared iPad, the academic organization must have access to *Apple School Manager*. Using Apple School Manager, the system administrator would create special *Managed Apple IDs* for each student. Using Apple School Manager, you prepare your device as a Shared iPad which enables remote monitoring and multi-user support on the device. All of the students' data is stored in *iCloud* under the Managed Apple ID within that institution's account.

Pro Tip   The various features of the *Apple Classroom app* and Shared iPad are outside of the scope of this book. If you are an educator who is interested in Apple School Manager and Shared iPad, please consult your institution's Apple representative for more information.

Summary

In this chapter, we laid the groundwork for managing iOS devices by configuring restrictions, network services, and Apple accounts. As you have noticed, setting up iOS device configurations one at a time can be pretty time consuming and error prone. In the next chapter, we will explore the *Apple Configurator* tool and how to use it to configure hundreds or thousands of devices using *Blueprints* and *Profiles*.

CHAPTER 5

Managing Devices with Apple Configurator

In Chapter 4, we explored the various ways to restrict or configure iOS devices interactively on the units themselves. As you have experienced, this manual approach can be problematic if you have more than a handful of devices to configure. Fortunately, we have tools like *Apple Configurator* that help us automate much of this process.

In this chapter, we will work with a couple of sample devices in Apple Configurator and develop a local workflow for preparing iOS devices for deployment. Along the way, you will be introduced to many concepts that we will use throughout the rest of this book including *Configuration Profiles*, *Mobile Device Management*, device *supervision*, and more.

Welcome to Apple Configurator

The first thing you need to know about *Apple Configurator* is that it is **not** a Mobile Device Management (MDM) solution. It is a **configuration** tool for iOS devices, and it was originally developed as a way for system administrators to configure identical *iPads* and *iPhones* in mass quantities.

© Drew Smith 2020
D. Smith, *Apple macOS and iOS System Administration*,
https://doi.org/10.1007/978-1-4842-5820-0_5

In 2012, I was directly involved in a large 1:1 *iPad* deployment for a chain of colleges across the continental United States. Over a few years' time, we had deployed over 30,000 *iPads* to students, staff, and faculty, and every single one of the devices had to function identically. We used Apple Configurator to achieve this level of standardization, and it worked very well.

The second thing to know about Apple Configurator is that it only runs on *macOS*. Therefore, the prerequisite for this section is that you have a Mac to install Apple Configurator on. The latest release supports iOS 13 and devices that were released alongside it, namely, the *iPhone 11* series. If you are going to run the latest version of Configurator, your Mac must be running at minimum *macOS Mojave* 10.14.6. As shown in Figure 5-1, you can download Apple Configurator 2 from the *Mac App Store* for free.

Figure 5-1. *Apple Configurator 2 is listed in the Mac App Store*

Third, to prepare a device in Apple Configurator, you need to connect it to the Mac using a USB cable. If you have a massive number of devices to configure, like I did with our 30,000-unit deployment, you should probably plan to buy some powered USB 2.0 hubs, iPad Carts that feature integrated USB hubs, or—if you are using the new *Mac Pro*—some PCI cards with eight or more USB ports per card. This will dramatically reduce the time it will take for the devices to prepare as Configurator will work on multiple connected devices simultaneously.

At this point, you should have a Mac running *Mojave* or later, at least one USB to Lightning cable, at least one iOS device that you can use to practice on, and Apple Configurator 2 installed in */Applications*. Let's get started by plugging in that iOS device and launching Apple Configurator.

Apple Configurator User Interface

When you launch Apple Configurator, your screen should look similar to Figure 5-2. If you just have a giant image of the connected iOS device, click the **View** pop-up menu on the toolbar and select **List**. Now you'll have your iOS devices listed in rows with the various column headers like I do.

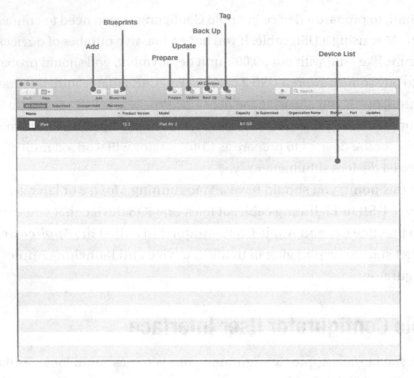

Figure 5-2. *The primary Apple Configurator window and toolbar*

There are a few key components of the toolbar as shown in Figure 5-2. Here's an explanation of a few of the major ones:

- **Add Button:** Use this button to install Apps, documents, media, or Configuration Profiles to the selected iOS device(s).

- **Blueprints Button:** Use this button to create or edit templates, called Blueprints, that we will use to build specific iOS devices for various groups of users.

- **Prepare Button:** This is the first button to press whenever we connect a new iOS device. This starts the *Prepare Devices Assistant* and steps through the activation and provisioning process.

- **Update Button:** This button will download and install the latest version of iOS for a given device.

- **Backup Button:** This button creates a backup of the selected device. This is essentially the same function that we covered in Chapter 4 using *iTunes* or *Finder* (*macOS Catalina*). The backups created in iTunes are compatible with the backups created with Configurator.

- **Tag Button:** This button allows you to tag specific groups of devices to easily identify them by color for specific purposes.

- **Device List:** This is the list of devices in Apple Configurator and their status. You can sort them in terms of **All Devices**, **Supervised**, **Unsupervised**, and when they are in **recovery** mode. You can also see some basic information in your list of devices. **Double-clicking** a device will provide more information including the *serial number*, *IMEI* number, *battery status*, *installed apps*, and more.

Pro Tip   You may be tempted to configure a set of devices exactly the same way through the integrated **Backup** and **Restore process** by configuring an iOS device exactly how you want it and then using the **Backup** button to prepare it for restore to other devices. There are a number of drawbacks to this method, including the fact that despite your best efforts, you can leave user-specific data on the device being used as the backup source. This also doesn't scale particularly well over time because if you need to make a single change, you have to create a whole new source backup. For these reasons and more, in this book, we are going to use **Blueprints** instead of Backup and Restore workflows.

Organization and Supervision Identity

Before you start configuring iOS devices, there are a couple of identity options that you will want to define in the application's **Preferences** dialog box. To access these options, click the **Apple Configurator 2** menu and choose **Preferences....** Then click the **Organizations** tab in the Preferences window. Figure 5-3 shows the Organizations tab. Click the + button to create a new Organization.

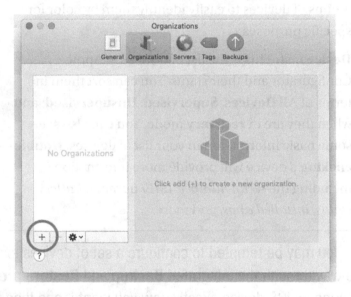

Figure 5-3. *The Organizations tab inside Apple Configurator's Preferences window*

As the information on the *New Organization* sheet explains, creating an Organization provides specific *contact information* and the *supervision identity* for supervised devices. You may be asking yourself, "What is a *supervised* device?" As we learned in Chapter 4, *iOS* is not designed as a multi-user operating system where many users can share the same device and have various unique identities and permissions like you do in *macOS*. Despite this fact, when large companies and schools purchase iOS devices and provide them to employees, students, or other end users, the IT Department still needs to implement basic information security controls.

Supervising a device is a way that system administrators can lock down specific parts of *iOS* from users in a way that is similar to having a local admin account and providing a limited environment for others. You will see later in this chapter that many security options are only available to devices that are supervised. Devices that are not supervised can still be managed, but the end user has the ability to change configuration settings, restore or reset the device, and remove restrictions.

You may be wondering when it is acceptable to **supervise** a device and when it is not. This is largely up to the organization and the use case for the device. The general rule of thumb that I have used is that if the device is owned by my organization, then I supervise it. If the device is owned by the end user, I will still attempt to manage it through *Configuration Profiles* or *ActiveSync*, but it is not going to be supervised so my security is considered *best effort*. Your mileage on this topic may vary depending on how restrictive the devices need to be in your particular case.

CREATING AN ORGANIZATION AND SUPERVISION IDENTITY

Go ahead and create an organization and a supervision identity as shown in Figure 5-4. When it prompts you to sign in to the *Device Enrollment Program*, **skip** that step. We cover this service in a later chapter of this book, and we will not be using that for this exercise. Enter the information about your organization such as the **name**, the **phone number** for your help desk, and **public address**. This information *will be* disclosed to end users or people who may find the device if it gets lost.

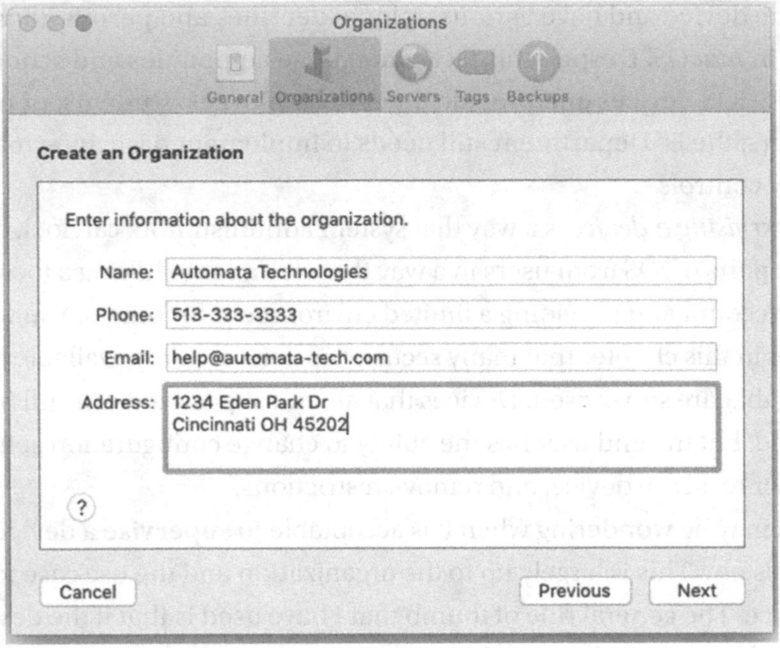

Figure 5-4. *Enter some contact information to define your organization*

Click the **Next** button to continue. Now we are going to create a new
supervision identity. This identity is basically a *trust certificate,* and you can
view it by clicking **Show Supervision Identity…** as shown in Figure 5-5. Now
that we have created an organization and a supervision identity, we are ready
to continue. Close out of the Preferences window and return to the main Apple
Configurator interface.

Figure 5-5. *An example supervision identity certificate*

Pro Tip   You can export your supervision identity using the little **gear** button next to the **+/-** buttons on the **Organizations** tab of the **Preferences** window. This will allow you to share the same supervision identity with other Macs that are being used with Apple Configurator. It is very important that all Macs that are enrolling devices share the same supervision identity for the same organization if you are using more than one machine to configure your *iPhones* and *iPads*.

Preparing Devices in Apple Configurator

Now that we have the supervision identity and organization out of the way, let's start by preparing our first device. We are going to create a supervised device in this exercise so that we have the ability to use the full extent of security options available to us.

PREPARE THE DEVICE

1. To get started, **select** the device in your list that you want to configure and click the **Prepare** button in the toolbar.

2. The Prepare Devices Assistant dialog box like the one shown in Figure 5-6 will prompt you select a method. We will use a **Manual Configuration,** and **supervise** the device, but **allow it to pair with other computers**. Click the **Next** button to continue.

3. We are not going to use an MDM in this chapter, so you can select **Do not enroll in MDM** in the next dialog box. Click the **Next** button to continue.

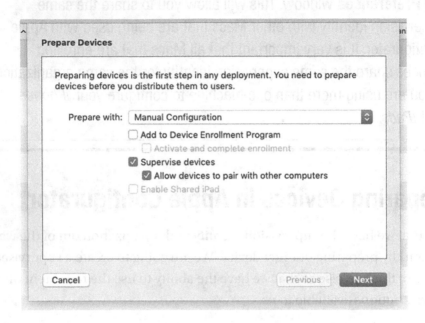

Figure 5-6. *Prepare the device as supervised*

4. Select your **Organization** from the pop-up menu. Click the **Next** button to continue.

5. When we are prompted to select which steps are shown during the *iOS Setup Assistant*, it is referring to the steps your end users must view and respond to when they boot their device for the first time. Many of these will seem familiar if you have recently installed a fresh copy of iOS and had to use the Setup Assistant. Please note that not all of these steps apply to every device. Let's choose **Show only some steps** from the drop-down and then **check** a few of them as shown in Figure 5-7.

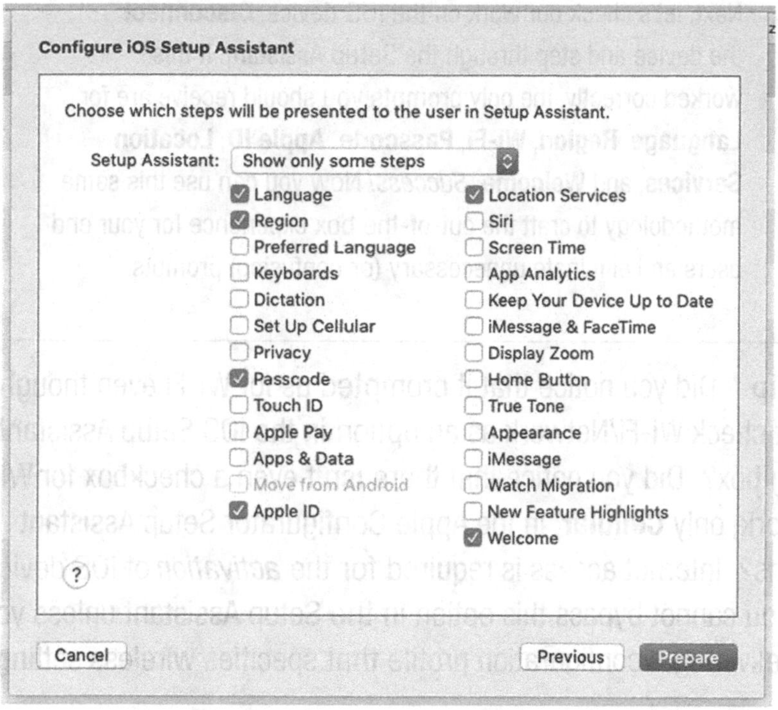

Configure iOS Setup Assistant

Choose which steps will be presented to the user in Setup Assistant.

Setup Assistant: Show only some steps

- ☑ Language
- ☑ Region
- ☐ Preferred Language
- ☐ Keyboards
- ☐ Dictation
- ☐ Set Up Cellular
- ☐ Privacy
- ☑ Passcode
- ☐ Touch ID
- ☐ Apple Pay
- ☐ Apps & Data
- ☐ Move from Android
- ☑ Apple ID

- ☑ Location Services
- ☐ Siri
- ☐ Screen Time
- ☐ App Analytics
- ☐ Keep Your Device Up to Date
- ☐ iMessage & FaceTime
- ☐ Display Zoom
- ☐ Home Button
- ☐ True Tone
- ☐ Appearance
- ☐ iMessage
- ☐ Watch Migration
- ☐ New Feature Highlights
- ☑ Welcome

Cancel   Previous   Prepare

Figure 5-7. *Select these steps to show to the user and skip the rest*

6. Click the **Prepare** button to set up the device. It will begin applying the configuration settings to the iOS device. When it completes, you will see that *Is Supervised* is now listed as **Yes** and your *Organization Name* is listed as shown in Figure 5-8.

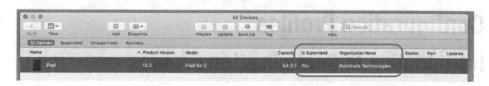

Figure 5-8. *Our device is now tied to our organization and supervised*

7. Next, let's check our work on the iOS device. **Disconnect** the device and step through the Setup Assistant. If this worked correctly, the only prompts you should receive are for **Language**, **Region**, **Wi-Fi**, **Passcode**, **Apple ID**, **Location Services**, and **Welcome**. *Success!* Now you can use this same methodology to craft the out-of-the box experience for your end users and eliminate unnecessary (or confusing) prompts.

Pro Tip   Did you notice that it prompted us for Wi-Fi even though we didn't check Wi-Fi/Network as an option in the iOS Setup Assistant dialog box? Did you notice that there isn't even a checkbox for Wi-Fi/Network, only **Cellular**, in the Apple Configurator Setup Assistant options? Internet access is required for the *activation* of iOS devices, and you cannot bypass this option in the Setup Assistant unless you are delivering a configuration profile that specifies wireless settings.

Once you have made it to the Home Screen, reset the test device back to default by going to *Settings* ➤ *General* ➤ *Reset* ➤ *Erase All Content and Settings*. Then plug the test device back into the computer using the USB cable. Once it has finished with the restore process, leave it at the Setup Assistant screen so we are ready for our next exercise.

Configuration Profiles
Introduction to Configuration Profiles

Configuration Profiles, often referred to by their file extension *∗.**mobileconfig** profiles,* are XML *Property Lists* that can be installed on iOS devices to disable and enable certain features or enforce various security restrictions. Configuration Profiles are made up of one or more payloads. A *payload* is a specific configuration, such as a minimum passcode security setting, that defines a requirement or restriction on the device. Some payloads are device specific, meaning that they apply at the device level, while some payloads are user specific, meaning that they apply only to specific users on that device (in the case of *macOS*). Payloads are available for *macOS*, *iOS*, *iPadOS*, *tvOS*, or some combination of these. In this chapter, we are going to focus specifically on *iOS* and *iPadOS* payloads.

Pro Tip   It is recommended by Apple that you create different Configuration Profiles for unique device types. This means that if you are creating a Profile to install exclusively on iOS devices, do not try to configure macOS payloads in that Profile. Create a unique set of Profiles targeted to each specific OS family instead of one monolithic Profile that could be applied to any OS.

YOUR FIRST CONFIGURATION PROFILE

The best way to learn about Configuration Profiles and their payloads is to create a few, apply them to your device, and see what the effect is.

1. To get started, choose **New Profile** from the **File** menu in Apple Configurator. You will see a window appear that looks similar to the one in Figure 5-9.

Figure 5-9. *Configuration Profile—General payload example*

2.   On the left side of the Configuration Profile editor, you will
     see various *payload categories*. When you **select** a category,
     you will be able to **add** a payload and configure it on the
     right side of the screen. Every Configuration Profile includes
     the mandatory **General payload**. Let's configure the General
     payload for this new Profile.

3.   Enter the information for the following fields:

     a. **Name:** The name of the Profile. This will be shown to end
        users if they browse to ***Settings ➤ General ➤ Profiles***
        on their device. This should be something descriptive and
        related to the payload being deployed.

b. **Identifier:** This is a unique string for each Configuration Profile. It doesn't matter what you use here as long as another Profile doesn't have the same identifier. Duplicate identifiers will trigger an overwrite of the previous one, allowing you to update your Configuration Profile without having to manually remove the old one first.

c. **Organization:** Enter a friendly name that will identify where this Configuration Profile came from and what organization it is associated with.

d. **Description:** Provide a brief description of what the payload(s) in this Profile does.

e. **Consent Message:** This is a message that displays when a user installs the Profile. For example, you may have various Profiles hosted on a web server for BYOD users, and you want to disclose what this does and ask them to agree to the changes being made to their device before it gets installed. Users will see this under *Settings ➤ Profile Download* when they attempt to install a Profile after downloading it from a web site or email attachment.

f. **Security:** If your devices are supervised, you can set a password here that is required to remove the Profile. For this one, let's keep the default **Always** option.

g. **Automatically Remove Profile:** This is useful if you are applying temp settings and want those settings or restrictions to expire after a set amount of time. **Never** is the default option.

4. Once you have finished entering the required information in the *General* payload, click the **Passcode** category and click the **Configure** button to define a Passcode payload.

5. We will now define our passcode security requirements for our devices. You can manipulate the options to your liking here as I have in Figure 5-10. Please note that if you want to cancel any payload, you simply click the **[–]** button in the top-right corner of the screen to delete it.

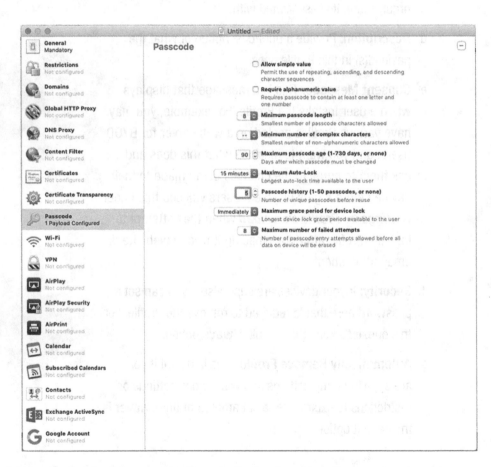

Figure 5-10. *My sample Passcode payload settings*

6.   Now that we have our payload settings defined and ready to
     go, we are ready to save the Configuration Profile so it can be
     applied to our device. Choose **Save...** from the **File** menu and
     save your Configuration Profile with a name and in a location
     you will be able to find later. After you have saved the file, **close**
     the Configuration Profile editor window.

Pro Tip   Notice how we have only configured one payload for this
Configuration Profile even though there are many more payloads
we could have added? As a best practice, it's better to have
multiple Profiles that are payload specific so that you can easily
change one setting without impacting other settings that might be
defined in the same Profile. For example, you may want to update
your passcode settings independently of the VPN settings. Having a
unique Profile for each allows you to change the passcode without
causing a potential problem for your VPN users. This methodology
also allows you to reuse the same Profiles for multiple different
groups of users. You can apply a passcode requirement Profile to
all users and then add the VPN Profile onto devices for only specific
users who use VPN.

---

7.   Next, it is time to apply this Configuration Profile to our test
     device. **Click** the device in the list to select it and then click
     Add ➤ Profiles as shown in Figure 5-11. Browse to the Profile
     we just created and saved and click the **Add** button to apply it
     to the iOS device per Figure 5-12.

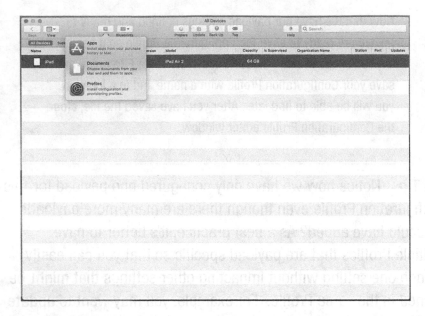

Figure 5-11. *Install the Profile from the Add toolbar button*

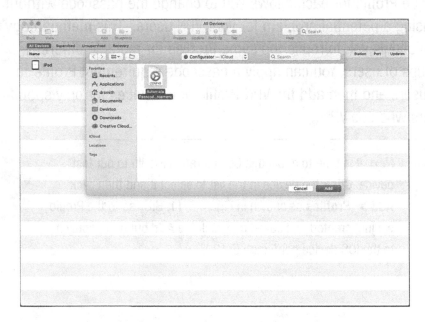

Figure 5-12. *Select the Configuration Profile we created with the Passcode payload*

8. When it is finished installing the Configuration Profile, **select** the test device to highlight it, and then let's **prepare** it again like we did in the previous section. Same settings as before, including the iOS Setup Assistant modifications. These are likely cached from the last time we did this, but if not, you can refer to Figure 5-7 from earlier in this chapter.

9. When it has completed the preparation and the Configuration Profile we created has been loaded, let's test our work. **Disconnect** the device and start stepping through the iOS Setup Assistant. This time, when you get to the passcode option, it should match Figure 5-13. See how it requires a strong passcode as defined in the payload we created? That is the power of Configuration Profiles.

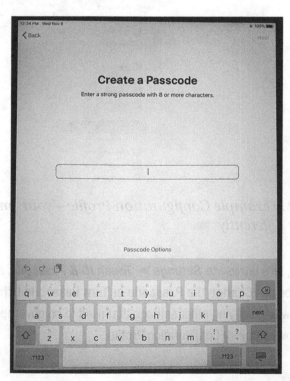

Figure 5-13. *Setup Assistant now requires a strong passcode*

10. Finish the iOS Setup Assistant, and when you get to the Home Screen, let's remove this Configuration Profile. Remember, we didn't specify a removal password, so as an end user, we have the power to remove this restriction. Browse to **Settings ➤ General ➤ Profiles** and tap our **Passcode Enforcement Configuration Profile**. Tap the **Remove Profile** button and follow the prompts to remove it as shown in Figure 5-14.

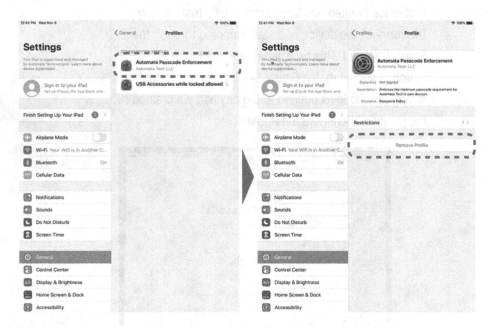

Figure 5-14. *My example Configuration Profile—yours may be named slightly differently*

11. Finally, let's browse to **Settings ➤ Touch ID & Passcode,** and now you can **Change the Passcode** or **Turn Passcode Off** along with modifying other settings that used to be governed by the (now removed) Configuration Profile.

Pro Tip   Notice how our Configuration Profile says "Not Signed" in bold red font? Some settings may not apply without a valid code-signed Profile. To code-sign your Configuration Profiles, before you save them in the Profile editor, choose **Sign Profile** from the **File** menu and select your **signing identity**. Please be aware that signed Profiles cannot be edited after the fact, so keep a saved copy that isn't signed for future modification. Going forward in this book, we will sign our Configuration Profiles.

In the previous exercise, we used Apple Configurator to apply a Configuration Profile to a supervised and company-owned iOS device. This is the simplest and most secure method, but it is far more common to find users wishing to use their own personal device for business instead of carrying around a second phone or tablet. In this case, we need to be able to provide end users with a Configuration Profile that they can install on their own device to make it compliant with company information security policy.

The challenge with BYOD devices is that they cannot be easily supervised, so end users can remove the restrictions we install at any time and without our knowledge. In this case, we need to come up with a *carrot* that will entice users to keep the Configuration Profile installed so that our security will stay in effect if the user wants to continue to use it for business purposes. That *carrot feature* is likely going to be dictated by your organization. I typically pair my security payload with VPN, Exchange account information, Enterprise Wi-Fi configuration, or all three to ensure that if the device is able to access company services, then it is secured. If the user removes the security, they also lose access to the company services from that device.

CREATE A USER-INSTALLABLE CONFIGURATION PROFILE

In this exercise, we are going to create a Configuration Profile that pairs our passcode security requirement with the configuration for the company VPN. In this particular company, all work must be done via VPN, so pairing these settings protects any endpoint that may be attempting to sign in through VPN.

1. Open Apple Configurator and create a new Configuration Profile by choosing **New Profile** from the **File** menu.

2. Enter the required information in the *General* payload section as shown in Figure 5-15, including the description and consent message. These are particularly important this time around because end users will be installing it.

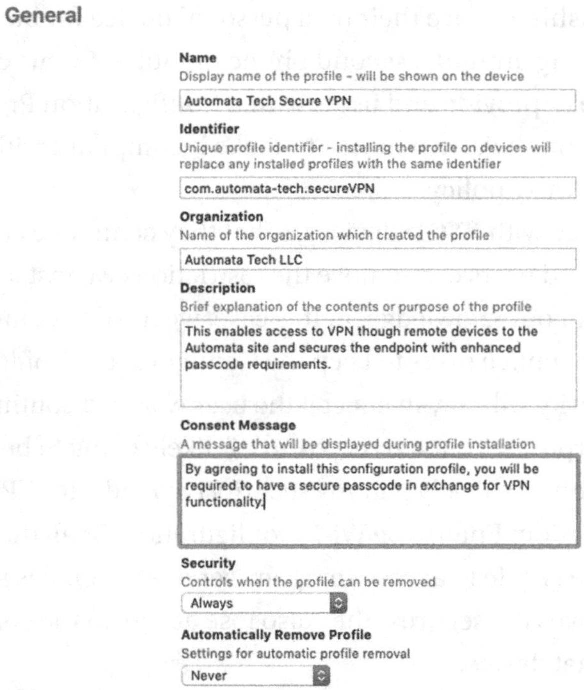

General

Name
Display name of the profile – will be shown on the device

Automata Tech Secure VPN

Identifier
Unique profile identifier – installing the profile on devices will replace any installed profiles with the same identifier

com.automata-tech.secureVPN

Organization
Name of the organization which created the profile

Automata Tech LLC

Description
Brief explanation of the contents or purpose of the profile

This enables access to VPN though remote devices to the Automata site and secures the endpoint with enhanced passcode requirements.

Consent Message
A message that will be displayed during profile installation

By agreeing to install this configuration profile, you will be required to have a secure passcode in exchange for VPN functionality.

Security
Controls when the profile can be removed

Always

Automatically Remove Profile
Settings for automatic profile removal

Never

Figure 5-15. Sample General payload information

3. Next click the *Passcode* payload and configure it like we did in
    the last exercise to require a **strong passcode**.

4. Next click the *VPN* payload and configure it with information
    similar to that in Figure 5-16. This is all dummy account
    information for this example, but in a real company, you would
    enter the legitimate VPN configuration settings.

Figure 5-16. *Sample placeholder data for the VPN payload*

5. Once we have populated the *General, Passcode*, and *VPN* payloads, we can save a copy of this for future editing. Choose **Save…** from the **File** menu and save it somewhere for future reference. Next choose **Duplicate** from the **File** menu to create the copy we will sign and distribute. Save the one we are planning to distribute to the **Desktop**.

Pro Tip   Did you see the message about requiring information to be added by the end user and therefore being unable to install on supervised devices? Because we are creating this Profile for exclusive use on BYOD devices, the warning about supervised devices can be ignored. If you were creating this Profile for use on supervised devices, you would need to specify the account information, so keep that in mind as you determine which devices you want to supervise vs. not supervise.

---

6. This time we are going to sign our Configuration Profile. Choose **Sign Profile** from the **File** menu and select the **signing identity** as shown in Figure 5-17.

Figure 5-17. *Selecting a signing identity for our Configuration Profile*

7. Now that we have our signed Configuration Profile ready to go, we could host this on a web server inside our organization or distribute it via email to specific users upon request. To simulate this, go ahead and email it from your Mac to your test device. Open your email and click the attachment ending in **.mobileconfig**. If successful, a dialog box will appear stating **Profile Downloaded** and **Review the profile in Settings if you want to install it**.

8. If we open up the *Settings* app, we will see the **Profile Downloaded** prompt as shown in Figure 5-18. Tap that button and step through the process to install the Profile. It will give you some warning messages relating to the use of VPN and the authenticity of our code signing (for this example, we are not using a known signing authority, but you will want to when you use these in a production environment).

Figure 5-18. *The steps to install the Configuration Profile interactively in iOS 13*

You will notice that our passcode requirement goes immediately into effect. To continue, we must create a new secure passcode. When it is finished installing, we can click the **Done** button. If we back out to the root of the

169

Settings app, you will see our newly installed **VPN** option with the **on/ off** switch as shown in Figure 5-19. This confirms our Configuration Profile worked! We have now secured the device with a new passcode and enabled access to the company VPN.

Figure 5-19. *The VPN switch is now available near my network configuration in Settings*

9. Finally, let's browse back to **Settings ➤ General ➤ Profile** and **remove** the Secure VPN Configuration Profile. Browse back to VPN, and you will notice that our configuration is gone. Thus, the user who removes our Profile also removes their VPN privileges. Classic catch-22!

Use **Reset ➤ Erase All Content and Settings** to default your test device before moving onto the next section.

Exploring iOS Configuration Profiles

Before moving onto the next section, spend some time exploring the various payloads that are available to iOS devices. **Create three separate, signed Configuration Profiles.** Name them and set the defined payloads as shown in the following. We will use those in a later section when we discuss *Blueprints*.

Profile #1 – Secure Passcode: Configure this profile to use the passcode settings similar to those found in Figure 5-20.

Figure 5-20. *Example Passcode payload*

Profile #2 – Home Wi-Fi: Configure this profile to use *your current location's* Wi-Fi settings. This will allow your iPad to auto-join this network rather than you having to select it manually on the device. It should be something similar to mine in Figure 5-21.

Figure 5-21. *My home wireless settings defined in the Wi-Fi payload*

Profile #3 – Student Restrictions: Pretend that we are giving these devices to students and they are not allowed to use **Camera**, **FaceTime**, **AirDrop**, **iMessage**, **Apple Music**, or **Radio** as shown in Figure 5-22.

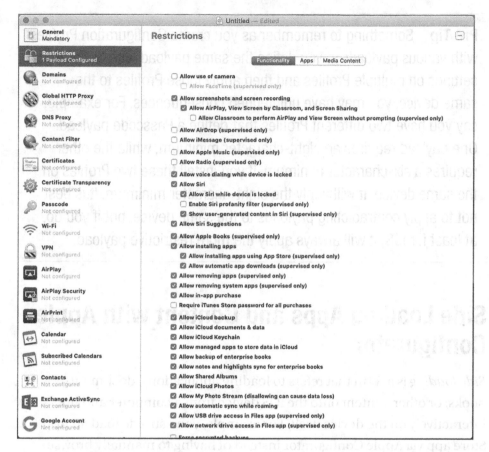

Figure 5-22. *Disable the options defined in the preceding text in the Restrictions payload*

You should now have three separate Configuration Profiles that are ready for us to deploy to any number of iOS devices. Save these to your **Desktop**. There are so many options for managing iOS devices, with new ones being added all the time. Apple maintains a list of payloads on their web site that should be a good reference as you begin to explore the possibilities:

```
https://developer.apple.com/business/documentation/
Configuration-Profile-Reference.pdf
```

Pro Tip   Something to remember as you create Configuration Profiles with various payloads: if you define the same payload with different settings on multiple Profiles and then apply those Profiles to the same device, you may have unintended consequences. For example, say you have two different Profiles that define a Passcode payload. One payload requires an eight-character minimum, while the other requires a six-character minimum. If you install these two Profiles on the same device, it will apply the eight-character minimum. It is best not to apply contradicting payloads to the same device, but if you do, at least for iOS, it will always apply the more restrictive payload.

Side Loading Apps and Content with Apple Configurator

Side loading is a term that refers to loading applications, documents, books, or other content onto the iOS device from a computer and not interactively on the device itself. For example, you can side load an App Store app via Apple Configurator instead of having to manually browse the App Store and download the App on the device interactively. You can also side load content before the iOS Setup Assistant is run, making it an ideal option for providing your users with preinstalled data without compromising the out-of-box experience.

Apps

Side loading Apps is pretty straightforward. The first thing you will want to do is connect an iOS device via USB and open Apple Configurator. **Click** the device to select it and then click the **Add** button in the toolbar and then **Apps** as shown in Figure 5-23.

Figure 5-23. *Click Add ➤ Apps to select Apps to load on the selected device*

You can load an App directly from your Mac by clicking **Choose from my Mac...** or you can **sign in** with an Apple ID that has Apps available. This could be a personal Apple ID like I'm using for this exercise or an *institutional Apple ID*. We will cover institutional Apple IDs and Volume Purchase Program (VPP) in Chapter 8.

Some organizations may have Apps that they create for internal institutional use only, and those will never be listed in the *App Store*. If you have Apps like this, you can load them directly from your Mac. We are going to choose to use Apps that are listed on the *App Store*, so **sign in** and you should see a list of the Apps that were purchased with your Apple ID as shown in Figure 5-24.

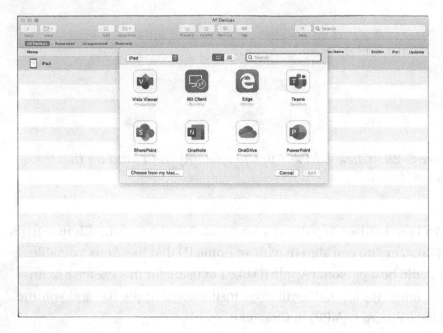

Figure 5-24. *Browsing Apps that have been purchased by my Apple ID*

Select the Apps you wish to add to the device from the App browser. You can select multiple by holding either the **shift key** or **command key**. Once you have selected two or three Apps, click the **Add** button. As you can see in Figure 5-25, the Apps we selected are being downloaded and installed on the test device.

Figure 5-25. *Downloading and side loading the Apps onto my connected iPad*

176

Depending on the size of the Apps and the speed of your Internet connection, this may take a few minutes or more to complete. Once the progress bar goes away, you can double-click the device and view the installed Apps as shown in Figure 5-26. As you can see, I chose to install the *Microsoft Office* Apps.

Figure 5-26. *Viewing the installed Apps to confirm they were copied to the iPad*

Pro Tip   Be careful which Apple ID you use to side load these Apps. While I used my personal Apple ID, if I give this device to someone, when they launch *Microsoft Word,* they will be prompted for my Apple ID and password before it will launch. They will also be prompted for my password when the App updates at some point in the future. I probably don't not want to give everyone in the office my personal Apple ID credentials when I hand them their iPad. There are a couple solutions for this that we cover in Chapter 8.

Documents

Similar to side loading Apps, we can also do the same with documents. Which documents you can load is going to depend on the Apps you have installed on the device. Select our test iOS device again and choose **Documents** from the **Add** button in the toolbar. I have four Apps listed that I can install documents into—*Books*, *Excel*, *PowerPoint*, and *Word* as you can see in Figure 5-27. Let's load a **PDF** file into the *Books* App.

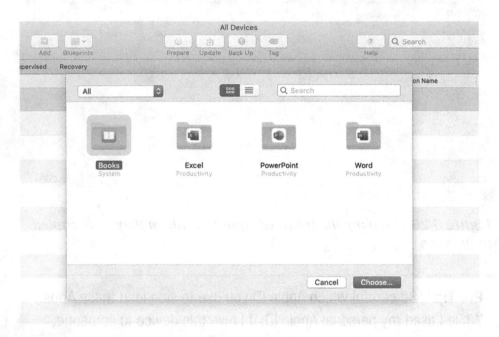

Figure 5-27. *Select an App to install the PDF document into*

Click **Books** to highlight it, and then click the **Choose** button to browse your Mac for a PDF document to upload. It doesn't matter what file you load for this exercise. I'm just using a random work file that I had lying around. Depending on the size of the PDF file, it should take just a few seconds to transfer the file to the *iPad*.

> **Pro Tip**   If you recall the structure of App packages from Chapter 4, because we chose to load the PDF into the Books App, it was copied into **Books** *package* ➤ **Documents** directory. If the Books App is deleted, the PDF file we pre-loaded will be deleted too.

Modifying iOS Devices in Apple Configurator

So far, we have configured iOS device settings, preinstalled Apps, and preinstalled some important documents. This is pretty cool, but there are a few more things we probably want to do to customize the out-of-box experience for our end users. For one, I don't know that I want every *iPad* on my network called "iPad," for example. Let's modify a few more settings on our test device.

Device Name

We can name one or many devices via Apple Configurator. If you select more than one device, you can add a token that will append a sequential number to the end of the name. In this case, let's just name our test device "Test iPad" (or iPhone, depending on your test device model). To do this, **click** the connected device to select it and then using the **Actions** menu choose **Modify ➤ Device Name...** and enter the **name** in the dialog box and click the **Rename** button, as shown in Figure 5-28.

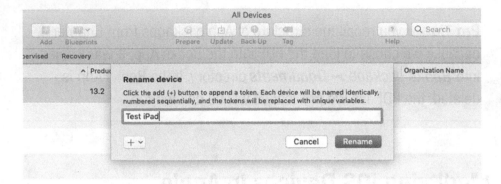

Figure 5-28. *Rename the device by entering a new name in the provided field*

Home Screen Layout

Now that we've got a few additional Apps installed on my test device, I may want to rearrange the Apps so that my users don't have to go searching for Microsoft Office. By default, *Word*, *Excel*, and *PowerPoint* are on the second Home Screen page, and I know that I'm going to get at least one help desk call from a user who doesn't think Office is installed on their *iPad*. Let's anticipate this issue and move these Microsoft Apps to the main Home Screen page.

Click the test device to select it and then using the **Actions** menu choose **Modify ➤ Home Screen Layout**. A window that looks similar to the one in Figure 5-29 should appear and allow you to move the icons around. I'm going to move *Excel*, *Word*, and *PowerPoint* to the main Home Screen and move *Stocks*, *Voice Memos*, and *Home* to the second screen. Simply drag and drop the Apps around the screen with the mouse and then click the **Apply** button when finished.

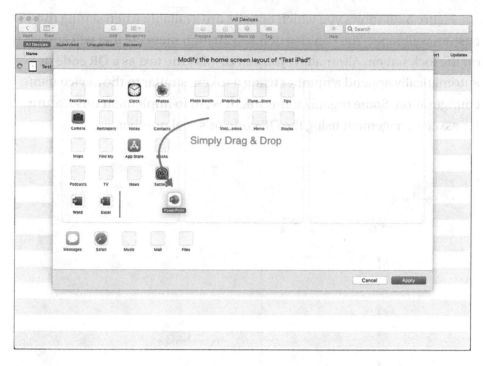

Figure 5-29. *Drag and drop icons around the window to rearrange them*

Wallpaper

Finally, the last modification we may want to make before handing the device to an end user is to customize the *wallpaper*. A lot of organizations like to identify their assets by customized wallpaper that cannot be removed. On a supervised device, by combining the wallpaper modification with a payload that restricts users from changing it, you can permanently brand your institution's devices in this way.

Figure 5-30 shows you which options are available when setting the custom wallpaper. You can also define a custom message that will appear on the lock screen. Alternately, you can display the text as a QR code or automatically append a number using a token, similar to the device name configuration. Some organizations might want to implement this feature for asset management using the QR code or serial number.

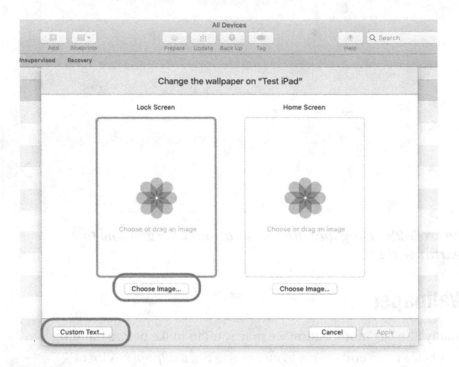

Figure 5-30. *The options for setting wallpaper and custom text*

Provisioning iOS Devices Using Blueprints

Now that you have used all of the various options available to prepare devices with Apple Configurator, it's time to put it all together into one repeatable, semiautomatic workflow. A *Blueprint*, as the name would suggest, is like a template for configuring multiple devices from the same basic set of instructions. In this exercise, we are going to create a Blueprint that will allow Apple Configurator to build us an iOS device to our exact specification.

We want to start with a completely clean test device, so if you haven't already, go ahead and erase and restore your test device. You can use **Settings ➤ Reset ➤ Erase All Content and Settings** directly on the device, or if you still have it attached to Apple Configurator, you can choose **Restore** from the **Actions** menu and the Configurator will download the latest iOS release and apply it to the selected device.

CREATE A BLUEPRINT

1.   To get started with Blueprints, click the **Blueprints** button on the toolbar and choose **Edit Blueprints** as shown in Figure 5-31.

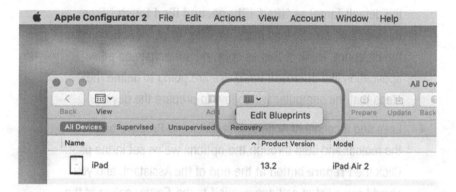

Figure 5-31. *Enter the Blueprint Editor by choosing Edit Blueprints in the toolbar*

2.   Once in the Blueprint Editor window, click the **New** button in the bottom-left corner of the screen to create a new Blueprint. Name the Blueprint "**Test Deployment**." Your screen should look something like Figure 5-32.

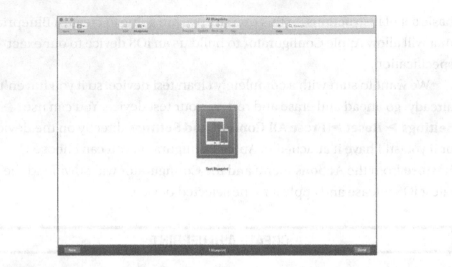

Figure 5-32. *Blueprints browser with the Test Blueprint document*

3. **Double-click** *Test Deployment Blueprint* to edit it. We can leave
   the default Target as "**iPad, iPhone, and iPod touch**." From
   this window, we can load Apps, Profiles, or script Actions into
   the Blueprint. Think of this as creating a *macro* in an office
   application like *Microsoft Word*. We are going to define the
   steps that the computer will follow to prepare the device.

4. Let's add a couple of Actions first. Click the **Prepare** button in
   the toolbar and step through the options we've set in the past.
   Click the **Prepare** button at the end of the Assistant, and you
   should see a list of settings applied to the *Setup* section of the
   Blueprint as shown in Figure 5-33.

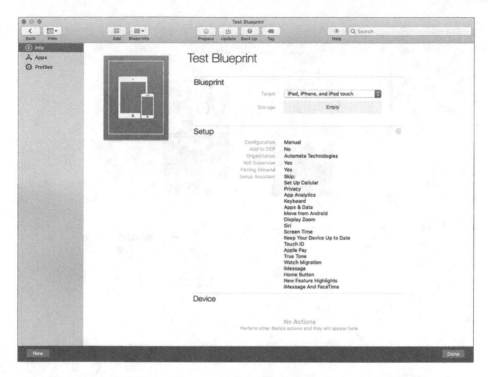

Figure 5-33. *The list of options we defined in the Prepare action*

5. Next, let's add some custom wallpaper. Like we did before with
    a single device, click **Actions** menu ➤ **Modify** ➤ **Wallpapers**.
    Add some custom images from your computer for the wallpaper
    and click the **Custom Text** button and enter **"My Company's"**
    + **Type** token. The result will say something like **"My
    Company's iPad"** or similar as shown in Figure 5-34. Click the
    Apply button, and you will see that the customizations we made
    have been added to the Blueprint under the *Device* heading.

Figure 5-34. *The customized wallpaper and lock screen previews*

Pro Tip   I like to use Apple's built-in macOS wallpapers for stuff like this. You can browse to **/Library/Desktop Pictures/,** and there are a number of suitable wallpapers that will work for this exercise.

---

6.   Next, we need to add some Apps. Click the **Apps** button in the left-side pane *or* click the **Add** button in the toolbar and choose **Apps**. Select a couple Apps like we did previously. I'm going to add *Word*, *Excel*, and *PowerPoint* again, myself. Depending on the Apps you loaded, you will see the storage bar fill up with some amount of data in use. In my case, it's 788 MB in use with those three Apps installed.

7. Up next, let's add some Configuration Profiles. Remember the three we created in a previous section? You should have the *Secure Passcode, My Home Wi-Fi Settings*, and *Student Restrictions* profiles ready to use. Click the **Add** button and choose **Profiles**. Select the three Profiles and click the **Add** button. Your screen should look similar to Figure 5-35.

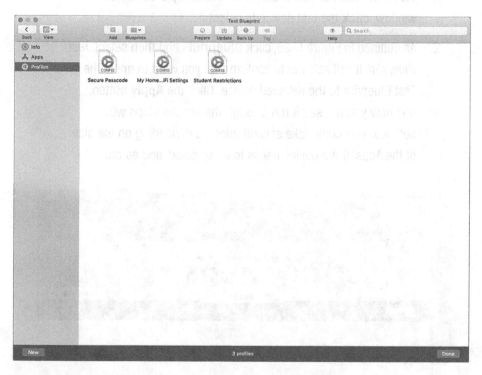

Figure 5-35. *Adding the three Profiles we created previously to the Blueprint*

8. At this point, we have created our Blueprint. Click the **Done** button in the bottom-right corner of the Blueprint window to exit the Blueprint Editor and return to the main Apple Configurator window. We now have a test Blueprint that we can apply to our test iOS device.

DEPLOY A BLUEPRINT

Next up, it's time to use the Blueprint we created to provision our test
iOS device.

1. If you haven't done so already, connect the test device to
    your Mac with the USB cable. In the main Apple Configurator
    window, **click** the test device to select it.

2. As outlined in Figure 5-36, click **Blueprints** and then select *Test
    Blueprint*. It will ask you to confirm that you want to apply the
    Test Blueprint to the selected device. Click the **Apply** button,
    and now you will see it run through the various steps we
    outlined. This could take several minutes depending on the size
    of the Apps, if the device needs to be updated, and so on.

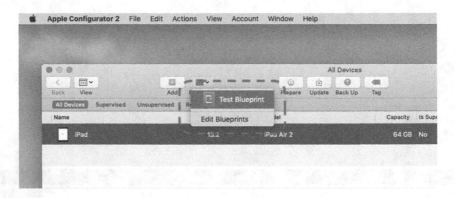

Figure 5-36. *Click the Blueprint we want to apply to the selected
device*

Pro Tip   You were probably prompted with a few consent messages
when the Mac was applying the Configuration Profiles. If you were
going to go into production with provisioning thousands of iOS
devices, you would probably want to remove the optional consent

language by deleting the text in the Consent Message field of the General payload so that you wouldn't need to agree to the alert every time the Blueprint runs. Ultimately, your goal should be an (mostly) unattended provisioning process.

3. Once the Blueprint completes, **disconnect** your test iOS device and step through the Setup Assistant to check your work. Did you notice something different this time? If you applied the correct Wi-Fi settings in the *Home Wi-Fi Profile* payload, it should have auto-joined your wireless network and skipped the prompt about connecting to a wireless network. *Cool!*

Once you have made it to the Home Screen, test a few things. Your lock and home screens should look like those in Figure 5-37. Notice how we have the Apps pre-loaded and our security settings have disabled the Camera and Messages Apps? Those are examples of the restrictions we enabled in the Student Restrictions Configuration Profile. *Pretty neat!*

Figure 5-37. *The completed configuration of my test iPad*

Pro Tip   We would call this testing process *configuration validation*. If you are testing this Blueprint for use in a mass deployment scenario, be sure to show this test device to all of your stakeholders so they can review and sign off on the end result before using the Blueprint to stage hundreds or thousands of devices.

Advanced Apple Configurator Tools

Side loading, Blueprints, and Configuration Profiles are the main reasons for using Apple Configurator; and they are pretty powerful tools. But there are a few additional hidden features inside Configurator that may be useful to device administrators. This section provides a brief overview of these advanced tools and when you may want to use them.

Single App Mode

In the *Accessibility* settings in Chapter 4, we covered the *Guided Access* feature. *Single App Mode* in Apple Configurator is very similar in that it locks the device into only being able to be used with one App. To place a device into Single App Mode, ensure the App is installed and available on the iOS device and connected to Apple Configurator via a USB cable. Click **Actions** menu ➤ **Advanced** ➤ **Start Single App Mode** and select the App you wish to use to activate the feature.

iOS Device Console

Sometimes in the course of troubleshooting an issue with a device, application, or even third-party online service, it can be helpful to view the *device logs*. To view these logs, we need to use the *console*. To access

the console, plug a device into Apple Configurator, **double-click** it, and
then choose **Console** on the left-side pane. You should see the live logging
output shown in Figure 5-38.

Figure 5-38. *Output from my test device's console. Wow, Gmail is
very chatty!*

Automator and Terminal Commands

Apple Configurator's Blueprints tool is pretty powerful for visually
scripting macros to automate the configuration of devices, but if you want
to step this up a notch, Apple also provides support for Automator and the
optional cfgutil command. If you use *Automator*, you'll find a number of
new *Actions* that get installed along with Apple Configurator.

To install the command line tool, choose **Install Automation Tools** from the **Apple Configurator 2** menu as shown in Figure 5-39.

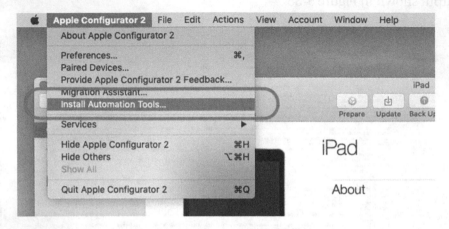

Figure 5-39. *Installing the optional command line tool*

For more information on cfgutil, you can use the man cfgutil command to read the manual. You can use cfgutil to write scripts to further automate the configuration of iOS devices.

Device Information Export

Apple provides two nifty features for exporting device data out of Configurator. As shown in Figure 5-40, if you are using some kind of internal enterprise App development, you can export data about devices in a format that easily can be uploaded to Apple's developer portal to whitelist the devices to run these in-house Apps. You can also export the data you select about each device into a *.csv that can be used for inventory management purposes.

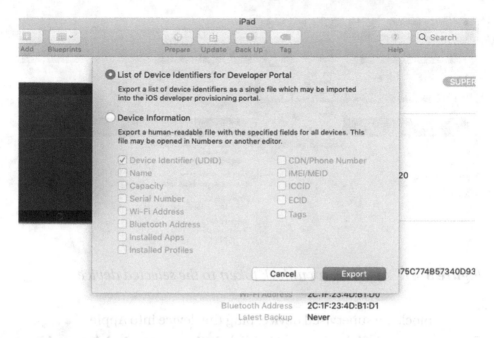

Figure 5-40. *Export data options for selected iOS devices*

Clearing Passcodes

Passcodes can be problematic, particularly in an office or school environment where staff or student turnover is high. Apple provides an option through Configurator to embed an *unlock token* into an iOS device so that it can be unlocked at a future date if the passcode that was set by the user is not known. Please note that this functionality is only possible for devices that are *supervised*.

To add an unlock token to the device, **click** the device to select it and then use **Actions** menu ➤ **Advanced** ➤ **Save Unlock Token** to apply it as shown in Figure 5-41. The unlock token can only be applied to a device that is currently unlocked, so you need to plan ahead if you want to use this functionality.

Figure 5-41. *Applying an unlock token to the selected device*

To unlock the supervised device, plug the device into Apple Configurator and **click** it to select it. Click **Actions** menu ➤ **Advanced** ➤ **Clear Passcode**.

In addition to clearing the device passcode, you can also clear the *Screen Time* passcode on supervised devices. The Screen Time passcode can be set by the user and does *not* have to be the same as the device passcode. If you need to clear the Screen Time passcode, plug the device into Apple Configurator, select it from the list, and click **Actions** menu ➤ **Advanced** ➤ **Clear Screen Time Passcode**.

Pro Tip   If you are provisioning a lot of supervised devices that may need to be unlocked at some point in the future, you should edit your Blueprint to add the **Save Unlock Token** action so that it gets added automatically in the initial setup process every time.

Revive Device

Apple has provided this function for reviving Macs that use the *T2 Security chip*. As discussed in Chapters 2 and 3, the T2 chip integrates a number of different logic board components to provide for a level of hardware security that isn't obtainable with software solutions alone. When the T2 chip has a problem, the entire system has a problem. Fortunately, if your T2 Mac is unresponsive, you may want to try to **revive** it using Apple Configurator. Apple provides instructions for doing so in a Knowledge Base article you can find here:

```
https://support.apple.com/guide/apple-configurator-2/revive-
firmware-in-mac-computers-apdebea5be51/mac
```

You should follow the specific instructions from Apple if you are going to attempt this. Each Mac with a T2 chip may have unique steps to follow depending on the model.

Summary

Apple Configurator is an excellent tool for automating the process of iOS device configuration. In this chapter, we learned how to create Blueprints that simplify and automate the setup of new devices. We also explored techniques that provide system administrators with powerful security controls in the form of supervision and Configuration Profiles.

The primary downside to using Apple Configurator is that it still requires IT personnel to touch each device and physically plug them into a Mac at least once. Later in this book, we will introduce the concept of over-the-air configuration, which requires even *less* direct interaction to stage new devices. In the next couple of chapters, we are going ***back to the Mac*** to learn how to remote manage *macOS* clients and build a server to use for Mobile Device Management.

CHAPTER 6

Managing macOS Clients with Apple Remote Desktop

Apple Remote Desktop (ARD) is a fundamental client management tool that Mac system administrators have been using for over 15 years. In this chapter, we are going to review the four main components of ARD—asset management, software distribution, client administration, and remote support. If you have more than a couple *macOS* clients to manage, ARD is a must-have tool.

Introduction to Apple Remote Desktop

Available on the *Mac App Store*, the current release of Apple Remote Desktop is version 3.9 and costs $79.99 as shown in Figure 6-1. While it is substantially more expensive than *Apple Configurator*, as far as commercial desktop management suites go, it is pretty affordable. If your organization doesn't already have a management solution for *macOS* clients, you could do a lot worse than ARD.

© Drew Smith 2020
D. Smith, *Apple macOS and iOS System Administration*,
https://doi.org/10.1007/978-1-4842-5820-0_6

Figure 6-1. *Apple Remote Desktop is available in the Mac App Store*

Pro Tip   There are a number of cross-platform desktop management tools out there like *Symantec Altiris* and *Microsoft System Center Configuration Manager (SCCM)* that can support macOS, Windows, or Linux clients that many large organizations have made substantial investments in. If you have a solution like that available to you and it meets your needs, ARD may not provide any additional functionality that you don't already possess.

Installing Apple Remote Desktop

When planning your use of Apple Remote Desktop, you need to determine where to install it. There are a couple of schools of thought about this. If you are the only Mac technician in your organization, you could just install it on your primary Mac desktop or laptop computer. This is going to give you the best experience as far as responsiveness for remote control tasks goes. You can store all of your scripts and installation files on your main computer, and you can back up your entire ARD system along with your main computer's data.

The downside to this solution comes when you need to schedule installations for a later time or date, particularly when you may not have your computer online or available. For example, let's say you want to schedule a software installation on your company's computers at 3:00 a.m. tonight, but you need to take your laptop home with you and it won't be on the corporate network at that time to push the installation files and run the tasks. In this case, you may want to either set up a *Remote Task Server* or install ARD directly on a dedicated Mac server and then use Screen Sharing or ARD to access that server from your workstation.

Remote Task Server

In Chapter 7, we will cover *macOS Server* in greater detail, but what you need to know right now is that unlike *Windows* where there are specific server and client versions that are different, *any* Mac can be a server. An ARD *Remote Task Server* refers to a computer that queues up or executes various tasks like software installations on a specified schedule. By default, Apple Remote Desktop makes the *Task Server* the local computer that the ARD application is installed on.

As mentioned in the installation section, there are some significant downsides to installing Apple Remote Desktop on your main workstation. One of those downsides is the need to keep your Mac online when pending task schedules are in progress. You can use a Remote Task Server as a way to mitigate this problem. By specifying a Remote Task Server, you can use ARD on your workstation, but all pending scheduled tasks get queued on the remote server.

To configure a Remote Task Server, you need to set up a Mac with a **static IP address** and install Apple Remote Desktop. Open ARD and choose **Preferences...** from the **Remote Desktop** menu. Figure 6-2 shows the **Task Server** tab and the option **Use Task Server on this computer,** and the checkbox for **Allow remote connections to this server** is checked.

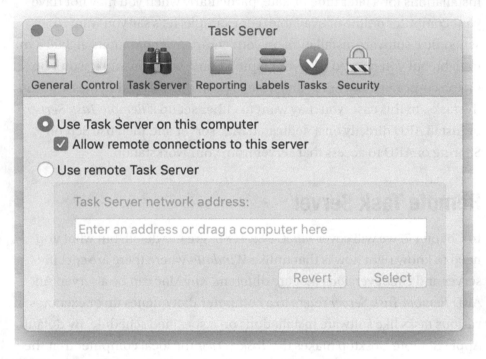

Figure 6-2. *The Task Server options in ARD's Preferences*

Next, on your technician workstation(s) with Apple Remote Desktop installed, launch ARD and choose **Preferences...** from the **Remote Desktop** menu. Click the **Task Server** tab as shown in Figure 6-3 and select **Use remote Task Server** and enter the **static IP address** of the server into the field and click **Select**. ARD will validate that it can communicate with the Remote Task Server and, if successful, will set all future tasks to run off the remote server.

Figure 6-3. *Configuring your technician workstation to use a Remote Task Server*

Server Installation

My preferred solution is to install ARD on a Mac server with a static IP address. This allows anyone on my team to access the ARD console and share all of the installation files or scripts. The installation process is very much like installing it on a single workstation, with the exception of making one change to the ARD Preferences.

By default, Apple has a security option set that you cannot use Apple Remote Desktop to remote control another Mac running Apple Remote Desktop. To disable this feature, choose **Preferences...** from the **Remote Desktop** menu and click the **Security** tab as shown in Figure 6-4. Check the box next to the **Allow control of this computer when this application is running** option.

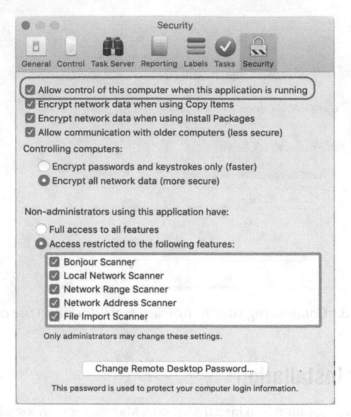

Figure 6-4. *Enable remote control of the computer using Apple Remote Desktop when ARD is also running on that remote computer*

Pro Tip When selecting a Mac to function as an Apple Remote Desktop server, I would recommend a machine with a good bit of onboard storage—either a *Mac Pro* with a couple extra SSD drives or a *Mac mini* configured with dual SSD drives. This will provide a good bit of space for the various installation packages that you'll be pushing to your Mac clients.

Interface Overview

Figure 6-5 highlights the main interface of the Apple Remote Desktop console.

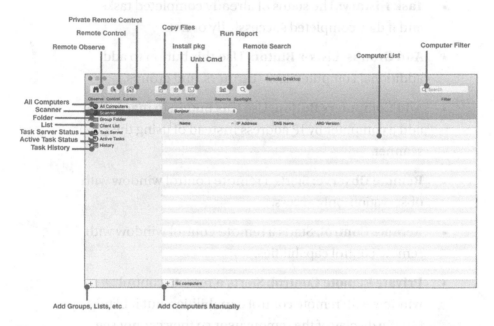

Figure 6-5. *Interface components in the main Apple Remote Desktop window*

- **All Computers List:** The default group showing all computers that have been added to ARD.

- **Scanner:** The scanner tool scans the local network and displays available computers that can be added to the ARD console.

- **Folder:** An organizational unit for containing lists of computers, tasks, scanners, and so on.

- **List:** An organizational unit for grouping computers.

- **Task Server Status:** The status of queued tasks on the local or remote Task Server.

- **Active Task Status:** The status of actively running tasks.

- **Task History:** The status of already completed tasks and if they completed successfully or not.

- **Add Groups/Lists + Button:** Use this button to add additional computer lists, scanners, and groups.

- **Add Computers Button:** Use this button to manually add a computer by IP address instead of using the scanner.

- **Remote Observe:** Starts a remote control window with observation-only access.

- **Remote Control:** Starts a remote control window with remote control capabilities.

- **Private Remote Control:** Starts a remote control window with remote control capabilities, but it blanks out the display of the remote user so they cannot see what is happening during the remote control session.

- **Copy Files:** Copies files from the Mac running ARD to one or more remote computers.

- **Install Package:** Installs an application from a ***.pkg** or ***.mpkg** file from the Mac running ARD to one or more remote computers.

- **Unix Command:** Runs one or more Unix commands on remote computers.

- **Run Report:** Opens the Report Viewer and displays information requested of one or more remote computers.

- **Remote Search:** Remotely searches remote computers for files based on specified criteria.

- **Computer List:** Displays all of the clients listed in the selected list.

- **Computer Filter:** Enter information into the search bar to filter the selected computer list.

Configuring macOS Clients for ARD

Before we can search and add Macs to our Apple Remote Desktop console, we need to enable the *Remote Management* service in the *Sharing System Preference*. As shown in Figure 6-6, click the **Remote Management** option. **Check** the box next to Remote Management to enable the service. It will prompt you to select the various options you want to enable. Go ahead and **check all the boxes** on this dialog sheet and then click the **Ok** button to dismiss the options.

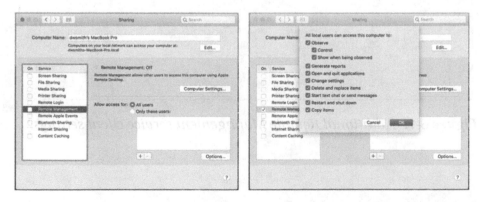

Figure 6-6. *Enable the Remote Management service and select all the ARD management options*

On the Remote Management service screen, you should see a *green circle* next to the service indicating that it is now running. Click the **Computer Settings...** button, and you will see some additional options as shown in Figure 6-7. If you are planning to allow users to see when they are being observed (we are) and you want to allow users to request assistance through the Remote Management menu bar extra (we do), check the box next to **Show Remote Management status in menu bar**.

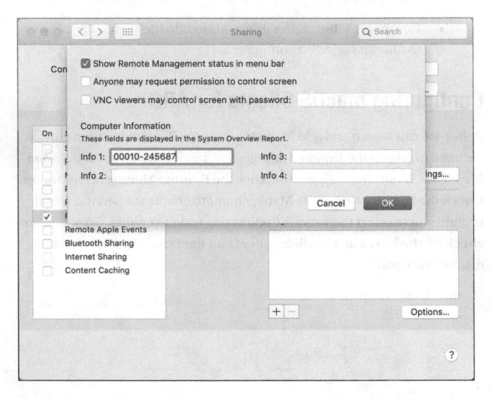

Figure 6-7. Additional Remote Management service client settings

We are also provided with four optional fields for collecting additional ad hoc information for our reports. There are a number of built-in device details that are able to be reported on such as processor speed, RAM, and network status. But what if we have something that is unique to our organization that we need to track?

I have a special property sticker on all of the MacBooks at my company with a serialized asset tag number. I would like to report on this information as well, so I can use the **Info 1** field to manually enter the asset tag information for this particular client. By doing this, when I pull a report in the future, I can also gather that data without having to physically visit every machine and inspect the sticker affixed to the bottom of the laptop.

Adding Clients Using the Scanner

Next, let's go back to our server machine running the Apple Remote Desktop console. Open ARD and click the **Scanner** button on the left side of the screen as shown in Figure 6-8. This starts a scan of the local area network, specifically my Wi-Fi network, and produces a list of clients on the network. It located my test laptop, *dwsmith's MacBook Pro*, that I want to add to the ARD console. To add this machine to the console, click the computer in the Scanner list and **drag and drop** it onto the *All Computers* icon on the left.

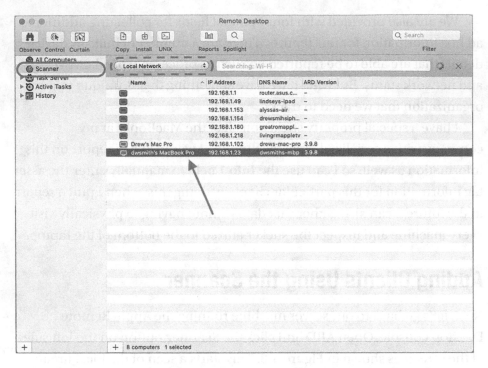

Figure 6-8. *The ARD console scanner tool identifying network devices including Macs with the Remote Management service running*

Pro Tip   Did you notice in the Scanner view that we are seeing both the *Name* and the *DNS Name* of our clients in ARD? In Chapter 2, we discussed the various names that your Mac uses including the friendly name (Name) and the hostname (DNS name). This is where we can start getting into trouble if our hostnames are all the same or are not adequately representative of the systems on the network.

Once you attempt to add one or more systems to the All Computers console list, ARD will prompt you to **authenticate** with a local administrator account from the client you are attempting to add. Enter the login info and click **Add** to continue as shown in Figure 6-9. Note that if you do not know the local password, you can still add the system to the console but you cannot run any tasks or remote control the system without authentication.

Pro Tip   If you have more than one computer to add, you can use the shift or command key modifier to select multiple computers and drag them all to the All Computers icon at once to add all of the systems simultaneously.

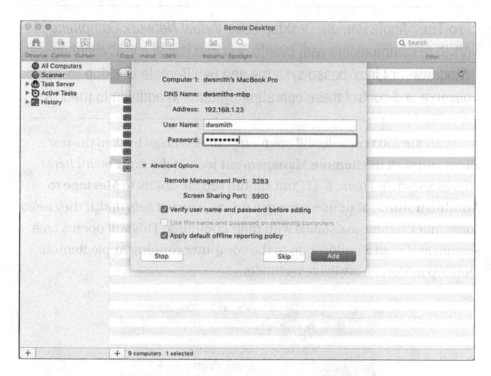

Figure 6-9. *Authenticate with the client's local Administrator account to add it to the ARD console*

After authenticating, the computer we added should be listed in the console under *All Computers* as shown in Figure 6-10.

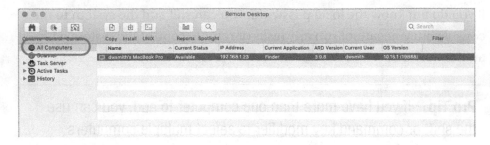

Figure 6-10. *The All Computers list with our added test Mac.*
The Current Status column should say Available

Pro Tip   Apple Remote Desktop uses *Virtual Network Computing*
(VNC) to communicate with clients. You can install a VNC client on
Windows- or Linux-based systems and use Remote Desktop to
observe and control these operating systems in addition to macOS.

With the ARD console still open on your server, go back to the test
client and click the **Remote Management** icon in the *extra menu items*
area as shown in Figure 6-11. You should see the ability to **Message to
Administrator....** Your users can use this as a sort of *help desk* if they need
some quick remote assistance with their computer. This will open a chat
session and send a notification to the computer running Apple Remote
Desktop to alert an available technician.

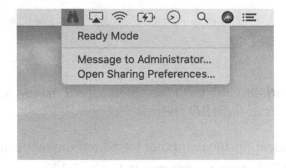

Figure 6-11. *The Remote Management menu item*

Organizing Clients in the ARD Console

With one Mac in the console, exclusively using the *All Computers* group is probably fine. However, you will probably have dozens or maybe even *hundreds* of Macs in your ARD console, and you'll want to have some organization around them so you can easily find them and manage them effectively.

Let's get organized with a couple of *Groups* and *Lists*. Using the **Add Groups/Lists + button**, create two **Groups**, one named **"Development"** and one called **"Production."** Then create two **Lists**, one called **"Test Macs"** and the other named **"Servers."** Using **drag and drop**, move the *Servers* list into the *Production* folder and move the *Test Macs* list into the *Development* folder. Finally, **drag and drop** the test Mac into the *Test Macs List* like I have in Figure 6-12 with **dwsmith's MacBook Pro**. When you are finished, your console should look similar to mine with the Computers, Lists, and Groups.

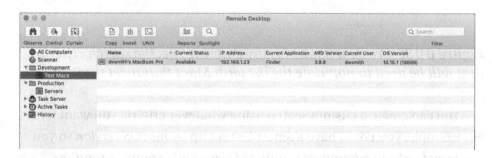

Figure 6-12. *Your console should look similar to this with nested Lists and Groups*

You can organize your console manually using *Lists* and *Groups* in any configuration that makes sense for you. You can also create **Smart Lists** that include dynamically assigned computers for various tasks. Computers can belong to more than one list, including more than one Smart List.

To create a Smart List, click the **Add Groups/Lists + button** and choose
New Smart List. You will be presented with a sheet like the one in
Figure 6-13.

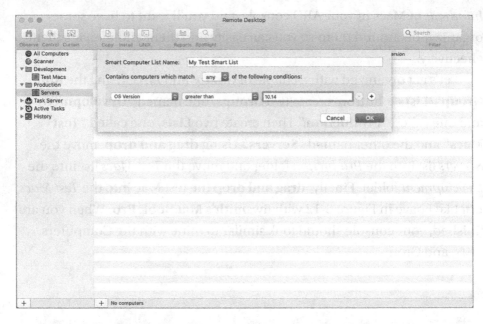

Figure 6-13. *Create a Smart List by entering specific search criteria
that will be used to populate the list with Macs that meet that criteria*

You can create a custom search using whatever criteria you want to.
For example, you could have a Smart List set up by *macOS version* so you
can target tasks to computers running Mojave and exempt computers
running Catalina. Click the **Ok** button to create the Smart List and then
click it to view the contents. Every time you use the Smart List, it will run
the query that you configured against your entire *All Computers* inventory
and populate the list with the matching systems.

Mac Remote Support

As the name implies, Apple Remote Desktop provides a robust toolset for remote controlling Macs. There are three main options when remote controlling a Mac client: *observation* mode, *curtain* mode, and *control* mode. You can initiate all three of these options from the main ARD console window. Select a computer and then click the **Observe**, **Control**, or **Curtain** button on the toolbar to open the remote control window as shown in Figure 6-14.

Figure 6-14. *The remote control window when connected to another Mac client*

When you are using the remote control window to remotely manage a system, you will notice a few options in the toolbar. You can switch between observation, curtain, and control modes. This allows you to start as an observer and then switch to curtain mode to do something securely, for example.

213

You can take a **screenshot** of the remote screen and save it as a file on your computer or **copy and paste** between the remote computer and the workstation that the ARD console is running on. Finally, you can adjust the quality of the image using the **slider** on the top-right corner of the window to improve performance on slower network connections if there is lag with higher-resolution imagery.

Observe

Observation mode is the simplest remote mode. You can view one or more systems without any interaction with the remote computer. This is helpful if you are talking with an end user and you want to shadow their Mac and have them demonstrate an issue they are having so you can better troubleshoot the problem. This feature has also been known to be used in classrooms or computer labs where the lab monitor or instructor wants to keep an eye on what the students in the class are doing with their computers during an assignment or a testing session.

Control

By default, when choosing to remote control another Mac using the ARD console, you will be in *shared* control mode. In this mode, your end user can continue to control their system, and you share control with them as the remote administrator. This can result in *fighting* over the mouse and keyboard, so if you need to take full control of the system and lock the user out of being able to control their system, you can toggle to *absolute* control mode by clicking the other control button as shown in Figure 6-15.

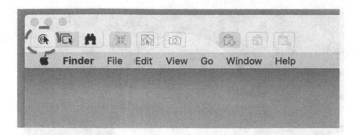

Figure 6-15. *The absolute control button*

Curtain

Curtain mode is a third form of remote control, similar to absolute control and shared control modes in that as a remote administrator you can control the user's desktop. However, the main difference with curtain mode is that it blanks out the remote screen so the end user cannot see what you are doing. This can be useful if you need to use any kind of secure procedure to resolve an issue and you don't want to disclose to the user what you are doing. An example might be mapping a secure network drive and browsing through sensitive data that you don't want a user to be able to see.

Pro Tip   When using **curtain** mode, ARD will prompt you to enter something into a dialog box that will be displayed to the end user when you take over their screen. This is useful for disclosing to the user that work is being done on their system and to show when the remote task is completed. Figure 6-16 provides an example of what the end user sees during this process.

System Administration in Progress, please wait...

Screen locked by Drew Smith

Figure 6-16. *An example of the message that end users see during curtain control procedures*

Chat

In addition to remote control, you can also chat with users remotely using the built-in instant messaging functionality in ARD. You can select a computer you want to interact with the user of and then choose **Chat** from the **Interact** menu to start a chat session. This will allow you to talk back and forth with the user in real time while you help troubleshoot their issue.

Lock Screen

The **Lock** and **Unlock Screen** feature found under the **Interact** menu is useful in schools and public lab environments where users may be found in violation of the school's acceptable use policy. For example, if a student is doing something in violation of the policy and they are remotely observed doing so, you can lock their screen and essentially catch them *red-handed* if you need to alert the school administration or authorities of the violation. When the screen is locked, it looks very similar to *curtain* mode, and the user cannot do anything save for powering down the system.

Client Administration

Apple Remote Desktop also provides a number of remote client administration features including power controls, remotely updating particular settings, and more. Most of these remote administration options are found under the **Manage** menu as shown in Figure 6-17.

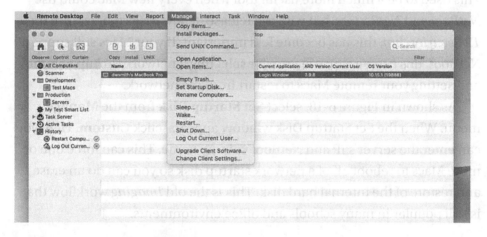

Figure 6-17. *The Manage menu provides most of the remote client administration commands*

Power Control

Select one or more remote computers and choose **Sleep…**, **Wake…**, **Restart…**, **Shut Down…**, or **Log Out Current User….** These are all pretty self-explanatory. When you select one of these power options, you are given a task window where you can choose *to immediately* require one of these actions to occur or *give the end user a warning and time to save and* *close out of anything they are currently working on* before the power task runs. Because this is a task, you can track the status through the *Active Tasks* list on the left side of the ARD console window.

Empty Trash

Another simple option. Select one or more computers and use this command to empty the trash on the remote machines.

Set Startup Disk

This used to be a much more useful tool when every new Mac could use *NetBoot* and *NetRestore*, but with the release of new Macs that feature the *T2 Security chip*, this has become less important. If your Macs still support NetBoot, this can be a nice feature for selecting a network startup volume and setting your remote Macs to restart from the network.

As shown in Figure 6-18, select **Set Startup Disk** from the **Manage** menu. When the Set Startup Disk window appears, click **Custom**. Here you can enter the server's IP and NetBoot volume name. This can force one or more Macs to reboot off of a network startup disk so you can do an erase and restore of the internal hard disk. This is the old *imaging* workflow that is still popular in many schools and office environments.

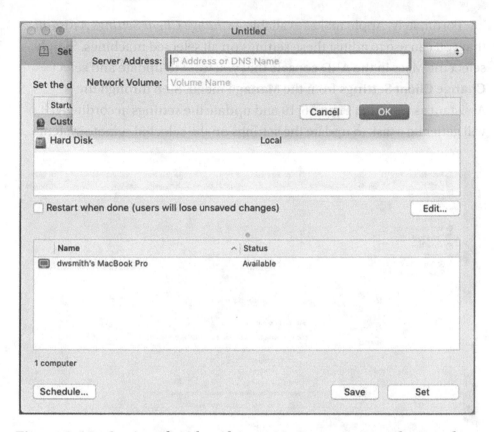

Figure 6-18. *Settings for identifying a NetBoot server and network volume for booting non-T2 Macs from the local area network*

Change Client Settings

Once you have several hundred Mac clients in your Apple Remote Desktop console, you may want to make a change to one or more settings that govern how ARD works. Even using remote control options, if you had to touch every single Mac in your organization and manually open the *Sharing System Preference* to make a change, it would be very time consuming.

Fortunately, Apple makes available a *Change Client Settings Assistant* that you can use to adjust these settings on all selected machines. Simply select the Macs in the ARD console that you want to update and select **Change Client Settings** from the **Manage** menu. Step through the Assistant as shown in Figure 6-19 and update the settings accordingly. It will generate a task to update the settings on the selected remote systems.

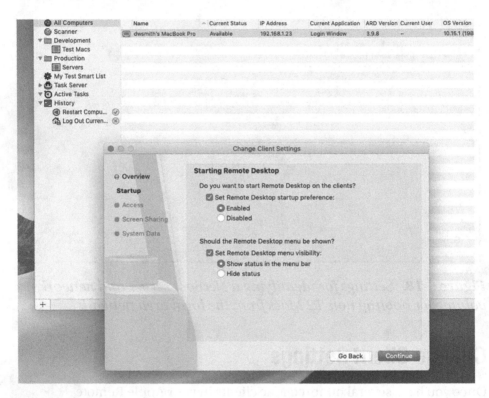

Figure 6-19. *The Change Client Settings Assistant*

Pro Tip   You should test this on at least one machine that is within physical proximity before you update the settings on multiple remote machines. If you make a mistake, you can correct it and try again, instead of pushing a setting that causes you to lose control of all of your remote systems. As a general rule of thumb, you really want to test until you have everything working flawlessly on a couple of machines before running any task or making a setting change on a massive scale.

Asset Management and Reporting

Apple Remote Desktop can help simplify the inventory control process for Mac system administrators by using various reporting features. The **Report** menu as shown in Figure 6-20 provides access to a number of common reports. You can experiment with these to see which reports work best for your particular scenario, but we are going to focus on three example reports in this chapter.

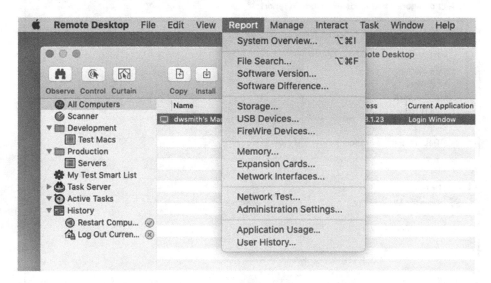

Figure 6-20. *The Report menu shows various common report options*

System Overview

The first report we are going to take a closer look at is the *System Overview Report*. This report gathers data from the client Macs selected and provides it in a report that can be viewed interactively via ARD, printed, or exported. In Chapter 1, we learned about how to use the *About This Mac* and *System Report* tools to find out just about anything we wanted to on a specific Mac. Using this System Overview Report, you can create a customized report from all of the Macs on your network by having ARD poll each machine for this info. Figure 6-21 shows the default options, but you can drill into each of these areas and add or remove specific columns based on need.

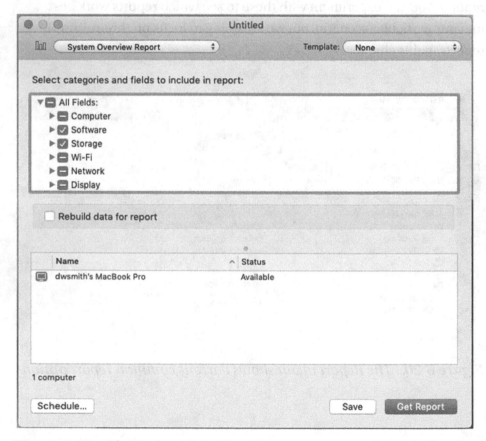

Figure 6-21. *The System Overview Report customization window*

Figure 6-22 shows the resulting report when run against one test machine on my network. You can scroll through the list horizontally or click a specific tab to jump to that information. You can also export this data using the button in the report toolbar.

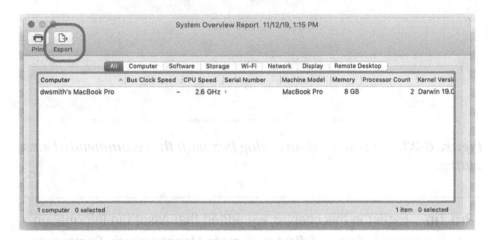

Figure 6-22. *The resulting System Overview Report*

You can export that data as a ***.csv** file as shown in Figure 6-23 and then import it into *Numbers* or *Microsoft Excel* to do further calculations on the data. This can be a very useful tool for life-cycle planning or identifying machines in your fleet that need RAM, storage, or other upgrades.

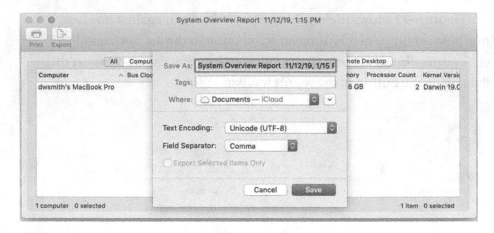

Figure 6-23. *The export data dialog box with the recommended ∗.csv settings*

Pro Tip   Earlier in this chapter, we added that asset tag information into the computer's **Info 1** field in Remote Management's Computer Settings option in the *Sharing System Preference*. If you look at the Remote Desktop tab, you will see the fields for Infos 1, 2, 3, and 4. In Info 1's column is the asset tag information we entered.

Software Version

The *Software Version Report* is particularly helpful if you are working to maintain software version parity across all of your various Mac clients. This is a great way to baseline your level of standardization and identify systems that are out of compliance. I typically install a copy of Apple Remote Desktop on a system I consider to be the baseline *reference system* that has all of the standardized software installed on it. That way I can compare my reference system against all of the other systems on the network. Figure 6-24 shows the configuration options for this report. I can select up to ten applications from the list and compare them to other Macs in my organization.

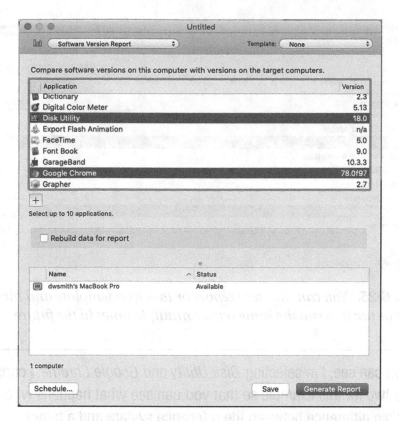

Figure 6-24. *The Software Version Report configuration window*

Pro Tip   Now would be a good time to mention **templates**. In the top-right corner of the report window, as shown in Figure 6-25, there is a *template pop-up menu.* You'll see this template menu in many task-related configuration windows. Let's say you want to check for the version of *Chrome* or *Disk Utility* on a regular basis. Instead of selecting those every time, you can **save** a template and choose to run that report again at any time from the template pop-up menu.

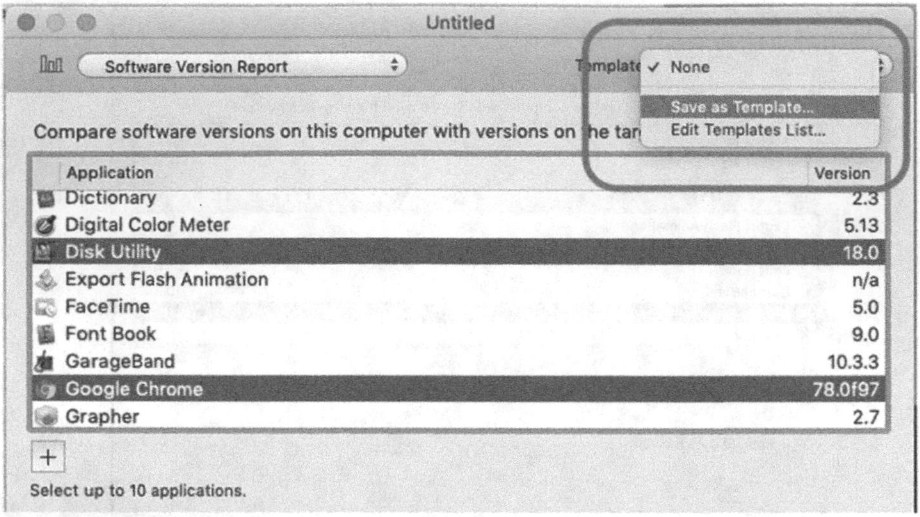

Figure 6-25. *You can save any report or task as a template and modify it later or use it to run the same report multiple times in the future*

As you can see, I'm selecting *Disk Utility* and *Google Chrome*. I chose these two for this example so that you can see what happens when there's a difference between the reference system and a target system for an application version (Disk Utility) vs. the application being missing from a target system (Google Chrome). Take a look at Figure 6-26. It found a newer version of Disk Utility on the target machine, which was expected because my target is running *Catalina* and my reference machine is still on *Mojave*. It also found that Chrome was not installed on the target machine, so if my goal is to have Chrome installed on every Mac in my organization, this target system is out of compliance and I'll need to install Chrome to fix that.

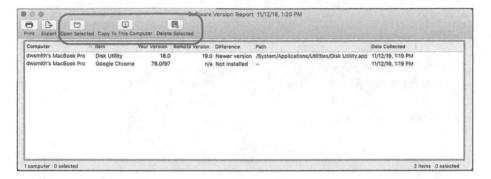

Figure 6-26. *The results of the Software Version Report and action buttons*

There's one more thing about this report that makes it kind of unique. Instead of simply providing me with data, there are three buttons in the report toolbar that I can interact with to act on this data. I can select the new version of Disk Utility and click the **Open Selected** button, and it will cause Disk Utility to launch on the remote machine.

I can click the **Copy To This Computer** button, and it will copy that new version of Disk Utility to the workstation I am currently running ARD on. Since Disk Utility is a self-contained application bundle, if my host OS supports it, I can run it on my Mac or install it into my /Applications/Utilities folder. If you are using this report to identify applications that you don't want on your network, like peer-to-peer file sharing applications, you can also select the application from the list and click the **Delete Selected** button and delete/uninstall it on the remote computer.

Application Usage

The final report we will examine is the *Application Usage Report*. This report allows you to select one or more Macs and input a date range as shown in Figure 6-27. It will then go out and poll all of the applications that have been used on the selected computer(s) and report back the date and time these were used and by which user. An example of this report is shown in Figure 6-28.

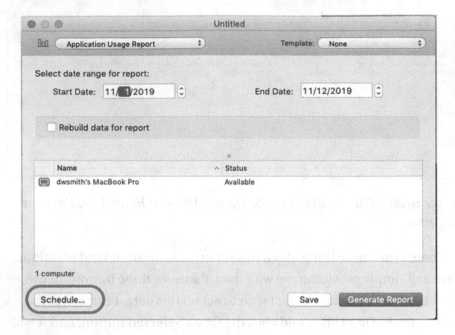

Figure 6-27. *The Application Usage Report configuration window*

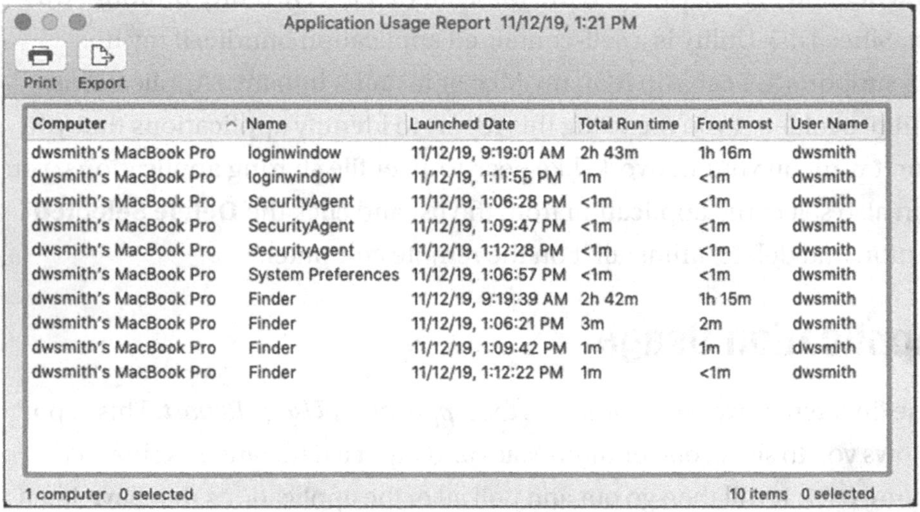

Figure 6-28. *The resulting Application Usage Report data from my test system*

This is an excellent report if you are paying per seat for applications and you are not sure if anyone is even using these applications or how often they are using them. This kind of report can provide valuable software metering information that can be used to make informed purchase and license renewal decisions.

Pro Tip   One more feature that you will find useful is setting a schedule for a task to run in the future or even repeat on a regular basis. As you can see in Figure 6-27, similar to the template pop-up menu found in each task window, there is also a **Schedule...** button. Clicking this button allows you to set a date/time for the task to run, and you can set it to repeat. In this way you can have reports run overnight or on a regular basis if you are doing ongoing software usage or compliance monitoring.

Software Distribution

The last, and arguably most useful function of Apple Remote Desktop, is as a tool for software distribution. The point of software distribution is to streamline the process of installing and upgrading software across your entire fleet of *macOS* clients. Yes, you could use a USB drive or a network share and go from Mac to Mac installing the software as you go, but this is really time consuming and error prone. Apple Remote Desktop provides a couple of features for mass installing applications across the network to all of your *Macintosh* endpoints.

Application Installers

There are three different types of application installers on macOS. The first is the *sandboxed* or *self-contained application* or App that you can download from the *Mac App Store* or you can install by dragging and

dropping the application directly from a *.**dmg** (disk image) into the
/**Applications** directory. An example of an application like this is *VLC
Media Player*, available at www.videolan.org and shown in Figure 6-29.
You can see that to install this kind of application, all you need to do is drag
the *VLC* icon into the alias of the */Applications* folder to install it.

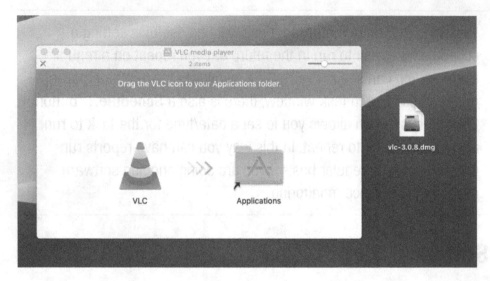

Figure 6-29. *VLC is an example of a self-contained application*

The second kind of installer is the *application install package* or *.**pkg**
file. These are very common and use Apple's macOS *Installer* helper
application to deploy them. These are used when support files need to
be installed in various areas of the hard disk and are not all contained
into a single folder or App bundle. I find these are most often used with
applications that support hardware peripherals like USB drawing tablets.

Figure 6-30 features a package installer for *Wacom* tablet drivers which
can be found at www.wacom.com. Instead of dragging and dropping the **Install
Wacom Tablet.pkg** file into the */Applications* folder, I need to **double-click**
the file and follow the *installer* prompts to install the application and its
supporting files into the correct places on my *Macintosh HD* volume.

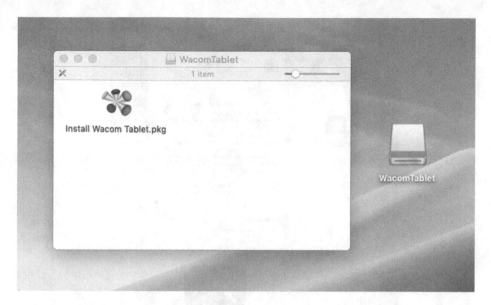

Figure 6-30. *An example of an installer package*

Finally, the third installer type is very similar to a ∗**.pkg** file and works in a similar fashion, but a commercial skin or another kind of front-end applet is used to install the application instead of Apple's macOS *Installer* helper. The most obvious example of this is the *Adobe Flash Player* installer, available at www.adobe.com/downloads. As you can see from Figure 6-31, if I use **Get Info** to see what kind of file this installer is, it tells me it is an **Application**. Installing this is the same process as the ∗**.pkg** except it launches a custom installer application that Adobe created to step me through the installation process.

Figure 6-31. *The Install Adobe Flash Player is an application, not a package*

Pro Tip   Sometimes there are still ***.pkg** files hidden inside these application bundles as in the case of *Install Adobe Flash Player*. Check it out, **right-click** the *Install Adobe Flash Player* application, and choose **Show Package Contents**. Browse to */Contents/ Resources/* and look—**Adobe Flash Player.pkg** is there. This doesn't mean that you can always just run that ***.pkg** file and the application will install correctly as there may be other dependencies that the commercial installer uses besides this single package.

As you have probably guessed, we need to approach the software deployment strategy a little differently for each of these different installer types.

Copy Items

The most straightforward method, using the *Copy Items* option, is best used for applications that are self-contained bundles like the *VLC Media Player*. To install this application on one or more Macs, open Apple Remote Desktop and select the target computers from one of your computer lists. Click the **Copy** button in the toolbar, and you will see the Copy Items window as shown in Figure 6-32.

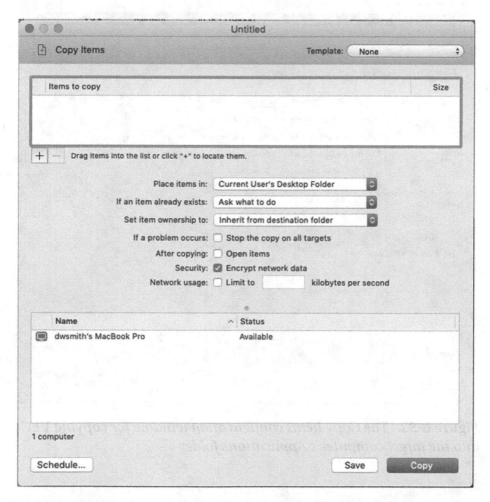

Figure 6-32. The Copy Items configuration window

Drag the *VLC* application from the disk image and **drop** it into the
Items to copy field. Select **Applications Folder** from the **Place items in:**
pop-up menu. Once you have finished setting up the file copy as shown in
Figure 6-33, click the **Copy** button to start the task.

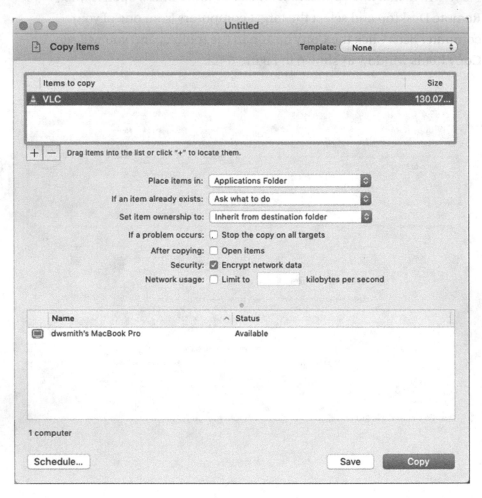

Figure 6-33. *The Copy Items configuration window for copying VLC
into the target computer's Applications folder*

The file copy will begin, and you will see a progress bar as shown in Figure 6-34.

Figure 6-34. *Progress on the active task of copying the application*

When the file copy completes successfully, go to your test machine and browse to */**Applications*** and **double-click** the *VLC* icon to launch the application. If it launched successfully as it did in Figure 6-35, then your application installation was successful.

Figure 6-35. *The VLC application installed successfully on the target computer*

Installing Packages

Installing packages is basically as straightforward as copying items. Select the computer(s) you want to install the package onto in the ARD console and then click the **Install** button in the toolbar. **Drag and drop** the *.pkg or *.mpkg file into the window and set the appropriate settings as shown in Figure 6-36. When you are ready, click the **Install** button, and the task will begin. Once it is complete, check the test computer by launching the application and making sure it works.

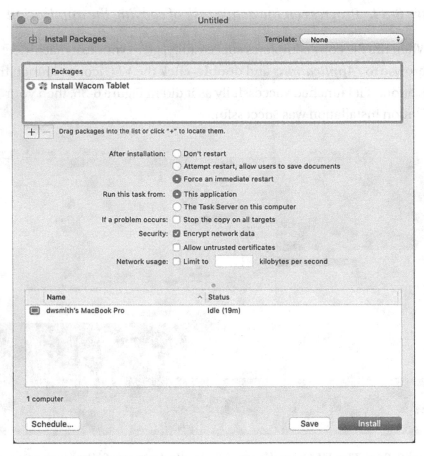

Figure 6-36. *The Install Packages configuration window for installing the Wacom tablet*

Pro Tip   Installing packages can take time, especially over the network where it can cause a lot of traffic. Notice the **Schedule** button on the install configuration window? Just like report tasks, install tasks can also be scheduled for a future date and time. Consider running massive installations during off-hours to limit the disruption that heavy network traffic could cause to your end users.

Running Unix Scripts

The last option that is probably the most complicated, but also quite elegant, is using the command line to write a script that installs a particular application. Since we were talking about *Adobe Flash Player* in the previous section as an example, I went digging into the commercial install package, and I found something very interesting. When you **right-click** the *Install Adobe Flash Player* application and choose **Show Package Contents**, you can browse to */Contents/MacOS/,* and there is a Unix executable called *Adobe Flash Player Install Manager* as shown in Figure 6-37. That is intriguing. I wonder if there is a manual for this command.

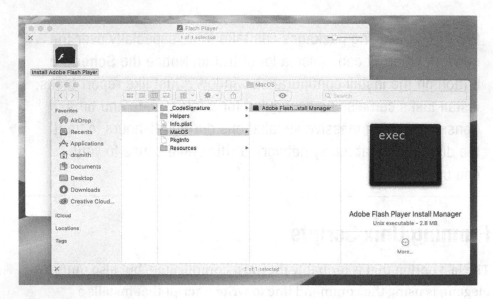

Figure 6-37. *The Unix executable buried in Adobe Flash Player installer application bundle*

I'm going to open a *Terminal* window, and then at the prompt I will type cd. Then I will drag and drop that **MacOS** folder that holds the *Adobe Flash Player Install Manager* Unix executable into the Terminal window. That will change my directory to the mounted disk image volume and the MacOS folder specifically, as shown in Figure 6-38.

Figure 6-38. *Using the cd command with a drag and drop of the directory we want to change our location to*

Now you will be at the **MacOS** directory in the *Terminal*. Type ls and you should see only one file in that directory, and it is Adobe Flash Player Install Manager. Next, let's see if there is a manual. Type man "Adobe Flash Player Install Manager" and press enter. Bummer. As seen in Figure 6-39, there is no manual provided for how to use the Adobe Flash Player Install Manager.

Figure 6-39. *No man page exists for this Adobe command line utility*

No worries, let's use our web browser and Google something like "Adobe Flash Player silent install for Mac" and see what we can find. The top hit is from Adobe's web site, and it says we can use this command with the `-install` flag to process a silent install. Let's give it a try! We are going to need to take a two-step approach to this. Our first step is to copy the installer to the target computer, and the second step will be to actually perform the installation by sending this Unix command.

Open Apple Remote Desktop and find our test computer in the *All Computers* group. Click it to select it and then click the **Copy** button in the toolbar. Drag the **Install Adobe Flash Player** application from the disk image and drop it in the **Items to copy** section. This time, when it asks where to place the items, click the button and choose **Specify full path;** and in the dialog box that appears, enter /**tmp** as shown in Figure 6-40. If your Copy Items window looks like mine, click the **Copy** button to copy this installer into the temp directory on the remote Mac.

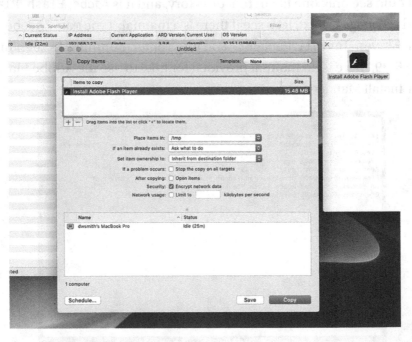

Figure 6-40. *Copy Items configuration window for copying the Flash Player installer to the /tmp directory on the remote test Mac*

When the file is done copying, you can verify that it exists by going to the test Mac and clicking **Go** menu ➤ **Go To Folder** and typing in **/tmp**. You should see the *Install Adobe Flash Player* application in the root of the temp folder as shown in Figure 6-41. The first part of the process is now complete. We now have a way of copying the Adobe Flash Player installer application to the temp folder on our Macs.

Figure 6-41. *The Install Adobe Flash Player application in the /tmp directory where we copied it*

Next, we need to write the Unix install script. The easiest way to do this and test it is interactively on a Mac. I'm going to use one of my test Macs for this. I'm going to open the *Terminal* app from the */**Applications**/ **Utilities** folder on my test Mac. Since I've already copied the installer to the **/tmp** folder, I'm going to **Show Package Contents** again on this installer and browse to */**Contents/MacOS**/* and then drag and drop the *Adobe Flash Player Install Manager* Unix command to my Terminal command prompt as shown in Figure 6-42.

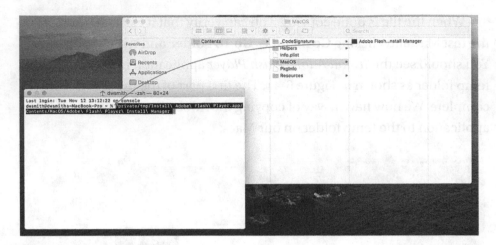

Figure 6-42. *Drag and drop the Unix command to the Terminal window as a shortcut vs. writing out the full path*

Next, we will amend a `-install` flag to the end of it per the instructions from Adobe's web site. My full command will look like that shown in Figure 6-43.

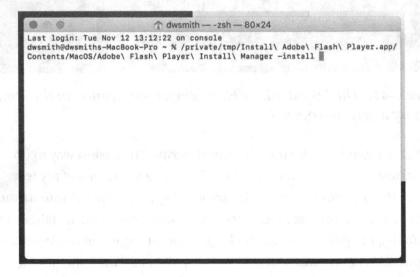

Figure 6-43. *Your Terminal window should look similar*

If you run this command interactively, it will prompt for your Administrator password. Once you enter it, the script will run, and you will get a message that says Install succeeded with exit code: 0. That means the installation completed. Browse to */Applications/Utilities,* and you will have a copy of the *Adobe Flash Player Install Manager* there as well as the *Adobe Flash Player plug-in* installed for your browser(s).

Great, now we know what command we need to run. We just need to write the script in ARD so we can use it on multiple machines to install *Flash Player* on multiple systems simultaneously. Let's go back to our Apple Remote Desktop system and select a different test system. Using the **Copy** command, copy the *Adobe Flash Player installer* application to **/tmp** so that the installer is on the machine.

Next, select the machine in the ARD console and click the **Unix** button on the toolbar. In the window that appears, enter the following command that we developed when testing:

```
/private/tmp/Install\ Adobe\ Flash\ Player.app/Contents/MacOS/
Adobe\ Flash\ Player\ Install\ Manager -install
```

Set it to run as **User: root,** and when your Send Unix Command window looks like the one in Figure 6-44, click the **Send** button to execute the command on the remote computer.

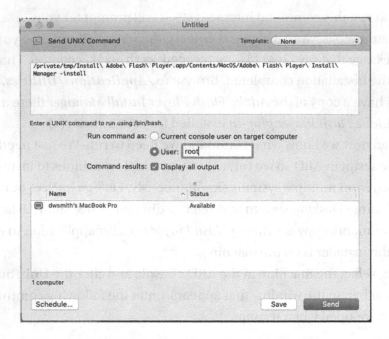

Figure 6-44. *The Send Unix Command window with our script*

The command will run on the remote computer, installing Adobe
Flash Player, and then you will get a dialog window back like the one in
Figure 6-45 that shows that it completed successfully. You can remote into
that test computer and verify that Flash Player is installed and is working
as expected.

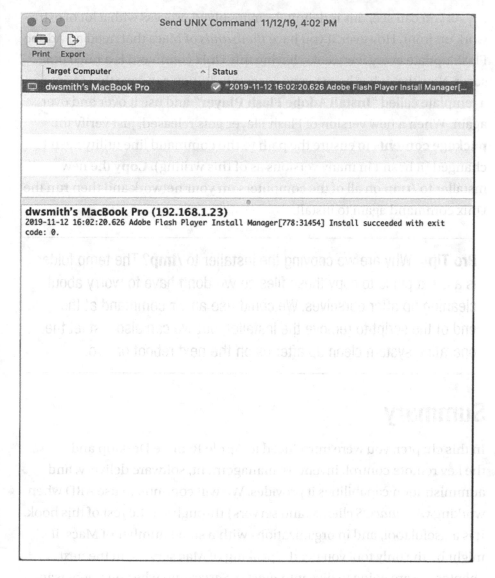

Figure 6-45. *The output from the Send Unix Command task*

As you can see, this is definitely an involved process with a lot of extra work up front. However, if you have *thousands* of Macs that need an Adobe Flash update every few weeks, having this Unix command is a huge time saver. Now that it has been tested successfully, you can save that script as a template called **"Install Adobe Flash Player"** and use it over and over again. When a new version of Flash Player gets released, just verify the **package contents** to ensure the path to the command line utility hasn't changed (it hasn't in many versions as of this writing). **Copy** the new installer to **/tmp** on all of the computers on your network and then run the Unix command again to install.

Pro Tip   Why are we copying the installer to **/tmp**? The temp folder is a great place to copy these files so we don't have to worry about cleaning up after ourselves. We could use an rm command at the end of the script to remove the installer, but we can also just let the operating system clean up after us on the next reboot or two.

Summary

In this chapter, you were introduced to Apple Remote Desktop and the key remote control, inventory management, software delivery, and administration capabilities it provides. We will continue to use ARD when working with *macOS* clients (and servers) throughout the rest of this book. It is a useful tool, and in organizations with a small number of Macs, it might be the only tool you need. Speaking of Mac servers, in the next chapter, we are going to dive into *macOS Server* and why you might want one (or might not even need one).

CHAPTER 7

macOS Server

The concept of a Mac server has changed quite extensively since the very first version of the software hit the scenes in the late 1990s. In this chapter, we are going to explore the server capabilities that Apple has built into the *macOS* client operating system, the services that are added when installing the *macOS Server* application, how to determine if you need a dedicated Mac server, and how to configure and manage the server if you do.

A Brief History of macOS Server

The original Mac OS Server was code-named "Rhapsody," and it was initially designed to be the first release of the next-generation Mac operating system that began development after Apple's purchase of NeXT in 1996. *Mac OS X* is the client operating system that was eventually released in the early 2000s, and along with it, Apple began selling an *OS X Server* as an application that ran on top of the client OS to provide it with server-class capabilities. Over the years, the features of the *Server* application have been scaled back or migrated into the base feature set of *macOS*. Today, there are only a handful of services that still remain exclusive to *macOS Server*.

Services

When it first debuted, *OS X Server* provided a number of useful features for managing your Mac clients. Apple included its own Lightweight Directory Access Protocol (LDAP) called *Open Directory (OD)* which was built to

© Drew Smith 2020
D. Smith, *Apple macOS and iOS System Administration*,
https://doi.org/10.1007/978-1-4842-5820-0_7

manage users and groups similar to Microsoft's (more popular) *Active Directory (AD)*. In addition to LDAP, it also included file sharing, printer sharing, and a web server based on *Apache*. As a popular solution for Mac system admins, OS X Server also included *NetBoot* and *Workgroup Manager* for managing fleets of Macs.

Inaddition to various management tools, *OS X Server* also provided *CalDAV*, instant messaging, a mail server, and a number of other productivity-related services. However, as more of these kinds of solutions began migrating to various cloud-hosted models, Apple moved most of them to iCloud or decided to sunset the service altogether.

As Apple started to move to more of a mobile-first administration principle with iOS devices, and then eventually Macs, they began to transform *macOS Server* into a tool for Mobile Device Management. Many of the core "server" services were moved into the base install of *macOS*. Today, *macOS Server* retains the *Open Directory* LDAP service, and *Workgroup Manager* has been dumped in favor of *Profile Manager*, which allows you to create and deploy Configuration Profiles to *iOS* and *macOS* clients.

Hardware

Apple server hardware has also changed dramatically over the years. Some of the original hardware that ran *OS X Server* included the *Power Mac G3* and *Power Mac G4* workstations. Apple briefly became very serious about dedicated server hardware and released the *Xserve* and *Xserve RAID* products for a time but eventually discontinued these models in favor of the *Mac Pro* workstation. As the need for a dedicated server OS was diminished, it no longer made sense for Apple to continue to develop and manufacture dedicated server hardware.

Introduction to macOS Server

In this chapter, we are going to explore the most common functions of a server operating system and how *macOS* or *macOS Server* can be configured for these purposes. Some of these features are going to be available in the standard install of the client operating system, and others will only be available after you purchase and install the *macOS Server* application.

Do I Need a Mac Server?

Before we begin building our Mac server, let's start by considering the use cases and if a dedicated Mac server is really necessary. As Apple has removed many of the services provided by a Mac server, they have also worked to build more cross-platform tools into *macOS* that allow it to fully participate as a client in other common networks, namely, those built on Microsoft and Linux technologies. More than likely, your organization already has some kind of LDAP, printer sharing, and file sharing solution, and you can use those with your *macOS* clients quite easily.

If you have been a Mac system administrator for a while, you may be familiar with the term *golden triangle*. This is where you would use a Mac server running *Open Directory* to sync with a *Windows* server running Microsoft's *Active Directory* to manage user accounts and then use *Workgroup Manager* to set Mac-specific permissions or settings. Today, you can bind your Macs directly to an Active Directory domain instead of even bothering with running a second LDAP specifically for your *macOS* endpoints. Configuration Profiles replace the *Workgroup Manager* component for restricting devices and locking down specific settings.

File sharing has also changed in recent releases. Apple used to utilize their *AppleTalk File Protocol* as the preferred file sharing technology for *macOS* clients. Today, *Samba* is the default file sharing protocol and works seamlessly with *Windows* and Linux clients. The point here is that if you are already running various *Windows-* or Linux-based servers, before you start building a Mac server to create redundant **Mac-only** versions of these existing file shares, consider how you might leverage these existing technologies with your *macOS* clients.

Beyond directory services or file/print sharing, there are a number of cloud-based solutions that may be a better fit for your organization. Web hosting is one that immediately comes to mind. Several years ago, using a Mac server for hosting your web site was very common, and in many ways it was a preferable solution over using Microsoft's *IIS*. While *Apache* is still available as an additional service in *macOS*, you could just as easily host your web site in the cloud using any number of low-cost web hosting solutions out there.

Here are some of the more common services that you may want to run on a Mac server, if you choose to deploy one. We will cover many of these in greater detail throughout this chapter:

- **File Sharing:** Starting with *macOS High Sierra*, Apple has integrated the *File Sharing Server* into the standard install of the operating system. You can enable this through the *Sharing System Preference*. This service allows you to share files and folders over the network.

- **Printer Sharing:** Starting with *macOS High Sierra*, Apple has integrated the *Print Sharing Server* into the standard install of the operating system. You can enable this through the *Sharing System Preference*. This service allows you to share printers over the network.

- **Apple Remote Desktop:** You can install Apple Remote Desktop in full console mode or as a *Remote Task Server* as described in Chapter 6 of this book.

- **Content Caching:** Starting with *macOS High Sierra*, Apple has integrated the *Content Caching Server* into the standard install of the operating system. You can enable this through the *Sharing System Preference*. This service caches copies of content from the *App Store* and other Apple-hosted services like *Software Update* to conserve bandwidth when installing updates or content on multiple devices.

- **Web Server:** *Apache* is integrated into the standard install of the Mac operating system. You can enable this through the command line.

- **Open Directory:** Included with the installation of the *macOS Server* application, Open Directory is an LDAP that allows you to configure network-based users and groups.

- **Profile Manager:** A basic Mobile Device Management solution that allows for the creation and assignment of *Configuration Profiles* to *iOS* and *macOS* clients— included with the *macOS Server* application.

- **Xsan:** Included with the installation of the *macOS Server* application that enables the creation and management of a Storage Area Network (SAN) solution.

- **DNS:** Starting with *macOS High Sierra,* Apple has removed DNS from the installation of *macOS Server*. You can use various other solutions including *BIND* or *Knot DNS*.

- **DHCP:** Starting with *macOS High Sierra,* Apple has integrated the *DHCP Server* into the standard install of the operating system. You can enable and manage this through the command line.

- **NetBoot/NetInstall:** Apple has continued to demote this service through the use of the T2 Security chip and the removal of these features in the more recent releases of

macOS Server. The core technology is still available in
macOS versions older than *Mojave*. If you are planning
to use this workflow, I would recommend looking at
DeployStudio as a solution (`www.deploystudio.com`).

So do you need a Mac server? To answer this question, it depends, but probably not. If you are a small business and you don't have any existing directory services or need a local file/print server, then it might make sense to deploy a dedicated Mac server.

If you are a larger organization with a lot of preexisting server solutions, try to integrate your Macs into that ecosystem instead of building a separate Mac-only environment. It will be easier for you and better for your end users to be able to participate as a first-class citizen on an existing corporate network. Increasingly, the main reason you would want a Mac server is to run *Profile Manager* unless your organization already has an effective Mobile Device Management solution from a third-party vendor like *JAMF*, *Mosyle*, or *Addigy*.

Deploying a Mac Server

If you have determined that a dedicated Mac server would be useful in your environment, we can begin configuring a Mac to function as a server.

Hardware Considerations

Depending on how you plan to use your Mac server, you should select the right hardware for the job. Typically this involves deciding between a *Mac Pro* and a *Mac mini*. Apple sells a *Mac mini* for as low as $800 as of this writing and features enough raw horsepower for most server roles. The onboard storage is relatively anemic at 128 GB of SSD space, so if you plan to use it for extensive file sharing, you should plan to purchase some kind of external Thunderbolt storage solution.

For the highest level of performance, the new 2019 *Mac Pro* can be configured with an insane amount of RAM, internal disk space, and up to 28 processor cores! It can also cost upward of the same price as a new car, so be sure that you are matching your needs with the correct specification. Most organizations can get by with a *Mac mini* of some variety. Even if you opt for the build-to-order variety and boost that internal disk to a 2 TB SSD, it will be a fraction of the cost of a Mac Pro.

One thing that you should also consider, particularly if you are planning to use the Mac primarily as a *Profile Manager* server, is the cloud-hosted model. There are a couple of vendors out there that provide Mac servers in the cloud. The most popular is **MacStadium**, where you can get access to a bare metal Mac server for a low monthly fee. You can explore these options at www.macstadium.com.

Backup

As we discussed in Chapters 2 and 3, you can either opt for a cloud-based backup solution or use *Time Machine* to back up your Mac server to an attached external disk. The only caveat in choosing a backup solution for your server is that it backs up the entire disk and any attached storage. You should be backing up all of the user data, the configuration, and any applications running on your Mac server. For this reason, stay away from solutions like *iCloud, OneDrive,* or *Dropbox* as those will only synchronize the user's home directory and not the entire disk.

Pro Tip   If you are going to use a *Time Machine* drive or some other kind of attached storage for backing up your servers, be sure to implement some kind of regimen of rotating those drives to a secure off premises storage facility. Many organizations have data recovery sites or third-party services that will store backup drives off-site in case of a fire or other natural disasters. You should do the same with your *Time Machine* drives on a regular basis.

Initial Configuration

At this point you should have selected a suitable solution for your Mac server, storage, and backup. The next thing we need to do is install a fresh copy of *macOS Catalina* on the server. So boot into *Internet Recovery* mode or use a bootable USB installer to boot your Mac, use *Disk Utility* to partition and/or format the drive, and then install a copy of *macOS*.

Once it has finished installing the OS, step through the **Setup Assistant.** Create a **local Administrator** account on the machine and sign into that account. Once you have reached the local Administrator user's Desktop, change the wallpaper to something that signifies that this is the server. I like to use some shade of gray, although some system administrators like to create a custom server wallpaper. Your server should look like mine does in Figure 7-1.

Figure 7-1. *macOS is installed on our server*

Pro Tip   Why do we care what the wallpaper is on our server? I tend to remote control into my servers and run them headless (without a monitor) in my data center. When I'm using a Screen Sharing window, it is helpful to remind me which system I'm on and to remind me to sign out after the session.

Next, run *Software Update* and install all the available patches and security updates available for your Mac. This will ensure we're running the latest security and bug fixes.

Finally, open the *Energy Saver System Preference* and set the computer to **never sleep**, **uncheck** the box to **put the hard disks to sleep whenever possible**, and **check** the box to allow it to **restart automatically after a power failure**. These settings will ensure that your server performs optimally and can reduce the risk of having the server go offline after a power-related event.

Network Settings

The first thing we need to do is configure a name for our server and a static IP address. Using the *Sharing System Preference*, name your server. I'm going to call mine "**MacServer**." If you have multiple existing servers, you may have a standardized server naming convention that you will want to use. This configuration assumes that you are simply sharing some data on the internal local area network.

Pro Tip   Double-check the Local Hostname and the Unix hostname and ensure these are the same. As you can see in Figure 7-2, I have configured all three of my server names to match.

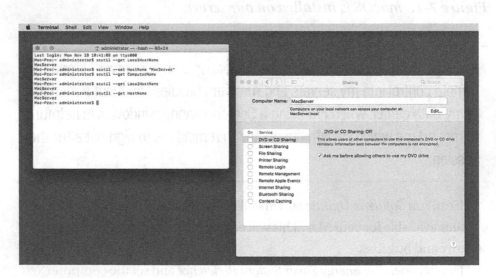

Figure 7-2. *Use the Terminal to verify the hostnames*

Next, we need to assign the static IP address to our server so that it remains consistent when we use services like file sharing. Open the *Network System Preference*, click the active network connection (**Wi-Fi** or **Ethernet**), and click the **Advanced** button and select the **TCP/IP** tab. We need to set a static IP address that isn't going to conflict with other computers on our network. You will need to consult with your Network Administrator or check your DHCP or router settings to determine the correct IP address, subnet mask, and gateway/router for this step. Figure 7-3 shows my complete IP address settings.

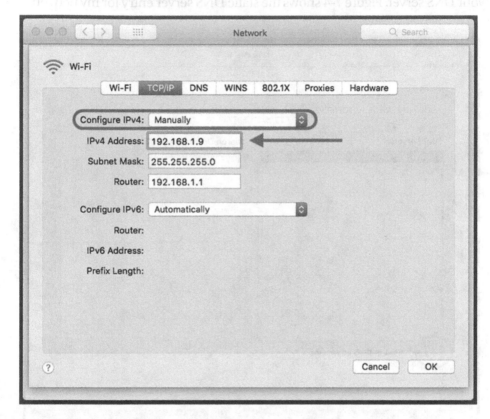

Figure 7-3. *Set a static IP address for our server*

Pro Tip   I have reserved the range of 192.168.1.2–192.168.1.9 for static IP addresses on my router. I'm going to use 192.168.1.9 as my static IP address for the MacServer.

In addition to configuring a static IP address, we also need to click the **DNS** tab and enter our DNS server information. In my network, my router is also my DNS server, so I'm entering 192.168.1.1 as my DNS server. You may also need to consult with your Network Administrator to determine the IP address for your DNS server. Figure 7-4 shows the static DNS server entry for my network.

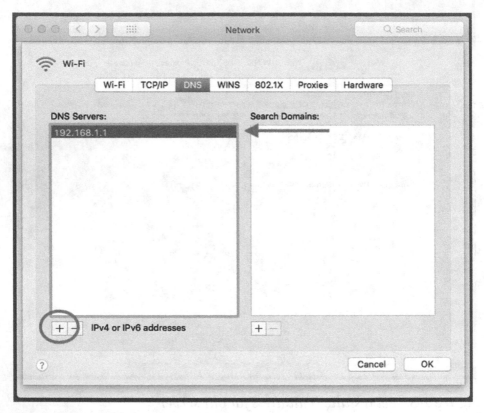

Figure 7-4. *Add a static DNS server*

Pro Tip   If you are unsure of your DNS settings, you can also switch your Mac back to DHCP temporarily and see what information is automatically populated in the DNS tab and then replicate that into the static DNS entry after changing back to the Manual address option.

Once you have set your DNS and static IP address information, open Safari and hit a web site like www.apple.com and make sure it resolves. You should see something similar to Figure 7-5 where you are able to successfully browse the Web. I would encourage you to use the **Network Utility** to ping various internal IP addresses and try to ping your server from another computer just to make sure everything is communicating properly on the local area network.

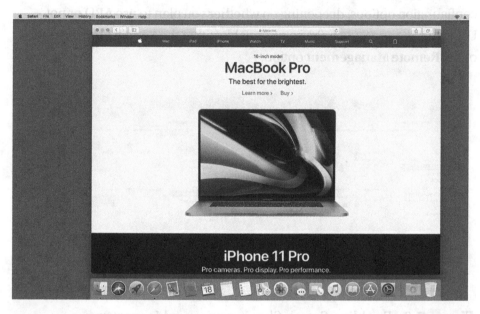

Figure 7-5. *Browse the Web to make sure your network settings are correct*

Pro Tip   If your Mac is going to be participating in a larger network, for example, a *Windows*-based network, make sure your Windows system administrator or Network Administrator creates a DNS entry for your hostname and a reverse DNS entry for the IP address. Your clients should be able to use **nslookup** or the **Lookup** option in the **Network Utility** and return the hostname by IP and the IP by hostname.

Configuring Remote Access

As I mentioned earlier, I typically run my servers without an attached monitor, keyboard, or mouse. When I need to interact with the server, I will use Screen Sharing or remote control from my primary workstation. You can use a VNC client or another Mac using the *Finder* to remote control the server, or you can use Apple Remote Desktop (ARD). Figure 7-6 shows the two different configuration options, deepening on whether you plan to use ARD or not. Using the *Sharing System Preference*, enable either the **Screen Sharing** option or the **Remote Management** option.

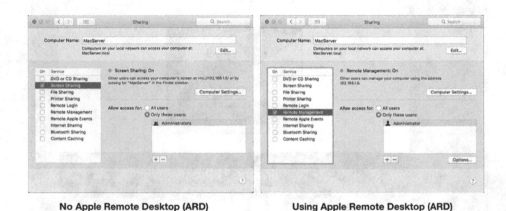

No Apple Remote Desktop (ARD)   **Using Apple Remote Desktop (ARD)**

Figure 7-6. *Enabling Screen Sharing on your Mac server*

Pro Tip   Another useful service to enable for remote administration is *Secure Socket Shell (SSH)*. The friendly name of that service in the *Sharing System Preference* is **Remote Login**. Enabling SSH can be useful for communicating with your Mac server via the command line interface.

I am planning to use Apple Remote Desktop, so I will configure that service; and then using the ARD application on my primary Mac, I will add the **MacServer** computer to my **server's computer list** using the same steps we followed in Chapter 6. If you are using ARD, you'll see something similar to Figure 7-7 when you have finished adding the MacServer to your console.

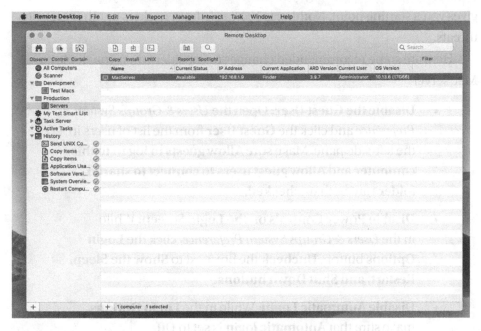

Figure 7-7. *Adding my server to the ARD console on my Mac workstation*

Pro Tip   Depending on the size and design of your network, your Network Administrator may have divided your network into various smaller subnets. In some cases, due to security reasons, servers are placed in a subnet that is separate from your client systems. If this is the case in your network, when you use the ARD scanner to search for a server, it may not find it. You may have to add the computer manually using the Add By Address option.

Server Security Considerations

When it comes to configuring a server, you really want to try to disable any services that are not going to be used. In this way, you are limiting the number of possible vulnerabilities that could exist and therefore be exploited. This is not an exhaustive list of things you must lock down to secure your server, but it gives you a starting point. Nothing is 100% safe from hackers or other security threats.

Here are some recommended changes to consider when you deploy a Mac server:

- **Disable the Guest User:** Open the *Users & Groups System Preference* and click the **Guest User** from the list of users in the left-side pane. Make sure **Allow guests to log in to this computer** and **Allow guest users to connect to shared folders** are both **unchecked**.

- **Disable Power Controls on the Login Screen:** While in the *Users & Groups System Preference*, click the **Login Options** button. **Uncheck** the box next to **Show the Sleep, Restart, and Shut Down buttons**.

- **Disable Automatic Login:** While in the **Login Options**, make sure that **Automatic login** is set to **Off**.

- **Disable the List of Users:** While in the **Login Options**, choose to *Display login window as* **Name and password**.

- **Enable Software Update for Security Patches Only**: Open the *Software Update System Preference* and click the **Advanced...** button. It is up to you if you want to automatically install all updates or not, but at bare minimum, make sure that the **Install system data files and security updates** box is **checked**. That way it will automatically patch your Mac server with important security updates.

- **Enable a Screen Saver Password:** Open the *Security & Privacy System Preference*. Click the **General** tab and **check the box** next to **Require password after sleep or screen saver begins**. Set the drop-down to **immediately**.

- **Enable FileVault:** Click the **FileVault** tab and enable FileVault encryption.

- **Enable the Firewall:** Click the **Firewall** tab. Turn on the Firewall and then use the Firewall options as detailed in Chapter 3 of this book to configure the level of security you want and any application exceptions.

- **Disable Location Services:** Click the **Privacy** tab and then click **Location Services** on the left-side pane. **Uncheck** the box next to **Enable Location Services**.

- **Disable Analytics:** While you are still on the **Privacy** tab, click the **Analytics** button on the left-side pane. **Uncheck Share Mac Analytics** and **uncheck Share with App Developers**.

- **Disable Bluetooth:** Open the *Bluetooth System Preference*. Click the **Turn Bluetooth Off** button to disable it.

- **Turn Off Wi-Fi:** Assuming you are using Ethernet to connect your server to the network, we should turn off the Wi-Fi radio. Open the *Network System Preference* and click the **Wi-Fi** button on the left-side pane. Click the **Turn Wi-Fi Off** button to disable it.

- **Log Out of iCloud:** If you signed into iCloud during the Setup Assistant process, go to the *iCloud System Preference* and **sign out** of iCloud.

Configuring Basic Server Services

Now that we have our Mac server ready to go, we can begin enabling some services. In this section, we are going to explore the server-class functions that are bundled with the core *macOS* client operating system. These are the most popular services found on Mac servers and include content caching, file services, print services, and web services.

Content Caching

One of the most popular features that was previously included in *macOS Server* but has been subsequently moved to the core *macOS* installation is *content caching*. This service runs on a device on your network and listens for clients that are downloading content from Apple or Apple-hosted services like the *iBooks*, *App Store*, *Mac App Store*, and so on. Then as that first client downloads the content, the computer running the content caching service downloads a copy and retains it. When the second, third, or any other device on the same subnet attempts to download that content, it gets copied from the cache server instead of being downloaded again over the Internet.

This solution has been extremely popular in businesses and schools that have multiple clients that share an Internet connection. I have used this with 1:1 iPad deployments and labs of Macs that need to download and install the same security updates or *macOS* releases, and it really speeds up the installation and saves on bandwidth utilization.

To enable the content caching service, open the *Sharing System Preference* and enable the **checkbox** next to **Content Caching** as shown in Figure 7-8. You can select which content to cache, and I usually stick to the default **All Content** option. If you are just wishing to use content caching with iOS devices connected physically via USB to Apple Configurator, click the box next to **Internet Connection**.

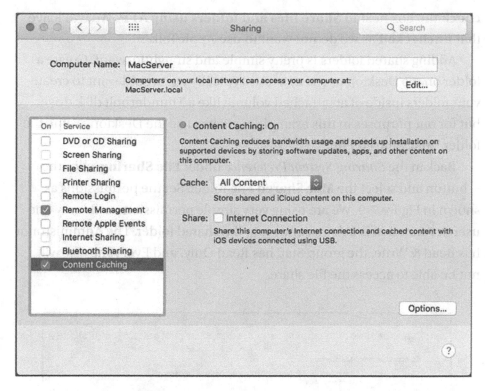

Figure 7-8. Enabling content caching on our server

Because this can take a fair amount of space on your server's hard disk, you can click the **Options...** button and choose how much disk space you want to devote to caching. Once the cache space is full, the service will make room for new content by deleting the oldest data first.

File Sharing

The next most common service that runs on Mac servers is file sharing. To enable local network file sharing, open the *Sharing System Preference* and click the **checkbox** next to **File Sharing**. By default, *macOS* shares files on the network using Samba. If for some reason you want to use the legacy AppleTalk protocol, you can click the **Options...** button and

check the box next to **Share files and folders using AFP**. We will leave that **unchecked** as we do not want to use AppleTalk.

Adding shared folders is pretty simple and straightforward. Create a folder on the Desktop to use as a test. Typically you would want to create your folders inside of an attached volume like a Thunderbolt disk drive, but for our purposes in this example, we'll just use the Desktop. Name the folder **"Mac Shared File."**

Back in the *Sharing System Preference* under **File Sharing**, click the + button and select the **Mac Shared File** folder. Set the permissions as shown in Figure 7-9. We are using very simple permissions with only one user account that is able to connect to the shared folder. The Administrator has Read & Write, the group Staff has Read Only, and Everyone else will not be able to access the file share.

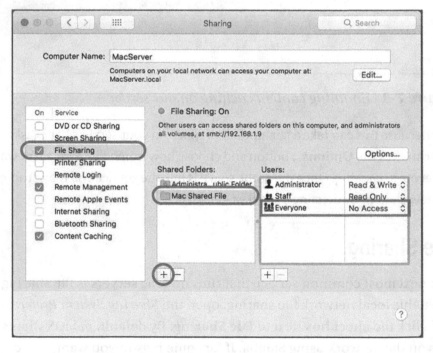

Figure 7-9. Enabling the file sharing service and configuring permissions

This is the simplest form of file sharing because we are limiting access to the share based on the single user account on this particular Mac—Administrator. There is only one member of the Staff group, and that is the Administrator account. If we were to create additional users on this Mac, and if they were members of the Staff group, they would be able to read the contents of the file share but not write to it.

Printer Sharing

Printer sharing is pretty simple and straightforward as well. The first step involves connecting a print queue to your Mac using the *Printers & Scanners System Preference*. As you can see in Figure 7-10, I have connected to an IP printer on my network, and now I want to share this printer queue with other Macs on my network.

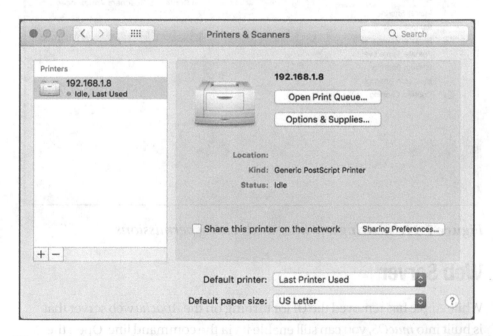

Figure 7-10. Add one or more print queues to the Printers & Scanners System Preference

To do this, open the *Sharing System Preference* and click the **checkbox** next to **Printer Sharing** to enable the service. You will see the list of print queues on my server in the next pane. **Check** the box next to the printer to share that queue and then set permissions with the rightmost pane. The default is **Everyone Can Print** as shown in Figure 7-11. You can also add additional users and groups and restrict access to these print queues by user or group.

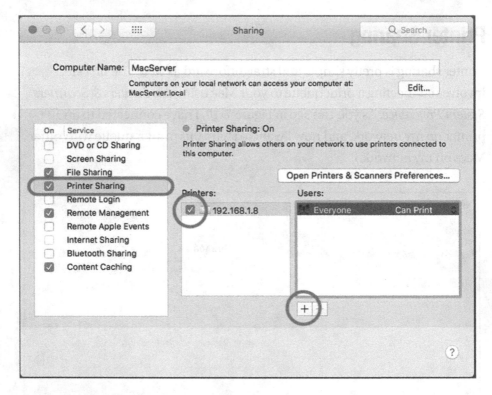

Figure 7-11. *Sharing a printer and setting permissions*

Web Server

While Apple has removed the UI for turning on the *Apache* web server that is built into *macOS*, you can still enable it via the command line. Open the Terminal and enter `sudo apachectl start` at the prompt to enable the built-in *Apache* web server as shown in Figure 7-12.

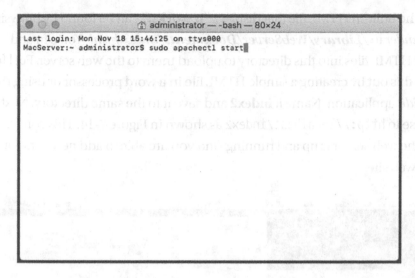

Figure 7-12. *The command to start the Apache service*

Enter your Administrator password, and this will turn the *Apache* web server on. We can test to make sure it is running by going to http:// localhost in the Safari browser as shown in Figure 7-13. It works!

Figure 7-13. *Confirmation that the web server is up and running*

The built-in HTML file that displays **"It works!"** can be found by browsing the *Finder* to */Library/WebServer/Documents/index.html*. You can add other HTML files into this directory to upload them to the web server. Feel free to try this out by creating a simple HTML file in a word processor or using the *TextEdit* application. Name it **index2** and save it to the same directory. Next, browse to `http://localhost/index2` as shown in Figure 7-14. This confirms that the web server is up and running, and you are able to add new content to your web site.

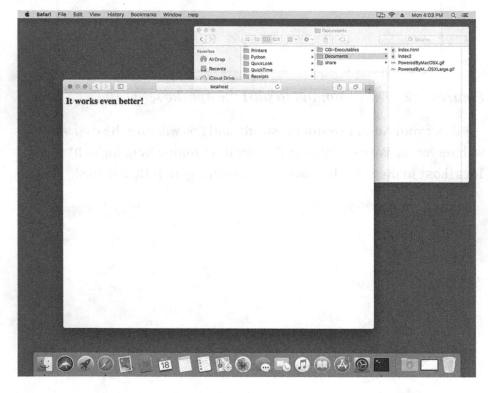

Figure 7-14. *Confirmation that you can upload new content to the web site hosted on your Mac*

You can also install *PHP, MySQL,* and other web technologies on your Mac web server if required. The configuration of those additional services is outside the scope of this book, but there are many good tutorials online that can step you through the process. If you are web developer and want to use your Mac workstation as a web server for development and testing purposes, there are also tools like *MAMP* that can install a *LAMP stack-*style development environment on your Mac in a snap. You can find out more by visiting `www.mamp.info/en/`.

Configure macOS Server Services

In this section, we will configure services that are only available after you purchase and install the macOS Server application.

Installing macOS Server

As you can probably guess, Apple makes the *macOS Server* application available for $19.99 on the *Mac App Store,* and the current version as of this writing is 5.9. Go ahead and purchase and download it as shown in Figure 7-15.

Figure 7-15. *Downloading the macOS Server application on the Mac App Store*

Pro Tip   Each time Apple releases a new version of their operating system, they release a new update to *macOS Server*. For this reason, the current version of *macOS Server* requires *Catalina*. If you attempt to install it on an older Mac that isn't running *Catalina*, you can opt for a slightly older version of *macOS Server*. The primary differences in the last few releases have been additional Profile Manager payloads that are specific to the more recent releases of *iOS* and *macOS*.

We are going to install *macOS Server* on *macOS 10.15* so we can take full advantage of all of the new payloads for *iOS* 13 and *macOS Catalina*. Once the application is finished downloading from the *Mac App Store,* browse to the */Applications* folder and open the *Server* application to continue with the installation and configuration.

Once you agree to the terms and conditions, the various services will be installed as shown in Figure 7-16.

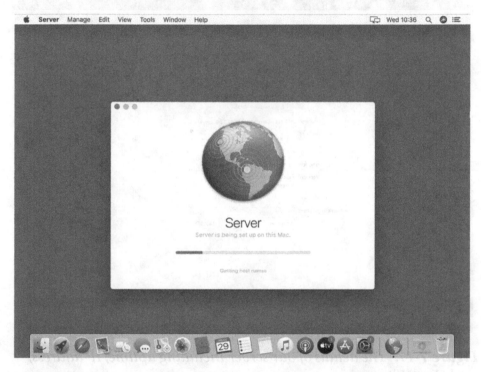

Figure 7-16. *Configuring your Mac for the first run of the Server application*

Once the Server application completes its configuration and installation, you will be presented with a window like the one shown in Figure 7-17. This is the main GUI for managing your server services including Profile Manager, Xsan, and Open Directory. There are also links to view the server logs, hardware statistics, and any alerts. You can see the Host Name, Computer Name, and if the server is reachable over the Internet.

Figure 7-17. *The details of our server including uptime, IP address, and Host Name*

Pro Tip   If your server's Host Name is not a fully qualified domain name (FQDN), you may need to click the **Edit Host Name** button and step through the Assistant to configure it as such. If you plan to use this server with Profile Manager, you should take this opportunity to register a domain name that will be used on the Internet and reconfigure your server name accordingly.

You can click the **Settings** tab and enable or disable remote access services. Note that you can enable *SSH* and *Screen Sharing* or Apple Remote Desktop here or in the *Sharing System Preference*. You can also allow access to the server using the Server app running on a remote Mac. That would allow you to install the Server app on the Mac in your office and then use it to control this server. The **Access** tab allows you to manage the users with permission to these remote access services and if they are reachable over the Internet or just on the local area network as shown in Figure 7-18.

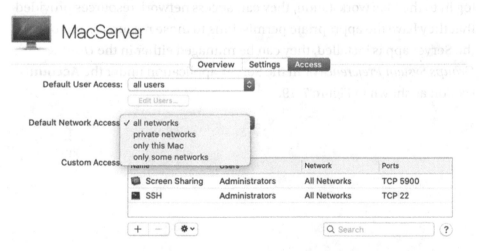

Figure 7-18. Configuring server access settings

Pro Tip   Internet reachability is Apple's term for which services (if any) can be reached on this server from the public Internet. This capability relies on your network configuration. I have an internal IP address configured on this server, but I also have configured my router to allow incoming connections to this server in my DMZ. If you plan to use this server as an MDM using Profile Manager, you will need to work with your Network Administrator to make the necessary changes to your network to allow this server to be reachable over the Internet. You can use Apple's Internet reachability test to validate those network settings and identify which services are available via the Internet.

In terms of *macOS Server*, there can be more than one directory domain. In the default installation, you will only have the Local Directory domain. This is where the users and groups exist that we create on our Mac using the *Users & Groups System Preference*. Members of this domain can log in to the Mac workstation, they can access network resources provided that they have the appropriate permissions to those resources, and once the Server app is installed, they can be managed either in the *Users & Groups System Preference* or in the Server application under the **Accounts** section as shown in Figure 7-19.

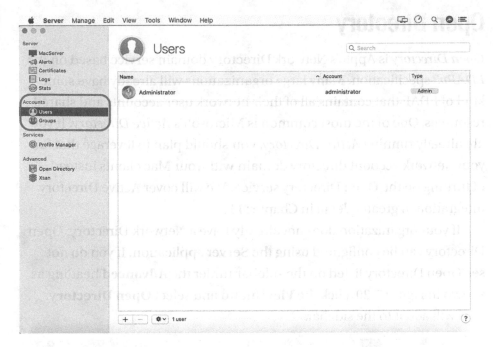

Figure 7-19. *The User Account window in macOS Server*

As you can see, we only have one user account, the local Administrator account. I could add additional users here or click the **Groups** section and add additional groups and populate members of those groups. These accounts only govern the resources on this specific computer. I cannot use accounts that I create here to access shared resources on another computer. This is why they are part of the Local domain.

If I want to create users and groups that govern access to resources on multiple machines, I need to create those accounts in a Network domain. Network accounts allow me to create a single user that can sign into other computers, access shared resources on this computer or other computers if they have the permission to those resources, and generally simplify the administration of user accounts and data security across my entire network. To use this Network domain, we must have a directory service available to contain these user accounts and groups.

Open Directory

Open Directory is Apple's Network Directory domain service based on the *LDAPv3* specification. Many large organizations will already have some kind of LDAP that contains all of their network user accounts and shared resources. One of the most common is Microsoft's *Active Directory*. If you are already running *Active Directory*, you should plan to leverage that for your network account directory domain with your Mac clients instead of turning on the Open Directory service. We will cover Active Directory integration in greater detail in Chapter 11.

If your organization does not already have a Network Directory, Open Directory can be configured using the Server application. If you do not see Open Directory listed on the sidebar under the **Advanced** heading as shown in Figure 7-20, click the **View** menu and select **Open Directory**. This will add it to the sidebar.

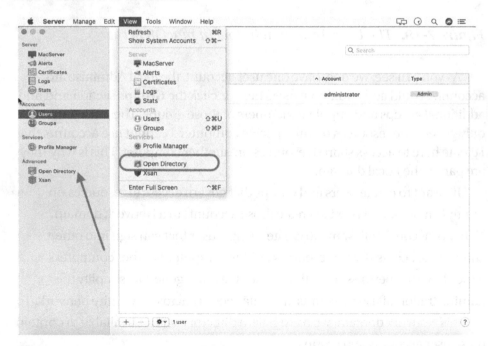

Figure 7-20. *Adding Open Directory as an available service if it doesn't already exist in the sidebar*

CREATE AN OPEN DIRECTORY MASTER

We are going to enable Open Directory on this server, so click the **Open Directory** button on the sidebar and then click the **on/off switch** in the top-right corner to enable the service. The *Configure Network Users and Groups Setup Assistant* will appear and prompt you to choose to create a new Open Directory domain, restore from an archive, or join an existing Open Directory domain as a replica. Select the option to **Create a new Open Directory domain** as shown in Figure 7-21 and click the **Next** button to continue.

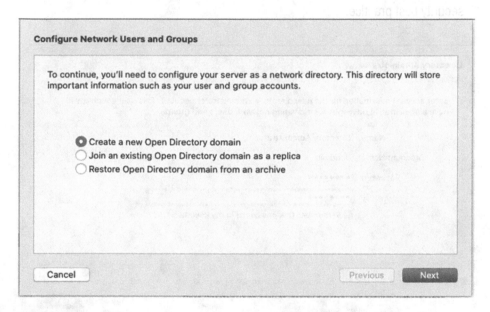

Configure Network Users and Groups

To continue, you'll need to configure your server as a network directory. This directory will store important information such as your user and group accounts.

- ◉ Create a new Open Directory domain
- ○ Join an existing Open Directory domain as a replica
- ○ Restore Open Directory domain from an archive

Cancel   Previous   Next

Figure 7-21. *Choose to create a new Open Directory domain*

Windows Pro Tip   Microsoft system administrators will recognize this idea of a master and a replica from *Active Directory*. Earlier implementations of AD included a server that functioned as the Primary Domain Controller and additional servers that were called Backup Domain Controllers. Open Directory is similar as you have an Open Directory Master and then multiple Open Directory Replicas that synchronize any directory changes or share the load when responding to requests.

The next step is to create an Administrator account for the new Open Directory domain. You can specify a username and password here or use the default **Directory Administrator** (**diradmin**) account. I am going to stick with the default for this example. Enter a secure password as shown in Figure 7-22 and click the **Next** button to continue. I recommend using a different password than the one you use for the local Administrator account to log in to the server as a security best practice.

Figure 7-22. *Create a username and password for the admin account for Open Directory*

Pro Tip   When you create Network Accounts in Open Directory, it is important to note that they should be unique to the Local Accounts on the client or server system. When the login window attempts to authenticate the user, it first looks for a matching account on the Local Directory domain of that Mac; and then if it doesn't find one, it goes up a level to the Network Directory domain and checks there. If you have an account in the Local domain that matches the account in the Network domain, it will always log in as the local account because it found a match in the Local domain and quit looking.

Step through the rest of the Setup Assistant and click the **Set Up** button to finish the initial configuration of the Open Directory Master. When the Assistant completes, you will see the Open Directory service is on; and if you click the **Users** or **Groups** button, you'll have a slightly modified interface that shows a drop-down menu for filtering your accounts and a column that designates the directory domain the account exists within as shown in Figure 7-23.

Figure 7-23. *After configuring Open Directory, we now have both a Local Directory and Network Directory*

At this point, we have configured our Open Directory Master. From here, you could configure additional servers to act as Replicas. If you have multiple locations and multiple servers, you may want to configure **Locales**. These can be configured in the Open Directory service window, and you can specify which servers should respond to requests from clients of a particular subnet. That way clients can query the nearest OD server depending on which network they reside on.

You can also view all of your Open Directory servers in the **Servers** section as shown in Figure 7-24. This is where you can select a particular server and **create an archive** of the Open Directory Master so that you can restore it later if something were to happen to it. You can also promote one of your Replicas as a new Master if required.

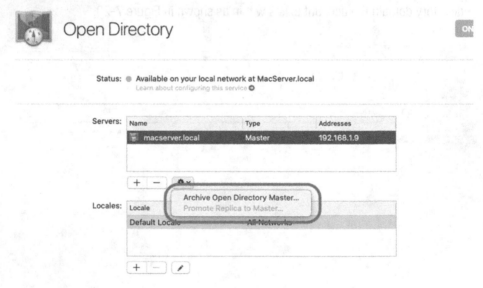

Figure 7-24. *Additional options for Replicas, Locales, and backing up your Master directory to an archive*

CREATE NETWORK USERS AND GROUPS

Next, let's start using this new directory by populating some Network users and groups. Click the **Groups** button in the sidebar and click the **+** button as shown in Figure 7-25. Create a group called **"Executive Team."** Make sure that the Directory option is **Local Network Directory** and not Local Directory. It should look something like Figure 7-26.

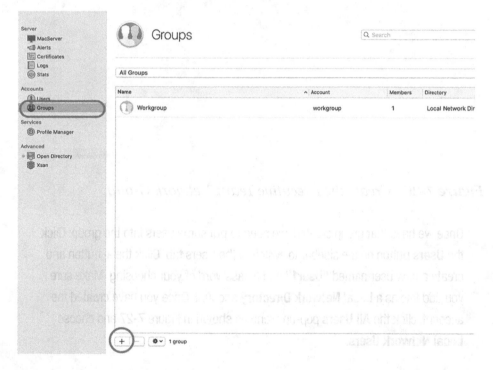

Figure 7-25. *Adding a new Group*

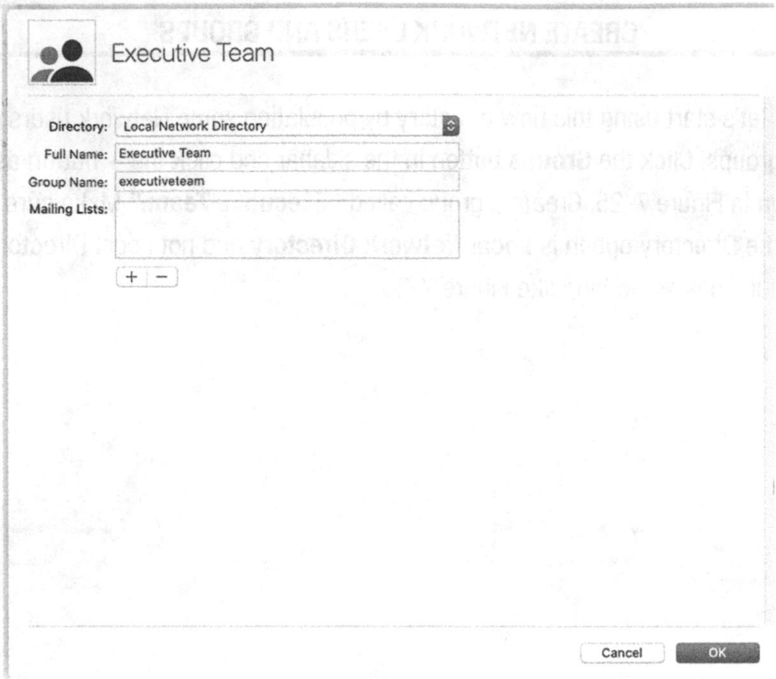

Figure 7-26. *Create the Executive Team Network Group*

Once we have that group created, we need to put some users into the group. Click the **Users** button on the sidebar to switch to the Users tab. Click the **+** button and create a new user named **"User1"** and a password of your choosing. Make sure you add this as a **Local Network Directory** account. Once you have created the account, click the **All Users** pop-up menu as shown in Figure 7-27 and choose **Local Network Users**.

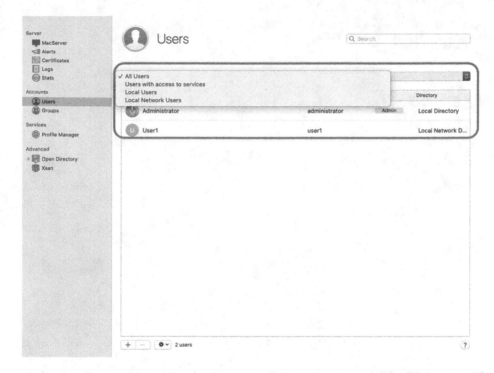

Figure 7-27. *Use the pop-up menu to filter out your local users*

Next, click the **gear** pop-up menu as shown in Figure 7-28 and choose the **Edit Password Policy…** option. We can use this to set a minimum-security policy for our end-user passwords. Go ahead and check the following boxes to set some basic requirements:

- Differ from account name

- Contain at least 8 characters

- Be reset every 3 months

Click the **OK** button to continue.

Figure 7-28. *The gear pop-up menu provides access to configure the network users' password policy*

Our next step is to modify our User1 account. **Right-click User1** in the **Local Network Users** screen and choose **Edit Access to Services…. Uncheck SSH** and **Screen Sharing** as shown in Figure 7-29 and then click **OK**.

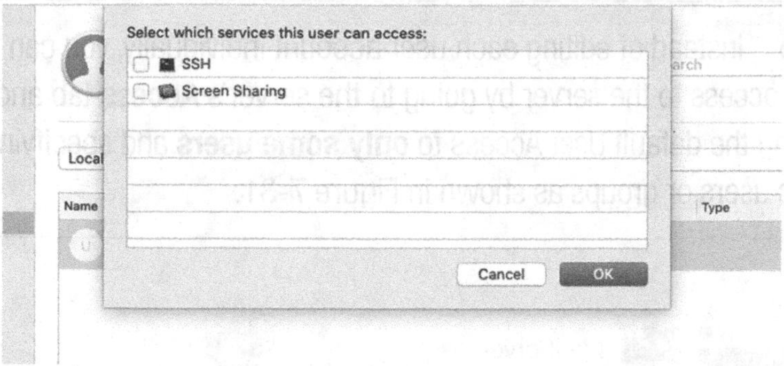

Figure 7-29. *Disable this user's access to SSH and Screen Sharing*

Next, **right-click** again the **User1** account and choose **Edit User**. In the **Groups** field, click the **+** button and start typing **"Executive Team"** into the field. This will add the user to the Executive Team group we created earlier. If the User1 is a member of the **Workgroup** group, click the Workgroup group to highlight it and then click the **–** button to remove it. When completed, your User1 should look like Figure 7-30. Click the **OK** button.

Figure 7-30. *Configure the User1 account as shown*

Pro Tip   Instead of editing each user account individually, you can also restrict access to the server by going to the server's **Access** tab and changing the default User Access to **only some users** and specifying specific users or groups as shown in Figure 7-31.

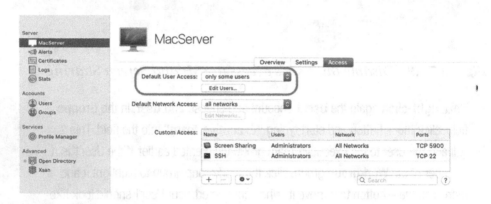

Figure 7-31. *Configuring Default User Access*

Finally, now that we have our User1 configured with the correct group, we are going to create a template from this user and create a couple more just like it. To create a template, click User1 to highlight it and then choose **Create Template from User...** from the **gear** pop-up menu as shown in Figure 7-32. When prompted, change the Template Name to **"Executive User Template"** and then leave the other settings as default and click the **Done** button to save the template.

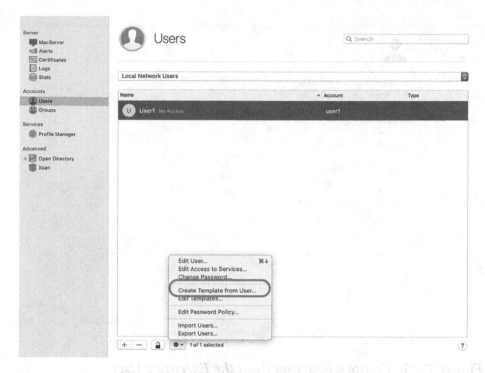

Figure 7-32. *Creating a template from the User1 account*

Now we are going to create two more users based on the Executive User Template. To do this, click the **+** button on the Users window, and this time you will see a pop-up menu in the New User window that that will allow you to create a user from a template as shown in Figure 7-33. Select **Executive User Template** and create User2 and User3 accounts.

Figure 7-33. *Create a new user from the Executive User Template*

Now that we have our three user accounts created, your Users window should look like the one in Figure 7-34. Don't forget to restrict their access to SSH and Screen Sharing too.

Figure 7-34. *You should have three user accounts—User1, User2, and User3*

Finally, let's explore the advanced options for a user. **Right-click User3** and choose **Advanced Options…** as shown in Figure 7-35. This will look familiar to you from the *Users & Groups System Preference*. Just like the local workstation, we can make adjustments like the home directory, login shell, and aliases. The option for configuring a Share Point URL is used for mapping a network drive at login, not to be confused with *Microsoft SharePoint*. We are not going to make any changes at this time, so click the **Cancel** button to continue.

291

Figure 7-35. *Advanced user settings for User3*

Pro Tip   We can see our three user accounts and a couple of groups, but did you know that there are many more users and groups than what we see here that have been placed in our directory by the OS? You can show or hide these System users and groups by **right-clicking** any user and choosing **Show System Accounts** or **Hide System Accounts** to toggle these groups on and off.

Now that we have created a few users and placed them into a group, we want to be able to log into a workstation with one of these accounts. To do this, we need to *bind* our *macOS* clients to the Open Directory domain. Binding a client to the domain allows it to search the list of Network Accounts in addition to the Local Accounts to find a match and allow a Network User to login to the computer. Any enabled user in the domain can sign into any computer bound to that domain.

BINDING MACOS CLIENTS TO OPEN DIRECTORY

Switch over to one of your test Mac clients and sign in as a local user with administrative rights. Open the *Users & Groups System Preference* and authenticate to unlock the preference pane. Click the **Login Options** button as shown in Figure 7-36. Next, click the **Join...** button next to the **Network Account Server** prompt.

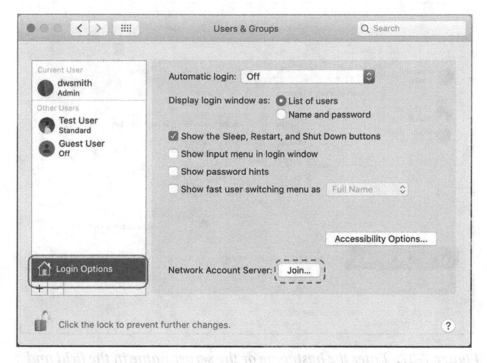

Figure 7-36. *Joining a Mac client to a Network Account Server*

You will be prompted with a dialog box to select or enter a server. You can enter an IP address or a hostname. If your network is small and simple like mine is for this example, you can also click the drop-down arrow as shown in Figure 7-37, and it may find the broadcasted host to select from the menu. Enter the server information and click the **OK** button to continue. If it prompts you to trust the Secure Socket Layer (SSL) certificates provided by the server, click the **Trust** button to continue.

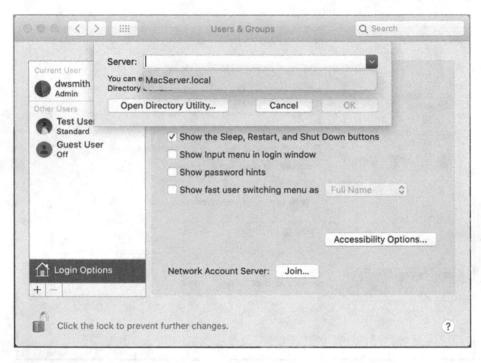

Figure 7-37. *Enter the hostname or the server name in the field and click OK*

You may receive a message that the server does not use Secure Socket Layer (SSL) authentication. You can click the **Continue** button past this message for now as we are not concerned with encryption for this exercise. It will prompt you for your local administrator account credentials, and then after a few moments of configuration, you will see your Open Directory server listed next to the Network Account Server and a green dot signifying that the connection is working. You may also want to make a couple changes to the login window as shown in Figure 7-38.

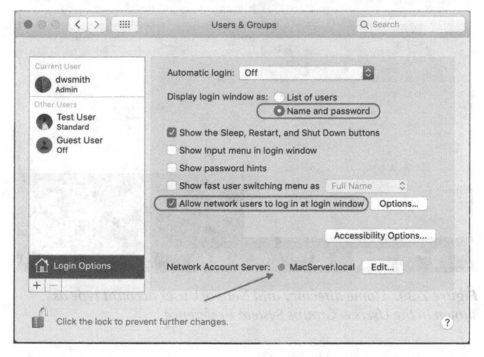

Figure 7-38. *Our client is now bound to our Open Directory domain, and you may want to change some login window options as shown*

Now that we have bound our Mac to the Open Directory, go ahead and **log out**
and then sign in using the User1 account. If all goes well, you should be prompted
with a couple of Setup Assistant questions on first login and then dropped into
a clean /**Users/User1/Desktop** directory with all the default new user settings
as a Network user. You can confirm this by going to the *Users & Groups System
Preference* or browsing to **/Users** to see your home directory as shown in Figure 7-39.

Figure 7-39. *Home directory and Network user account type as
shown in the Users & Groups System Preference*

Congratulations! You have successfully created an Open Directory domain,
populated it with users, bound a client Mac to the domain, and signed in
successfully with a Network user account.

Pro Tip   A quick note about file sharing and Open Directory: Prior to *macOS Mojave*, you could share files and folders and set permissions for Open Directory Network accounts. If you have shared folders on an Open Directory Master or Replica, you won't be able to map those shares even if you are using the local user account, because it will not authenticate. If you plan to create shares on a Mac and share them with other Macs, the host cannot be running the Open Directory service; and even if you bind that Mac to the Open Directory domain, you cannot authenticate to those shares using Network accounts. The reason for this is because the ACL groups are no longer created in the directory for file sharing access like they used to be in older versions of Server. There are unofficial fixes out there for this, but that is outside the scope of this book.

Certificates

When you completed the steps to bind your Mac client to Open Directory, you may have received a message stating *This server does not provide a secure (SSL) connection. Do you want to continue?* In that case, because we were setting up a test server, we chose to ignore this message and continue. However, in a production environment, you will want to use SSL to secure your client's communication with the server to prevent man-in-the-middle attacks, among others. Even if you are not using Open Directory and you are only deploying your server for use with Profile Manager, you will need some basic understanding of certificates and how to change them in macOS Server.

FallBack SSL Certificate

The most basic certificate that Apple provides is the *Fallback Certificate*. It gets created when you install the Server application, and it is available but not often used. You can find this certificate by opening the *Keychain Access* utility on your Mac server and clicking the **Certificates** for the **System** keychain.

Self-Signed Certificates

In the case of Open Directory, Apple provides a self-signed certificate that you can use that is generated when the Open Directory service is installed. Self-signed certificates will prompt users to trust them and are not usually the best choice for production installation. We can adjust the certificate that is being used for Open Directory if we want to replace this with a trusted third-party certificate.

Managing Certificates

We can change out the certificates we are using for any service at any time. Before we do anything with these certificates, we need to stop the services that are using them. In this case, we need to temporarily turn off the Open Directory service by clicking the on/off toggle switch in the top-right corner of the Open Directory window as shown in Figure 7-40.

Figure 7-40. *Disable Open Directory before attempting to make any changes to certificates*

Now that the service has been disabled, click the **Certificates** button in the sidebar. You will probably have something similar to Figure 7-41 with some kind of mix of certificates and the **Secure services using** pop-up menu. Using this menu, we can select which services are using which certificates.

Click the **Secure services using** pop-up menu and choose **Custom**. You will be presented with some services and their matching certificates. I have two certificates to choose from. Both of these were generated automatically for me by the server, but only one is valid. I'm going to select the **MacServer** certificate in the **Certificate** column and click **OK** to continue.

Figure 7-41. *Selecting the certificate you want to use for a particular service*

Now you will see that I'm securing my Open Directory service using my MacServer certificate. The last step is to open the Keychain Access application and search for the **OPENDIRECTORY_SSL_IDENTITY** identity preference. **Double-click** it to open it and select a new **Preferred Certificate** as shown in Figure 7-42. Click the **Save Changes** button to close it.

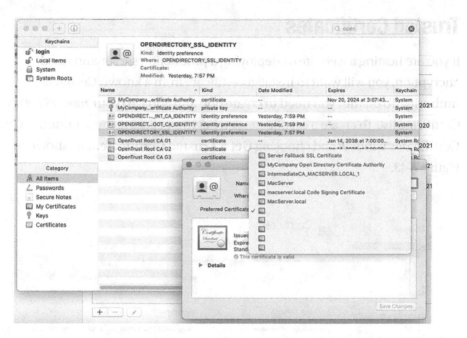

Figure 7-42. *Selecting the certificate for the SSL identity for the Open Directory service*

Go back to the Open Directory settings and restart the service by flipping the switch back to the **on** position. If you go back to your test Mac and unbind it from our domain and then join it again, you will be prompted to trust the new certificate.

Pro Tip   To unbind a Mac from the domain, log in as a user with local administrative privileges and use the *Users & Groups System Preference* ➤ **Login Options** dialog and click the **Edit** button, similar to how you joined the domain but in reverse. In the sheet that slides out and displays the Open Directory server, highlight that server and click the – button to remove it.

Trusted Certificates

If you are hosting a web site or deploying a production server and need encryption, you will want to install a certificate from a known Certificate Authority. To do this, you need to create one and add it to your *macOS Server* Certificate list. To create a certificate, you begin by clicking the + button on the **Certificates** window and choosing **Get a Trusted Certificate...** as shown in Figure 7-43.

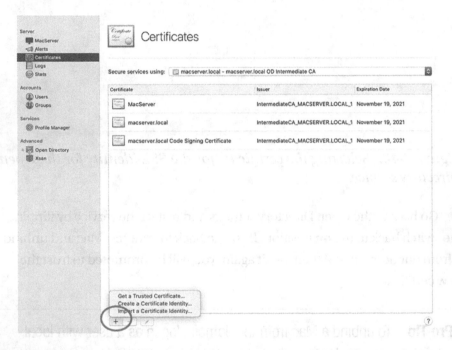

Figure 7-43. *Starting the process to get a trusted certificate*

This will open the *Get a Trusted Certificate Assistant*. Step through the prompts to provide your personal information and click the **Next** button to continue. This will bring you to the *Certificate Signing Request (CSR)* window. The CSR includes the information you need to provide to your chosen signing authority as shown in Figure 7-44 so they can generate the certificate for your server. You can copy/paste this string, or you can click the **Save** button to save the *.csr file. Since this is the end of the first step, you can click **Finish to close the dialog box**.

Get a Trusted Certificate

Your certificate signing request (CSR) has been generated below. Provide it to your certificate vendor when prompted.

```
-----BEGIN CERTIFICATE REQUEST-----
MIICzjCCAbYCAQAwgYgxIDAeBgkqhkiG9w0BCQEWER3c21pdGg5OEBtYWMuY2
9t
MRowGAYDVQQDDBFNYWNTZXJ2ZXIwMS5sb2NhbDEMMAoGA1UECgwDTi9BMQswCQ
YD
VQQLDAJJVDETMBEGA1UEBwwKQ21uY21ubF0aTELMAkGA1UECAwCT0gxCzAJBg
NV
BAYTAlVTMIIBIjANBgkqhkiG9w0BAQEFAAOCAQ8AMIIBCgKCAQEAs/
8c893SF+/8
//Zjh2DPUQ0TPgAULCQfQydGrT21t4QvPIu9tIpTAJFsL/
1qu8MIk7OLgEWoEzoI
XfHvdaIlmRh18DSshHU+CbwmXxpw7zldlEZamQs5hGRYbyDRaLbG5oCztx204G
/b
/
REViNZATqeMYv9N5EhNTPB+9inIiYMxFmVUvi0efs1dfmMTUX1YOKVq97qGuuI
```

Cancel   Finish

Figure 7-44. *The CSR string that you need to provide to your signing authority*

Next, you will notice that it created a placeholder for this certificate while you contact the signing authority. Once you have completed the validation process and you have received your SSL certificate, **double-click** the placeholder certificate and **drag and drop** the **SSL certificate and/or cert bundle** into the placeholder's **Certificate Files** section as shown in Figure 7-45. Click **OK** to save it, and now you can use the third-party certificate with your server.

Figure 7-45. *Double-click the placeholder certificate once you receive the file(s) from the signing authority and drop it into the highlighted field*

Pro Tip   If you are planning to use a trusted certificate in a production environment, make sure that your server hostname is unique on your network or, in the case of web sites, the public Internet. For SSL to work properly, it is not recommended to have a server hostname that ends in .local. If you need to change your Host Name for any reason, do so within the Server application so that the associated services get updated with the new name. You should also restart any services or the server itself after changing the Host Name.

Profile Manager

The final service we will configure in *macOS Server* is really the main reason to have a Mac server these days—Profile Manager. Profile Manager is a Mobile Device Management (MDM) solution that integrates with Apple's cloud services like *Device Enrollment Program* (DEP) and *Volume Purchase Program* (VPP) that we've touched on throughout this book so far. We will be using Profile Manager to create Configuration Profiles to provision and manage iOS devices and Mac clients *over the air* in Chapters 8 and 9.

Before we begin, there are a couple of prerequisites that you need to be aware of when using Profile Manager. First, the server must be accessible over the Internet. For my test server, I enabled *Apache* temporarily and made sure I could hit the "It works!" page from both inside and outside of my network. I also created a domain and made sure that I could get to the server on the public Internet by DNS name, not just the IP address. Once you have tested it, you can disable the *Apache* service again. Second, once you have a functional web server, it also needs to be SSL encrypted. So you'll need to procure a signed certificate from a Certificate Authority of your choice.

Pro Tip   I have used namecheap.com or godaddy.com as my SSL certificate vendors for a small fee. There are also alternatives such as letsencrypt.org that you can use to get signed free SSL certificates.

We are going to get started with configuring the Profile Manager service by clicking the **Profile Manager** button in the sidebar and then clicking the **on/off** switch to turn it **on** as shown in Figure 7-46.

This will begin the *Configure Device Management Assistant*. Step through the first dialog box to enter your **Name**, **Email Address**, **Phone Number**, and **Physical Address**. This will be disclosed to your end users on their managed devices, much like when we created an Organization in Apple Configurator.

Figure 7-46. *Turn on the Profile Manager service to initiate the Configuration Assistant*

The next step is to **select** the **trusted certificate** from a third-party Certificate Authority. If you are planning to use Profile Manager as an MDM, which we will be doing throughout the rest of this book, you must have a certificate that is signed by a Certificate Authority. If you use a self-signed Certificate, it will not work.

Next, you will need an *Apple ID* to use for **Apple Push Notifications**. You should not use a personal *Apple ID* here; you should use one that you configured solely for business use. Enter that information in the fields and click **Next** as shown in Figure 7-47. Once you have entered your *Apple ID*, click the **Finish** button to enable Device Management on this server.

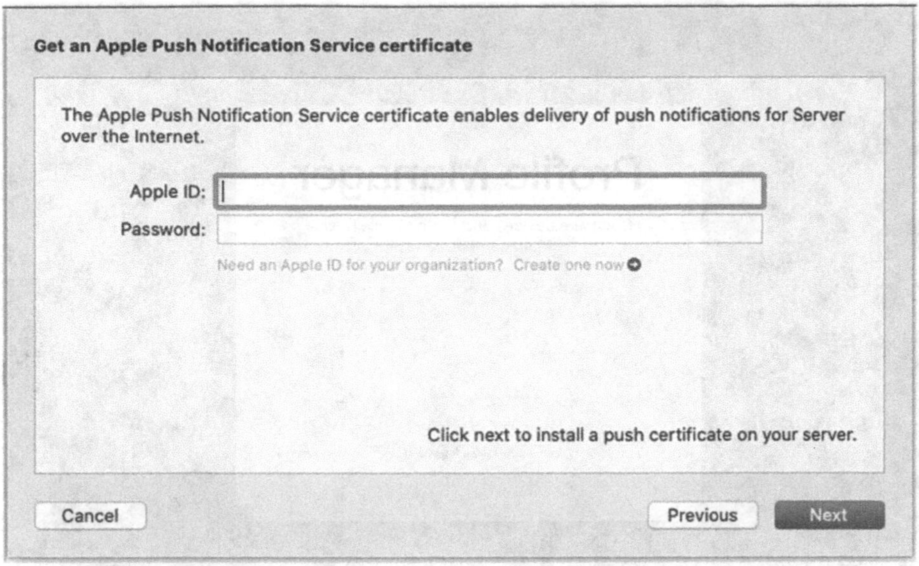

Get an Apple Push Notification Service certificate

The Apple Push Notification Service certificate enables delivery of push notifications for Server over the Internet.

Apple ID: |

Password:

Need an Apple ID for your organization? Create one now ●

Click next to install a push certificate on your server.

Cancel   Previous   Next

Figure 7-47. *Enter your institutional Apple ID for use with Push Notifications*

At this point, the service is on, and you should be able to open the Profile Manager web site. We need to test this by browsing to the site in three different ways. First, launch a browser on the server and browse to the //localhost/profilemanager site and make sure it brings you to the Profile Manager login screen. Next, open a browser on another computer on your internal network and make sure you can get to the server's internal IP /profilemanager. In my case it's 192.168.1.9/profilemanager. Finally, hit the server from an external device via the name you registered over the Internet—in my case it's http://579testing.com/profilemanager. If all is well, you should not receive any certificate errors, and you should see a login screen as shown in Figure 7-48.

Figure 7-48. *The Profile Manager login window via a web browser*

Pro Tip   If you go back to the server's main status screen by clicking
the button in the sidebar with the server's name, you should see a green
dot under Internet reachability. You can also click the Reachability Details
button and make sure that Profile Manager is showing as available over
the Internet as shown in Figure 7-49. If you are not seeing that, you
should contact your Network Administrator and have them check the
router or firewall configuration.

Figure 7-49. *Use Apple's reachability service to confirm that Profile Manager is available from the public Internet*

At this point, we have enabled the Profile Manager service and confirmed that it is working both internally and externally. There are additional options that we can configure for integration with *Apple School Manager, Device Enrollment Program,* and *Volume Purchase.* I will cover those in the next chapter when we discuss these various services within the larger topic of MDM.

Summary

In this chapter, we discussed the need for a dedicated Mac server, the server-class solutions built right into the core *macOS* client operating system, and the advanced services provided by installing the *macOS Server* application. While every organization is going to have different needs, it is clear that Apple has promoted the use of existing industry standard directory and file sharing and print sharing technologies over proprietary Mac-only solutions whenever possible.

As you can see, *macOS Server* has primarily become a tool for enabling Mobile Device Management through the Profile Manager tool. The case can be made that unless you want to use Profile Manager, you may not need a Mac server at all. If you do need Profile Manager, it could be the only service you need to run on your server, and it is not dependent on Open Directory or any other service.

In the next chapter, we will explore MDM concepts including *User Approved MDM, Device Enrollment Program,* and *Volume Purchase Program.* These solutions form the foundation for developing a next-generation deployment and support model for Apple-branded devices.

CHAPTER 8

Mobile Device Management

The concept of Mobile Device Management (MDM) has been around for nearly two decades, but it has become increasingly more popular in recent years due to the "bring your own device" model and the capability to now manage traditional desktop computers like Macs or Windows PCs. MDM solutions work through the Application Programming Interfaces (APIs) that the operating system vendor makes available as a means to configure, control, secure, and manage a device *over the air*. In this chapter, we are going to explore the various services and APIs that Apple makes available to MDM vendors that form the foundation for managing modern *iOS* and *macOS* endpoints.

An Apple MDM Primer

There are typically a handful of things that all Mobile Device Management solutions provide. Inventory management and reporting is one; remote (over-the-air) security, configuration, and management is another; and remote software deployment is the third. There are three main components that provide these capabilities on Apple products. Inventory management is handled through the Device Enrollment Program (DEP), security and configuration is handled through Configuration Profile payloads, and software deployment is enabled through the Volume Purchase Program (VPP). We will cover each of these areas throughout this chapter.

© Drew Smith 2020
D. Smith, *Apple macOS and iOS System Administration*,
https://doi.org/10.1007/978-1-4842-5820-0_8

There are many third-party MDM solutions on the market today. All of the big players integrate with VPP and DEP and provide remote management using Configuration Profiles. You may have heard of *JAMF*, *Cisco Meraki*, or *Addigy*. These are some of the most popular MDM solutions, and each of them has unique features that differentiate them from the competition. Through *macOS Server*, Apple also offers a first-party MDM solution with Profile Manager. Since all of these various management solutions use the same APIs, we will use Profile Manager in this book to demonstrate the concepts of MDM, DEP, and VPP which will translate to any MDM solution you may choose to use in your organization.

Pro Tip   Since we will be discussing a number of Apple-hosted services throughout this chapter, this is a good time to introduce you to Apple's **System Status** page. You can browse to this page at `www.apple.com/support/systemstatus`. Here you will see all of the various Apple-hosted services and if they are available or if they are having issues. Sometimes an issue with activation, DEP, VPP, or other services can be the result of a service outage on Apple's side. This is a good page to consult when troubleshooting various issues.

Device Enrollment Program (DEP)

Apple's Device Enrollment Program (DEP) is a service that they provide when you purchase devices directly or through participating Apple Authorized Resellers. The way that this works is when your organization purchases an Apple device, a record is created in a database that is hosted by Apple. The record includes the model information, serial number, and membership (if any) into a specific MDM server for each device. Customers interact with DEP through one of two customer portals—*Apple School Manager* or *Apple Business Manager*. These online portals allow you to look up new devices and assign them to specific MDM servers. As new devices are purchased and shipped, Apple populates the database with new device records.

Pro Tip   If you have an existing device that you want to add to your organization's DEP database, you can do so manually in *Apple Configurator*. This is also useful if you purchased a device from a reseller that does not participate in DEP. You will have 30 days to remove the device from DEP before it is locked in as a device owned by your organization. While it may be tempting, it is not recommended that you add any BYOD or end-user-owned devices into your organization's DEP database.

Device Enrollment Program has two very specific features. First, it provides a proof of purchase history for all of your Apple devices. You can look up any device by serial number and see when it was added to DEP (approximate purchase date), the make/model of the device, and the purchase order and/or account number that was used to make the purchase. This is particularly useful information for when you need to contact *AppleCare* and they are looking for proof of purchase validation. The second feature is the ability to assign devices to an MDM server so that you can apply Configuration Profiles during the Setup Assistant process.

As Figure 8-1 illustrates, this process is transparent to the end user. You can use DEP to assign a device to an MDM server and configure the device's restrictions, configuration settings, and Apps through that MDM, and when the user steps through the Welcome screens and does the device activation through Apple, it contacts your MDM server and applies the required configuration settings before the user even gets to the Home Screen or the Desktop—thereby effectively managing the device without the IT staff ever having to touch it.

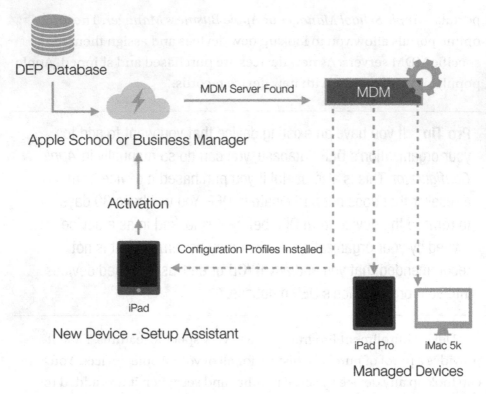

Figure 8-1. *A diagram of how DEP and MDM work together to configure new devices over the air*

Volume Purchase Program (VPP)

Let's say that you are in a situation where you need to install the *Microsoft Office* suite on every iPad and Mac in your organization. You want to be able to do this automatically and without end-user interaction by pushing these down from the *App Store* and *Mac App Store*, respectively. You also want to make sure that users can update the Apps when prompted using their *Apple ID* and not a single shared institutional *Apple ID*. Apple provides a solution for this scenario called Volume Purchase Program (VPP).

Apple's VPP allows a system administrator to *purchase* any number of free or paid Apps from the App Store and assign a license for that App to a specific *Apple ID*. At any time, the license to that App can be removed from a specific user and then assigned to another user. This allows an organization to purchase a pool of licenses for any participating App and assign them to users when they need them and remove the licenses when they no longer do. When a license is removed, it is placed back into the pool where it can be assigned to another user.

Pro Tip   You can use *Managed Apple IDs* or personal *Apple IDs* with VPP. When you remove a license to the App, the user will receive a notice that the App license has been removed, and they will have up to 30 days to export the data from the App's container or purchase a license on their own to continue using the App. After the 30-day grace period, the App will disappear from the device.

Developers must opt in to have their App available for purchase through VPP. There are sometimes VPP discounts if Apps are purchased in bulk quantities, or if you are part of an academic organization, education discounts could also apply. This is entirely up to the discretion of the App developer or publisher (iBooks).

Pro Tip   In the case of iBooks, licenses to textbooks or other books can be purchased in bulk, but unlike Apps, they cannot be assigned and then removed and reassigned to another *Apple ID*. Once a book is assigned to a user, it is theirs to keep and cannot be returned to the pool.

Supervision and User Approved MDM

As we already discussed, Mobile Device Management is an over-the-air solution for configuring, securing, and deploying devices to end users as well as managing the devices without IT needing to physically touch those devices. In general, this idea of unified device management is very appealing in that I can manage my *macOS* clients the same way that I manage my iOS devices, but it is important to note a few differences between platforms.

Device Supervision

In Chapter 5 we discussed supervision as it relates to iOS devices and *Apple Configurator*. Because *iOS* was conceived as a single-user operating system, there are not independent Standard users and an Administrator user to lock down specific parts of the OS for the sake of security and support considerations. Supervision is a way to manage organization-owned devices as a system administrator might do with an administrator account on a desktop computer. Just like we did in *Apple Configurator*, you can supervise an iOS device through an MDM solution and gain access to the full catalog of payloads for restricting and securing devices.

User Approved MDM

In *macOS*, there is no Supervision mode because it is built as a multi-user operating system. You can apply Configuration Profile payloads to a Mac client, and as long as the user is not a local Administrator, they cannot remove it. It is important to note that any user with local Administrator privileges on the Mac can remove any Configuration Profile using the *Profiles System Preference*. If you are using MDM to secure your Macs, be sure that your user accounts are **Standard** or **Managed**.

Pro Tip   The *Profiles System Preference* will only be visible once a Configuration Profile is installed.

Most of the Configuration Profiles that you will install on a *macOS* client will take effect as soon as they are assigned. There is one subset of Configuration Profile payloads that are special and require the end user to approve them before they will take effect. These payloads are tied to Apple's Transparency, Consent, and Control (TCC) initiative. Specifically, these are the Privacy Preferences Policy Control payload and the Kernel Extension (kext) Policy payload.

There are two ways to install Configuration Profiles with these kinds of payloads. One is interactively on the device by double-clicking the ***.mobileconfig** profile and stepping through the installation and approval dialog boxes. The other is by pushing the Configuration Profile out via an MDM solution where the device was enrolled via DEP.

Pro Tip   Apple is very adamant that TCC-related payloads require the end user to approve them physically on the device. To this end, they have even disabled the ability to interact with the *Profiles System Preference* to approve the Profiles remotely using Apple Remote Desktop or Screen Sharing.

Here are a few payload examples that require User Approved MDM to manage:

- Photos
- Camera
- Microphone
- Reminders

317

- Address Book (Contacts)
- Accessibility

Pro Tip   Both the Camera and Microphone access can only be disabled/denied using the payload. The user must approve access to these devices whenever they are used for the first time with a specific application.

In Chapter 3 we covered the topic of third-party kernel extensions (kexts) and the need for end users to use the *Security & Privacy System Preference* to approve these kexts the first time they run. If our devices are User Approved, we can define and automatically whitelist these kexts to run without prompting the end user to approve them. Another way to think of User Approved MDM is that the system administrator is electing to approve these kinds of things on behalf of the end user. User Approved MDM is a topic we will continue to demonstrate in Chapter 9 as we enroll and manage devices with Profile Manager.

Pro Tip   There are no special management capabilities that you gain by supervising a macOS device. The Administrator account still supersedes Configuration Profiles on *macOS* as of this writing. Likewise, there is no *iOS* equivalent of User Approved MDM as this is a Mac-only concept.

Apple School Manager/Apple Business Manager

As mentioned earlier in this chapter, Apple School Manager and Apple Business Manager are very similar administration portals that Apple provides to organizations for the purpose of managing MDM/DEP and VPP. Apple School Manager has a few additional academic-only features like *Classroom* or *Shared iPad* options that we will not be covering in this book. I will be using Apple School Manager to demonstrate the common features of these two portals and how to use them in conjunction with your MDM solution.

Configuring Apple's Management Portal

The first step in getting started with Apple School Manager or Apple Business Manager is creating an institutional *Apple ID* that Apple will use to create an institutional Administrator account. This *Apple ID* must be protected via multi-factor authentication and should not be tied to a single employee's account. Once Apple grants you access to either the Apple School Manager or Apple Business Manager portal, you can use this account to sign in and begin setting things up. Figure 8-2 shows the login windows for http://school.apple.com and http://business.apple.com depending on the type of organization you belong to.

Figure 8-2. *The login portals for Apple School Manager and Apple Business Manager*

Once you are signed into the portal, you will see something similar
to Figure 8-3. Here you can manage your organization's locations,
users, devices, and content. You can create additional user accounts
and give them various roles such as Content Administrator or Account
Administrator privileges to assist with managing your Apple devices and
user accounts.

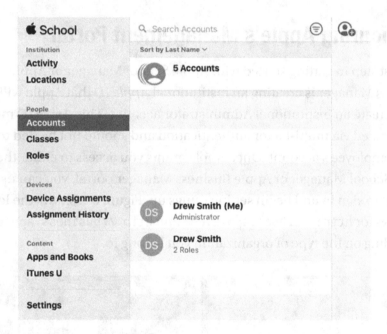

Figure 8-3.   *The main Apple School Manager home page*

Feel free to explore and familiarize yourself with the options available
under each of these headings:

- **Activity:** A history of recent activity in the management
  portal.

- **Locations:** If you are a company or school with multiple locations, you can add locations for each of your buildings and define a unique password policy by location. In an academic environment, you may want password restrictions that are different for K-6 vs. high school, for example.

- **Accounts:** This is where you manage user accounts.

- **Roles:** This is where you manage the permissions for various roles like site manager or staff.

- **Device Assignments:** This is the area where you interact with the Device Enrollment Program database and assign devices to specific MDMs.

- **Assignment History:** This is the history of MDM device assignments.

- **Apps and Books:** This is where you interact with Volume Purchase Program and make bulk purchases of content to distribute through your MDM solution.

Click the **Settings** button in the lower-left corner of the window, and you will see the options as shown in Figure 8-4. Here you can define some of the settings for VPP, MDM, and Customer Information. The **Device Management Settings** button will display your active Customer Number(s) for purchases directly from Apple or Reseller IDs if purchasing through a participating third-party.

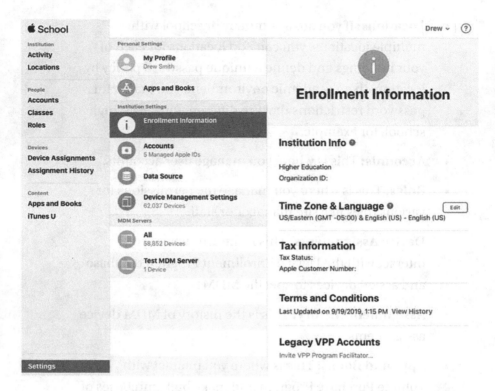

Figure 8-4. *Customer and institutional information*

MDM Server Integration

The very first thing we are going to do is to create an MDM server record to link our server to our instance of Apple School Manager. This will allow us to assign specific devices to our *macOS Server* running Profile Manager and manage them.

CONFIGURING PROFILE MANAGER AND DEP

1. The first step is to browse to **Settings** in the Apple School
   Manager/Apple Business Manager management portal. Click
   Device Management Settings and then click the **Add MDM
   Server** button as shown in Figure 8-5.

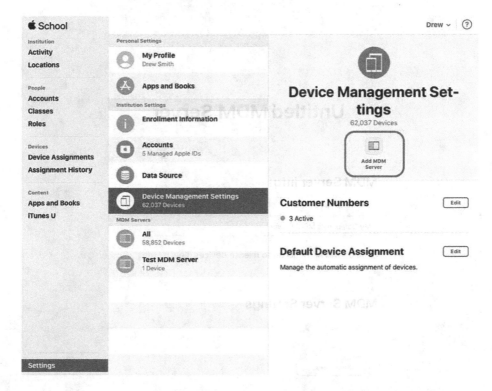

Figure 8-5. *Click Add MDM Server in Device Management Settings*

2. To configure the MDM server info, you need to provide a few
    items including a name and a public key to create a secure
    connection between DEP and your MDM server. Name this
    MDM server something descriptive. I'm going to call **mine "My
    Company's MDM Server**." I am going to leave the **Allow this
    MDM Server to release devices** box checked. Your screen
    should look similar to Figure 8-6.

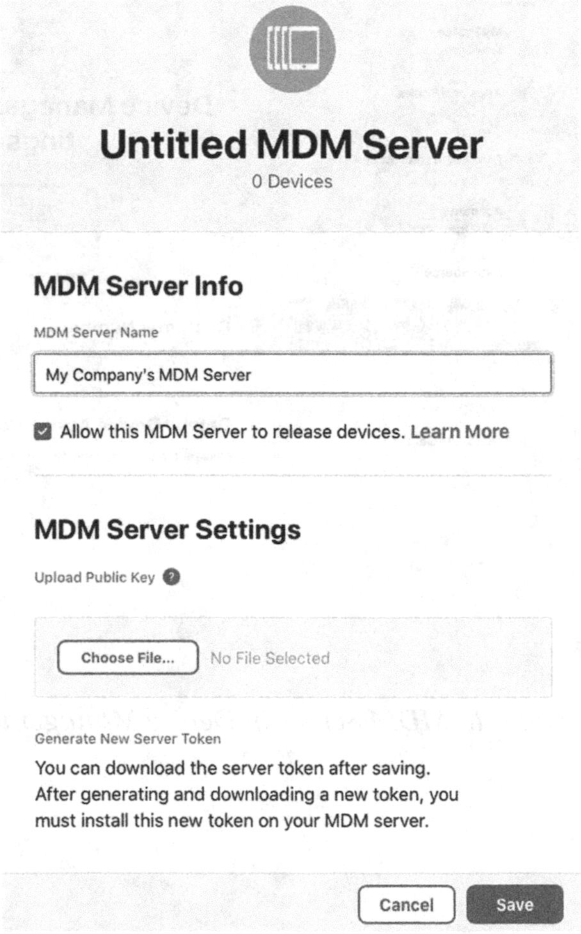

Untitled MDM Server
0 Devices

MDM Server Info

MDM Server Name

My Company's MDM Server

☑ Allow this MDM Server to release devices. Learn More

MDM Server Settings

Upload Public Key ❓

Choose File...   No File Selected

Generate New Server Token
You can download the server token after saving.
After generating and downloading a new token, you
must install this new token on your MDM server.

Cancel   Save

Figure 8-6. *Name your server and upload a public key*

Pro Tip   When your organization purchased devices, they were automatically placed in the DEP database. If your organization wants to sell or dispose of the device, Apple requires you to remove the device from the DEP database as part of the Apple School Manager/Apple Business Manager terms of service. Releasing the device is the term Apple uses for removing the device from your organization's DEP database.

3. Next we need to get that public key from our Profile Manager instance running on our Mac server. Switch over to the **Server** application and click the Profile Manager service. Under the **Deployment Programs** section, there are a number of options as shown in Figure 8-7. Depending on the program your organization belongs to, you will want to choose either **Apple School Manager** or **Apple Business Manager** and click the **Configure...** button under one of those options.

Figure 8-7. *Click the Configure... button under the Deployment Program that aligns to your organization*

Pro Tip   Now is a good time to check the *Date & Time System Preference* on your Mac server. You will need to make sure that the time zone, date, and time are all accurate before continuing, or you may run into errors configuring the secure connection to the cloud hosted service.

4. I will be using **Apple School Manager**, so I'm clicking the **Configure...** button under that heading. The very first thing the Configuration Assistant will do is remind you that you need to have access to the online management portal at business. apple.com or school.apple.com before you proceed. Click **Next** to continue.

5. On the next dialog box, you will be presented with a **public key** that can be used on the Apple School Manager site. This is the key we need to continue configuring our MDM connection. Click the **Export...** button as shown in Figure 8-8. Save it to the Desktop.

Figure 8-8. Export your server's public key

6. Next, go back to Apple School Manager and click the **Choose File** button under the **MDM Server Settings ➤ Upload Public Key** option as shown in Figure 8-9. Select the ***.pem** file you downloaded to your Desktop from the Profile Manager Configuration Assistant. Click the **Save** button after adding the public key.

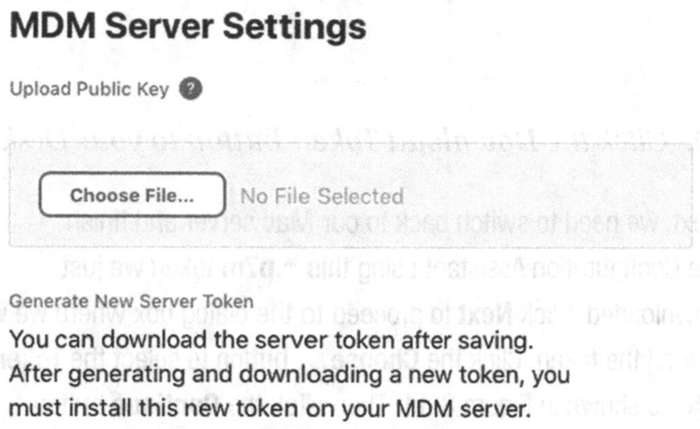

MDM Server Settings

Upload Public Key ❓

Choose File...   No File Selected

Generate New Server Token
You can download the server token after saving.
After generating and downloading a new token, you
must install this new token on your MDM server.

Figure 8-9. *Upload the public key from your server to this section of the management portal*

7. Once you click the **Save** button, the page will refresh, and you will have an option to download a token as shown in Figure 8-10. Click the **Download Token** button and save the file to your Desktop. It will warn you that downloading the token will reset any existing ones in use. Since we don't have any existing ones, we can ignore this warning and click the **Download Token** button to continue.

Figure 8-10. *Click the Download Token button to your Desktop*

8. Next, we need to switch back to our Mac server and finish
    the Configuration Assistant using this ***.p7m** token we just
    downloaded. Click **Next** to proceed to the dialog box where we will
    upload the token. Click the **Choose…** button to select the **Token
    File** as shown in Figure 8-11. Then click the **Continue** button.

Figure 8-11. *Choose the Token File you downloaded to the Desktop
from the management portal*

9. Once that has completed successfully, click the **Done** button to
    finish the configuration. You should now have a green dot next
    to the selected Deployment Program as I do in Figure 8-12.

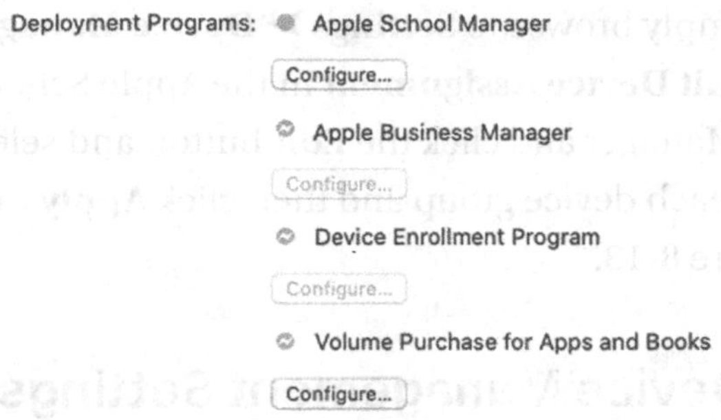

Deployment Programs: ● Apple School Manager

[Configure...]

○ Apple Business Manager

[Configure...]

○ Device Enrollment Program

[Configure...]

○ Volume Purchase for Apps and Books

[Configure...]

Figure 8-12. *Apple School Manager has a green dot on my server indicating that it is running*

Pro Tip   You should definitely make a note of when your tokens are set to expire (every 365 days) so you can renew them without causing a service outage. You should also pay attention to the updates that Apple makes to its terms and conditions for your Apple School Manager or Apple Business Manager account. These usually update when there are major new features or new operating system releases. You will need to periodically go into the management portal and agree to these new terms, or the DEP/VPP services may fail to work properly until you do.

Managing DEP Clients

Now that we have our MDM server configured, we need to add a couple of clients from the DEP database to our specific server. Because I can have multiple MDM servers in my organization, I need to manually move devices into the server I want to use. If you have one MDM server and you want to manage all of your devices with that single server, you can move all of the devices into that single server and set it up as the *Default Device Assignment* so any newly purchased devices automatically get assigned to this MDM server.

To do this, simply browse to **Settings ➤ Device Management Settings ➤ Default Device Assignment** in the Apple School Manager/Apple Business Manager and click the **Edit** button and select the specific MDM server for each device group and then click **Apply** to save changes as shown in Figure 8-13.

Device Management Settings

62,037 Devices

Add MDM
Server

Customer Numbers   [Edit]

● 3 Active

Default Device Assignment   [Revert] [Apply]

iPad

[My Company's MDM Server ◇]

iPhone

[My Company's MDM Server ◇]

iPod

[My Company's MDM Server ◇]

Mac

[My Company's MDM Server ◇]

Apple TV

[My Company's MDM Server ◇]

Figure 8-13. *Configuring the Default Device Assignment by product*

Next let's assign a test iPad and a test MacBook Pro to our newly created MDM server. To get started, click the **Device Assignments** link under the **Devices** heading in Apple School Manager. You should see something similar to Figure 8-14.

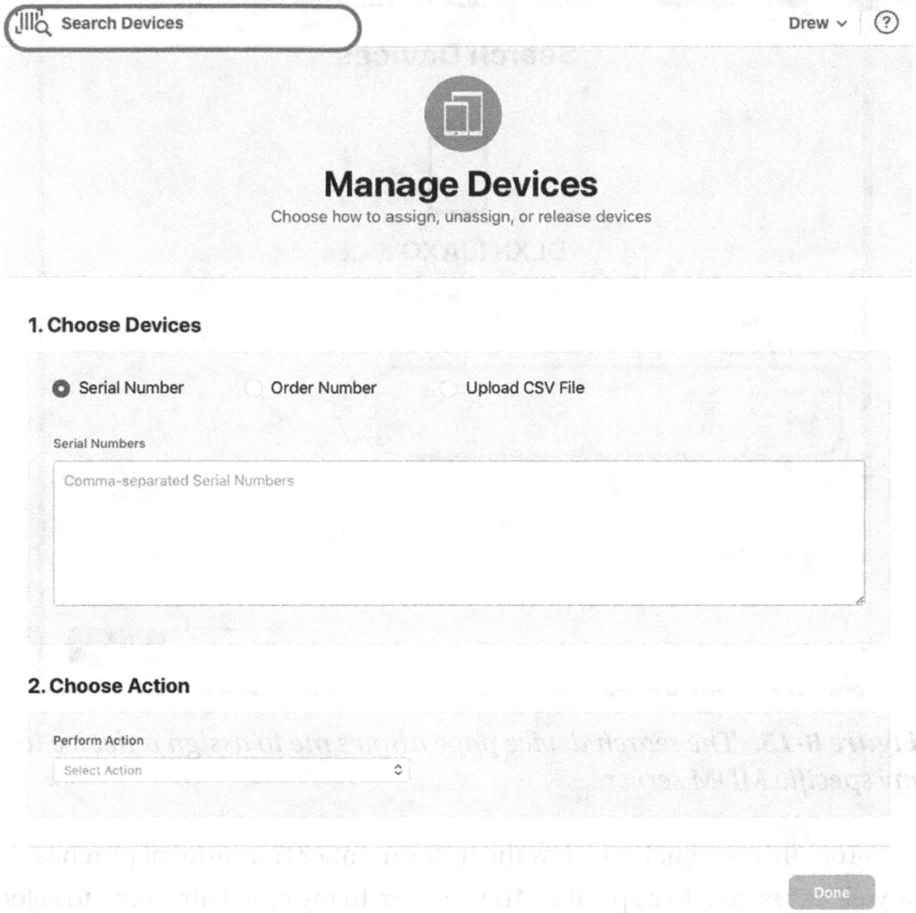

Figure 8-14. *The Manage Devices page in Apple School Manager*

From this screen, you can either select devices individually by searching for them or entering their serial number, or you can upload a ***.csv** file to assign them in bulk. Since we only have two devices to assign, we are going to click the **Search Devices** link in the top-left corner of the screen and manually search for our devices by serial number. I entered my serial number for an *iPad Air* that I have, and it found the device in the DEP database as shown in Figure 8-15.

331

Search Devices

DLXNTJAXGXXX

Order Number
1003225658

MDM Server
None

Date Assigned
None

Release Devices

Back   Done

Figure 8-15. *The search device page allows me to assign a device to
my specific MDM server*

From this screen, I can view the order number (for proof of purchase)
as well as assign it to a specific MDM server. In my case I am going to select
"My Company's MDM Server" from the pop-up menu. I can also release
this device by clicking the **Release Device** button. I'm going to assign this
to my MDM server and then click the **Done** button.

Apple School Manager will update the device assignment, and I
can click the **Done** button again to exit. To confirm that my device was
assigned, I can browse to **Settings ➤ My Company's MDM Server**
and ensure that it lists **1 iPad** under the **Devices** section as shown in
Figure 8-16. Repeat this process for additional iOS devices and at least
one test Mac.

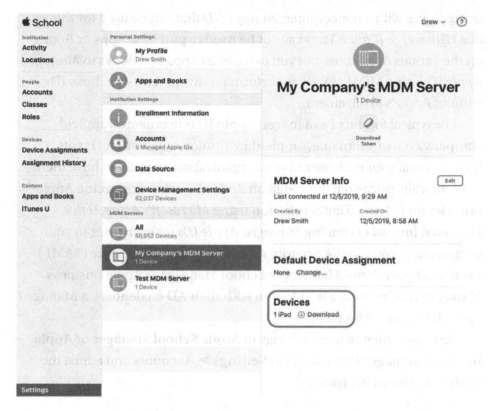

Figure 8-16. *Confirmation that our test device got assigned to the new MDM server*

Now that we have at least one Mac and one iOS device connected to our MDM, we are all set to begin managing these devices in Profile Manager. We will explore Profile Manager in detail in Chapter 9.

Managed Apple IDs

I have touched on *Managed Apple IDs* a few times throughout the various chapters in this book. *Managed Apple IDs* are those that are created by and tied to your organization through Apple School Manager and Apple Business Manager. This allows your organization to provide each student or employee with a noncommercial *Apple ID* that can be used for things like *iTunes U* or *iCloud*. They cannot be used to purchase Apps or Books on the various App Stores, but you can assign Apps and Books to *Managed Apple IDs* using MDM as well as perform password resets for those IDs without Apple's involvement.

The typical format of a Managed Apple ID is username@appleid. company.com or username@appleid.institution.edu. You can create these manually for each user in your organization, or you can have them automatically provisioned through an *Active Directory* connector. Apple provides for federated authentication using *Microsoft's Azure Active Directory*. Instead of creating *Managed Apple IDs* for every user in your organization, you can use Security Assertion Markup Language (SAML) to connect your *Azure AD* to Apple School Manager or Apple Business Manager. The first time a user logs in with their AD credentials, a *Managed Apple ID* is created for them.

You can configure these settings in **Apple School Manager** or **Apple Business Manager** by browsing to **Settings ➤ Accounts** and adjust the settings as shown in Figure 8-17.

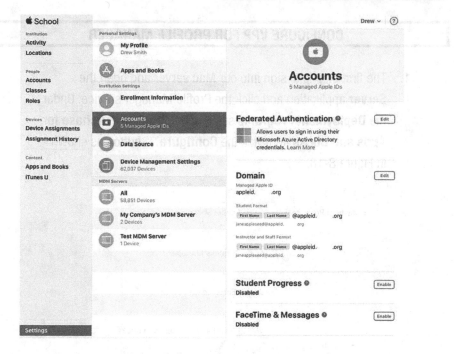

Figure 8-17. *Account settings for Managed Apple IDs and Azure AD*

Redeeming Apps and Books with VPP

Finally, the last thing we need to configure for use with Profile Manager is
Volume Purchase Program (VPP) so we can redeem and assign Apps and
Books to our devices. This is similar to the process we followed to create
our MDM connection to Profile Manager.

CONFIGURE VPP FOR PROFILE MANAGER

1. The first step is to sign into our Mac server and open the
    Server application and click the Profile Manager service. Under
    the **Deployment Programs** section, find **Volume Purchase for
    Apps and Books** and click the **Configure...** button as shown
    in Figure 8-18.

Figure 8-18. *Click the Configure... button under the VPP section*

2. You will be prompted to choose a VPP token. Open **Apple
    School Manager** or **Apple Business Manager** and browse
    to **Settings ➤ Apps and Books**. Scroll down to the bottom
    section under the **My Server Tokens** heading and click the
    Download button next to your organization's Location name as
    shown in Figure 8-19 to save the file to your Desktop.

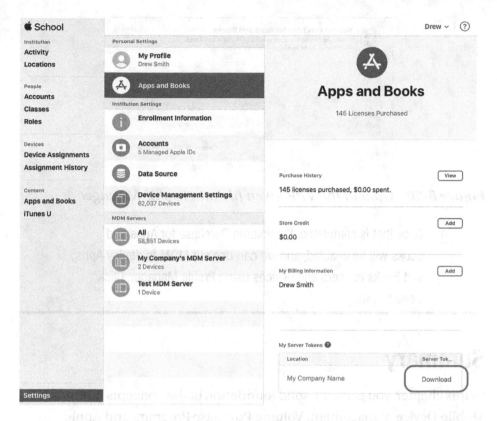

Figure 8-19. *Click the Download button on the Apps and Books pane*

3. Once it downloads the ***.vpptoken** file to your computer, click the **Choose...** button in the Volume Purchase Configuration Assistant and then select the VPP token file, as shown in Figure 8-20, and click **Continue**.

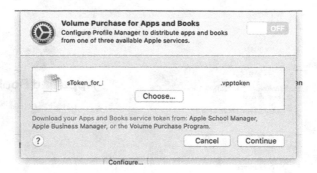

Figure 8-20. Upload the VPP token file into Profile Manager

4.   Once that is completed, the Volume Purchase for Apps and
Books will be enabled, and we can use our MDM to deploy Apps
and Books to users and devices using Profile Manager. Click
Done to exit.

Summary

In this chapter, you gained a solid foundation of the concepts around
Mobile Device Management, Volume Purchase Program, and Apple
School Manager/Apple Business Manager. Now that we have configured
a connection to our Profile Manager server and added a couple of test
devices, we are ready to move forward with the over-the-air management
of these test endpoints.

In Chapter 9, we will use the concepts we have learned to remotely
configure our *iOS* and *macOS* devices using Profile Manager as our MDM.

CHAPTER 9

Profile Manager

While it is not mentioned much in Apple's marketing materials, they do offer their own first-party Mobile Device Management (MDM) solution. *Profile Manager* is a service that is included with the *macOS Server* product. For small- to medium-sized *macOS* and *iOS* deployments, it does the job well enough that your organization may not need to purchase their own third-party MDM. Regardless of the choice of MDM, the concepts are universal, and we will be using Profile Manager in this chapter to explain the basic functions that are found in all commercial MDM solutions.

Introduction to Profile Manager

This chapter picks up where we left off in Chapters 7 and 8 . At this point, you should have your *macOS Server* configured with Profile Manager. It should be available on the public Internet with DEP and VPP configurations in place. Finally (and most importantly), your Profile Manager service is using a signed certificate from a trusted Certificate Authority.

You should also have at least two test devices assigned to your MDM server in Apple School Manager/Apple Business Manager—one Mac and one iOS device. With all of this in place, open the web browser of your choice from any computer and browse to `https://yourdomain/profilemanager/`. For example, in my case I'm going to `https://579testing.com/profilemanager` like we did at the end of Chapter 7 . Sign in with your server's admin account to continue.

© Drew Smith 2020
D. Smith, *Apple macOS and iOS System Administration*,
https://doi.org/10.1007/978-1-4842-5820-0_9

Pro Tip   In a production environment, you will want to create
a Standard user account on your server and sign in with that
when using Profile Manager on the Web instead of the local
Administrator account.

The Profile Manager User Interface

When you first sign into Profile Manager, it can be somewhat overwhelming
with checkboxes, tabs, and lists all over the place. Figure 9-1 and the
accompanying bullet points provide a quick overview of what all of these UI
widgets do. We will be working with most of these options throughout this
chapter with some hands-on exercises.

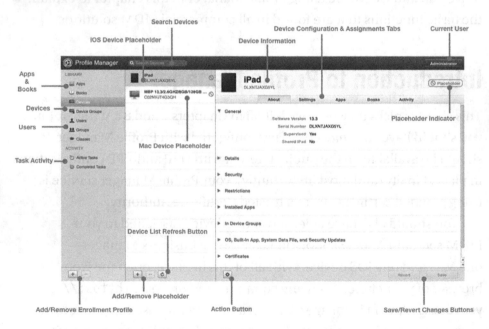

Figure 9-1. *The Profile Manager UI*

- **iOS Device Placeholder:** This is a device that runs *iOS* but has not yet connected to your MDM and is not currently managed.

- **Mac Device Placeholder:** This is a device that runs *macOS* but has not yet connected to your MDM and is not currently managed.

- **Placeholder Indicator:** This indicator shows that the device record is simply a Placeholder. Once we have installed an Enrollment Profile on the device and it has checked in with the MDM, this message will disappear.

- **Add/Remove Placeholder:** Allows you to manually create a Placeholder for any device based on serial number, UDID, IMEI, and MEID.

- **Search Devices Field:** Allows you to search all of your devices for a specific one.

- **Device Information:** A quick summary of the selected device including the name and serial number.

- **Device Configuration and Assignment Tabs:** This is the section where we assign specific Configuration Profile payloads, Apps, and Books to the selected device.

- **Current User:** Indicates the current user signed into the Profile Manager web site. Clicking this button reveals other account options including logoff.

- **Save/Revert Changes Buttons:** Allow you to save and apply configuration changes or cancel changes you made.

- **Action Button:** This button allows you to send a command to a managed device. A few of the more common actions include Clear Activation Lock, Fetch Device Location, Clear Passcode, Wipe, and Lock. The actions available to you will depend on the device type (*iOS* vs. *macOS*) and if it is supervised or not.

- **Device List Refresh Button:** Profile Manager is always synchronizing in the background with VPP and DEP through Apple School Manager or Apple Business Manager. Clicking this button forces an immediate sync of data between services.

- **Add/Remove Enrollment Profile:** These buttons allow you to create or remove custom Configuration Profiles that can be applied to a system manually to enroll them into your MDM.

- **Task Activity:** Provides status on current tasks and provides a history of tasks that have been applied to devices.

- **Users or Groups:** Manage device settings, profiles, and Apps on a per-user or per-group basis.

- **Devices or Device Groups:** Manage device settings, profiles, and Apps on a per-device or per-device-group basis.

- **Apps and Books:** The interface for adding or viewing VPP entitlements that you can apply to users, groups, or devices.

Enrollment Settings

We are going to explore the Users and Groups areas later in this chapter, but we do need to make one quick setting change before we can begin enrolling devices into our MDM. Click the **Groups** button in the sidebar on the left side of the Profile Manager window. Click the **Everyone** group and expand the **Restrictions** option under the **About** tab to reveal the settings shown in Figure 9-2. Make sure the boxes that are checked in this example match what you have, specifically the **Allow enrollment during Setup Assistant for devices configured using Device Enrollment Program** option. We will need this to be in place for the DEP enrollment exercises to work. Click the **Save** button to apply the changes if you made any.

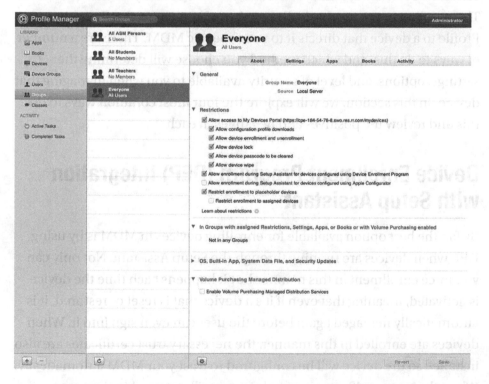

Figure 9-2. Enrollment settings for the Everyone group

Pro Tip   I would also recommend checking the box next to **Restrict enrollment to placeholder devices** so that only devices that you have created Placeholders for are actually able to enroll. This will help with device organization and also keep rogue devices from appearing in your **Devices** list. Remember that your Profile Manager instance is available from the public Internet so random people could enroll themselves if this is unchecked.

MDM Enrollment

There are several ways that you can enroll devices into your MDM solution. The enrollment process basically consists of applying a Configuration Profile to a device that directs it to your specific MDM. There are a number of ways to do this, and which method you choose will determine the settings, options, and level of security available to you when managing that device. In this section, we will explore the four most common ways to do this and review the positives and negatives in each.

Device Enrollment Program (DEP) Integration with Setup Assistant

By far, the best option available for enrolling devices in MDM is by using DEP when devices are running through the Setup Assistant. Not only can you force enrollment in this manner but it happens each time the device is activated, meaning that even if it's a device that is reset or restored, it is automatically managed again before the user can even sign into it. When devices are enrolled in this manner, the necessary trust certificates are also installed so the device will be configured to trust your MDM automatically. When the trust certificates are in place, we will not need to sign our Configuration Profiles when pushed through our MDM solution.

The main downside to this enrollment method is that you need to have either Apple School Manager or Apple Business Manager configured with your MDM and the devices must be in your DEP database. If you do have DEP integration configured with your MDM and you are purchasing your devices from Apple directly or through a participating Apple Authorized Reseller, then this is the option you should go with.

MDM ENROLLMENT USING DEP

For this example, we are going to enroll a test iPad into our Profile Manager MDM using the Setup Assistant integration. Picking up where we left off in a previous chapter, we should have a test iOS device already added to our MDM as a placeholder. Profile Manager's **Devices** should look similar to Figure 9-3 with at least one iOS device listed.

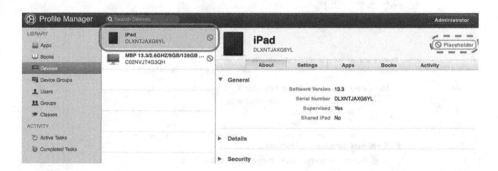

Figure 9-3. *iPad placeholder created by DEP when we assigned the device to our MDM server in Apple School Manager*

1.   The first step to enroll the device is to click the iPad placeholder in the Devices list and then click the Settings tab.

2. Scroll down to Enrollment Settings ➤ Enrollment during Setup
    Assistant as shown in Figure 9-4. Check the following boxes:

    i. **Prompt user to enroll device during Setup Assistant**

    ii. **Do not allow user to skip enrollment step**

    iii. **Supervise**

    iv. **Allow pairing with a Mac (deprecated)**

These settings will force the device to enroll during the Setup Assistant, and it
will allow any end user to enroll it. Once it is enrolled, it will also be supervised
so we can use the full suite of configuration tools to manage it.

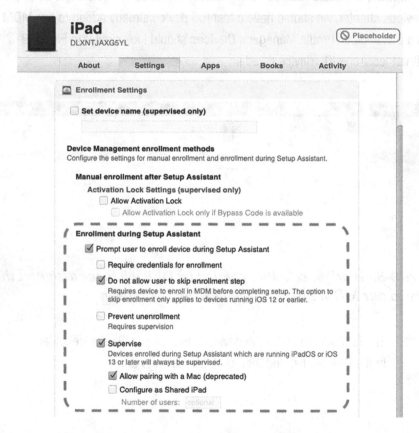

Figure 9-4. *Enrollment during Setup Assistant settings*

346

3. Next, scroll down a little further to the Setup Assistant Options section as shown in Figure 9-5. Uncheck everything except the following:

    i. **Passcode Lock**

    ii. **Appearance**

    III. **New Feature Highlights**

    iv. **Welcome**

4. We will use this setting to test that enrollment worked by skipping all but the passcode lock setup, prompting for dark mode, the *iPadOS* feature demo, and the Welcome screen. Click the **Save** button in the bottom-right corner of the window.

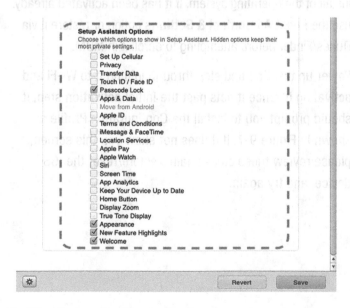

Figure 9-5. *The Setup Assistant Options*

5. You can click the **Activity** tab and confirm that the DEP Profile
    for the iPad was uploaded to Apple School Manager/Apple
    Business Manager so it is ready for enrollment during Setup
    Assistant as shown in Figure 9-6.

Figure 9-6. *Confirmation that our setting changes uploaded to ASM*

6. Next, grab the test iPad and make sure that it is running a fresh
    install of the operating system. If it has been activated already,
    use the **Reset All Content & Settings** option or restore it via
    iTunes/Finder before attempting to enroll it in MDM.

7. Power up the iPad and step through joining it to Wi-Fi and
    activating it. Once it gets past the initial activation step, it
    should prompt you to install the Configuration Profile as
    shown in Figure 9-7. If it does not show you this screen,
    please review these steps again, restore/reset the iOS
    device, and try again.

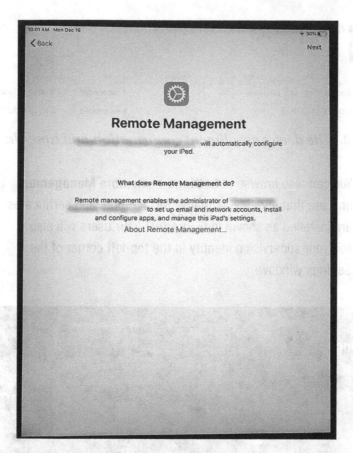

Figure 9-7. *The Remote Management prompt on our test iPad*

8. Click **Next** to step through the configuration process. It will take a few minutes to configure and enroll the device in MDM. Then it should prompt you to set a passcode, select light or dark mode, tell you about *iPadOS* features, and then greet you with Welcome and the Get Started button to bring you to your Home Screen.

9. If you go back to Profile Manager, you will see that the **Activity** tab will state that the device was enrolled and the Placeholder label has been removed from my device as shown in Figure 9-8 indicating that it is now managed.

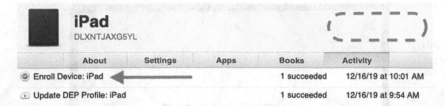

Figure 9-8. *The device enrollment confirmation and time/date stamp*

10. You can also browse to **Settings ➤ Remote Management**
and see that our "MyCompany" MDM Profile and certificates
are installed as shown in Figure 9-9. Your users will also
see your supervision identity in the top-left corner of the
Settings window.

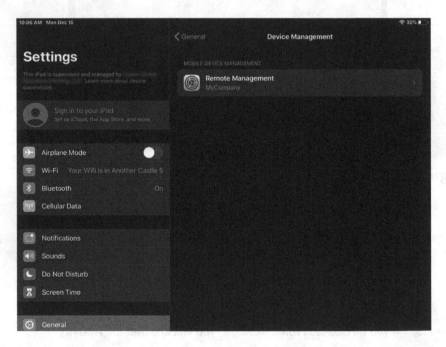

Figure 9-9. *Our Management Profile is installed, and the device is
supervised*

Pro Tip   One thing you will want to keep in mind if you are mass deploying iOS devices on a wireless network that uses Network Address Translation (NAT) is that Apple can restrict multiple over-the-air activations of iOS devices from the same public IP address if they happen in rapid succession. For example, in large organizations like schools where you may have tens or hundreds of devices activating at the same time, you may run into failed activation issues. I would recommend speaking with your organization's Apple rep about whitelisting your public IP addresses to avoid this issue.

This process is very similar for *macOS* clients with the exception of a few unique Mac-only features. Explore the basic enrollment settings and configure your Test Mac to enroll during Setup Assistant and skip all but the Terms and Conditions prompt. You should be able to easily enroll your test Mac client into MDM using DEP. Give it a shot!

My Devices Portal

The next way to enroll your devices is to use the self-service *My Devices Portal* built into Profile Manager. There are a couple of caveats with the Device Portal Enrollment method. This is really meant to be used in "bring your own device" (BYOD) deployments, so your iOS devices will not be able to be supervised. In addition to that limitation, the MDM enrollment can be removed at any time by the end user without your knowledge. The main benefit of using the My Devices Portal is so that your organization's users can enroll in MDM without needing to hand their device over to you (the IT department) for configuration.

To configure self-service enrollment, we need to make a couple of quick adjustments. I would recommend that you disable the ability for the Everyone group to access the My Devices Portal as shown in Figure 9-10.

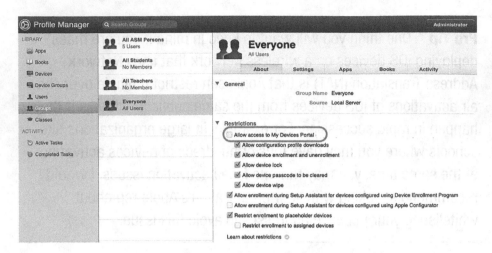

Figure 9-10. *Uncheck the Allow access to My Devices Portal option*

I would also recommend creating a new User Group called **BYOD** or **Self Service** and restricting access to the My Devices Portal to users that are members of that group. You should implement some kind of access management process like a web form or a trouble-ticket to your IT department whereby a user requests BYOD access and provides you with their device serial number so you can set up a Placeholder for the device and add the user to the BYOD group. That way you won't have any rogue devices being added without your knowledge or consent.

Pro Tip   If you are using Apple School Manager or Apple Business Manager, you should manage your Users and Groups using the management portal or configure Azure AD integration. Otherwise, you can use Users and Groups in the Server app to create these accounts.

Once you have the required users and groups in place, ensure that the new BYOD group that you created has the ability to access the My Devices Portal and associated settings as shown in Figure 9-11 for my All ASM Persons group. Next, we need to configure a Placeholder for the personal device and associate it with our end user.

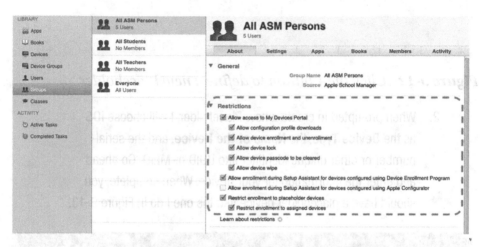

Figure 9-11. *Configure the restrictions on your self-service group to allow for My Devices Portal access*

CREATE A PLACEHOLDER DEVICE FOR BYOD ENROLLMENT

For this example, I'm going to set up my personal iPhone as the placeholder and assign it to my user in Apple School Manager.

1. The first thing we need to do is configure a Placeholder for this iPhone. Click the **Devices** button in the sidebar and then click the **+** button and choose **Add a Placeholder** to create a new Placeholder as shown in Figure 9-12.

353

Figure 9-12. *Click the + button to define a new Placeholder*

2. When prompted to create a new Placeholder, I will choose **iOS** as the **Device Type**, the **Name of the Device**, and the serial number or other unique identifier like UDID or MEID. Go ahead and enter the information for your device. When complete, you should have a placeholder device like the one I do in Figure 9-13.

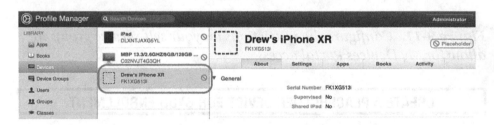

Figure 9-13. *The placeholder I created for my personal device*

3. Now that we have a placeholder device, we need to assign that device to our user. I have created a test user named **Drew Smith** in Apple School Manager. In Profile Manager, select **Users** in the sidebar, and then select your test user and click the **Devices** tab as shown in Figure 9-14. Click the **+** button ➤ **Add Devices** and then in the pop-up dialog box add the BYOD placeholder device to the user. Click the **Done** button, and then click the **Save** button to continue.

Figure 9-14. *Add the placeholder device to the test user*

Now that we have configured everything, let's test this out as if we were the end user. Go to your personal device and open Safari or another browser of your choice and go to `http://yourdomain/mydevices`—where *yourdomain* is the domain you are using for Profile Manager. In my case, it's `http://579testing.com/mydevices`. Sign in using the username associated with the placeholder device as shown in Figure 9-15.

Figure 9-15. *The My Devices Portal on my iPhone*

Once you have signed in, you will want to do two things. First, you will want to enroll the device, so click the big blue **Enroll** button and follow the prompts to download the Enrollment Profile as shown in Figure 9-16.

Figure 9-16. *Click the Enroll button to download the Enrollment Profile*

Next, click the **Profiles** tab and click the big **Install** button to install
a **Trust Profile** for your organization as shown in Figure 9-17. This will
ensure that all of the Profiles and commands sent from your MDM to the
device will be trusted by the device.

Figure 9-17. *Download the Trust Profile for our MDM to the device*

Finally, close Safari and open the **Settings** app and browse to **General ➤ Profiles** and find the **Remote Management Profile** we downloaded. Click the **Install** button to enable MDM on the test device as shown in Figure 9-18. You can confirm that it is installed on the device by browsing to **General ➤ Device Management**, and you will see our **Remote Management** server information here.

Figure 9-18. *Install the Mobile Management Profile*

We can also confirm that the device has been added successfully in Profile Manager. Open the Profile Manager console again and click the **Devices** button in the sidebar. You should see our new device is now there and is no longer a placeholder as shown in Figure 9-19.

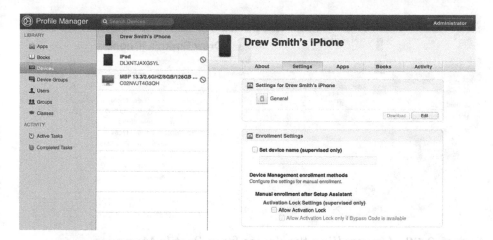

Figure 9-19. *My iPhone is now enrolled in my MDM and can be managed*

At this point, we can manage this device as long as the end user doesn't remove the Management Profile. Please note that since this is not a supervised device, the ability to apply certain payloads will be restricted.

Before we move on, this is a good place to demonstrate how to *unenroll* a device using the Profile Manager console. There are a number of reasons why you may want to do this. For example, if this is a BYOD device and the user has left your organization, you will probably want to remove the device, especially if the user wasn't savvy enough to remove the Management Profile when they left.

To remove a device, open Profile Manager and click the **Devices** button in the sidebar. Select the device you want to remove to highlight it and then click the – button as shown in Figure 9-20.

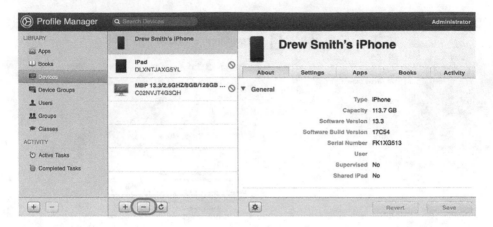

Figure 9-20. *Unenrolling the device from Profile Manager*

Profile Manager will prompt you to choose to **Unenroll** the device or **Revert to Placeholder** as shown in Figure 9-21. If you know that the Management Profile was already removed by the user, you can choose to **Revert to Placeholder**. If you are not sure if the Profile was already removed, select Unenroll, and that will revert the device to a Placeholder and remotely remove the Management Profile from the device. We will click the **Unenroll** button.

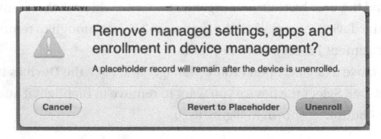

Figure 9-21. *When prompted, choose to Unenroll if you don't know if the user has removed the Management Profile themselves*

After a few minutes, the device will return to the Placeholder label status, and you can confirm on the device directly via **Settings** app ➤ **General** that the Device Management Profile is now gone. Since this is a BYOD device, we can click the Placeholder device and then click the – button again and confirm that we want to remove the Placeholder as well.

Apple Configurator

The third way to enroll devices into MDM is through Apple Configurator. In Chapter 5, we skipped the MDM prompts with a promise we would cover those in a later chapter, and here we are. The main downsides to using Apple Configurator to enroll devices into MDM are that **(a)** it is limited to iOS devices and **(b)** you still have to physically touch every device. The nice thing about Apple Configurator is that if you are already physically touching every device, applying Blueprints, and so on, then adding MDM support to enable future over-the-air updates to the configuration is quick and easy.

ENABLE MDM ENROLLMENT IN APPLE CONFIGURATOR

We need to make a few setting tweaks so we can begin using Apple Configurator with our MDM.

1. The first change we need to make is to select a supervision identity for use with Apple Configurator. Log in to your Mac server and open the Server application. Click the **Profile Manager** service from the sidebar and then click the **Configure...** button under Apple School Manager or Apple Business Manager, depending on your service.

2. Click the Supervision tab and then check the box next to **Use Apple Configurator to configure enrolled devices**. Next, select your signed trust certificate from the Supervision Identity drop-down menu as shown in Figure 9-22. Click the **Done** button to continue.

Figure 9-22. *Configure the supervision identity for Apple Configurator MDM enrollment*

3. Next, open Apple Configurator from the Applications folder on your Mac that you plan to use to configure devices. Select **Preferences...** from the **Apple Configurator** menu and then click the **Servers** tab as shown in Figure 9-23.

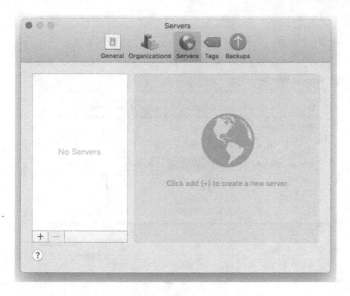

Figure 9-23. *The Servers tab in the Apple Configurator preference pane*

4.   Click the **+** button to add a new MDM server to Apple Configurator. Name the server something descriptive and then edit the Host name or URL field to substitute "myserver. local" with the domain of your server. For example, mine is 579testing.com as shown in Figure 9-24. Be sure to leave the other part of the URL intact when you update the domain.

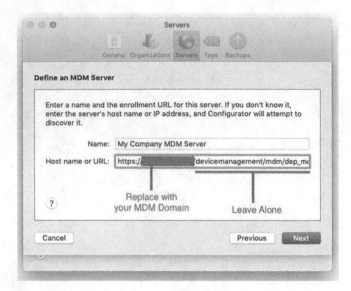

Figure 9-24. *Edit the domain to point Apple Configurator to your MDM*

5. Click the Next button to complete the configuration.

6. Next, let's test our MDM configuration with another iOS device. Connect the test device to Apple Configurator using a USB cable. Once it appears, select it and click the **Prepare** button in the toolbar.

7. In the Prepare Devices Assistant dialog box that appears, check the box next to **Supervise devices** and click the **Next** button to continue.

8. In the Enroll in MDM Server option, select our server from the pop-up menu as shown in Figure 9-25. Click **Next** to continue.

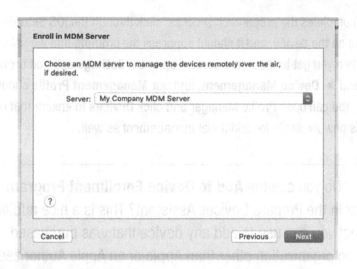

Figure 9-25. *Select your MDM server when prompted*

9. When prompted, sign into DEP using your Apple School Manager/Apple Business Manager Administrator *Apple ID* and password.

10. When prompted, select which iOS Setup Assistant screens you want to prompt the user with and then click the **Prepare** button.

Pro Tip   If you are using the same test device that you used for DEP enrollment through Setup Assistant, you should remove that device from your MDM and delete the Placeholder before attempting to activate the device using Apple Configurator. Otherwise, when the device gets to the activation step, it will give you an error stating that you need to use DEP to activate and enroll the device in MDM.

Once it completes the preparation process, click through the iOS Setup Assistant on the device, and it should suppress the prompts that we selected for it. When you get to the Home Screen, open the **Settings** app and browse to **General ➤ Device Management,** and our **Management Profile** should be present. You can open Profile Manager and click **Devices** to ensure that our device is now available for additional management as well.

Pro Tip   Do you see the **Add to Device Enrollment Program** checkbox in the Prepare Devices Assistant? This is a nice additional option that you can use to add any device that was purchased through an organization other than Apple or an Apple Authorized Reseller that supports DEP. When you check this box, it will add the device to the DEP database.

Manual Install or Using an Install Script

The last option is to manually create and download Enrollment Profiles and then interactively install them on your devices. For Macs, this can be done with a script using Apple Remote Desktop, and for iOS devices, you can host them on an internal web site or email them to end users. The main drawback to using this method is that it is the least automated, and in the case of macOS clients, using a script will result in additional interactivity to enable User Approved MDM.

ADDING DEVICES USING ENROLLMENT PROFILES

1. The first thing we need to do is create our Enrollment
    Profile. Open Profile Manager and click the **+** button ➤ **New
    Enrollment Profile**. Name the Enrollment Profile, and for now
    we will **uncheck the Placeholder requirement**, as shown in
    Figure 9-26, so that any device we install this on gets added to
    our MDM.

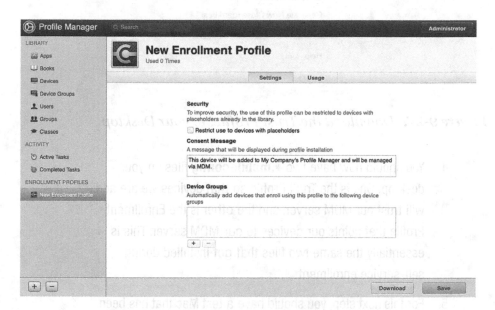

Figure 9-26. *Creating a new Enrollment Profile*

2. Click the **Save** button and then click the **Download** button
    to download the *Enrollment Profile*. It will download a new
    *.mobileconfig profile to your Mac. If it attempts to install it,
    cancel and then move it out of the Downloads folder and onto
    the Desktop.

3. Next, we need to download a copy of the *Trust Profile*. Click the **Logged In User** button in the top-right corner of the Profile Manager window and choose **Download Trust Profile** as shown in Figure 9-27. Again if it attempts to install it, cancel and then drag the Trust Profile out of the Downloads folder and into the Desktop.

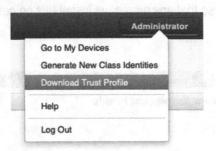

Figure 9-27. *Download the Trust Profile. to your Desktop*

4. You should now have two ***.mobileconfig** files on your desktop. One is the Trust Profile so that devices we are adding will trust our MDM server, and the other is the Enrollment Profile that points our devices to our MDM server. This is essentially the same two files that get installed during self-service enrollment.

5. For this next step, you should have a test Mac that has been added to Apple Remote Desktop. We are going to write a script to install these two Profiles on that remote Mac. Go ahead and copy the two ***.mobileconfig** files to **/tmp** on the remote computer using the **Copy** command as shown in Figure 9-28.

Figure 9-28. *The Copy File dialog box in Apple Remote Desktop*

6. Next, we can go ahead and choose to send a Unix command
   to the test Mac to install these Profiles. We are going to use
   the `profiles` command that is found in ***/usr/bin/***. In the
   Unix window in ARD, enter the following command, specifying
   the name of the two ***.mobileconfig** files if they are named
   differently than mine:

   ```
   /usr/bin/profiles -I -F /tmp/Trust_Profile_for_MyCompany.
   mobileconfig
   ```

   ```
   /usr/bin/profiles -I -F /tmp/New_Enrollment_Profile.
   mobileconfig
   ```

   The `-I` stands for install and the `-F` stands for file then followed by
   the path to the file to be installed. Your **ARD Send Unix Command**
   window should look like Figure 9-29.

369

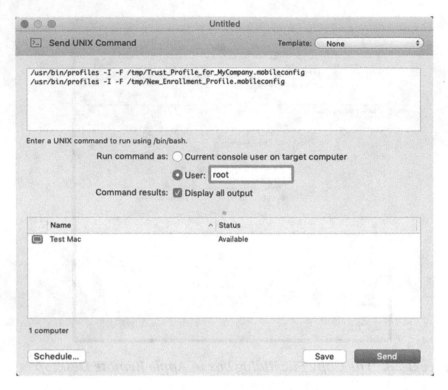

Figure 9-29. *The Send Unix Command window in Apple Remote Desktop*

7. **Send** the command to the test Mac. We can save this as a template if we want to run it again in the future.

8. Next, let's log in to the test Mac and see if the Profiles installed. If the script ran correctly, you should see a new *Profiles System Preference*. Click the *Profiles System Preference,* and you should see two **Device Profiles** as shown in Figure 9-30.

Figure 9-30. *The newly installed Device Profiles*

9. Go back to Profile Manager and look at the list of devices. You
should have a new Mac listed in your Devices list like I do in
Figure 9-31. This represents the Mac we just added using a
script from Apple Remote Desktop.

Figure 9-31. *Our test Mac has been added to Profile Manager*

10. Now go back to the test Mac and browse back to the *Profiles System Preference*. Click the **Remote Management Profile**. Do you see how there is an alert that *states "Functionality may be limited until this profile is approved."* This is referring to User Approved MDM (UAMDM). We discussed UAMDM briefly in Chapter 8. So, while this Mac is now listed in Profile Manager, there are some limitations to the types of payloads we can use until we convert this Mac to User Approved status.

11. There is only one way to convert this device to User Approved MDM, and that is clicking the **Approve…** button interactively directly on the device. There are no scripts that you can use to convert; you can try to Screen Share or use ARD's remote control option to click the **Approve…** button, but Apple has it blocked. You will need to sit down at that specific machine and click the **Approve…** button. Click the **Approve…** button and confirm like I did in Figure 9-32.

Figure 9-32. *Click the Approve button to enable User Approved MDM*

We have now configured MDM manually using a script on a test macOS client.

Pro Tip   The only way to successfully enroll a *macOS* device into
MDM and have it automatically configured as User Approved is
through the DEP enrollment method. If you use DEP to push your
Enrollment Profile during the Setup Assistant, the device will be User
Approved without any additional interaction required.

iOS Management with Profile Manager

Now that we have had some experience with the various ways to enroll and
remove enrollment from both *macOS* and *iOS* clients, let's explore some
of the management capabilities available to us in the Profile Manager
console. In this section, we will focus on iOS capabilities and payloads. If
you haven't yet, go ahead and use your favorite method to enroll a test iOS
device into Profile Manager and make sure it is supervised.

iOS Payloads

Time to have some fun. Let's begin by selecting our test device in
the **Devices** area of Profile Manager. Click the **Settings** tab where we
configured activation and enrollment options. At the top of the Settings
page, you should see a **Settings for iPad** section as shown in Figure 9-33.
Click the **Edit** button.

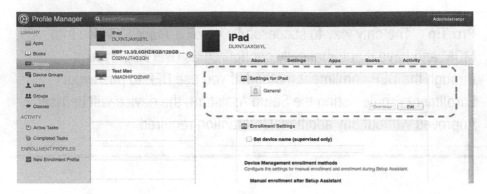

Figure 9-33. *Click the Edit button to access the Configuration Profile settings for our test device*

The Settings for iPad window will look very familiar to you from Apple Configurator. This is basically the same list of *iOS*-compatible payloads that we have used in previous chapters. Go ahead and configure the **General** payload as is required, making sure that **Automatic Push** is selected as the **Profile Distribution Type**. Next, we are going to configure a few payloads that change the visible configuration of the Home Screen for demonstration purposes.

Scroll down to the **Home Screen Layout** payload. Click the **Configure** button to customize the payload settings. Use the + button under the **Dock** field to add the **App Store**, **Mail**, and **News** to the Dock as I have done in Figure 9-34.

Figure 9-34. *Configuring the Home Screen Layout payload*

Next, click the **Lock Screen Message** payload. Click the **Configure** button and enter the **lost message** and **asset tag info** that you want to display on the lock screen. Finally, click **Restrictions** and then click **Configure** to customize these options.

We are going to uncheck the following items:

- Allow FaceTime (supervised only)

- Allow iMessage (supervised only)

- Allow Apple Music (supervised only)

- Allow Radio (supervised only)

- Allow removing Apps (supervised only)

- Allow removing system Apps (supervised only)

- Allow in-app purchase

Your screen should look similar to Figure 9-35. Click the **OK** button to continue.

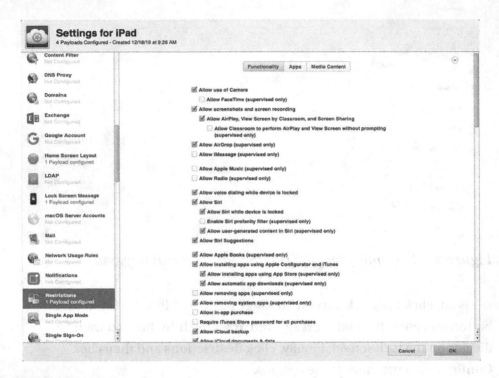

Figure 9-35. *Configure the Restrictions payload*

Now you will see the various payloads we configured listed under the **Settings for iPad** section. Click the **Save** button to apply these settings to our test iPad. If your iPad is powered on and sitting at the Home Screen, after a few seconds you will see a few changes take place. The Dock will update with the three Apps we identified, Messages and FaceTime Apps will disappear completely from the device, and just try to delete any installed app. Good luck! Your device should look similar to Figure 9-36.

376

Figure 9-36. *Our managed iPad with specified restrictions and settings*

Exit to the lock screen, and you will see a message about contacting support and an asset tag number.

Next, let's go back to Profile Manager and reverse some of these settings. Click the **Edit** button under the device's **Settings for iPad** section. Click the **–** button under the **Restrictions** payload to remove it and then click **OK** to continue. Click the **Save** button to apply these changes over the

377

air to the test iPad. After a few seconds, FaceTime and Messages Apps will return to the Home Screen, and you can now delete nearly any App that you want to. Delete the Stocks app just to be sure. Excellent!

This is very similar to how we configured and deployed payloads in Apple Configurator, but with the added benefit of being able to update the device in real time without it being connected to our Mac with a USB cable. This is the power of MDM. At this point, you can experiment with all kinds of *iOS* payloads and apply them or remove them from your test iOS device just to see how it reacts. There are a lot of really great options available to you, so I encourage you to take the time to try these out and see how they may fit into your overall deployment and management strategy.

iOS Remote Management

In addition to applying Configuration Profiles, there are a number of nice remote management features available in the **Actions** button's submenu. To demonstrate, interactively on your test iOS device, set a passcode. It doesn't matter what the passcode is or how complex it is. Return the device to the lock screen and verify that it is secure. Once it is locked, go back to Profile Manager and select the test iOS device from the **Devices** list. Click the **Action** button and select **Clear Passcode** as shown in Figure 9-37.

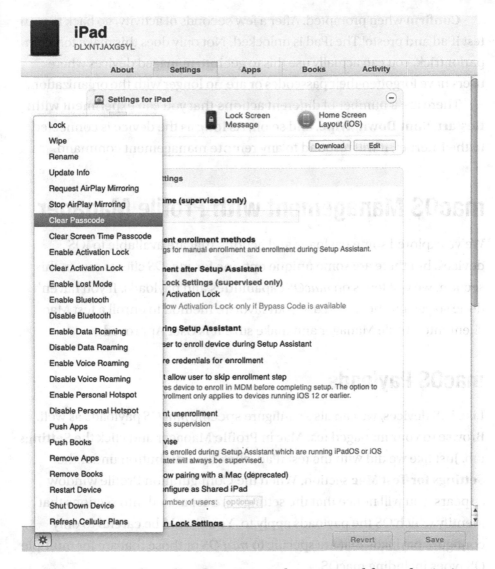

Figure 9-37. *Sending the Clear Passcode command from the Actions submenu*

Confirm when prompted. After a few seconds of activity, go back to your test iPad and presto! The iPad is unlocked. Not only does this make for a fun parlor trick, you can actually use this to get into managed devices where users have forgotten their passcodes or are no longer with the organization.

There are a number of different actions that you can experiment with: **Restart**, **Shut Down**, **Wipe**, and so on. As long as the device is connected to the Internet, it will respond to any remote management command.

macOS Management with Profile Manager

We've explored some payloads and actions that are available to iOS devices, but there are some unique options for *macOS* clients too. In this section, we will focus on *macOS* capabilities and payloads. If you haven't done so yet, go ahead and use your favorite method to enroll a test Mac client into Profile Manager and make sure it is User Approved.

macOS Payloads

Like iOS devices, we can also configure specific *macOS* payloads as well. Browse to your managed test Mac in Profile Manager and click the **Settings** tab. Just like we did with the test iPad, click the **Edit** button under the **Settings for Test Mac** section. When the Configuration Profile window appears, you will notice that the settings are separated into sections that identify which OS the payloads apply to. You should be careful to only configure payloads that are specific to *macOS* or those that are for multiple OS types including macOS.

Begin by configuring the **General** payload and ensure that **Automatic Push** is selected for the **Profile Distribution Type**. Next, let's scroll down to the **macOS**-only section of possible payloads and click **Login Window**. Click the **Configure** button and customize the settings as I have in Figure 9-38.

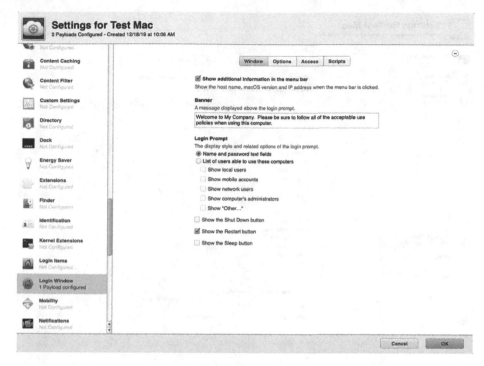

Settings for Test Mac
2 Payloads Configured - Created 12/18/19 at 10:06 AM

| Window | Options | Access | Scripts |

☑ Show additional information in the menu bar
Show the host name, macOS version and IP address when the menu bar is clicked.

Banner
A message displayed above the login prompt.

Welcome to My Company. Please be sure to follow all of the acceptable use policies when using this computer.

Login Prompt
The display style and related options of the login prompt.
◉ Name and password text fields
○ List of users able to use these computers
  ☐ Show local users
  ☐ Show mobile accounts
  ☐ Show network users
  ☐ Show computer's administrators
  ☐ Show "Other..."
☐ Show the Shut Down button
☑ Show the Restart button
☐ Show the Sleep button

Left sidebar:
- Content Caching — Not Configured
- Content Filter — Not Configured
- Custom Settings — Not Configured
- Directory — Not Configured
- Dock — Not Configured
- Energy Saver — Not Configured
- Extensions — Not Configured
- Finder — Not Configured
- Identification — Not Configured
- Kernel Extensions — Not Configured
- Login Items — Not Configured
- Login Window — 1 Payload configured
- Mobility — Not Configured
- Notifications — Not Configured

Cancel   OK

Figure 9-38. *The Login Window payload settings*

Next, we can scroll down to **Security & Privacy** and click the
Configure button to edit the payload. Click the **Privacy** tab and customize
to match my settings in Figure 9-39. What we are doing here is adding
the Finder application to the *~/Documents* folder and setting it to
always allow the Finder to access it without prompting the user to allow
it whenever it is accessed by a new user account. This is one of the new
Transparency, Consent, and Control features in *Mojave* and *Catalina* that
you will want to spend some time configuring and testing.

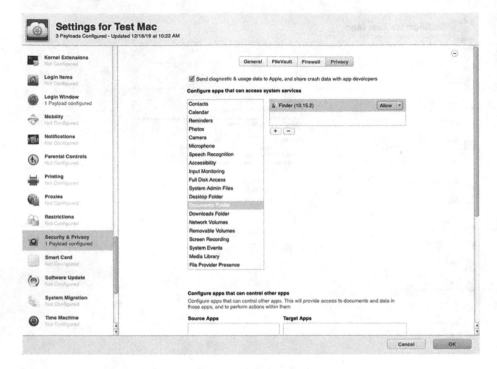

Figure 9-39. *The TCC/PPPC settings in in the Security & Privacy payload*

Finally, click **Restrictions** and click the **Configure** button to edit the payload. In the **Preferences** tab, choose to **Restrict items in System Preferences** and then uncheck **Startup Disk** and **Software Update** like I have done in Figure 9-40.

Settings for Test Mac
4 Payloads Configured · Updated 12/18/19 at 10:22 AM

Figure 9-40. *Disable access to specific System Preferences*

Click **OK** to save the **Settings for Test Mac** and then click the **Save** button to apply them.

After a few minutes, let's take a look at the *macOS* client we have been testing with and see what has changed. If you **log out**, you will see that the login window has changed to simple username and password fields; and clicking the clock in the top-right corner of the screen will allow you to toggle through the name of the computer, IP address, and so on. The ability to **shut down** the computer from the login window is also disabled, but you can still **restart** the computer if needed.

Log in as a local user and open the **System Preferences** from the **Apple** menu. As shown in Figure 9-41, the *Startup Disk* and *Software Update System Preferences* are disabled and grayed out.

Figure 9-41. The disabled System Preference panes are grayed out

Pro Tip   If you are going to restrict System Preferences using Profile Manager, there is one setting you are going to want to adjust in the **Login Window** payload to allow local Administrators to be able to access these disabled System Preferences. As shown in Figure 9-42, you should enable the **Computer administrators may refresh or disable management** setting under the **Options** tab. Once this is applied, when a local Administrator signs in, they should hold down the **option key** or the **left shift key** until the Mac prompts them with the dialog box shown in Figure 9-43. Choosing **Disable Settings** in this dialog box will re-enable all disabled System Preferences. This modifier key only works with user accounts that have Administrator access.

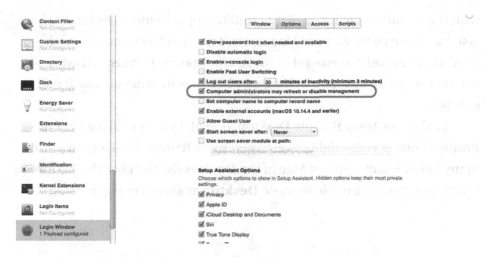

Figure 9-42. *Ensure this setting is checked if you plan to disable any System Preferences with Profile Manager*

Figure 9-43. *Select Disable Settings to re-enable the System Preferences*

macOS Remote Management

Just like *iOS*, there are specific functions that you can invoke using the Actions menu. You can test this out by selecting your test Mac in **Devices** and then clicking the **Action** menu near the bottom of the Profile Manager window and selecting one of the functions. You can experiment with these, and you will notice that unlike Apple Remote Desktop, which also has these controls, your Mac doesn't need to be connected to the local area network to respond to these commands. Because MDM is live on the public Internet, as long as a Mac has Internet access, it will execute.

Speaking of Apple Remote Desktop, one of the very cool features of Profile Manager is the ability to activate Apple Remote Desktop on one or many Macs. Select your test Mac in the **Devices** list and click the **Action** button and choose **Enable Remote Desktop** as shown in Figure 9-44.

Figure 9-44. *The list of actions available for macOS clients*

After a few seconds, open the *Sharing System Preference* on your test Mac, and you should see that the **Remote Management** option is checked as shown in Figure 9-45. If you click **the Options...** button, you will see that all of the options are enabled.

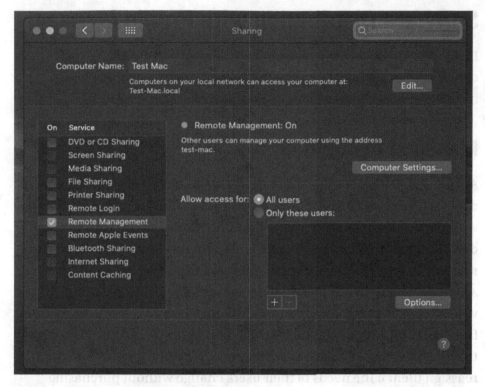

Figure 9-45. *The Sharing System Preference after the Enable Remote Desktop action is executed*

Now you can go into your Apple Remote Desktop console to add the device to your ARD computer list. If you are enrolling your *macOS* devices through DEP during Setup Assistant, once they are live in your MDM, you can turn on Apple Remote Desktop and then push various scripts and additional packages via ARD. This provides a complete end-to-end solution for staging systems remotely from activation through account creation and package installation.

Software Distribution with Profile Manager

In addition to managing devices, Profile Manager also works in conjunction with Volume Purchase Program (VPP) to enable remote installation of Apps from the App Store and Mac App Store.

Managed Distribution

Apple uses a concept called *Managed Distribution* to provide licenses to devices for Apps that are deployed via Profile Manager. The way that this works is that an organization purchases App Store credit, which is kind of like a really big *iTunes Gift Card*, and then uses that credit to redeem multiple licenses of Apps. For example, you can purchase ten copies of *Angry Birds* and then assign them to ten separate iPads, regardless of who is using them. Then a few months later, you can remove *Angry Birds* from four of the iPads and then install it on four other iPads. This way the organization can assign specific Apps to specific devices and then reassign them if the needs of their users change without purchasing additional licenses.

Redeeming Apps

The first thing we want to do when assigning our Apps is to redeem a pool of licenses. For the purposes of this exercise, instead of purchasing *App Store credit*, we can just pick a few free Apps to play around with. Open **Profile Manager** and click the **Apps** icon in the sidebar. In the lower-right corner of the screen, click the **Get More Apps** link. It should redirect you to Apple School Manager or Apple Business Manager. Go ahead and sign in with your institutional admin account.

Once you are signed in, click the **Apps and Books** link under the **Content** heading in the sidebar as shown in Figure 9-46. You will see that I have a pool of various free licenses already here, and we are going to add a few more. Use the **search bar** near the top of the screen to begin searching the *App Store*. For this exercise, we will focus on *iOS*, but we can also find *macOS* Apps here as well.

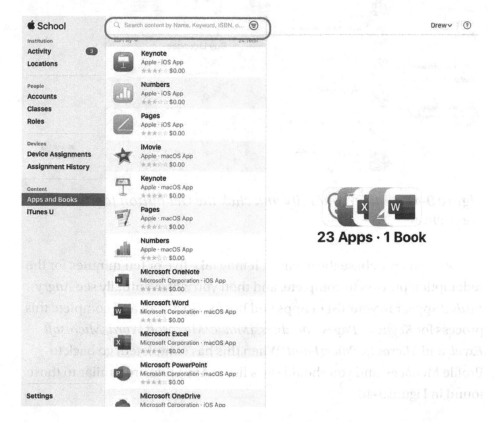

Figure 9-46. *The Apps and Books section of Apple School Manager*

Let's stick with our *Angry Birds* example just for fun and enter **"Angry Birds"** into the search bar. Select *Angry Birds 2* near the top of the search results list. Upon clicking it, you will get a prompt to **Buy Licenses** for the App. Select the **Organization** from the pop-up menu and enter a quantity. We'll pick up **three** of them in this case. Your screen should look similar to Figure 9-47. Click the **Get** button to purchase the licenses and add them to our Managed Distribution pool.

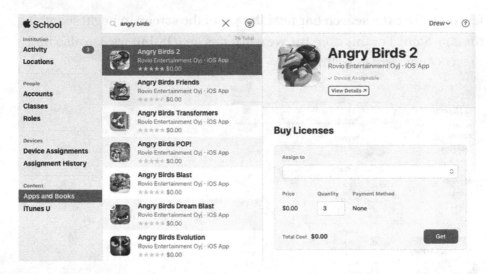

Figure 9-47. *Enter a quantity and click the Get button to purchase the licenses*

Once you purchase the licenses, it may take five or ten minutes for the redemption process to complete, and then you will eventually see *Angry Birds 2* appear in your list of Apps and Books. Go ahead and complete this process for *Keynote, Pages, Numbers, iMovie, Microsoft Word, Microsoft Excel,* and *Microsoft PowerPoint.* When this has completed, go back to Profile Manager, and you should see a list of Apps that are similar to those found in Figure 9-48.

Figure 9-48. *The Managed Distribution pool of Apps available to us in Profile Manager*

Pro Tip   Profile Manager and VPP/DEP synchronize pretty regularly, but if you are not the patient type, you can force a sync by clicking Devices and then clicking the refresh button next to the add/remove Placeholder buttons.

App Distribution

Now that we have our Apps redeemed and available in Profile Manager, it is time to assign them to our test device. Click the **Devices** icon in the sidebar and then select our test iOS device. In my case, it's the iPad we've been using throughout this chapter. Click the **Apps** tab and then click the + button as shown in Figure 9-49.

Figure 9-49. *Assigning Apps to our test device*

When prompted, we are going to check the boxes next to **Angry Birds 2**, **Keynote**, and **Microsoft Excel**. You will notice there are also options for installation mode. To see the differences, choose **Automatic** for one, **Tethered** for another, and **Manual** for the third. Your window should look similar to Figure 9-50. Click the **OK** button to continue and then click the **Save** button to apply to the device.

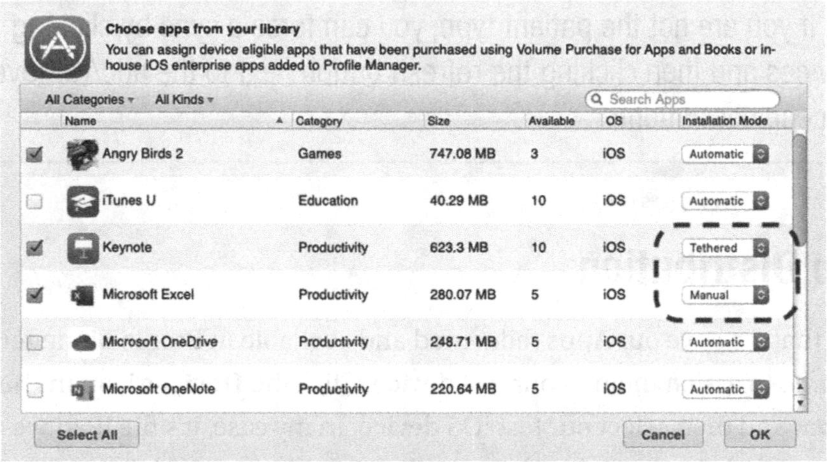

Figure 9-50. *Select different Installation Mode options to see the differences between them*

If you take a look at the test device, you will see *Angry Birds 2* should be downloading and installing on the Home Screen. Depending on your Internet speed, this may take a few minutes. You will not see the other two because they are not set to Automatic. Because *Excel* was set to Manual, the user has to go to the App Store and download it manually unless they are prompted on the device to install at some point. *Keynote* will only download if we are using **Tethered Content Caching**, which we are not.

Pro Tip   Tethering is a great feature for schools or businesses with a lot of devices and limited shared bandwidth. For large Apps like *iMovie* or *GarageBand*, it may be preferable to force the Apps to only install on the device if the device is on a subnet with a Mac configured with the **content caching** service running.

Let's force all three of these to install **automatically**, so make the necessary changes to the **Installation Mode** options and click **Save** again to update as shown in Figure 9-51. All of the Apps will now install onto the iPad.

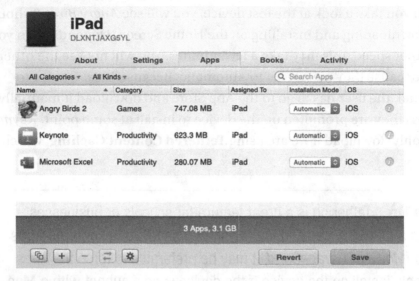

Figure 9-51. *Update the installation mode to Automatic for all of the assigned Apps*

As you might expect, assigning Books to the device is done in the exact same fashion. Another item of note is that while we have been applying Apps, Books, and Configuration Profiles to devices in this chapter, you can also apply these to specific users or groups of users as well. The only caveat with assigning Books is that unlike Apps, once you distribute a Book to a user, you cannot reclaim the license. If your organization creates custom *iBooks Textbooks* using the *iBooks Author* application, you can distribute those books using Profile Manager, but you can only assign them to users, not devices.

In addition to using Managed Distribution with Managed *Apple IDs* through Apple School Manager, you can also provide licenses to Apps that were purchased by your organization to users with non-Managed *Apple IDs*. To enable this functionality, click the **Groups** button in the Profile Manager sidebar and then select the **Everyone group**. Scroll down

and expand the **Volume Purchasing Managed Distribution** section and
check the box next to **Enable Volume Purchasing Managed Distribution
Services** as shown in Figure 9-52.

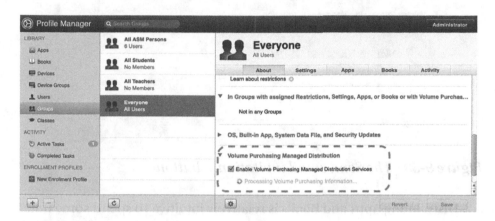

Figure 9-52. *Enabling Volume Purchased Managed Distribution for
Apple IDs outside of your organization*

Once you have enabled this, create a new User account for this user
and send them an **email invitation** to join *Volume Purchase Managed
Distribution* with your organization using the button shown in Figure 9-53.
When they receive the email, they will be prompted to sign into the *App
Store* with their personal *Apple ID*. You can then assign Apps to that user
the same way you do with Managed Apple IDs or devices.

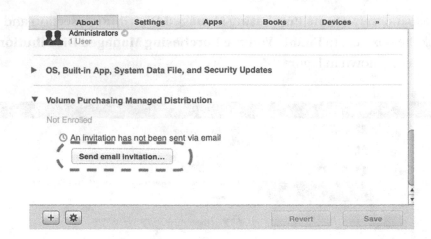

Figure 9-53. *The Send email invitation... button*

Distributing Apps and Books is relatively intuitive so spend some time testing this on a *macOS* client as well. The process is basically the same, but with applications from the *Mac App Store* instead of *iOS* Apps.

Summary

In this chapter, we covered a lot of the core functionality of Mobile Device Management with Profile Manager. There are so many useful payloads and features that *macOS* and *iOS* system administrators can use to make their life easier, and we barely scratched the surface! Take some time to experiment and become more familiar with the effects of the various payloads and commands available to you before you move onto the next chapter.

CHAPTER 10

Automated macOS Application Deployment Using Munki

In this chapter, we are going to be working with an open source solution called *Munki* from *Walt Disney Animation Studios* (`www.munki.org`). *Munki* is a simple, effective, and freely available software deployment solution for managing Macs in medium and large organizations.

Introduction

Munki was written in *Python* and runs as an application on your Mac clients. At its most basic level, the client software checks into a specified web server every hour to see if anything has changed. Then it syncs, downloads, and installs software packages. This allows one technician at the Munki Admin console to package and deploy applications on a set schedule to any number of Macs across a nearly unlimited number of locations.

© Drew Smith 2020
D. Smith, *Apple macOS and iOS System Administration*,
https://doi.org/10.1007/978-1-4842-5820-0_10

As we work through this chapter, we will be building a web server for use with *Munki*, configuring our Munki Admin workstation, packaging a few applications for deployment, and then deploying those applications to a test Mac running the *Munki Managed Software Center* application. I have found that due to the various underlying changes that Apple has made to *macOS*, using a tool like this to deploy software is the best alternative to the now-obsolete task of monolithic imaging.

One of the best features of Munki is that it stores all of the data in XML files like **∗.plists** which can easily be synced between multiple servers. This allows for load balancing and multilocation support without having to worry about centralized databases or other complexities found in commercial solutions. I have personally used Munki to manage software deployments to over ten thousand *macOS* clients across 50 locations. I think you will find it to be a powerful addition to your arsenal of Mac deployment and support tools.

Configuring an Apache Web Server for Munki

Let's get started by building our Munki web server. Before we begin this exercise, go ahead and stage a Mac that will be used as our web server. Your server does not need to be running *macOS Server* as the built-in tools in the client version of *macOS* will provide all of the necessary features we need. You may be tempted to use your existing Profile Manager server; however, this is not recommended because both services use the Apache web server and could conflict with each other.

The Munki server only needs to be available on the internal network and will work best without any other services running on it. If you are building out a production Munki server, you may want to consider a machine with adequate disk space as the main requirement because all of your installation packages will reside on this box.

Pro Tip   If you are serious about a production Munki server, you may want to configure a Linux- or Windows-based web server with redundancy, RAID storage, and fast I/O. You could also purchase a 2019 Mac Pro for this, but from a cost perspective, you may be best served with standard non-Apple hardware. For the exercises in this book, a small Mac mini or a Mac virtual machine will work fine.

Configuring the Web Server

Once you have installed *macOS Catalina,* step through **Setup Assistant** to configure the local user accounts and then configure the wallpaper, date and time, and a static IP address. Finally, name your server something simple like **MunkiServer01**. At this point, you should have a server ready to go with a name, static IP address, Internet access, the ability to ping your clients (and your clients should be able to ping it), and all the necessary server security hardening completed. You can reference Chapter 7 for this step if needed.

CONFIGURING THE APACHE SERVER SETTINGS

The first thing we need to do is make some changes to the Apache configuration file before we turn on our web server service. Open the **Terminal** and step through this exercise to configure and start the web server:

1. Before we begin, use the Terminal to change our user to root using the sudo command. In the past we used sudo before each single command to run as root, but in this case, we will be doing many steps that require root access, so by entering the sudo su command as shown in Figure 10-1, we are going to be able to lock in our root access for the extent of this session. Please note that the command prompt has changed to reflect that I'm now the root user.

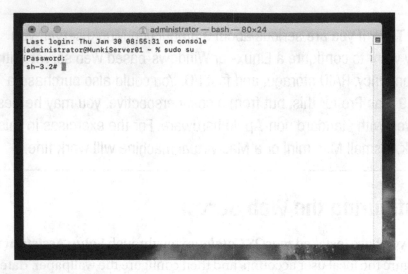

Figure 10-1. *Using the Terminal as root changes the command prompt to sh-3.2#*

2. The next thing we need to do is change to the */etc/apache2/* directory via **Terminal** so we can modify the **httpd.conf** configuration file located there. Go ahead and use the command cd to change the directory and then use the ls command to confirm you have located the directory with the *httpd.conf* file as shown in Figure 10-2.

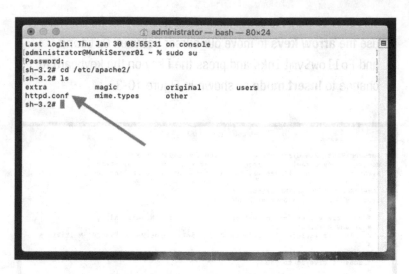

Figure 10-2. *Locate the httpd.conf file via Terminal*

3.   Our next step is to open and edit this file in the built-in Unix
     text editor, **VI** (*vee-eye*). To do this, type vi httpd.conf and
     press **enter** to open the configuration file in **VI**.

4.   In **VI**, you will see the contents of the ***httpd.conf*** file. You can
     read through this document if you would like. It explains that
     this file is the main Apache HTTP server configuration file. You
     can use the **arrow keys** on your keyboard to navigate around
     the document.

5.   As you scroll through, there are two lines we need to pay
     attention to. The first one is DocumentRoot "/Library/
     WebServer/Documents". That is the path on our Mac to
     the root of the web server where we would place our files and
     folders.

6.   The second line is in the Options section just below it and
     reads Options FollowSymLinks Multiviews. We need
     to edit this line because by default this is configured to parse
     and display files as web pages, but for Munki we want our web

401

server to display the contents as *folders and files*. So we will use the **arrow keys** to move our cursor between Options and FollowSymLinks and press the **i** key on the keyboard to change to **Insert mode** as shown in Figure 10-3.

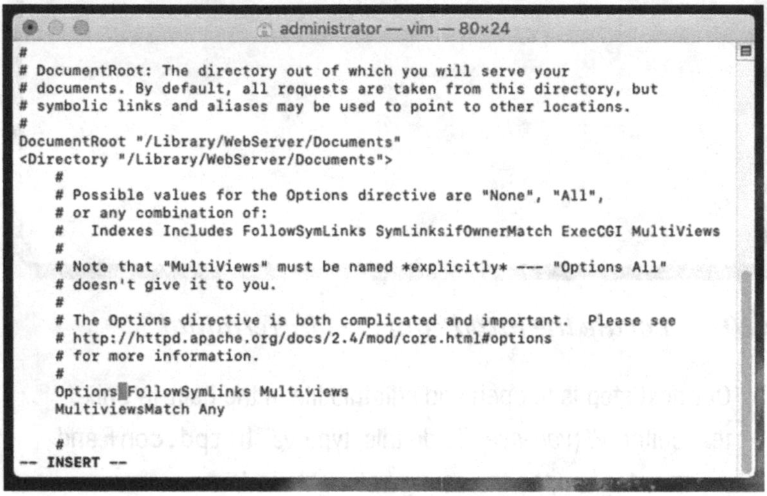

Figure 10-3. *Enabling Insert mode in VI to edit the httpd.conf file*

7. Next, enter Indexes in this line so it now reads Options Indexes FollowSymLinks Mulitviews which will enable us to see files and folders on our web server and not HTML content. Once you have made that change, press the **escape** key to exit out of **Insert mode**. Your Terminal window should look similar to Figure 10-4.

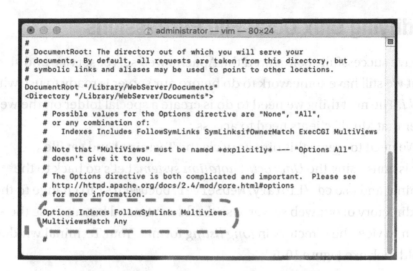

```
● ● ○                    administrator — vim — 80×24
#
# DocumentRoot: The directory out of which you will serve your
# documents. By default, all requests are taken from this directory, but
# symbolic links and aliases may be used to point to other locations.
#
DocumentRoot "/Library/WebServer/Documents"
<Directory "/Library/WebServer/Documents">
    #
    # Possible values for the Options directive are "None", "All",
    # or any combination of:
    #   Indexes Includes FollowSymLinks SymLinksifOwnerMatch ExecCGI MultiViews
    #
    # Note that "MultiViews" must be named *explicitly* --- "Options All"
    # doesn't give it to you.
    #
    # The Options directive is both complicated and important.  Please see
    # http://httpd.apache.org/docs/2.4/mod/core.html#options
    # for more information.

    Options Indexes FollowSymLinks Multiviews
    MultiviewsMatch Any

    #
```

Figure 10-4. *Your Options line should now look like this*

8. Now that we have made the required changes and have taken
    note of the path to the web server's root directory, we can write
    our changes and quit the document. To do this in ***VI***, type **:wq** and
    press **enter**. The **colon** (**:**) identifies that a command is coming,
    w signifies **writing** the changes (saving), and the **q** will **quit** the
    document and drop us out of ***VI*** and back to the command prompt.

9. Back at the command prompt, we can now enable our web
    server service. Enter `apachectl start` to enable the service.
    Open a browser window and type `http://localhost/`, and
    you should see a message that says **"It works!"** as shown
    in Figure 10-5. We have now configured the web server and
    started the service.

```
 Safari   File   Edit   View   History   Bookmarks   Window   Help
● ● ●   < >   □                              localhost                        ○
```

It works!

Figure 10-5. *Confirming that our web server service has started*

Modifying Unix Octal File Permissions

We have successfully configured the Apache web server service and started it, but we still have some work to do before our server is ready to use with *Munki*. The next thing we need to do is create a special folder on the web server that Munki clients need to access.

We need to create this directory via the **Terminal** and set file permissions using the *Unix octal notation system*. Let's go back to the Terminal and use cd /Library/WebServer/Documents/ to change to the root directory of our web server. Use the ls command but also use the -l option to view the directory in *long listing* format. Your Terminal window should look like Figure 10-6.

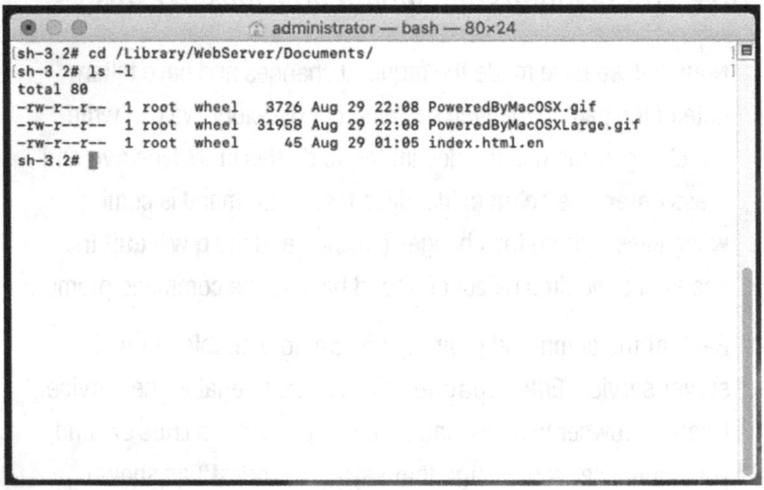

```
● ● ●                    🔒 administrator — bash — 80×24
[sh-3.2# cd /Library/WebServer/Documents/
[sh-3.2# ls -l
total 80
-rw-r--r--  1 root  wheel   3726 Aug 29 22:08 PoweredByMacOSX.gif
-rw-r--r--  1 root  wheel  31958 Aug 29 22:08 PoweredByMacOSXLarge.gif
-rw-r--r--  1 root  wheel     45 Aug 29 01:05 index.html.en
sh-3.2# ▋
```

Figure 10-6. *The output from the long listing command*

You should see three lines, one for each file in this directory. The first column indicates the octal file permissions for each file, which are called *octets*. The second column indicates the number of hard links, while the third column is the owner of the file and the fourth column is the group. The fifth column is the file size, the sixth is the last modified date/time, and the final column is the filename itself.

As you can see, **root** is the owner of these files, and **wheel** is the group. These will align with the permissions we can view in the *macOS* GUI's **Get Info** dialog box that we used in Chapter 3. We are going to create a new directory here. *Munki* requires a folder called **munki_repo** which is the repository of all of the Munki XML files and install media that our clients will access during the software installation. Let's use the `mkdir` command to create this directory. Enter `mkdir munki_repo` and press **enter**. Now do another `ls -l` command to see that our new folder has been created and the permissions that are set by default. Your Terminal window should look similar to Figure 10-7.

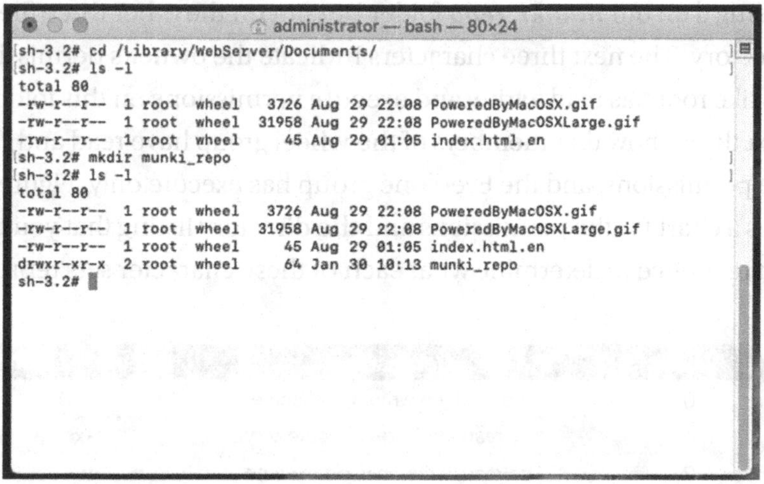

```
● ● ●                  administrator — bash — 80×24
[sh-3.2# cd /Library/WebServer/Documents/
[sh-3.2# ls -l
total 80
-rw-r--r--  1 root  wheel   3726 Aug 29 22:08 PoweredByMacOSX.gif
-rw-r--r--  1 root  wheel  31958 Aug 29 22:08 PoweredByMacOSXLarge.gif
-rw-r--r--  1 root  wheel     45 Aug 29 01:05 index.html.en
[sh-3.2# mkdir munki_repo
[sh-3.2# ls -l
total 80
-rw-r--r--  1 root  wheel   3726 Aug 29 22:08 PoweredByMacOSX.gif
-rw-r--r--  1 root  wheel  31958 Aug 29 22:08 PoweredByMacOSXLarge.gif
-rw-r--r--  1 root  wheel     45 Aug 29 01:05 index.html.en
drwxr-xr-x  2 root  wheel     64 Jan 30 10:13 munki_repo
sh-3.2# 
```

Figure 10-7. *The long listing output with our new directory included*

Let's take a look at our new directory's octets for a moment. By default, we see `drwxr-xr-x`, so what does that mean as it relates to permissions? Great question! This alphabet soup indicates the *read, write, and execute* privileges for the *owner* (in this case root), the *group* (in this case wheel), and the *Everyone* group. As we learned in Chapter 3, the Everyone group really means *everyone else*. Figure 10-8 is a good visual representation of the breakdown between directory, owner, group, and everyone permissions.

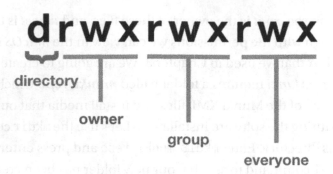

Figure 10-8. Understanding the octets of a directory's file permissions

The **d** identifies that this is a directory and not a file. That is why there is a leading d on our ***munki_repo*** folder but not on the other three files in this directory. The next three characters indicate the owner's permissions. It looks like root has read, write, and execute permissions on this folder. The next three show that members of the wheel group have read and execute permissions, and the Everyone group has execute only. Figure 10-9 provides a chart for the permissions and the directory listing that you can use as a reference to determine what each of these character sets represents.

Value	Permission	Directory Listing
0	no read, no write, no execute	-
1	no read, no write, execute only	-x
2	no read, write only, no execute	-w-
3	no read, write & execute only	-wx
4	read only, no write, no execute	r-
5	read and execute only, no write	r-x
6	read and write only, no execute	rw-
7	read, write, and execute	rwx

Figure 10-9. Octal file permissions quick reference

We need our ***munki_repo*** directory to be read/write accessible to our Mac clients for *Munki* to function properly, so we will need to change the file permissions to this folder. To do this, we will be using the chmod command. If you spent some time reviewing the man pages for chmod and chown earlier in the book, you are probably aware that we can change a file's owner and permissions with these commands. Using the chmod command and referencing the table in Figure 10-9, we can assign one of eight possible values to owner, group, and everyone that represent their permissions to this folder. As you can see, if we use the value of 7, it will grant read, write, and execute permissions; and this is what we want for the owner, group, and everyone for our ***munki_repo*** folder.

Go ahead and enter chmod -R 777 munki_repo/ at the prompt and press **enter**. What we are doing with this command is modifying the ***munki_repo*** directory's permissions to allow root, wheel, and everyone read, write, and execute permissions. Let's use ls -l again and make sure that the changes we made took effect. Your Terminal window should look like Figure 10-10.

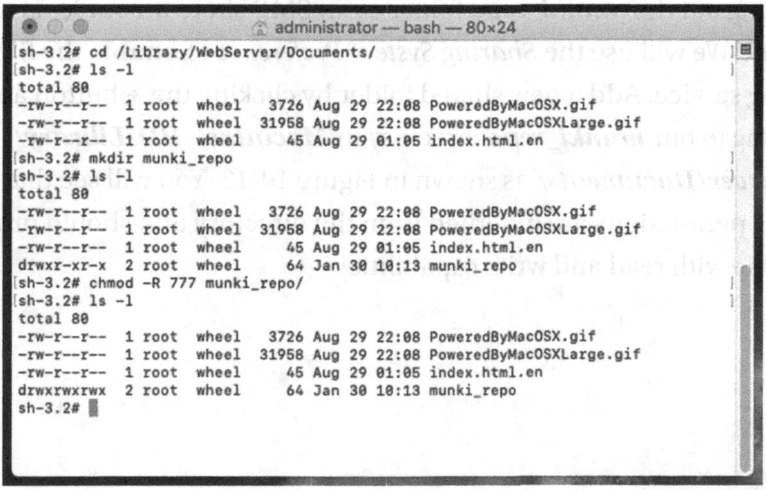

```
● ● ●                    administrator — bash — 80×24
sh-3.2# cd /Library/WebServer/Documents/
sh-3.2# ls -l
total 80
-rw-r--r--  1 root    wheel    3726 Aug 29 22:08 PoweredByMacOSX.gif
-rw-r--r--  1 root    wheel   31958 Aug 29 22:08 PoweredByMacOSXLarge.gif
-rw-r--r--  1 root    wheel      45 Aug 29 01:05 index.html.en
sh-3.2# mkdir munki_repo
sh-3.2# ls -l
total 80
-rw-r--r--  1 root    wheel    3726 Aug 29 22:08 PoweredByMacOSX.gif
-rw-r--r--  1 root    wheel   31958 Aug 29 22:08 PoweredByMacOSXLarge.gif
-rw-r--r--  1 root    wheel      45 Aug 29 01:05 index.html.en
drwxr-xr-x  2 root    wheel      64 Jan 30 10:13 munki_repo
sh-3.2# chmod -R 777 munki_repo/
sh-3.2# ls -l
total 80
-rw-r--r--  1 root    wheel    3726 Aug 29 22:08 PoweredByMacOSX.gif
-rw-r--r--  1 root    wheel   31958 Aug 29 22:08 PoweredByMacOSXLarge.gif
-rw-r--r--  1 root    wheel      45 Aug 29 01:05 index.html.en
drwxrwxrwx  2 root    wheel      64 Jan 30 10:13 munki_repo
sh-3.2# █
```

Figure 10-10. *Modifying the file permissions for the munki_repo folder*

Next, let's make sure we can get to the ***munki_repo*** folder from our web server. Open a browser window and enter `http://localhost/munki_repo`, and you should see an index of the empty directory as shown in Figure 10-11.

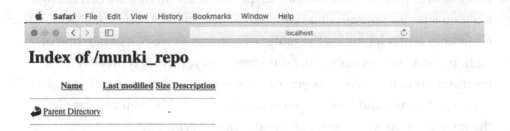

Figure 10-11. *The listing via http of our munki_repo folder*

Go ahead and close out of the browser and exit from the Terminal app.

Creating a Network File Share for Munki

The last step we need to take to prepare our server for use with *Munki* is sharing out the ***munki_repo*** folder as an SMB share on our local area network. We will use the *Sharing System Preference* to **enable** the **file sharing** service. Add a new shared folder by clicking the + button and browsing to our ***munki_repo*** directory in ***Macintosh HD/Library/ WebServer/Documents/*** as shown in Figure 10-12. You will see that the file sharing permissions are inherited from the directory and should provide everyone with read and write capabilities.

Figure 10-12. *Sharing the munki_repo folder as a network file share*

Close out of System Preferences. At this point, we should do a quick validation from another computer on our network to make sure that everything is working as expected. I'm going to use my admin workstation to map the ***munki_repo*** folder as a share as well as click the ***munki_repo*** directory via a web browser.

Use the **Connect to Server** option in the Finder as shown in Figure 10-13 and authenticate to mount the SMB share of the ***munki_repo*** folder.

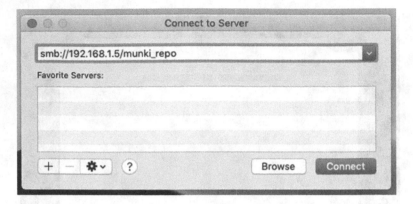

Figure 10-13. *Map the munki_repo share using the SMB protocol*

I'm also going to open my Safari web browser and hit
`http://192.168.1.5/munki_repo/`. If everything is configured properly,
you should be able to browse the directory with the network share and via
the web browser as shown in Figure 10-14.

Figure 10-14. *Browsing the munki_repo directory on a remote
computer via Safari and the Finder*

Congratulations! Your web server is now configured for use with
Munki!

Pro Tip   If you are looking to support multiple sites with Munki, you can repeat these same steps for each location's server and then use a utility to sync the munki_repo directories between servers. Because there is no centralized database or proprietary files to worry about, simply syncing the flat files and folders between servers will allow you to scale your Munki environment with ease.

Configuring the Munki Admin Workstation

Now that we have our server up and running, our next step is to configure the workstation that our *Munki* system administrator will use to create packages, upload data to the server, and manage the *Munki* environment. I typically use the same workstation where I have *Apple Remote Desktop* installed so I have all of my Mac management tools in one place.

Installing MunkiTools and MunkiAdmin

The first thing we need to do is download a couple of installer packages. The first one is the official *MunkiTools* release from the *Munki Project's GitHub* page. You can find the client installers at https://github.com/munki/munki/releases, and I'm going to be downloading the **Munki 3.6.4** release which supports *macOS 10.10 Yosemite* to *macOS 10.15 Catalina*.

Pro Tip   Munki recently released version 4.x on their GitHub page, which includes its own Python support instead of relying on Apple's embedded version. You should assess the support for legacy versions of macOS with this release and determine if you should install Munki 4 or continue to use the 3.x variant based on the age of your Mac fleet. We will be using the stable release of 3.6.4 for the exercises in this chapter.

Download **munkitools-3.6.4.3786.pkg** from this page and save it to your Desktop. Next, **double-click** the downloaded package and follow the prompts to **install** it. If *Gatekeeper* gets in the way, you may need to **right-click** the package and choose **Open** from the contextual menu and agree to open a file from an unknown developer. It will require a restart when finished. Go ahead and **restart** when prompted.

We are also going to download the *MunkiAdmin* tool and install it on this workstation. *MunkiAdmin* is another open source project. It is a GUI tool for managing your *Munki* environment. The current release is 1.7.1, and this can be found at https://github.com/hjuutilainen/munkiadmin/releases/. Download this version and save it to your Desktop. Expand the disk image and **drag and drop** the *MunkiAdmin* application to either your */Applications* or */Applications/Utilities* folder to install it. I am going to install it into the */Applications* folder on my workstation.

Configuring the Munki Client on the Admin Workstation

Once we have restarted our administrative workstation, go ahead and reconnect to the ***munki_repo*** network share and make sure you can still browse it via the Finder. Next, we need to do some post-installation configuration via the Terminal to point our administrative workstation to our *Munki* repository. Go ahead and open the Terminal again and enter munkiimport --configure at the command prompt as shown in Figure 10-15.

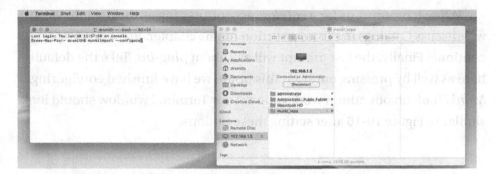

Figure 10-15. *Invoking the configuration command line utility in Terminal*

We will need to answer some questions as we step through the command line configuration utility. The first thing it asks is for the Repo URL. This can be deceiving because what it wants here is the path to our *munki_repo* share, not the URL to the web server. Enter the full path in this format smb://192.168.1.5/munki_repo/ where the IP address is the domain name or IP of your *Munki* web server.

Pro Tip   I'm using an IP address because I did not create a DNS record for this demo server. However, in a production environment, you would likely want to enter the FQDN as part of the path to your munki_repo share.

Next, it will ask us what file extension we prefer to use for the *pkginfo* files. These are the files that Munki reads to determine how we want the various installers to run. We will keep the default as *.plist*, so press **enter** to accept the default. Now it will prompt us to choose an editor for the *pkginfo* files. We are going to be using the GUI *MunkiAdmin* application so we can accept the default here. Press **enter** to continue.

When it prompts us for a *catalog*, accept testing as the default. We will discuss Catalogs in the next section of this chapter. Press **enter** to continue. Finally, the last prompt will ask about *plug-ins*. Take the default here as well by pressing **enter**. At this point, we have finished configuring *MunkiTools* on our admin workstation. Your Terminal window should look similar to Figure 10-16 after setting these options.

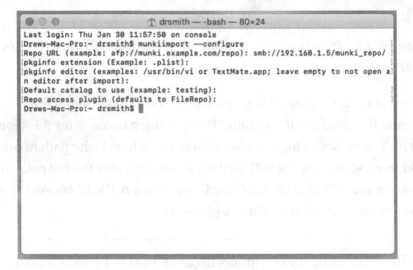

Figure 10-16.   *The recommended responses to the configuration prompts*

Munki Components

There are a number of components that *Munki* uses to function on a client machine. All of the functionality of *Munki* resides on the client software installed as part of *MunkiTools*. Later in this chapter, we will install and configure *MunkiTools* on a test client so we can see it in action. Before we do this, it is important to understand the main components of the *Munki* client software:

- **Managed Software Center:** This is a GUI utility that gets installed into the */Applications* directory by the MunkiTools package. This allows end users to select authorized software titles and install them on their Macs without requiring local Administrative rights.

- **Installer Items:** These are packages or disk images that reside on your *Munki* server for applications that are to be installed and managed via the *Munki* client or *Managed Software Center.*

- **Catalogs:** These are lists of software that are imported into *Munki* by the administrator and include metadata about how the application should be installed, scripts, and specific settings. We will have a testing catalog of applications we are not ready to install on end user systems and a production catalog for applications that are approved for mass installation.

- **Manifests:** This is a list of what software should be installed on a given machine. You can have a manifest for each machine, location, or workgroup. In general, it is a best practice to have as few manifests as possible to keep things simple and consistent.

- **Receipts:** While not specific to *Munki,* when a package is installed on a Mac, a receipt is created. *Munki* determines what needs to be installed vs. what is already installed on the client workstation using receipts. If one exists for a given package, Munki will not try to install it again.

- **Bill of Materials:** Like receipts, the Bill of Materials is not unique to *Munki* and is created when a package is installed. This is a list of components for a given software application that *Munki* references to remove software and related dependencies during the uninstall process.

Importing the MunkiTools Package

The first thing we are going to do is import our first package into *Munki* from the command line so we can see how this works. We can go ahead and start with the *MunkiTools* package since it is conveniently sitting on our Desktop and ready to go.

```
IMPORTING OUR FIRST INSTALL PACKAGE
```

1. Start by opening the Terminal again and at the command prompt enter munkiimport and then **drag** the **munkitools. pkg** file from the Desktop and **drop it** into our command line. Your Terminal window should look similar to Figure 10-17.

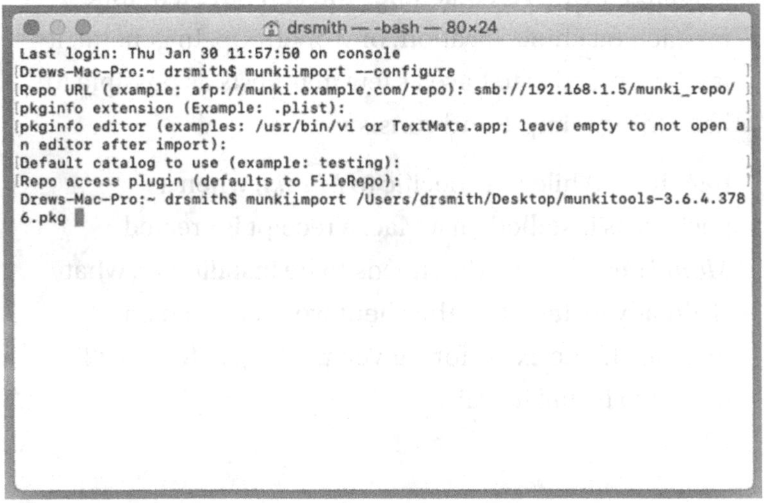

```
Last login: Thu Jan 30 11:57:50 on console
[Drews-Mac-Pro:~ drsmith$ munkiimport --configure
[Repo URL (example: afp://munki.example.com/repo): smb://192.168.1.5/munki_repo/
[pkginfo extension (Example: .plist):
[pkginfo editor (examples: /usr/bin/vi or TextMate.app; leave empty to not open a]
n editor after import):
[Default catalog to use (example: testing):
[Repo access plugin (defaults to FileRepo):
Drews-Mac-Pro:~ drsmith$ munkiimport /Users/drsmith/Desktop/munkitools-3.6.4.378
6.pkg █
```

Figure 10-17. *Using the munkiimport command and the path to the *.pkg file*

416

2. Next, press **enter** to execute the munkimport command on our package file. It will now start prompting us to edit or accept the default options through the import command line utility. We will go into more detail on each of these items when we package our other applications later in this chapter, but in the meantime configure yours as follows:

    Item name: munkitools
    Display name: MunkiTools
    Description: Client software for the Munki service.
    Version: 3.6.4.3786
    Category: Utilities
    Developer: Open Source
    Unattended install: False
    Unattended Uninstall: False
    Catalogs: testing

3. If your Terminal window looks similar to Figure 10-18, go ahead and answer **y** to the **Import this item?** prompt.

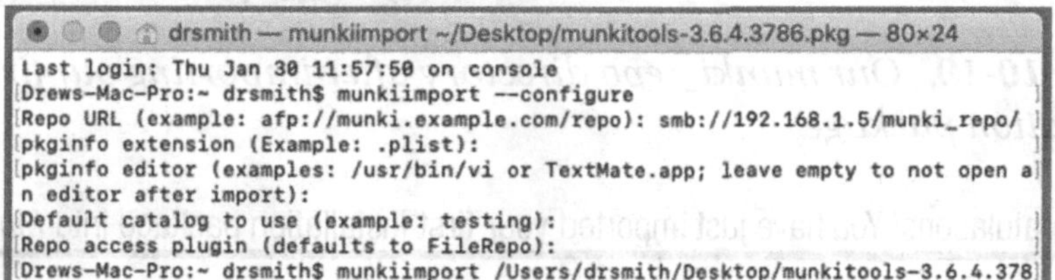

Figure 10-18. Configuring the installer package using the munkiimport command line utility

4. When prompted to `Upload item` to subdirectory `path`, press **enter** to accept the default.

5. When prompted to `Attempt to create a product icon?`, answer **y** and press **enter**. You will see it output some text about importing and copying the package to our server.

6. When it prompts you to `rebuild the catalogs`, answer y and press **enter**. It will provide some output, and if you take a look at your *munki_repo* share, you will see that a number of new folders have now appeared as shown in Figure 10-19.

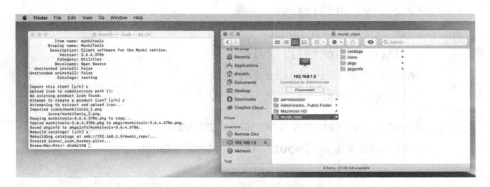

Figure 10-19. *Our munki_repo directory after importing our first installation package*

Congratulations! You have just imported your first installation package into *Munki*.

Introduction to MunkiAdmin

Now that we have a package imported into *Munki* and a few folders have been created at the root of our *munki_repo* directory, let's open the *MunkiAdmin* application. When you open *MunkiAdmin,* it is going to prompt us to point it to our *munki_repo* network share. Browse to the share, click it to select it, and then click the **Open** button as shown in Figure 10-20.

Once you have selected the ***munki_repo*** share, you'll see the main *MunkiAdmin* console interface with our *MunkiTools* package already in the list.

Figure 10-20. *When prompted by MunkiAdmin, point it to the SMB share of our munki_repo*

Figure 10-21 and the following descriptions will give you a quick reference to the MunkiAdmin interface.

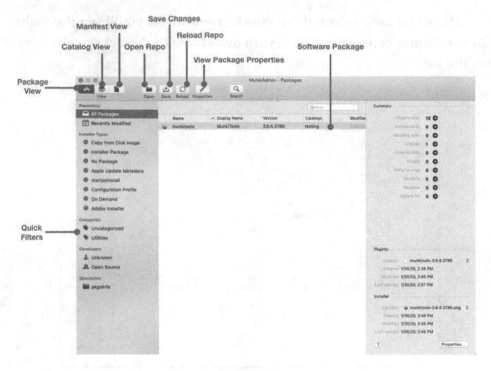

Figure 10-21.   *The MunkiAdmin interface*

- **Package View:** The view that lists all of the software
  packages imported into *Munki.*

- **Catalog View:** The view that shows all of the Catalogs
  and allows us to manage our Catalogs.

- **Manifest View:** The view that shows all of the Manifests
  and allows us to manage our Manifests.

- **Open Repo:** Press this button to connect to a specific
  munki_repo network share.

- **Save Changes:** Saves the changes made to the current
  package, Catalog, or Manifest to the munki_repo.

- **Reload Repo:** Refreshes the *MunkiAdmin* console after changes are saved to the munki_repo.

- **View Package Properties:** Loads the dialog box with all of the package install options.

- **Software Packages:** The list of available software packages imported into *Munki*.

- **Quick Filters:** This sidebar will populate based on the category or developer and will filter your list of software packages based on that search criteria. For example, if you wanted to isolate just the Adobe packages, you would click the Adobe developer filter.

Packaging Software into Munki

Now that our administrative workstation is ready to go, we need to start packaging some software. *Munki* will support importing and installing packages in the standard *macOS Installer* ***.pkg** format, ***.dmg** disk image installation, and *Adobe CC* packages without any special repackaging requirements. *Munki* can also create uninstall packages as well, so you can use it to remove software when it is time to upgrade from an old version to a new one.

Pro Tip   If you are experienced with software installation on Microsoft Windows systems, you can think of Apple's native *.pkg installation packages as the *macOS* equivalent of a Microsoft *.msi setup file.

Importing Software into Munki

In this section, we are going to build out a catalog of installer packages. Before we begin, you should hit the Internet from your administrative workstation and download the following installers to your Desktop. In the case that these applications may be available both via the *Mac App Store* and directly from the developer's web site, download the version from the developer instead of the *App Store* version:

- **Adobe Reader:** https://get.adobe.com/reader/

- **Adobe Flash Player:** https://get.adobe.com/flashplayer/

- **VLC:** www.videolan.org/vlc/download-macosx.html

- **Mozilla Firefox:** www.mozilla.org/en-US/firefox/new/

- **Google Chrome:** www.google.com/chrome/

- **Audacity:** www.audacityteam.org/download/

IMPORT SOFTWARE PACKAGES

You should have your ***munki_repo*** network share mapped to your computer and the six *****.dmg** files on your desktop, one for each of the preceding applications listed. In this exercise we are going to import these software applications into *Munki.* We will begin with *Firefox* and *Adobe Flash Player* because they both use a different kind of installation process. *Firefox* is a simple drag and drop of the application into the ***/Applications*** folder, while *Adobe Flash* uses an installation package file.

1. We are going to start with Firefox. Go ahead and open a new Terminal window and enter munkiimport at the command prompt and then drag and drop the Firefox *.dmg file into the window as shown in Figure 10-22. Press enter on the keyboard to begin the command line munkiimport utility.

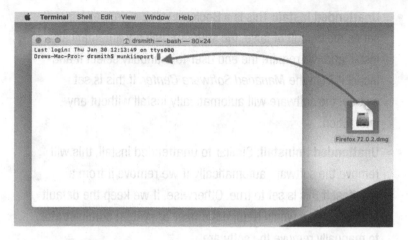

Figure 10-22. *Using the munkiimport command with a *.dmg file*

This will look similar to the process we used to import *MunkiTools* earlier in this chapter. Go ahead and step through the options via the command line. Here's a little more information on what each of these options is used for:

- **Item Name:** The name of the package in *Munki*.

- **Display Name:** The title of the software shown in the *Managed Software Center*.

- **Description:** The description of the software provided in the *Managed Software Center*.

- **Version:** The version of the software. *Munki* will attempt to determine the version from the package, but if it cannot, you would need to provide a version number manually. Version numbers are important as *Munki* will need to reference this when we need to upgrade software at a future date.

- **Category:** This will place the software in a specific category for filtering in *MunkiAdmin* and *Managed Software Center*.

- **Developer:** This will place the software in a specific developer group for filtering in *MunkiAdmin*.

- **Unattended Install:** This is a Boolean value of true or false. If set as the default of false, the software will not automatically install and will require the end user to manually select it and install it from the *Managed Software Center*. If this is set as true, the software will automatically install without any interaction.

- **Unattended Uninstall:** Similar to unattended install, this will remove the software automatically if we remove it from a manifest if this is set to true. Otherwise, if we keep the default of false, then it would require the user or system administrator to manually remove the software.

- **Catalogs:** Identifies which catalog(s) the software should be listed in. We can also modify this later in *MunkiAdmin*.

Go ahead and answer these questions to match what I have shown in Figure 10-23.

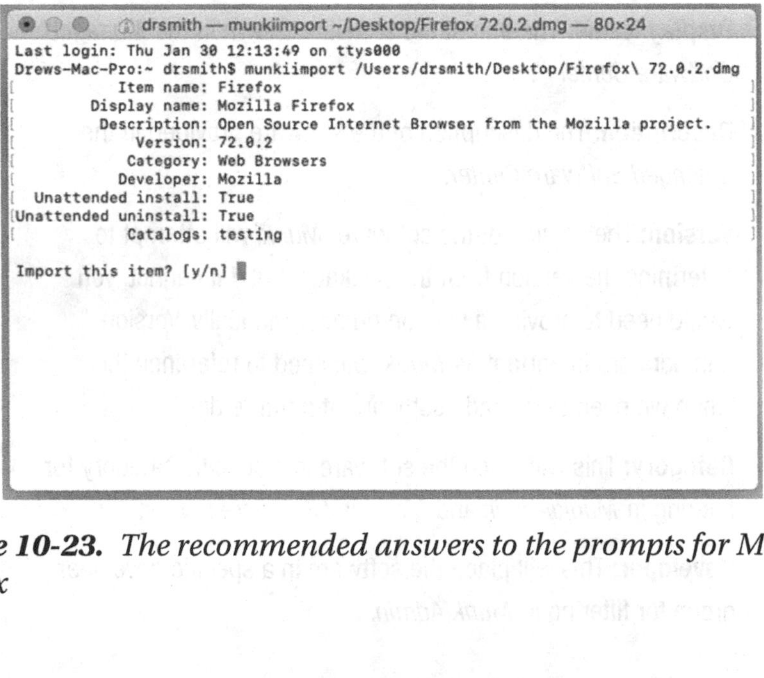

Figure 10-23. *The recommended answers to the prompts for Mozilla Firefox*

2. When you are prompted to import the item, enter y to continue.

3. When it asks to upload the item to a subdirectory path, we are going to take the default. We will not be placing our software packages in various subdirectories, only in the single default directory on our *munki_repo* share in the *pkgs* directory. Press **enter** to accept the default and continue.

4. Next, it will prompt you to attempt to create a product icon. Answer y to this one to continue. Munki will attempt to create an icon if it finds one in the package and will display that icon in the *Managed Software Center*.

5. It will now copy the package to the *munki_repo* share and save the required **pkginfo.plist** data based on what it found in the installer package and our command line input. It will ask you to rebuild the catalogs, and since we just made a change to the catalog by adding a new application, we will answer with a **y** and press **enter** to continue.

Once it completes the rebuild of the catalog, we have successfully imported the *Firefox* application. If you want to double-check your work to ensure that the application is available, you can open the *munki_repo* network share and browse the */pkgs* and */pkgsinfo* directories to see that *Firefox* is available. You can also hit your *munki_repo* page from a web browser to ensure that the packages are available via the Web. Finally, you can open *MunkiAdmin* and **reload** the repo to see that *Firefox* is available. As you can see from Figure 10-24, everything is available and synchronized on my workstation.

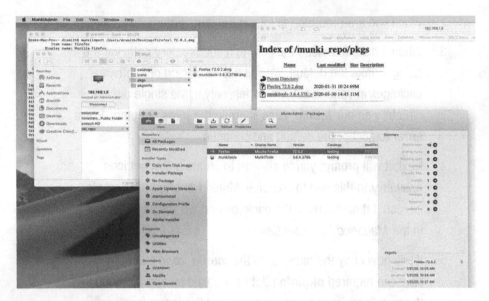

Figure 10-24. *The Firefox package is available in MunkiAdmin and the munki_repo share and via the web server*

6. Next, we can import *Adobe Flash Player*. **Double-click** the
    Install Flash Player *.dmg file to mount the disk image to
    the desktop. Inside you will need to **right-click** the **Install
    Adobe Flash Player** application and choose to **Show Package
    Contents**. Next, browse the */Contents/Resources/* directory
    and find the **Adobe Flash Player *.pkg** file as that is our
    installer. Use the `munkiimport` command and **drag and
    drop** the *.pkg file into the Terminal window to specify the
    path. Press **enter** to begin the import process like we did with
    Firefox.

7. When prompted, enter the information as shown in
    Figure 10-25. Please note that we will need to modify a few
    of these options.

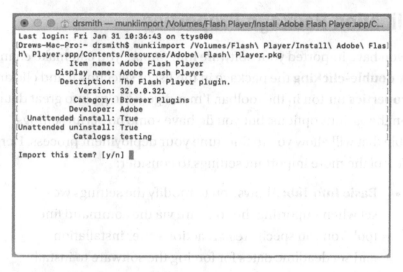

```
●  ○  ●  ⬆  drsmith — munkiimport /Volumes/Flash Player/Install Adobe Flash Player.app/C...

Last login: Fri Jan 31 10:36:43 on ttys000
[Drews-Mac-Pro:~ drsmith$ munkiimport /Volumes/Flash\ Player/Install\ Adobe\ Flas]
h\ Player.app/Contents/Resources/Adobe\ Flash\ Player.pkg
[             Item name: Adobe Flash Player                                        ]
[          Display name: Adobe Flash Player                                        ]
[           Description: The Flash Player plugin.                                  ]
[               Version: 32.0.0.321                                                ]
[              Category: Browser Plugins                                           ]
[             Developer: Adobe                                                     ]
[    Unattended install: True                                                      ]
[Unattended uninstall: True                                                        ]
[              Catalogs: testing                                                   ]

Import this item? [y/n] ▮
```

Figure 10-25. *Recommended settings for the Adobe Flash Player installation packag*

8. When prompted, import the item accepting all defaults. Answer **y** when prompted about the icon and rebuild the catalogs.

9. Once it finishes the import of the software into *Munki*, go ahead and verify that everything copied correctly.

10. Repeat the import process for the other four software titles, setting them all as unattended install/uninstall when prompted. When you are done, reload the ***munki_repo*** in *MunkiAdmin,* and your software list should look like Figure 10-26.

Figure 10-26. *The complete list of imported software titles*

Application Package Properties

Once you have imported your software into *Munki*, you can make changes to it by **double-clicking** the package in the list or selecting it and clicking the **Properties** button in the toolbar. I'm not going to go into great detail here on the various options, but you do have some powerful settings available that will allow you to fine-tune your deployment process. Here are a few of the more important settings to consider:

- **Basic Info Tab:** Allows you to modify the settings we set when importing the software via the command line tool. You can specify restart actions after installation and set deadline dates for forcing the software to install if necessary.

- **Requirements Tab:** This allows you to set dependencies based on existing software installed on the system and minimum OS and maximum OS versions for each individual package. This is particularly nice if you want to provide an older version of an application to clients running on older OS and a new version of the software for users on a more current OS.

- **Install Scripts Tab:** Here you can specify scripts to run before and after the software installation runs. This is a powerful way to customize applications after the software installs.

- **Uninstall Tab:** Here you can specify the uninstall process including using an uninstall script and scripts both before and after the uninstall process runs.

Creating a Munki Package to Execute a Script

If you recall from Chapter 6, we were able to send scripts to remote machines using the **Send Unix Command** tool. Any command or a script of multiple commands that we can send via *Apple Remote Desktop* can be packaged and executed by *Munki*. In this section, we will explore how to create a custom package that delivers a script.

We will be using a new tool in this section for creating a custom package. There are many utilities out there that will create a *∗*.**pkg** file. We will be using one called *Munki-Pkg*, which is available here: https:// github.com/munki/munki-pkg. *Munki-Pkg* is a command line utility so there is no GUI. We will simply download it, extract it, and copy the resulting folder to the Desktop. We will run it from the Terminal by changing to the *~/Desktop/munki-pkg-master/* directory.

CREATING A PACKAGE TO RUN A SCRIPT

In this exercise we are going to create a package that runs a script that will force the client Mac to immediately reboot.

1. The first thing we will want to do is develop our script. This one is very simple because it is a single command, but you could create a more advanced script with multiple commands, variables, and more. Using Terminal or Apple Remote Desktop, test this command to ensure it immediately restarts the computer:

    ```
    shutdown -r now
    ```

The computer should immediately restart. If that works successfully, we now have our script ready to package in *Munki*.

Pro Tip   The purpose of this exercise is to demonstrate how you can create a custom package to run a script. This example restart script is not recommended for production use with Munki as it could cause your client systems to restart without notice to the end user.

2.   Open Terminal and then open the ***munki-pkg-master folder*** on the Desktop and then **drag and drop** the ***munkipkg*** Unix executable into the Terminal to execute the *Munki-Pkg* utility as shown in Figure 10-27. Do not press enter yet as we have to add some options to make the `munkipkg` command work.

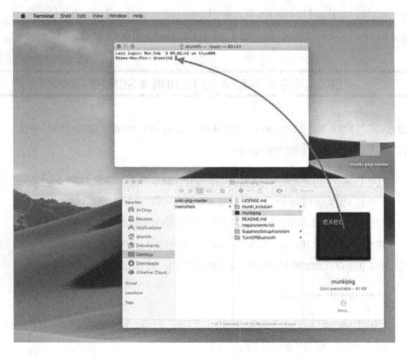

Figure 10-27. *Drag the Unix exec to the Terminal*

3. We are going to go ahead and create a new empty package. After the path to the `munkipkg` executable, add `--create RestartClientScript` into the command line and press **enter** as shown in Figure 10-28. This will create a new empty package called ***RestartClientScript***.

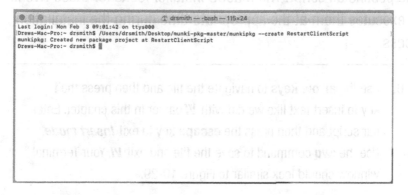

```
●●●                              ⚙ drsmith — -bash — 115×24
Last login: Mon Feb  3 09:01:42 on ttys000
[Drews-Mac-Pro:~ drsmith$ /Users/drsmith/Desktop/munki-pkg-master/munkipkg --create RestartClientScript
munkipkg: Created new package project at RestartClientScript
Drews-Mac-Pro:~ drsmith$ █
```

Figure 10-28. *The full munkipkg create new project command*

4. If successful, it will have created a folder at the root of your home directory called ***RestartClientScript***, and inside that folder you will see folders for *build*, *payload*, and *scripts*. We are going to ignore the payload folder and focus on the scripts folder. Go ahead and change directories in the Terminal to the scripts folder by entering `cd /RestartClientScript/ scripts/`.

5. Once you are in the scripts folder, we are going to use *VI* again to create a file that will run our script. Enter `vi postinstall` to create a new file in the *VI* text editor called ***postinstall***. The file must be named ***postinstall*** to package and run properly when we execute the script.

> **Pro Tip**   Software packaging is outside of the scope of this book, but there are many good articles online about creating custom install packages and how they work. You will find that there are two scripts that can run in any package. One is the preinstall script and the other is the postinstall script. The *macOS Installer* looks for these two files and executes them at the appropriate time during the installation process.

6. Use the **arrow keys** to navigate the file and then press the **i** key to insert text like we did with *VI* earlier in this chapter. Enter our script and then press the **escape** key to exit *Insert mode*. Use the **:wq** command to save the file and exit *VI*. Your Terminal window should look similar to Figure 10-29.

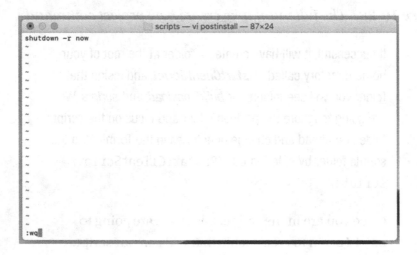

Figure 10-29. *Use VI to write our script*

7. You can browse the scripts folder in the Finder or an `ls`
    command on the **/scripts** directory, and you will see that we
    now have a **postinstall** file in that directory. The last step is to
    package this project into a *.**pkg** file that can then be uploaded
    into *Munki*. **Drag and drop** the munkipkg executable to the
    Terminal window again like we did earlier. **Next, drag and
    drop** the **RestartClientScript** folder to the Terminal window to
    append the path to our project or enter the path to the project
    file. When your Terminal window looks like Figure 10-30, press
    enter to create the **RestartClientScript.pkg** file.

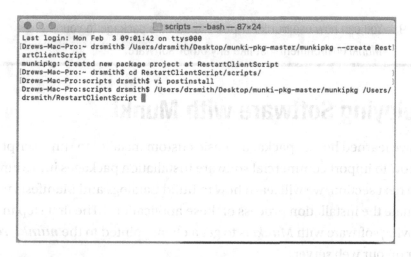

Figure 10-30. The entire command to create our *.pkg file

8. When the command runs successfully, we should see the
    output in the Terminal that a *.**pkg** file was created in the
    /build folder of our **RestartClientScript** project folder. If you
    browse to that directory, you will see the **RestartClientScript-
    1.0.pkg** file as shown in Figure 10-31.

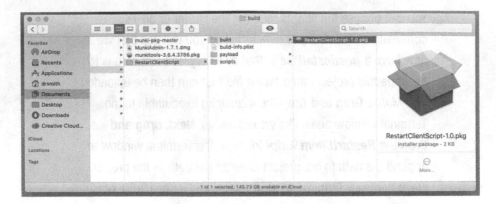

Figure 10-31. *The finished *.pkg file that only executes a script*

9. You can now use munkiimport to add the package to your
    Munki environment just like any other software.

Deploying Software with Munki

We have learned how to package a basic custom installer to run a script
and how to import commercial software installation packages into Munki.
In the next section, we will learn how to build Catalogs and Manifests to
automate the installation process of these applications. The first step in
deploying software with *Munki* is to get a client pointed to the ***munki_repo***
folder on our web server.

Installing and Configuring Munki on Client Workstations

We are going to begin by installing the *MunkiTools* application on a test
client machine. You can do this interactively on your client system by
running the *MunkiTools* package we downloaded earlier in the chapter, or
we can use *Apple Remote Desktop*. Most likely, you will be installing *Munki*
on multiple Macs in a production environment, so let's use ARD for this task.

INSTALLING MUNKITOOLS WITH ARD

Before you begin this exercise, grab a test Mac and add it to your ARD console if it's not already there.

1. The first step is to install MunkiTools. Open ARD and **click** your test Mac to select it. Click the **Install** button in the toolbar and add the **munkitools.pkg** installer to the list of packages. Click the **Install** button as shown in Figure 10-32.

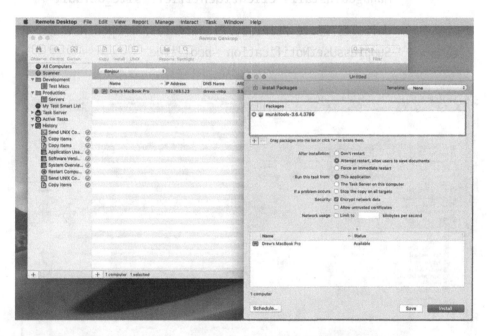

Figure 10-32. *Use ARD to install the MunkiTools package on your test Mac*

2. Once it finishes the installation, it will force the computer to restart. The next thing we need to do is run a script that will modify a few keys in Munki's **ManagedInstalls *.plist** file stored on the client in */Library/Preferences/*. **Select** the client

in ARD and click the **Unix** button in the toolbar. Enter
the following lines into the script window as shown in
Figure 10-33. Don't forget to set the command to run as **root**:

```
#!/bin/sh
```

```
defaults write /Library/Preferences/ManagedInstalls
SoftwareRepoURL "http://192.168.1.5/munki_repo"
```

```
defaults write /Library/Preferences/
ManagedInstalls ClientIdentifier "site_default"
```

```
defaults write /Library/Preferences/ManagedInstalls
SuppressUserNotification -bool true
```

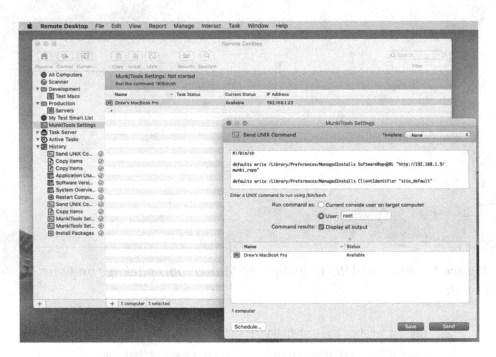

Figure 10-33. *Enter the script into the Send Unix Command window*

Let's step through what each of these lines does. The first line is required for any script, identifying it as a shell script. Lines 2–4 use the `defaults write` command to modify keys in the **ManagedInstalls.plist** file found in */Library/ Preferences/* folder.

The `SoftwareURL` key points the client to my web server. You should make sure this points to your *Munki* web server's ***munki_repo*** folder via http.

The `ClientIdentifier` points to the Manifest this client will be using to determine which software is available to them. We will cover Manifests in more detail later in this chapter.

The `SuppressUserNotification` key is a Boolean value where we are going to change it from the default of **false** to **true**. Depending on your environment, you may want to keep the default. What this will do is provide a notification (or not) to your end users when new applications are available to them to install/update in *Munki*. Because we are going to automate the install and upgrade process, we are setting this to true which will *not* provide a notification to the end user.

After you have entered the script, you can click the **Send** button to execute it on the client.

Pro Tip   If this is going to be the default settings for all (or most) of the clients in your organization, consider using the **Save** button here to save this script to run again on future installs of Munki.

---

3. Once the script has run successfully, we can double-check our settings on the client by browsing to */Library/ Preferences/* and using the **QuickLook** option in the Finder to view **ManagedInstalls.plist**. You should see that the `SoftwareURL` has updated to point to our ***munki_repo***. Your **ManagedInstalls.plist** file should look similar to Figure 10-34.

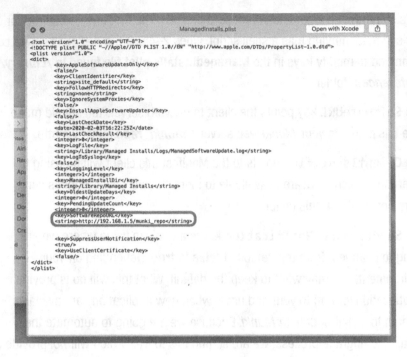

Figure 10-34. *The ManagedInstalls.plist file with our customizations*

4. If everything looks correct, go ahead and restart your test
   computer as it will need to stop and start the Munki service
   using the new preferences before we can continue. We have now
   successfully installed and configured Munki on our test Mac client.

Manifests

As you may recall from earlier in this chapter, a *Manifest* is a list of software
that needs to be installed on a given machine. We can create as many
Manifests as we need to, but the recommendation is to maintain a small
number of these to keep your *Munki* environment as lean and simple
as possible. In this section, we are going to build a Manifest called ***site_
default*** because that is the Manifest we pointed our test client to.

Before we begin, we need to create a *manifests* folder in our *munki_ repo* directory. Make sure you have mounted the *munki_repo* network share on your Mac administrator workstation and then open the Terminal. Use the cd command followed by dragging the *munki_repo* share to the window to change the directory to the network share. Type ls -l and you should see the directory shown in Figure 10-35.

```
● ● ●                   munki_repo — -bash — 80×24
Last login: Mon Feb  3 09:12:23 on ttys000
[Drews-Mac-Pro:~ drsmith$ cd /Volumes/munki_repo
[Drews-Mac-Pro:munki_repo drsmith$ ls -l
total 128
drwxr-xr-x  1 drsmith  staff  16384 Jan 30 14:46 catalogs
drwxr-xr-x  1 drsmith  staff  16384 Jan 31 10:55 icons
drwxr-xr-x  1 drsmith  staff  16384 Jan 31 10:55 pkgs
drwxr-xr-x  1 drsmith  staff  16384 Jan 31 10:55 pkgsinfo
Drews-Mac-Pro:munki_repo drsmith$ █
```

Figure 10-35. *Using the Terminal to browse the munki_repo share*

Next, enter mkdir manifests to create a new folder called *manifests* in the *munki_repo* share. Use ls -l or view the share via the Finder to confirm the folder now exists as shown in Figure 10-36.

Figure 10-36. *Confirming that our new directory is now available*

439

Now, let's open *MunkiAdmin* and connect to our ***munki_repo***.
Click the **Manifests** tab in the toolbar. We are going to create a new
Manifest by choosing **New Manifest** from the **File** menu. When
prompted, name it ***site_default*** and save it to the ***manifests*** folder on
our ***munki_repo*** share as shown in Figure 10-37.

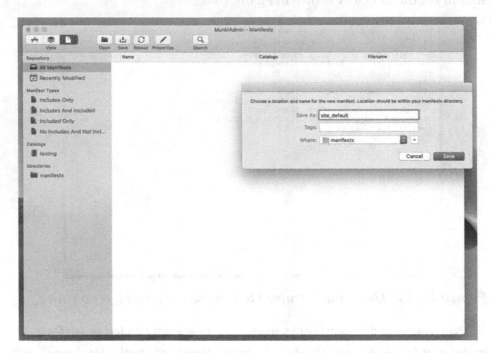

Figure 10-37. *Creating a site_default Manifest in MunkiAdmin*

From the *MunkiAdmin* **Manifest** view, you should now see a
site_default Manifest. **Double-click** it to open the **Manifest Properties**.

CUSTOMIZING A MANIFEST

In this exercise, we are going to customize the **site_default** Manifest.

1. Starting in the **General** tab, we will assign a Catalog to this
    Manifest. We currently have one available Catalog, **testing**. Click the
    checkbox to the left of the testing catalog to point this manifest to
    the software listed in the testing catalog as shown in Figure 10-38.

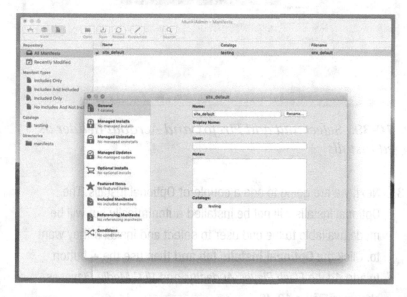

Figure 10-38. *Adding the testing Catalog to the site_default Manifest*

2. Next, we are going to select the **Managed Installs** tab.
    Using the **+** button in the bottom part of this window, we
    can add specific applications to this list that will be available
    to the client using this Manifest. Since these packages are
    set to install without user interaction, these will be installed
    automatically when *Munki* runs again. We will add *Firefox* and
    Acrobat Reader to this list of **Managed Installs**. **Select and
    add them** as shown in Figure 10-39.

Figure 10-39. *Select and add Firefox and Acrobat Reader as Managed Installs*

3. Next, we are going to add a couple of Optional Installs. The Optional Installs will not be installed automatically but will be made available to the end user to select and install if they want to. Click the **Optional Installs** tab and then use the **+** button to add *Adobe Flash Player*, *Audacity*, and *VLC Media Player* as shown in Figure 10-40.

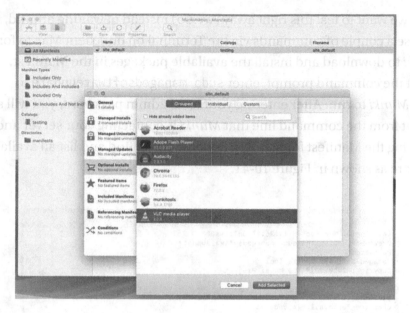

Figure 10-40. *Selecting Flash Player, VLC, and Audacity as Optional Installs*

4. After making these changes to the **site_default** Manifest, click the **Save** button and then the **Reload** button in the toolbar to publish our changes and refresh the *MunkiAdmin* console.

Now that we have configured our Manifest, the *Munki* client software running on our test Mac will be able to look at the **site_default** Manifest and execute the items in this list. It will automatically install *Firefox* and *Acrobat Reader* the next time that *Munki* runs, which will be sometime in the next hour or so.

Pro Tip   By default, the Munki agent checks in with the server approximately once per hour. At that time, it looks for any changes on the server and then downloads and installs any packages or runs any scripts that have been placed into production since the last time it checked in.

If we want to test this right away (we do) instead of waiting around, we can use a couple of commands via the Terminal on our client Mac to force *Munki* to download and install the available packages in the Manifest.

At the command prompt, enter sudo managedsoftwareupdate to force *Munki* to run. After entering your local admin password, you will see output from the command line that *Munki* is contacting your server and checking the Manifest for pending updates. It will find and list all available software as shown in Figure 10-41.

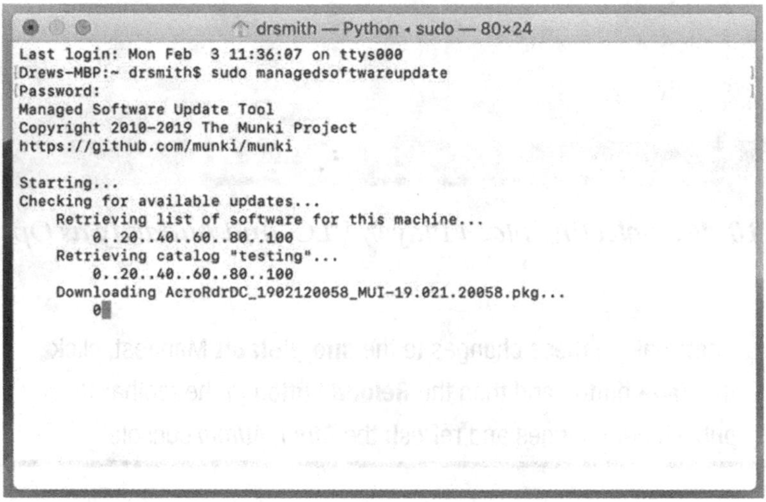

Figure 10-41. *Munki is running and checking the available updates for our test machine*

Next, we can enter sudo managedsoftwareupdate --installonly, and it will begin installing the software that we listed in the Manifest as Managed Installs. Figure 10-42 shows the progress that the command line will output as it runs the installer in the background and installs *Adobe Acrobat Reader* and then *Firefox*.

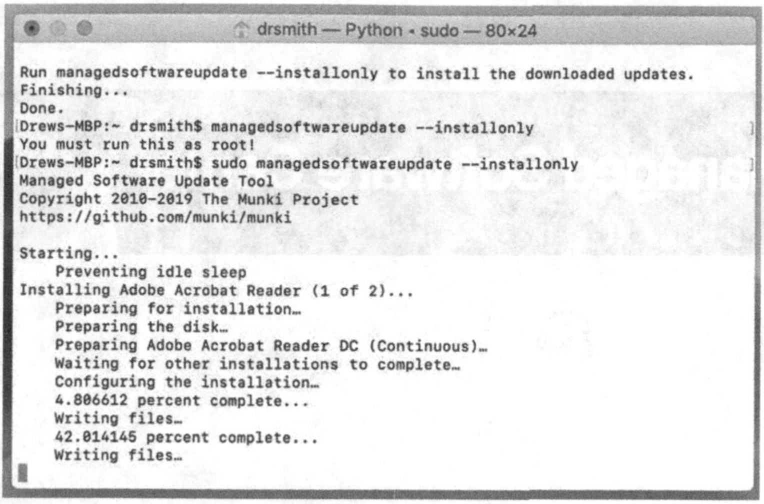

```
● ● ●                    ⌂ drsmith — Python · sudo — 80×24

Run managedsoftwareupdate --installonly to install the downloaded updates.
Finishing...
Done.
[Drews-MBP:~ drsmith$ managedsoftwareupdate --installonly               ]
You must run this as root!
[Drews-MBP:~ drsmith$ sudo managedsoftwareupdate --installonly          ]
Managed Software Update Tool
Copyright 2010-2019 The Munki Project
https://github.com/munki/munki

Starting...
    Preventing idle sleep
Installing Adobe Acrobat Reader (1 of 2)...
    Preparing for installation…
    Preparing the disk…
    Preparing Adobe Acrobat Reader DC (Continuous)…
    Waiting for other installations to complete…
    Configuring the installation…
    4.806612 percent complete...
    Writing files…
    42.014145 percent complete...
    Writing files…
▌
```

Figure 10-42. *Installing the software packages*

Once complete, browse your */Applications* directory, and you should see *Adobe Acrobat Reader* and *Firefox* are now available. Feel free to open them to ensure that they installed successfully and work as expected.

Managed Software Center

We have successfully installed the Managed applications, but where are the **Optional Installs** that we made available to the end users who can choose if they want to install them or not? Your end users can browse these applications and install them via the *Managed Software Center* application which is installed as part of *MunkiTools* and found in */Applications*. On your test Mac client, open the *Managed Software Center* as shown in Figure 10-43.

Figure 10-43. *The Managed Software Center application for end-user interaction*

Managed Software Center looks like the *Mac App Store* application and functions very similar. It provides a shopping cart experience for users to select optional applications, and they can simply click the **Install** button under any application that is assigned to their computer via the Manifest to install it. They do not need Administrator access to install, and they can manage their own updates on their own timeline. Go ahead and install *Adobe Flash Player*, *Audacity*, and *VLC Media Player* on our test Mac so you get a feel for how this works.

Pro Tip   Do you see how the various categories we used when importing the software package into *Munki* are leveraged in the Managed Software Center? If you plan to use this tool for a large number of applications, those categories will be very useful as you build out your testing and production Catalogs.

Catalogs

Now that we have been working with Manifests and deploying software to a test machine, we should discuss *Catalogs* in a bit more detail. With the goal of keeping our *Munki* environment as simple as possible, we should think about how many Catalogs we will need. I typically use two Catalogs: one for testing and one for production. My testing Catalog is only used on my non-production machines to ensure that a package installs and runs as expected before it gets installed on all of the machines in my organization.

In *MunkiAdmin*, click the **Catalog** button in the toolbar to switch to the Catalog view. We should see our **testing** Catalog in this list. I always like to use the testing catalog as the default place to import our software packages. After testing is completed, I add those packages to the production Catalog. Let's create a ***production*** Catalog so you can see how this will work. Choose **New Catalog** from the **File** menu. When prompted, name this catalog ***production*** as shown in Figure 10-44.

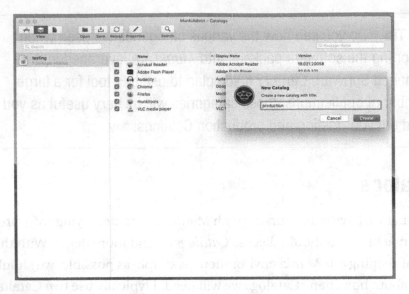

Figure 10-44. *Creating a new Catalog named "production"*

By default, no packages are enabled in a new Catalog. Click the new **production** Catalog in the left sidebar to select it and then **check the boxes** next to the packages we want to put into production. We will check the box next to every application except *Adobe Acrobat Reader* and *MunkiTools*. Your *MunkiAdmin* window should look similar to Figure 10-45.

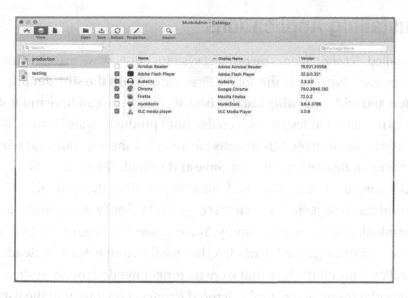

Figure 10-45. *Selecting the applications that will be listed in our production Catalog*

Save the changes to the Catalogs and **reload** the *MunkiAdmin* console. Next, we are going to edit the **site_default** Manifest and remove the **testing** Catalog and replace it with the **production** Catalog. This will ensure that only approved applications that are included in production are applied to clients that are subscribed to our **site_default** Manifest.

Open the Properties of the **site_default** Manifest and make a small change to the **General** tab. **Uncheck** the **testing** Catalog and **check** the **production** catalog. Go to the **Managed Installs** tab and remove *Acrobat Reader* from the list. **Save** and **reload** the *MunkiAdmin* console. The next time that *Munki* runs on a client machine, it will only look for available software in the **production** Catalog.

Pro Tip   Because we removed the *Adobe Acrobat Reader* from the production Catalog, that does not mean it will uninstall it from any clients that already have it installed. It will only prevent it from installing on future runs.

Uninstalling Applications

We installed *Acrobat Reader* on our test system, but now we want to uninstall it. We can use *Munki* to do this for us. First, we can **edit** the **site_default** Manifest and add the **testing** Catalog back in. Since you can have multiple Catalogs in each Manifest, we will enable both production and testing. Next, we can go to the **Managed Uninstalls** tab and click the + button and select *Adobe Acrobat Reader* from the list. **Save** and **reload**. On the test client, force *Munki* to run, and it will uninstall *Acrobat Reader* from the system.

I used the managedsoftwareupdate --installonly command via the Terminal, and it ran successfully. You can see from Figure 10-46 that as it scanned through the Bill of Materials for the Adobe Acrobat Reader uninstaller, it found the files that were no longer needed on my system and removed them. Since *Adobe Acrobat Reader* is no longer in the list of Managed Installs, it will not attempt to reinstall the software.

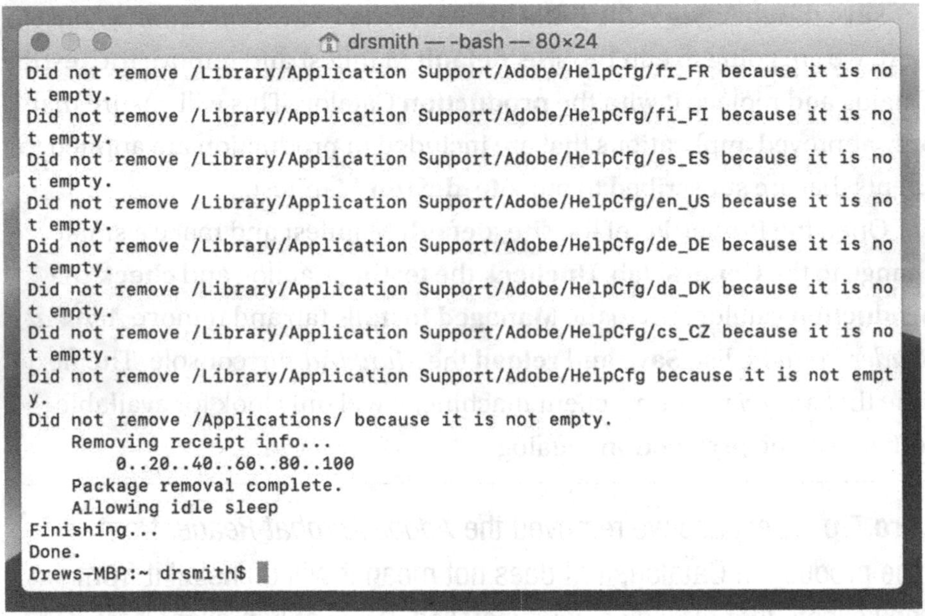

```
● ● ●                    🏠 drsmith — -bash — 80×24
Did not remove /Library/Application Support/Adobe/HelpCfg/fr_FR because it is no
t empty.
Did not remove /Library/Application Support/Adobe/HelpCfg/fi_FI because it is no
t empty.
Did not remove /Library/Application Support/Adobe/HelpCfg/es_ES because it is no
t empty.
Did not remove /Library/Application Support/Adobe/HelpCfg/en_US because it is no
t empty.
Did not remove /Library/Application Support/Adobe/HelpCfg/de_DE because it is no
t empty.
Did not remove /Library/Application Support/Adobe/HelpCfg/da_DK because it is no
t empty.
Did not remove /Library/Application Support/Adobe/HelpCfg/cs_CZ because it is no
t empty.
Did not remove /Library/Application Support/Adobe/HelpCfg because it is not empt
y.
Did not remove /Applications/ because it is not empty.
    Removing receipt info...
        0..20..40..60..80..100
    Package removal complete.
    Allowing idle sleep
Finishing...
Done.
Drews-MBP:~ drsmith$ ▉
```

Figure 10-46. *Uninstalling Adobe Acrobat Reader*

Pro Tip   Notice that it also removed the Receipt info for *Adobe Acrobat Reader*? If at a later date we want to add *Acrobat Reader* back onto this machine, *Munki* will see that there is no longer a Receipt for this package and schedule it to install again.

Summary

Munki is a very powerful tool, and we have only scratched the surface when it comes to using all of the capabilities it provides. If you are planning to use *Munki* to manage all of your software deployments in a production environment, I would recommend visiting the *Munki* GitHub page to learn more. There is a very active community of *Munki* administrators out there that can provide you with many ideas as you plan your deployment strategy and build out the *Munki* environment.

CHAPTER 11

Microsoft Integration

Apple has continued to update their operating systems to work better
in heterogeneous environments over the past decade. In this chapter,
we are going to explore the various ways that a Mac or iOS device can
integrate seamlessly into a corporate network that is based primarily on
technologies from Microsoft Corp. Apple provides a number of built-in
solutions that help with this multi-platform integration, but there are some
third-party solutions available that go even further. In this chapter, we will
discuss several of the built-in solutions and related strategies to support
Apple products on a corporate network with minimal reconfiguration
or cost.

Introduction to Apple-Microsoft Integration

Over the last several iterations of *macOS* and *macOS Server*, Apple has
chosen to demote or completely remove first-party services in favor of
industry standard solutions. For example, for decades *AppleTalk* was the
standard networking protocol for the Mac. Apple File Protocol (AFP) was
the file sharing standard in the Mac operating system. However, more
recently Server Message Block (SMB) file sharing has taken over as the
default file sharing protocol in *macOS*. AFP still exists, but it has been
demoted to a solution that you can use if you need it, but the preference is
to use the same file sharing solution as Linux and Windows clients do.

© Drew Smith 2020
D. Smith, *Apple macOS and iOS System Administration*,
https://doi.org/10.1007/978-1-4842-5820-0_11

Pro Tip   Server Message Block (SMB) is a protocol for sharing data over the network. Microsoft adopted this protocol in *Windows 95*. Linux and macOS clients use an SMB-compatible solution called Samba to access SMB-shared resources.

Beyond adopting SMB file sharing in *macOS* instead of Apple File Protocol, we can see the continued demotion of Open Directory in favor of Active Directory and the removal of a DHCP server, mail, messaging, and CalDAV server solutions in *macOS Server*. Many of these services have been replaced with cloud-hosted versions like *iCloud*, *Office 365 (O365)*, and *Google Docs*. This actually works to our favor as Mac system administrators, because we can more easily integrate Apple devices into existing systems instead of having to stand up special Apple-only technologies or implementing complex and expensive middleware.

My Microsoft Environment

Before we get too deep into the details of integrating Apple platforms into our enterprise Microsoft environment, it would be a good idea to give a quick overview as to what my current network looks like. Figure 11-1 provides a visual overview of the corporate network before I begin adding Macs and iOS devices to the mix.

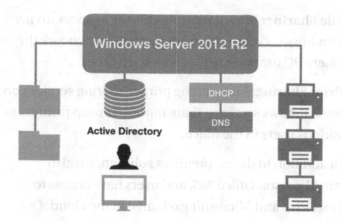

Figure 11-1. *My Microsoft Network, services, printers, and shares*

- **Microsoft Active Directory:** On premises Windows domain named MyCompany.local. I have several organizational units (OUs) by location with a minimal Group Policy applied for the purposes of this demonstration.

- **User Accounts and Group Membership:** I have several user accounts and a couple of groups to control access to various network file shares and printers. Each user authenticates to their PC with their domain account.

- **Group Policy:** For the purpose of this demonstration, I have an OU with a basic Group Policy (GPO) applied that controls the default home page in my Internet Explorer (IE) browser.

- **DNS:** I am running DNS server on my Windows server providing DNS to my network of PCs.

- **DHCP Server:** I'm running Microsoft's DHCP server and providing DNS to my network of PCs via this service.

- **File Sharing:** I'm running file sharing services on my Windows server to share out a couple of network drives where PC users share files with each other.

- **Print Sharing:** I'm running printer sharing services on my Windows server to share out workgroup printers to various users in the office.

- In addition to the on premises solution, we also run Microsoft Office 365, and users have access to OneDrive and Microsoft Exchange in the cloud. Our email is delivered via Exchange on O365.

Now that we have our Microsoft environment defined, we need to plan our Apple platform integration and determine which services our Mac and iOS users will require.

Microsoft Services Required for Apple Users

We are going to add a *MacBook Pro* to our network for the company president. He will need access to the following services:

- The ability to sign in on his Mac both in the office and remotely

- Access to shared files in the main corporate office server

- The ability to print to the shared HP LaserJet printer in his office

- Access to Exchange email

- Access to Microsoft OneDrive

- The Microsoft Office suite (including Microsoft Outlook) natively on his Mac

- Default access to the company Intranet when he opens Safari

- Migration of his existing Internet Explorer Favorites, Outlook Personal Folders, and data from his old Windows laptop

We are going to provide an *iPhone 11* to our company president as well. He will need access to these services from his iPhone:

- Access to Microsoft OneDrive

- Access to his Exchange email

- Contacts from his Exchange account available in the Phone app

- Access to open and edit Word and Excel documents on the iPhone

Finally, we are going to provide an *iPad* to our corporate sales manager, and she needs to be able to update a couple of reports every day on the main corporate office file server. She will need to be able to map the network drive from her iPad and update a couple of Excel files there:

- Access to Microsoft Excel on the iPad

- Access to shared files in the main corporate office server

Throughout this chapter, we will use these three scenarios to integrate an *iPad* running *iPadOS*, an *iPhone*, and a *Mac* into our existing corporate network.

Active Directory Integration for macOS

In this first section, we are going to focus on Active Directory authentication for macOS clients. Before getting started on this exercise, you should have a Mac with a clean OS install and a local Administrator account configured. Using the *Sharing System Preference*, go ahead and name this new Mac **101-2019MBP**, which identifies it as a *2019 MacBook*

Pro in our main office 101. Open the **Terminal** and set the Local Hostname and hostname to match. For Active Directory integration to work properly, we need all three of the Mac's names to be the same.

Pro Tip   You probably have some kind of corporate naming convention at your organization. While Apple devices will attempt to name themselves after the first user account that is created on the machine, you will want to name your Macs in the same fashion that you name your Windows PCs.

Our Mac is now ready to be joined to the MyCompany domain. Let's switch over to our Domain Controller and open **Active Directory Users and Computers** to get started.

PREPARE A DOMAIN CONTROLLER FOR MAC CLIENTS

As a best practice, I prefer to create records for my macOS clients in Active Directory *prior* to adding them to the domain. This serves a couple of purposes in that it guards against the Mac joining into the wrong OU and proactively avoids any odd errors where a Mac client is unable to write a new computer record in AD when it joins to the domain. In this exercise, we are going to prepare a place in Active Directory for our new MacBook Pro.

1. Open **Active Directory Users and Computers**. As shown in Figure 11-2, I have an OU called *Main Office Computers*. Inside that OU, I have a *Windows 10 PCs* OU that houses the computer records for all of my Windows PCs in the main office. This is also where I apply specific Windows 10 GPOs for the main office computers. Create a new OU here for our Macs and name it **macOS PCs**.

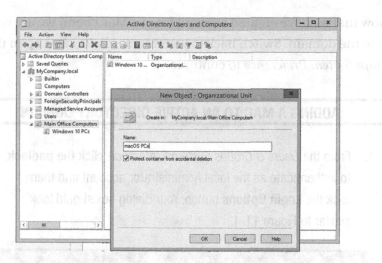

Figure 11-2. *Creating the macOS PCs organizational unit*

2. Now that we have our OU created, we can populate it with computer records for our Macs. With the *macOS PCs* OU selected, **right-click** anywhere in the right-side panel and choose **New ➤ Computer** and name it **101-2019MBP** as shown in Figure 11-3. Click **OK** to create the record.

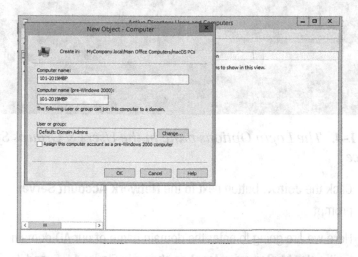

Figure 11-3. *Add a new computer record in Active Directory*

Now that we have created a record for our Mac client, we are ready to add it to the domain. Switch back to your MacBook Pro and open the *Users & Groups System Preference* to continue.

ADDING A MAC TO AN ACTIVE DIRECTORY DOMAIN

---

1. From the *Users & Groups System Preference*, click the **padlock** to authenticate as the local Administrator account and then click the **Login Options** button. Your dialog box should look similar to Figure 11-4.

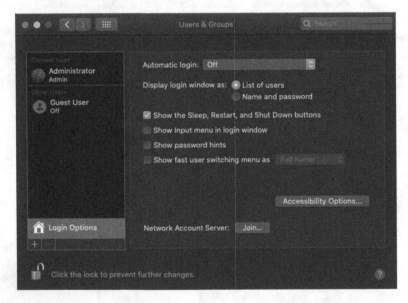

Figure 11-4. *The Login Options pane in the Users & Groups System Preference*

2. Click the **Join…** button next to the **Network Account Server** prompt.

3. Here we are going to enter the domain name of our AD domain. I will enter **MyCompany.local** as shown in Figure 11-5, and it will begin to search for the domain.

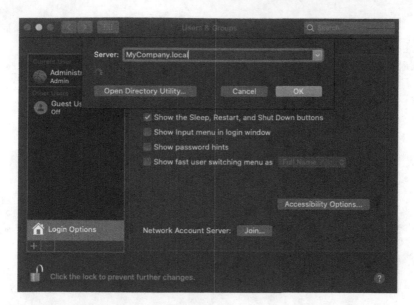

Figure 11-5. *Enter the name of the domain in the Server field*

Pro Tip   If you are experiencing an issue finding the domain, you should check your DNS settings on your Mac to make sure that it's getting DNS from your Windows server and make sure you can resolve the IP and domain name both backward and forward. If you have multiple DNS servers, make sure that your Windows server is the primary DNS server.

---

4. Once it finds the domain, it will prompt you to enter a Computer Name and credentials. If we set up our Local Hostname and hostname properly, it will auto-fill the Computer Name that we want to use as shown in Figure 11-6. Enter your Domain Admin username and password into the next field and click **OK**.

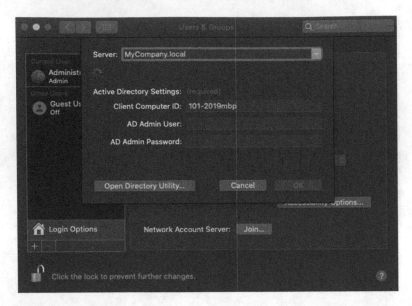

Figure 11-6. *Confirm the Computer Name and authenticate with a Domain Admin account*

5.   Next, it will prompt you to modify the directory configuration on your Mac and ask you to enter your local Mac Administrator account username and password. Enter that information and click the **Modify Configuration** button to continue.

6.   Your Mac will now begin configuring Active Directory, and after a minute or so, you will see a green dot next to the name of your Windows domain as shown in Figure 11-7. This indicates that your Mac is now successfully joined to the MyCompany domain.

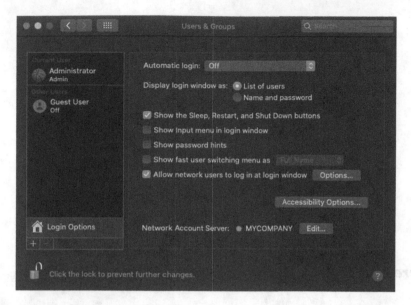

Figure 11-7. *The green dot next to the domain name confirms that our Mac has successfully joined*

Pro Tip If you are getting errors when joining to your domain, one thing to check is the time zone, date, and time of both your Domain Controller and your Mac. Often times your client or server is a few minutes off, and that will cause the domain binding to fail with various cryptic error messages.

Now that our Mac is on the domain, we should log out of the local Administrator account and log in as a Network Account user from our Windows Active Directory domain. *Don President* is the name of our lucky user who gets this brand-new *MacBook Pro.* Let's test this login with his account as shown in Figure 11-8.

Figure 11-8. *Signing in with a Network user account*

After stepping through the Setup Assistant, we are placed into the default new user's home directory. Browsing with the **Finder** to **Home** reveals that we are in as the *dpresident* user. Your screen should look similar to Figure 11-9. Excellent! Go ahead and sign out and sign back in as Administrator.

Figure 11-9. *The default new user Desktop in macOS Catalina*

Let's try something. Go ahead and disable Wi-Fi and ensure that your MacBook Pro is no longer connected to the network. Log out and then attempt to sign in again with the Network user account. You are going to have a little problem. You won't be able to authenticate because the domain is unreachable. There's a red indicator button on the login screen in the top-right corner showing that we are disconnected from the network as shown in Figure 11-10.

Figure 11-10. *The red dot indicates that the Windows domain is unreachable*

One of the requirements of setting up this laptop was the ability for Don President to sign in while off of the network. To fix this issue, we need to convert the *dpresident* account to a Mobile account on this Mac. Log in as the local Administrator account and re-enable network access. Sign out and make sure you can sign back in as the *dpresident* user. Once you are logged in as Don President, go to the *Users & Groups System Preference* as shown in Figure 11-11. Notice how the current user listed is a **Network** type? We need to convert this to a **Mobile** account type.

Figure 11-11. *Notice the user account type designation for Don President*

Click the **padlock** and authenticate as the local Administrator. Then click the Don President user as shown in Figure 11-12. Click the **Create...** button next to the **Mobile account** prompt.

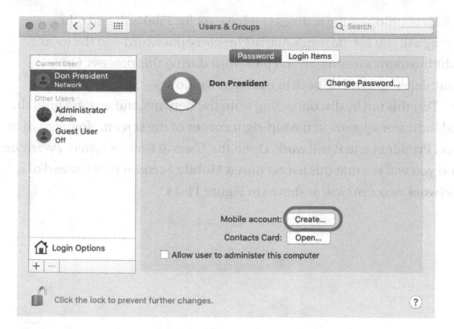

Figure 11-12. *Converting the Don President Network account to a Mobile account*

Place the home directory in the **Macintosh HD (Startup disk)** option when prompted and click the **Create** button to continue. It will warn you that it is about to log you off to create a local home folder as shown in Figure 11-13. Click the **Create** button to continue.

Figure 11-13. *Follow the prompts to log out and create the Mobile account*

Depending on the settings you have set for FileVault and others, it may ask you for the user's Active Directory password and the local Administrator's username and password during this process. Once it completes, you will be back to the login window.

Test this out by disconnecting from the network and waiting until the red indicator appears in the top-right corner of the screen. Now sign in as Don President and it will work. Open the *Users & Groups System Preference,* and you will see that this user is now a **Mobile** account type instead of a **Network** account type as shown in Figure 11-14.

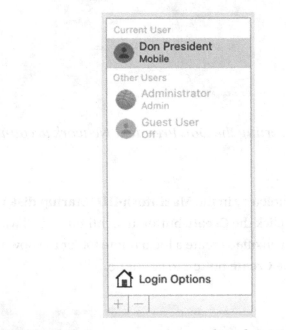

Figure 11-14. *The user account is now listed as Mobile*

Pro Tip   Please note that if multiple Network users need to access this Mac while it is offline, you would need to convert each user account on this Mac from Network to Mobile. Right now, the only Active Directory user who can sign into this MacBook Pro when it's disconnected from the network is Don President.

As we have demonstrated, adding a Mac to a Windows domain requires almost no additional configuration on the Windows server and no extensions to Active Directory to simply allow for authentication and support for cached credentials using the Mobile user account type in *macOS*. We have added the Mac to the domain interactively, but we can also automate this task by using a Configuration Profile or via a script.

USING A CONFIGURATION PROFILE TO ADD A MAC TO ACTIVE DIRECTORY

Before you begin this exercise, you should start with a clean install *macOS* on a test Mac. You should name it and create a computer record in Active Directory to match. Then using the method you prefer, you should enroll it in MDM and promote it to User Approved so we have full access to all of the Configuration Profile options.

I have built a test Mac called **101-2019MPRO** and named it accordingly (including the Local Hostname and hostname). I have added it to Profile Manager, and I have created a computer record in AD for it, but have not yet joined it to the domain.

1. Open Profile Manager and browse to our **101-2019MPRO** Mac in the **Devices** section. Click the **Settings** tab and then click the **Edit** button to apply a new Configuration Profile setting.

2. Configure the **General** payload as we have in the past, ensuring that **Automatic Push** is enabled, and enter an optional profile description.

3. Scroll down to the **macOS** section of the available payloads and choose the **Directory** payload and click the **Configure** button.

4. Customize the payload as shown in Figure 11-15. Note that we are provided with a few new options including one to create Mobile accounts at login for all of our domain users the first time they sign into this Mac. Because we already have a computer record in AD, we will not specify the path to the specific OU.

Figure 11-15. *Configure the Directory payload for binding to our Active Directory domain*

Pro Tip   There are some optional settings under **Mappings** and **Administrative** tabs that we will leave at the default for this exercise, but I encourage you and your Windows system administrator to look at these and determine the best settings for your particular environment. The option for how often the domain password changes (the default is every 14 days) on the client computer is particularly interesting if your machines will be off of the local area network for longer periods of time.

5. Once you have customized the payload, click the **OK** button to save the configuration and close out of the Configuration Profile editor. Click the **Save** button in Profile Manager to apply the settings to the **101-2019MPRO** client as shown in Figure 11-16.

Push Settings: 101-2019MPRO
1 of 1 in progress

Target	Settings	Status	Last Updated
101-2019MPRO	Settings for 101-2019MPRO	In Progress	12/30/19 at 11:39 AM

Figure 11-16. *Applying our domain payload to our test Mac using MDM*

It should complete the Push Settings task successfully, and your Mac will now be configured to sign into the domain. Note that upon signing in for the first time, it is converting Don President to a Mobile account type on the machine automatically.

Pro Tip   You may also want to configure payloads for things like
Active Directory certificates or the login window to further customize
the user experience or apply any required security certificates and
include those along with your Directory payload.

USING A SCRIPT TO BIND A MAC TO ACTIVE DIRECTORY

Apple also provides a command line tool called dsconfigad for scripting
the Active Directory configuration. Using this command within Apple Remote
Desktop's **Send Unix** task can be effective for joining multiple Macs to the
domain at once and further automates the process. This is particularly useful if
you are not using an MDM solution at your organization.

Before you begin this exercise, you should start with a clean install *macOS*
on a test Mac. You should name it and create a computer record in Active
Directory to match. I have built a test Mac called **101-2013MPRO** and named
it accordingly, but this time I have left the hostname as *unset* so I can share a
shortcut with you during this exercise. I have created a computer record in AD
for it, but have not yet joined it to the domain.

1. We are going to interactively develop this script on our test Mac
    using the Terminal app, but once you have perfected it, you can
    create a template in Apple Remote Desktop and apply it to your
    entire Mac fleet. Open the **Terminal** on your **101-2013MPRO** to
    get started.

2. We are going to write a quick little script that will capture the
    Mac's Computer Name and save it as a variable, and then
    using the `scutil --set` command, it will set the hostname
    accordingly. So at the command prompt in the Terminal, type

    `HOSTNAME=$(network setup -getcomputername) scutil`
    `--set HostName $HOSTNAME`

    Press **enter** and then press **enter** again when prompted with
    the `HostName [computer name]` output and then enter
    the local Administrator password when prompted. Once it
    completes that change and you are at the command prompt
    again, enter `scutil --get HostName`, and it should now
    match the others as `101-2013MPRO`. If you use this script in
    Apple Remote Desktop, it will always change the hostname on
    the Mac client to match the Computer Name. At this point, your
    Terminal window should look similar to Figure 11-17.

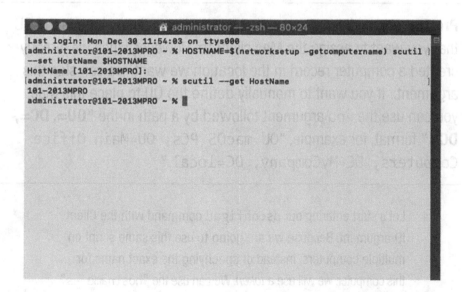

Figure 11-17. *Using the script to copy the Computer Name to the*
hostname

3. Now that our Computer Name and hostname are consistent, we are ready to join the domain using the dsconfigad command. You can look at the manual for dsconfigad to read more about what this command does and additional options, but for this exercise we will stick to the basics. We need to define four arguments:

   a. The **Client ID** (-c) represents the name we want to use to join the Mac to the domain.

   b. The **Administrator account** (-u) represents the username of a Domain Admin account.

   c. The **Administrator password** (-p) represents the password for that Domain Admin account.

   d. The **Domain** (-domain) represents the domain we are adding our Mac to.

Pro Tip One additional option that you can also define here is the OU that you want to assign the Mac client to. However, since we already created a computer record in the location we want, we can skip this argument. If you want to manually define the OU to place this Mac, you can use the -ou argument followed by a path in the **"OU=, DC=, DC="** format, for example, "OU=macOS PCs, OU=Main Office Computers, DC=MyCompany, DC=local."

---

4. Let's start entering our dsconfigad command with the Client ID argument. Because we are going to use this same script on multiple computers, instead of specifying the exact name for this computer, we will use a *token*. We can use the "hostname -s" token so that it automatically applies the hostname of this Mac

as the Client ID in the script. This will mimic the behavior of the GUI when we join a Mac to the domain using the *Users & Groups System Preference*.

5.   Next, we will specify the username and password for the Domain Admin account for our MyCompany.local domain. Finally, we will add the argument that specifies the domain name. Your finished script with all of the arguments should look something like Figure 11-18.

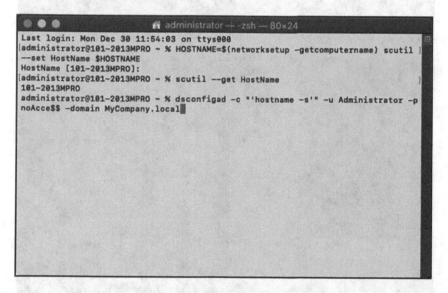

Figure 11-18.   *The full script that renames the computer and adds it to the domain*

```
dsconfigad -c "'hostname -s'" -u Administrator
-p noAcce$$ -domain MyCompany.local
```

6.   It will prompt you to enter the password of the local
     Administrator account. After a minute or two, it will complete
     successfully. Open the *Users & Groups System Preference* and
     click the **Login Options** button to confirm that the Windows
     domain is now listed with a green indicator icon next to the
     Network Account Server as shown in Figure 11-19.

Figure 11-19. *After the script runs, we can confirm that our Mac is*
on the domain in the Users & Groups System Preference

Pro Tip   There are additional commands that you can use with
`dsconfigad` to set additional settings like `-mobile enable` to
support the Mobile account options and `-passinterval` to adjust
the frequency that the domain computer password changes so that
systems that are off of the network for prolonged periods of time do
not fall off of the domain. If you have questions about this, consult
with your Windows system administrator to determine if there is a
need for this or other options.

We have successfully configured Active Directory and joined our Mac
using three different methods. Now that we have our Mac on the domain,
we can access other resources on our Windows server.

Using Profile Manager to Mimic Microsoft Group Policy

We are starting to check off these various integration tasks for Don
President's MacBook Pro. He can sign in with his Active Directory
credentials, and he can log in while his machine is offline. However, we
still need to configure his Mac to conform to our corporate standards.
That could include a number of things defined in our Windows Group
Policy including the default wallpaper, how long it takes for a screen saver
to begin, if a screen saver requires a password, energy saver settings like
when to put the computer or display to sleep, and the default home page
just to name a few.

Fortunately, most of these options are available to us in Profile
Manager, and we can use a Configuration Profile to provide these settings
to Don's Mac and *mimic* the settings we have built into our company's
GPO. For the purposes of this demonstration, we will simply set the energy
saver and some custom Safari settings. To do this, open Profile Manager

and browse to our **101-2019MBP** computer in **Devices**. Click the **Settings** tab and then click **Edit**.

Let's configure the Energy Saver payload first. Click **Energy Saver** and then click the **Configure** button to define the settings for this payload. Your settings should look similar to mine in Figure 11-20.

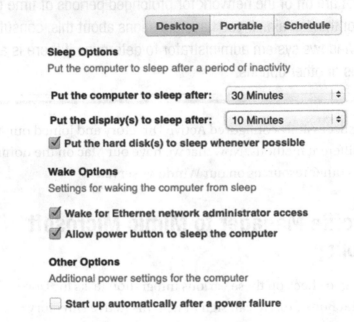

Figure 11-20. Configure the Energy Saver payload

Next, we need to do something a little more customized to configure Safari's settings. We are going to add a new payload called **Custom Settings**, and we will configure it as shown in Figure 11-21. The way that this works is that we are going to override the local user's settings with ours for a specific application—in this case, Safari. We are going to enter **com. apple.Safari** into the **preference domain** field, and then we can add items and define specific behaviors on a per-key basis as if we were creating our own custom *.plist** xml file.

Figure 11-21. Creating custom keys and values for Safari to customize the user experience

You may wonder where I found these options that I am using to override the default behavior of Safari. This is going to vary by application, but typically I look for the corresponding ***.plist** file in the *~/Library/ Preferences/* directory. The easiest applications to modify are those that save their settings there, and then I can simply upload the modified ***.plist** file into the **Custom Settings** payload in Profile Manager using the **Upload File** button. Unfortunately, some applications (like Safari) are a bit trickier.

Safari has a file called **com.apple.Safari.manifest** in Safari.app bundle ➤ **Contents** ➤ **Resources** ➤ **com.apple.Safari.manifest** ➤ **Contents** ➤ **Resources**. I know, it's buried! If you open this xml file in TextEdit, you will see various keys and their matching options as shown in Figure 11-22.

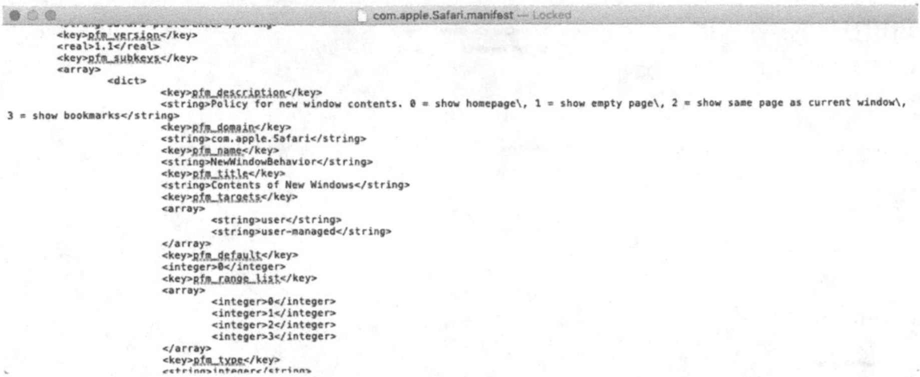

Figure 11-22. *The key and value options for overriding the Safari preferences*

I picked a few of these to add to my **Custom Settings** payload and manually added them by clicking the **Add Item** button and entering the values. As for the MyCompany home page, I used a **string** type to define the URL to www.msn.com. For the purposes of this demonstration, we will call that our company's "Intranet home page." You could put any URL in here and apply it as the new default home page in Safari.

Pro Tip   When you choose to upload a *.**plist** preference file for a specific application, it will allow you to adjust the Property List Values in a way that is similar to using a Group Policy Administrative Template. Creating Custom Settings payloads for applications can take a lot of time, but it is worth the effort if you have hundreds or thousands of Macs to manage.

Click the **OK** button to close the Configuration Settings window and then click the **Save** button to apply the settings to our Mac. Switch back over to Don's MacBook Pro and launch Safari. You will see that our new window and new tab behavior is now set to load the home page instead of favorites, and the home page that loads is `www.msn.com` as we defined in our Custom Settings payload. Your screen should look similar to Figure 11-23.

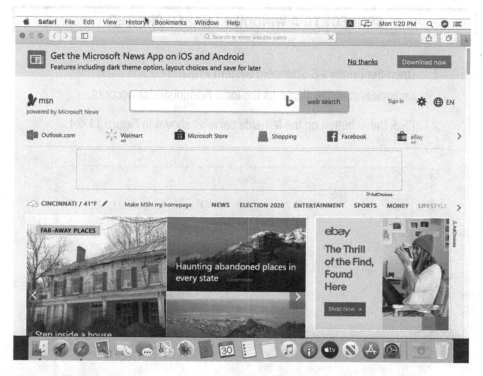

Figure 11-23. *Our customized settings applied to Safari on our test Mac*

Windows Printer Sharing Integration

The next item on our to-do list for Don is to map his network printer to his Mac. We have an HP LaserJet 9050 printer in the main office that is shared from our Windows server. Don has permission to print to the shared printer, and all we need to do is connect to it from his Mac. You can perform this task while signed in as Don.

CONNECT TO A WINDOWS SHARED PRINTER

1. Open the Printers & Scanners System Preference and click the padlock and authenticate as the local Administrator account.

2. Click the + button on the left-side pane as shown in Figure 11-24.

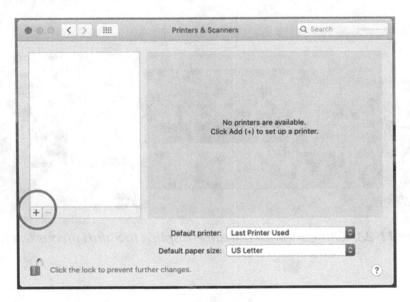

Figure 11-24. *Add a new printer using the Printers & Scanners System Preference*

3. The Mac will search for available network printers in the
    directory domain and will list them. We will select our printer
    from the list, and the under the Use pop-up menu, we will
    choose Select Software and then browse for the HP LaserJet
    Series PCL driver. Once your window looks like Figure 11-25,
    click the Add button to finish the process. Print a test page to
    make sure it worked.

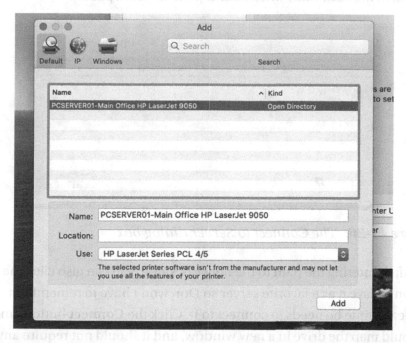

Figure 11-25. *Find our network printer and select the proper driver*

Windows File Sharing Integration

Next up, we have some Windows file sharing to configure. Don will need
access to the **Executive Shared** drive on his Mac, and the sales manager
will need to access the same network drive on her *iPad* so she can update
the daily sales report that Don reviews. We will start with connecting to the
network share on Don's Mac.

macOS File Sharing

While signed in as Don, we can use the **Go** menu ➤ **Connect to Server**
option to manually map the **Exec Shared** drive that is hosted on our
Windows server. As shown in Figure 11-26, enter the entire path to the
share. As a best practice, you may want to use the FQDN when defining the
server name and note that on the Mac, we need to use the *forward-slash*
instead of the *back-slash* when defining the network path.

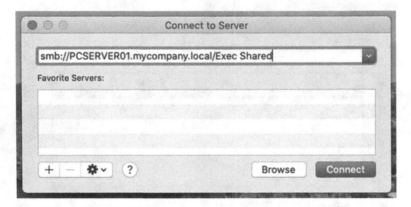

Figure 11-26. *The Connect to Server dialog box*

After entering the path to the network share, you can also click the +
button to save it as a favorite server so Don won't have to remember the
path each time he needs to connect to it. Click the **Connect** button, and
it should map the drive in a new window, and it should not require any
additional authentication as we are already signed into the MacBook Pro
with Don's domain account.

Pro Tip   Most likely you will want to automatically map Don's network drives at login like we do on Windows. To do this, you can go to the *Users & Groups System Preference* ➤ **Login Items** tab; and using the **+** button, you can add the network volume to the list as shown in Figure 11-27. That way upon logging into the Mac, it will attempt to connect to these drives automatically.

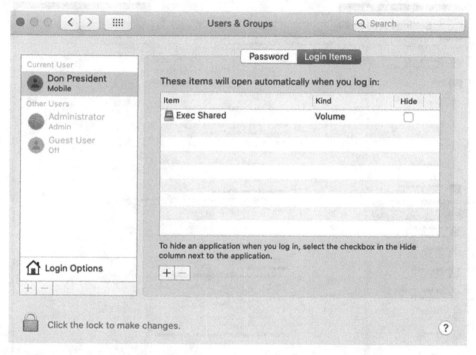

Figure 11-27. *Adding the Exec Shared volume to the Login Items for Don President*

Pro Tip   You can also configure an MDM payload for mapping network drives automatically at login. As you can see in Figure 11-28, you can select to add an **Authenticated Network Mount** and then specify the file sharing protocol, the server name, and the name of the share.

Figure 11-28.   *Adding a Mount Point in the Login Items payload via Profile Manager*

iPadOS File Sharing

Now that Don is all set on his Mac, let's switch over to Sally's new iPad.
Since she is running *iPadOS*, she has an additional option in the Files app
that allows her to connect to a network share. To access this option, open
the Files app from the Home Screen and then tap the **...** button and select
Connect to Server as shown in Figure 11-29.

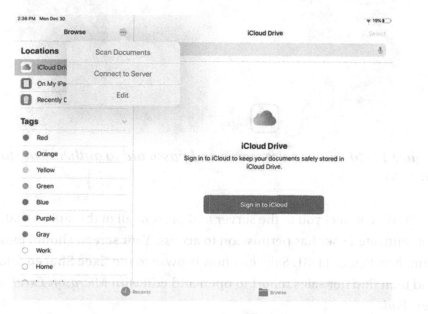

Figure 11-29. *Accessing the Connect to Server option in the Files App*

When it prompts for a server path, enter **smb://PCSERVER01.
mycompany.local** (or the server's IP address) into the **Server** field and
tap the **Connect** button. It will prompt you to authenticate, so go ahead
and enter the username and password for someone who has access to the
Windows shares. I'm using *sjones* in Figure 11-30, but *dpresident* would
also work. After entering the user's credentials, click the **Next** button to
continue.

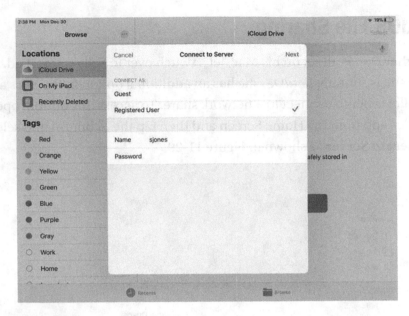

Figure 11-30. *Enter a username and password to authenticate to the file server*

It will connect you to the server and present all of the shares that your authenticated user has permission to access. Your screen should look similar to Figure 11-31. Sally can now browse to the **Exec Shared** folder and then find her sales report to open and edit with *Microsoft Excel* on her *iPad*.

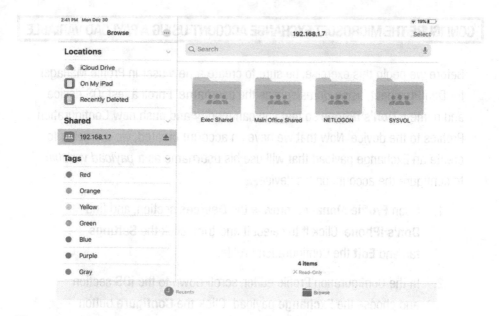

Figure 11-31. *Browsing our network file share from the iPad*

We have successfully configured local Windows file sharing on both *macOS* and *iPadOS* clients. Users of Apple devices can seamlessly share data with users on Windows PCs.

Microsoft Exchange Integration

Apple provides *Microsoft Exchange* integration at the operating system level on both *macOS* and *iOS*. You can use a Configuration Profile to configure the Exchange account settings for Mail, Contacts, Calendars, and Tasks. For Don's new *iPhone 11*, we will simply configure the Exchange settings for his device remotely using Profile Manager. For his Mac, he wants to use Microsoft Outlook, so we will need to configure that manually after we download and activate the Office 365 applications in the next section.

CONFIGURE THE MICROSOFT EXCHANGE ACCOUNT USING A PAYLOAD VARIABLE

Before we begin this exercise, be sure to create a new user in Profile Manager
for Don President, using *dpresident* as the username. Enroll a test iOS device
and name it **Don's iPhone** so that you can modify and push new Configuration
Profiles to the device. Now that we have an account created, we are going to
create an Exchange payload that will use his username as a *payload variable*
to configure the account on his device.

1. Open **Profile Manager**, browse the **Devices** section, and find
   Don's iPhone. Click it to select it and then click the **Settings**
   tab and **Edit** the Configuration Profile.

2. In the Configuration Profile editor, scroll down to the **iOS** section
   and choose the **Exchange** payload. Click the **Configure** button
   to specify the settings.

3. Enter the Exchange server information into the various
   fields as required by the Exchange payload as shown in
   Figure 11-32. For the username, we will use **%short_
   name%** instead of *dpresident*. What that will do is allow
   us to apply this payload to other users in our organization,
   and at the time that the Configuration Profile is applied, the
   %short_name% variable will resolve to the current user's
   username, in this case *dpresident*.

Figure 11-32. *Setting the Exchange settings by using a payload variable*

4. Scroll down to the **Enabled Services** section of the payload and ensure all of these are checked as shown in Figure 11-33. This will enable the entire *iOS* to access data from Microsoft Exchange, including the Phone app's Address Book.

491

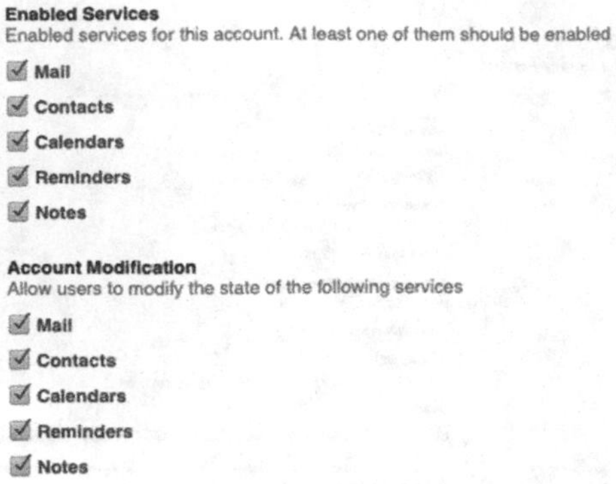

Enabled Services
Enabled services for this account. At least one of them should be enabled

☑ Mail

☑ Contacts

☑ Calendars

☑ Reminders

☑ Notes

Account Modification
Allow users to modify the state of the following services

☑ Mail

☑ Contacts

☑ Calendars

☑ Reminders

☑ Notes

Figure 11-33.   Configure which services are enabled

5.   Click the **OK** button to save the configuration payload and then click **Save** to apply. It will prompt the user for their password when the Profile applies, and then Exchange will be completely configured.

Pro Tip Note that if your company is using some of the MDM features included in ActiveSync, those will also apply to the device. For example, things like minimum passcode requirements will apply to the device, and whichever payload has the greater restriction will take precedence over the others. For example, if you require a minimum passcode length of four characters in Profile Manager but ActiveSync is set to require a minimum of six characters, the device will prompt the user to set a new six-digit passcode before Exchange data will begin to sync to the device.

Whether you are using BYOD or you are managing company-owned devices in Profile Manager, you can see how using a Configuration Profile to apply specific settings like Microsoft Exchange would be preferable to manually configuring every individual device.

Microsoft Office 365 Applications and OneDrive

The next step is to install the Office 365 applications to Don's MacBook Pro. While we are at it, we can install Word and Excel on his iPhone too. Using Profile Manager, browse to the specific device and use the **Apps** tab to apply copies of Word, Excel, PowerPoint, Outlook, and OneDrive to his Mac as shown in Figure 11-34.

Figure 11-34. *Installing the Microsoft Office 365 applications on Don's MacBook Pro*

This is pretty simple and straightforward because it's the same process we followed in Chapter 9. Set the **Installation Mode** to **Automatic** and click the **Save** button to push the configuration and begin the application installation process. It will take a fair amount of time to install all of these applications, and you can use the Active Tasks window to monitor the progress until they have completed.

Activating the Office 365 Applications

Once the Office applications have finished installing on Don's MacBook Pro, we can launch one of them and use the activation wizard to authenticate with our O365 account and activate the software license as shown in Figure 11-35.

Figure 11-35. *Click the button to sign into an existing O365 account to activate*

While we have Microsoft Outlook open, we can follow the prompts to configure the Exchange information and finish syncing with the mail server. We now have Don's email fully configured and ready to go. We can let it sync his inbox in the background while we configure his OneDrive.

Pro Tip   If your user still has Personal Folders (***.pst**) files, once you have migrated those files to the Mac, you can import them into Outlook for Mac using the **Import** function under the **Outlook** menu.

Configuring OneDrive for Business

While Outlook is busy refreshing his inbox in the background, we can open **OneDrive** from the */Applications* folder. When prompted, enter Don's email address and Office 365 password to continue. We will choose the */Users/dpresident/* directory for the location of our OneDrive folder as shown in Figure 11-36. Choose to **Open at login** to allow Don's files to sync automatically and follow the prompts to complete the setup wizard.

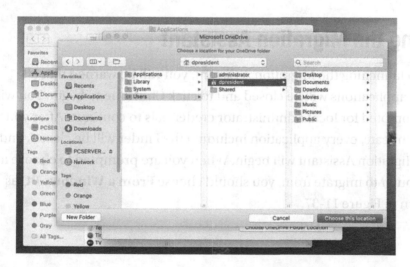

Figure 11-36. *Select Don's home directory as the location for his OneDrive folder*

We have now finished configuring Office 365 and Microsoft OneDrive for Business on Don's MacBook Pro.

Migrating Users from Windows to macOS

If he was using OneDrive to store all of his data and wasn't using **.pst** files on his Windows PC, there may not be much left to migrate. However, many users will still have data on their old PC that needs to be moved to their Mac. To check the last box on this PC to Mac migration for Don President, we need to migrate any remaining data over to his Mac.

Fortunately, Apple provides a pretty useful migration tool to assist in this process. To get started, make sure both his new Mac and his old PC are connected to the same network and then browse to the */Applications/ Utilities/* folder on Don's Mac and open the **Migration Assistant** utility.

Using the Migration Assistant

Upon launching the Migration Assistant, you will be warned that all open applications will be closed and to click **Continue** to begin. You will be prompted for local Administrator credentials to continue. After you authenticate, every application including the Finder will be closed, and the Migration Assistant will begin. When you are prompted to choose a computer to migrate from, you should choose **From a Windows PC** as shown in Figure 11-37.

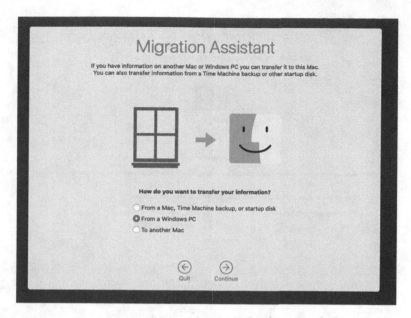

Figure 11-37. *The Migration Assistant using the Windows PC option*

On Don's old Windows PC, open a browser and go to www.apple.
com/migrate-to-mac and download the **Windows Migration Assistant**.
When prompted, go ahead and **run** the **setup.exe** that downloads and step
through the setup wizard to complete the installation and any additional
components that are required. Once it is finished with the installation,
open the **Windows Migration Assistant** application from the Start menu
or the Windows Desktop. Follow the prompts to until you see the name of
the PC appear on your Mac as shown in Figure 11-38.

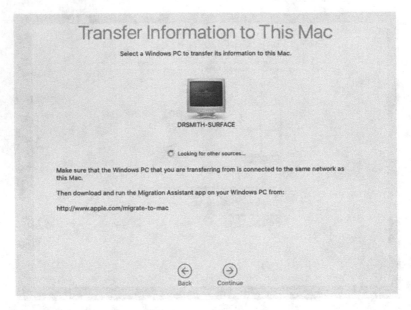

Figure 11-38. *Selecting the PC to migrate from*

When the computer you want to migrate from appears, **select it** and then click **Continue**. Switch back to the Windows PC and ensure that the security codes match between the Mac and Windows PC. Once you confirm that they do, click the **Continue** button on the Windows PC. It will begin gathering data and communicating with the new Mac. This may take several minutes.

When you are prompted to select various files and user accounts, **select the relevant information** as shown in Figure 11-39. Once you have selected the information to migrate, click the **Continue** button.

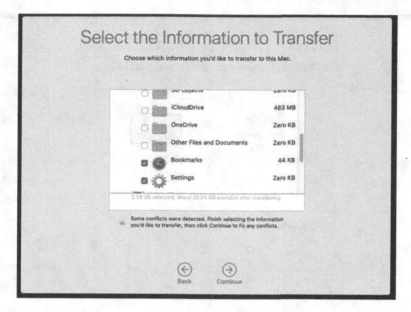

Figure 11-39. *Select the files and settings you wish to migrate*

It will prompt you to authenticate as the Administrator on the
Mac. Click the **Authorize** button when prompted and enter the local
Administrator credentials. Then click the **Continue** button to proceed. It
will now begin transferring the data over the network from the old PC to
the new Mac as shown in Figure 11-40.

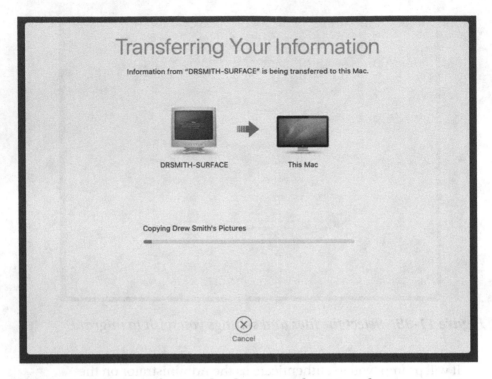

Figure 11-40. Transferring the data over the network

Moving the Migrated Data into Place

By default there will be some cleanup to do after the data is migrated if you use the Migration Assistant. When it completes, you'll be able to sign in with the new local user account, and all of the data will be available in the new home directory. To finish with the migration, we will need to use the **Get Info** settings on the migrated user's **home** directory and then apply **read-only permissions** to the *entire directory* for the **Everyone** group on this computer. You can do this using the **Sharing & Permissions** section of the **Get Info** dialog box and choosing to **apply to enclosed items** from the **Advanced Settings pop-up menu** as shown in Figure 11-41.

Figure 11-41. *Using the Get Info* ➤ *Sharing & Permissions option to change permissions to the migrated folders*

Now we can sign in as Don President and browse the old user folder and collect any data we may want including files in the ***migrateduser/ Library/Safari/*** directory which includes our old Internet Explorer Favorites shown in Figure 11-42. **Drag and drop** that directory into ***dpresident/Library/Safari*** folder to restore access to them.

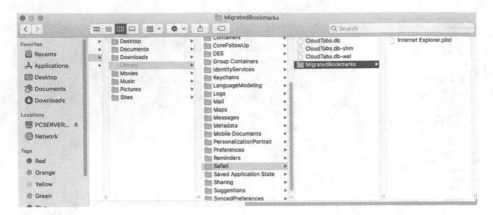

Figure 11-42. *Moving Safari data from the migrated Library folder*

Once we have copied all the user data, confirm that the migrated data is user accessible as shown in Figure 11-43. Next, we can open the *Users & Groups System Preference* and delete the migrated user account from the Mac. The migration is now complete.

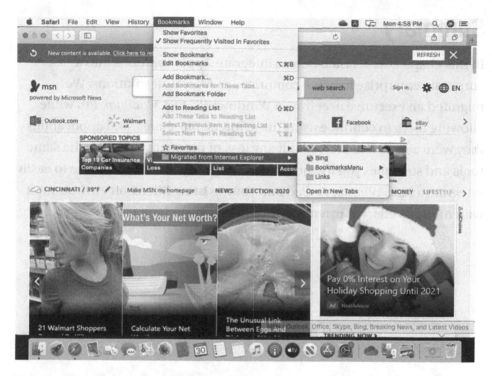

Figure 11-43. *Confirming that the migrated IE Favorites are available in Don's Safari Bookmarks menu*

Pro Tip   Unless I have a lot of data to migrate, I prefer to use OneDrive to move the user's data off of the old PC and onto the new one. I will export the Internet Explorer Favorites using the **File ➤ Export** option in IE and then save them to a single directory. I can then import them into Safari on the new Mac. This method backs up the user's data in Microsoft's cloud and speeds up the restore process because I don't have to copy data between two home directories and delete the user account that was created by the Migration Assistant.

Summary

In this chapter, we learned how to integrate Apple solutions into a corporate enterprise network comprised of Microsoft solutions. We migrated an executive user from a Windows PC to a *MacBook Pro* while allowing them to continue using the printers, file shares, and applications they were accustomed to without any loss of productivity. Using the same tools and strategies you learned in this chapter, you should be able to easily integrate a Mac, iPhone, or iPad into your existing Microsoft environment with minimal effort or extensive IT infrastructure changes.

CHAPTER 12

Mass Provisioning of iOS Devices

Introduction

Up to this point, we have been working with one or two test devices, but
now we are going to configure our Profile Manager MDM to facilitate
a mass deployment of iOS devices. In this chapter, we are going to put
some of our iOS skills to use in a couple of real-world scenarios. The
first scenario is a standard BYOD deployment where we will configure
employee-owned devices into our MDM and provide basic management.
The second scenario is the configuration and deployment of ten company-
owned devices that will be given to a remote sales team and need to be
managed from a distance using over-the-air MDM tools.

Planning Your Deployment

It is always a good idea to sit down and logically plan out your deployments
before developing the technology solution(s) that will ultimately be put
into production. Before we begin working in Profile Manager, let's spend
some time reviewing the requirements, goals, and support needs for each
of our sample scenarios.

© Drew Smith 2020
D. Smith, *Apple macOS and iOS System Administration*,
https://doi.org/10.1007/978-1-4842-5820-0_12

The BYOD Scenario

The first step in any technology deployment is to determine the primary goal(s) that the new service will achieve. The primary goal in this scenario is to reduce the corporate budget that is currently being spent on acquisition and support of company-owned iPhones for employees. The proposed solution is to adopt a bring your own device (BYOD) model that will allow employees to do company work on their personal iPhones. This will enable the employee to select the iPhone model they prefer, they will no longer need to carry two devices, and they will instead get a small monthly stipend added to their take-home pay to help defer the cost of their personal device.

The next step is the requirements gathering phase. You have met with various leaders in your organization, and everyone agrees that instead of continuing to provide company-owned iPhones to each employee, the best strategy going forward is to allow employees to use their personal iPhones on the corporate network. You have discussed the various security requirements, data loss prevention policies, and device recovery scenarios with executive leadership. You have concluded that users will need to onboard their personal devices into your MDM solution to ensure that devices comply with these requirements.

To secure these personal devices and ensure compliance with corporate information security standards, we have determined that any BYOD device must have the following controls in place:

- Minimum passcode lock that changes every 90 days

- Remote wipe capabilities in case the device is lost

- Configuration of corporate office Wi-Fi access

- Configuration of VPN services when working remotely

- Force encrypted backups to secure company data in the event of a local backup

- Disable Notifications on the lock screen to protect potentially sensitive data (e.g., email previews)

We will need to ensure that our BYOD Configuration Profile provides all of these features later on in this chapter.

iPad Deployment to the Remote Sales Team

Similar to the BYOD scenario, our first step is to determine the goals of the technology project. The goal of this deployment is also fairly simple. The company has ten remote sales people, each located in different parts of the country and always on the move. The VP of Sales and Marketing has asked IT for an iPad for each member of the sales team so they can stay in touch while on the road. This has been budgeted, approved, and purchased. The iPads are ready for deployment and configuration for each remote user.

As part of the requirements gathering process, the VP of Sales had a couple of requests from IT. First, they wanted the devices to be configured in such a way that the sales team had to use approved tools and channels to communicate with clients. For example, they want them to use Salesforce CRM and Zoom so that the communications can be tracked and managed.

The VP of Sales was concerned that having FaceTime, Messages, and things like that available to the sales team may lead to customer contact and communication that falls outside of the company standard. Along those same lines, the VP has requested that only approved Apps be allowed on the iPads and that the App Store should be locked down. Finally, it is important that the devices can be remotely managed and if necessary wiped and rebuilt over the air if there was any software issue with the devices. These sales people travel and cannot be without their device for any considerable length of time, and they are not always near an *Apple Retail Store*.

To enable these restrictions and provide over-the-air configuration/reconfiguration, we need to ensure that the following options are set in Profile Manager for these devices:

- Minimum passcode lock that changes every 90 days

- Remote wipe capabilities in case the device is lost

- Configuration of corporate office Wi-Fi access

- Configuration of VPN services when working remotely

- Enabled MDM enrollment via DEP during the Setup Assistant

- The ability to use iMessage and FaceTime disabled

- The App Store disabled

- Zoom and Salesforce pre-installed

We will need to ensure that our sales team iPad Configuration Profile provides all of these features later on in this chapter.

Anticipated Support Needs

At this point, we have developed our goals and technology strategy for these two deployments. While it is difficult to predict every possible support need, we can anticipate a few things and have a plan in place to address these. For the BYOD scenario, the most common support requirement will be the MDM enrollment process. We will be creating and distributing a company-wide email to our end users that will walk them through the process of onboarding their device, including a web form that allows them to request BYOD services and enrollment step-by-step guide.

For the sales team iPad scenario, we will train our help desk to walk the sales team through the Setup Assistant and provide some basic software troubleshooting including a full reset of the device in the event that it is required. Because we are using over-the-air configuration, anytime a full reset is done on the device, it will automatically configure the correct settings, install the required Apps, and apply any device restrictions. At this point, we are ready to begin the technical work inside Profile Manager.

Configuring Profile Manager for the BYOD Scenario

There are a number of things we need to do to prepare Profile Manager for a BYOD deployment. The first thing we are going to do is to create a device group. Open **Profile Manager** and click the **Device Groups** button on the left sidebar as shown in Figure 12-1.

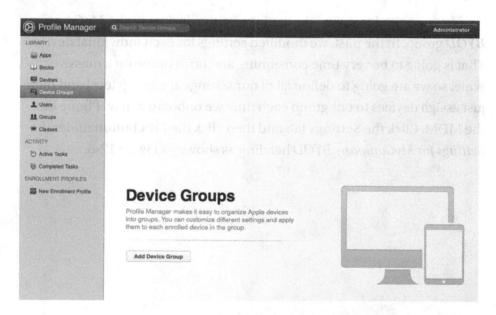

Figure 12-1. *Viewing the Device Groups in Profile Manager*

Go ahead and click the **Add Device Group** button or click the + button on the lower part of the Device Groups pane. **Double-click** the name and rename it *MyCompany BYOD* as shown in Figure 12-2. Click **Save** to apply the name change.

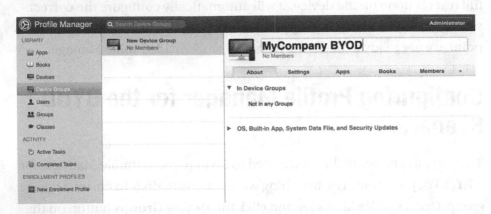

Figure 12-2. *Create a new Device Group*

Next, we need to define the settings for the devices in the *MyCompany BYOD* group. In the past, we modified settings for each individual device. That is going to be very time consuming and error prone on a massive scale, so we are going to define all of our settings at a group level and then just assign devices to our group each time we onboard a new iPhone into the MDM. Click the **Settings** tab and then click the **Edit** button under the *Settings for MyCompany BYOD* heading as shown in Figure 12-3.

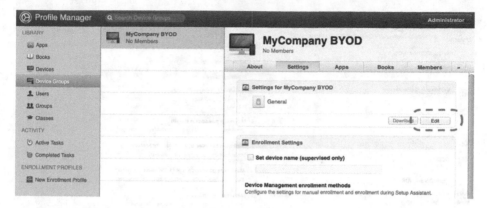

Figure 12-3. *Edit the Configuration Profile for our new Device Group*

Now we are going to configure the Mobile Configuration Profile the same way that we have with individual devices, but this time at the group level. The General payload is similar to what we have done in the past. Just set it to Automatic Push and provide a basic BYOD description. We'll take the default security options because these will not be supervised devices anyway.

Next, we will need to start configuring our payloads to match our requirements from earlier in the chapter. It's important to note that we won't need to configure anything special to enable remote wipe or remote management capabilities as that is automatically set when the device joins our MDM. We do need to configure the other security options.

First up, click the **Passcode** payload, and let's configure that to our corporate standards with the **complex passcode** and the requirement to **change it every 90 days** as shown in Figure 12-4.

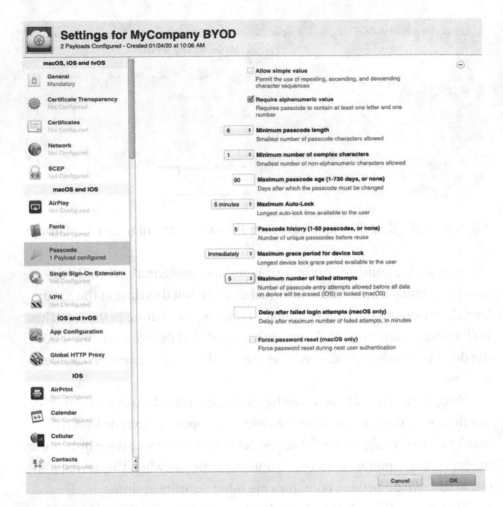

Figure 12-4. *Set the Passcode payload*

Next up is wireless. Click the **Network** payload, and we can configure our corporate wireless network as shown in Figure 12-5. Your settings will vary depending on your network, SSID, security configuration, and so on.

Figure 12-5. *Configure your corporate wireless settings*

Next, we need to configure VPN so click the **VPN** payload and
configure it as shown in Figure 12-6.

Figure 12-6. Configure the VPN payload

Finally, we need to configure a couple of the restrictions. Click the **Restrictions** payload and scroll through the options on the **Functionality** tab. We will need to *enable* **Force encrypted backups** and *disable* **Show Notification Center in Lock screen** as shown in Figure 12-7.

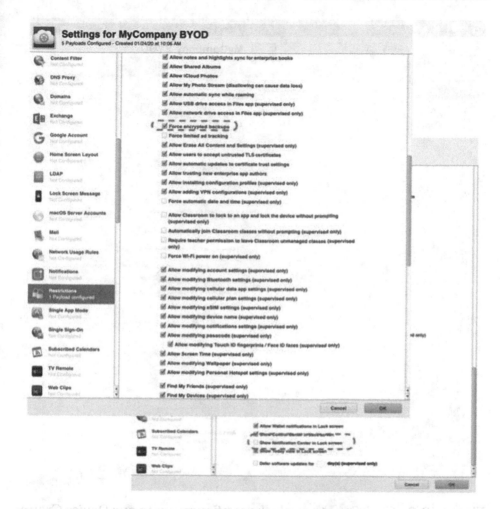

Figure 12-7. *Configure the Restrictions payload*

Now that we have everything configured with our five payloads, click the **OK** button to save the configuration and then click the **Save** button as shown in Figure 12-8 to apply the new settings to the *MyCompany BYOD* device group.

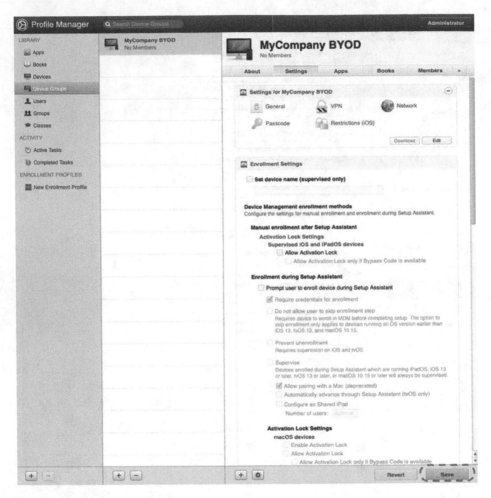

Figure 12-8. *Click Save to apply the configuration to our Device Group*

Excellent! Now we have our BYOD group ready to go, and all devices we add to this group will gain these settings and requirements. The next thing we need to do is add some placeholders for our devices into our MyCompany BYOD device group. Fortunately, this is easily done through the process we defined for our end users to submit a ticket via our web form to request this access.

Pro Tip   You can do this any number of ways depending on the size of your company and the process around stipends, approvals, and so on. This is really up to each individual company. I have seen it where IT just emails out a configuration profile to each user, and I've seen it where there is an entire process where several approval steps occur before IT is given the go-ahead to enable enrollment for a given device.

We have three pending requests for new BYOD members. Let's go ahead and fulfill those requests now by creating matching Placeholders and add those to our MyCompany BYOD device group. You will do this just like we did in previous chapters with one additional step—assigning the placeholder to a device group instead of configuring the settings individually for each device.

Click the **Devices** button on the left sidebar and then click the + button in the lower area of the Devices pane and choose **Add Placeholder**. Enter the placeholder information as shown in Figure 12-9. We'll use Serial Number as our identifier.

Figure 12-9.   *Create a Placeholder for each BYOD device*

Once you have the placeholder for *Dan's iPhone* listed in your Devices column, click the **Device Groups** button on the left sidebar again and click the **MyCompany BYOD** device group to select it. Next, on the **Members** tab, click the + button as shown in Figure 12-10 and select **Add Devices**.

Figure 12-10. *Adding device members to a Device Group*

Click the **Add** button next to *Dan's iPhone* and then click the **Done** button to dismiss the dialog box as shown in Figure 12-11. Click the **Save** button to save the changes we made to the group membership for our *MyCompany BYOD* device group. Repeat these steps for two more placeholder devices and make sure one of them has a serial number that matches your physical test device so we can try this out and see the results.

Figure 12-11. *Add the placeholder to the group*

Now that we have our placeholder devices assigned to the device group, it is time to provide an enrollment profile to our users so they can add their device to the MDM and receive our configuration settings. There are a couple of ways to do this. If your Profile Manager server is connected to a company LDAP such as Active Directory, you could associate ***Dan's iPhone*** with his user account and allow him to onboard the device using the ***My Devices Portal*** and restrict the enrollment to assigned devices as shown in Figure 12-12.

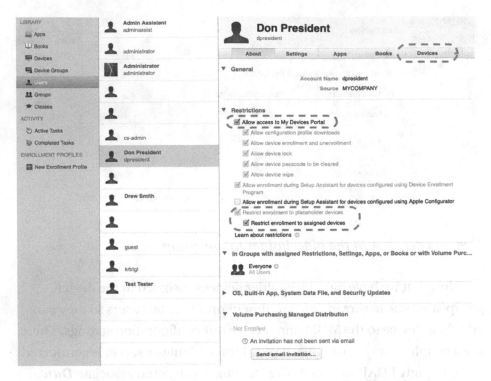

Figure 12-12. *Select an existing user account and assign the device to the user and allow them to access the My Devices Portal*

You could also simply create a new Enrollment Profile and email it to the user so they can access it from their phone as an attachment and follow the prompts to install it. Alternately, you could house the Enrollment Profile on an internal web server and point users to that location to download and install it.

Finally, you can point users to the *My Devices Portal* and configure the **Everyone** group to allow enrollment but ensure that **Restrict enrollment to placeholder devices** is *enabled* as shown in Figure 12-13. Any of these options are acceptable, and you will need to decide what will work best for your particular case.

Figure 12-13. Configuring the Everyone group for device self-enrollment

For our example, we will use the *My Devices Portal* option for the **Everyone** group. Go ahead and jump on your test iPhone and browse to your MDM server's /mydevices subdirectory. For example, my URL would be https://579testing.com/mydevices. Authenticate, and when the page loads, tap the blue **Enroll** button and follow the prompts to download and install the Enrollment Profile. At this point, it will find the matching Placeholder and begin applying our payloads.

When this is completed, browse your device to ensure that the Wi-Fi, VPN, and applied restrictions are in place. Feel free to wipe the test device using the management options in Profile Manager or remove the profile manually on the device to see the immediate effect. This is the kind of behavior you can expect from a non-supervised BYOD device.

Pro Tip   As the needs of your business change, you may need to update, modify, or add new configuration settings and payloads. You can always modify the settings for the MyCompany BYOD device group and immediately apply those changes to all devices that are a member of the group.

You have now enabled a large-scale BYOD solution. Going forward, all you will need to do is create additional placeholders and have your end users self-enroll, and the MDM will take care of the rest of the work for you.

Configuring Profile Manager for the Sales Team iPad Scenario

Configuring the sales team iPads are also pretty straightforward as we will create a device group and apply the appropriate settings for this scenario as well. The main difference here is that because these are company-owned devices, we will use supervision and DEP to assign the devices to a specific device group and force enrollment during the Setup Assistant activation step.

Let's get started by opening **Profile Manager** and browsing to the **Device Groups** section again. Click the + button to add a new Device Group. This time we will call it *Sales Team iPads*. Click the **Sales Team iPads** device group to select it and then click the **Settings** tab. Click the **Edit** button under the **Settings for Sales Team iPads** section as shown in Figure 12-14.

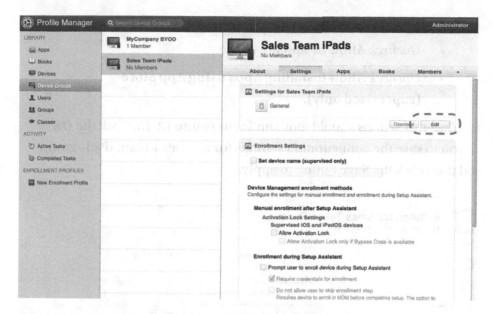

Figure 12-14. *Assigning configuration settings to our new device group*

The first thing we need to do is configure all of the same VPN, Network, and Passcode payloads that we did for the BYOD group. You can go ahead and configure those payloads to match.

Pro Tip   If you have a very large organization and every device will share similar wireless and passcode requirements, you may want to create a Device Group called "Security Standard" or something similar. Next, you can add new Device Groups as members of the Security Standard group in a sort of nested group scenario so you don't have to configure the same settings on multiple groups each time.

Next up, we need to restrict the use of iMessage, FaceTime, and the App Store. Configure the **Restrictions** payload as follows:

- *Uncheck* **Allow iMessage (supervised only)**.

- *Uncheck* **Allow FaceTime (supervised only)**.

- *Uncheck* **Allow removing Apps (supervised only)**.

523

- *Uncheck* **Allow removing system Apps (supervised only)**.

- *Uncheck* **Allow in-app purchase**.

- *Uncheck* **Allow installing Apps using App Store (supervised only)**.

Your restrictions should look similar to Figure 12-15. Click the **OK** button to save the configuration settings for the Sales Team iPads group and then click the **Save** button to apply.

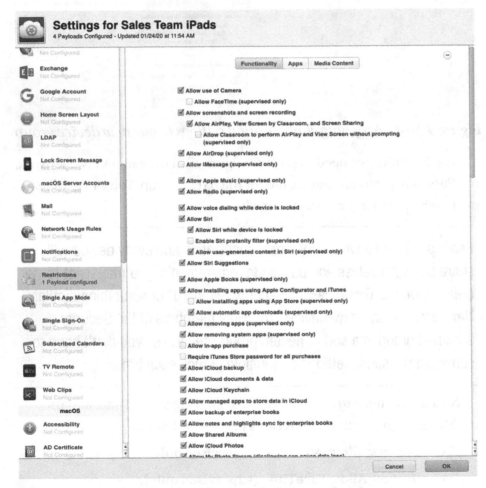

Figure 12-15. *Configuring the Restrictions payload*

Now that we have configured our restrictions and configuration settings, we need to configure the enrollment and Setup Assistant options. From the **Settings** tab, scroll down to the ***Enrollment during Setup Assistant section*** and change the settings to match those in Figure 12-16.

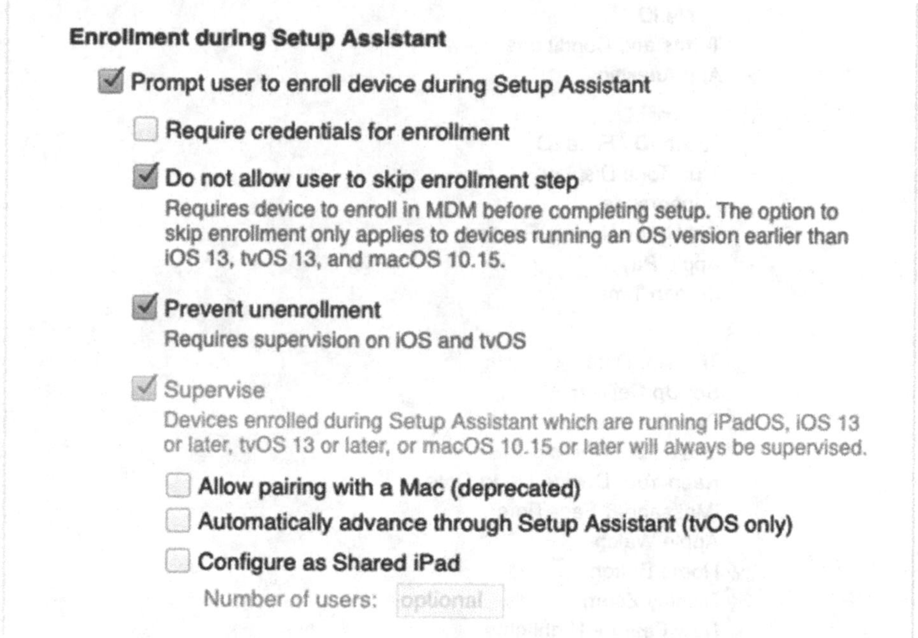

Enrollment during Setup Assistant

☑ Prompt user to enroll device during Setup Assistant

☐ Require credentials for enrollment

☑ Do not allow user to skip enrollment step
Requires device to enroll in MDM before completing setup. The option to skip enrollment only applies to devices running an OS version earlier than iOS 13, tvOS 13, and macOS 10.15.

☑ Prevent unenrollment
Requires supervision on iOS and tvOS

☑ Supervise
Devices enrolled during Setup Assistant which are running iPadOS, iOS 13 or later, tvOS 13 or later, or macOS 10.15 or later will always be supervised.

☐ Allow pairing with a Mac (deprecated)
☐ Automatically advance through Setup Assistant (tvOS only)
☐ Configure as Shared iPad
Number of users: optional

Figure 12-16. *Settings for enabling enrollment during Setup Assistant*

Scroll down a bit further and change the ***Setup Assistant Options*** to suppress a number of settings. This will make it simpler for the end user to step through the device and will hopefully save time and additional calls to your IT help desk. Change your settings to match those in Figure 12-17.

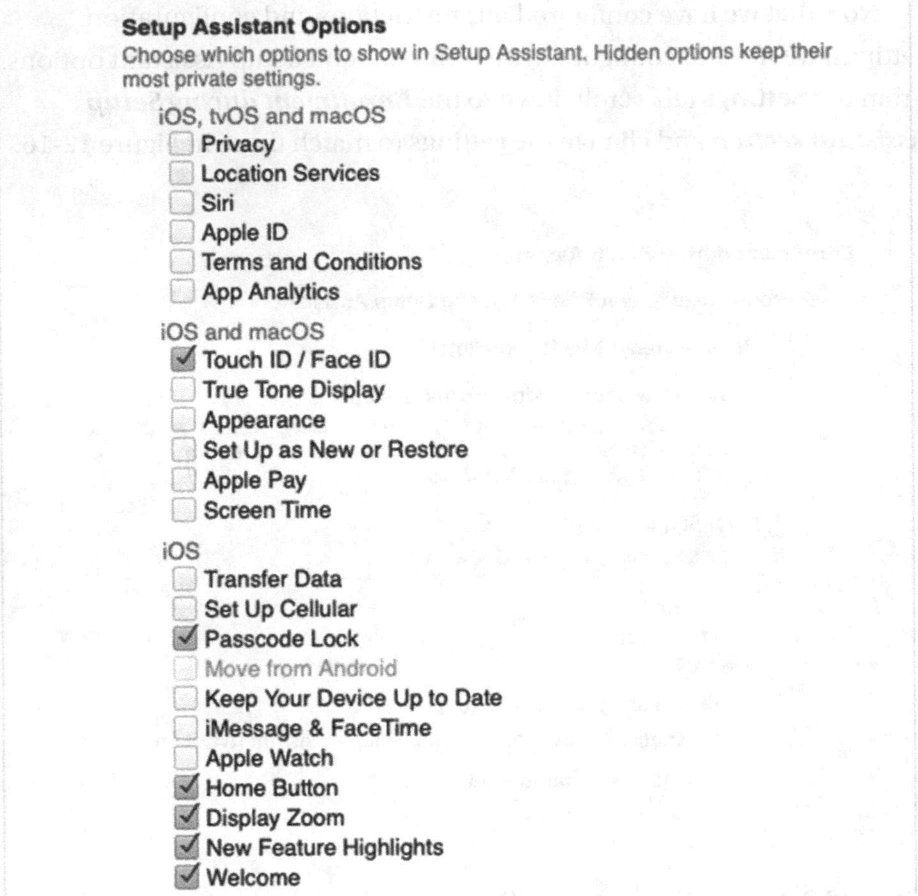

Setup Assistant Options

Choose which options to show in Setup Assistant. Hidden options keep their most private settings.

iOS, tvOS and macOS
- ☐ Privacy
- ☐ Location Services
- ☐ Siri
- ☐ Apple ID
- ☐ Terms and Conditions
- ☐ App Analytics

iOS and macOS
- ☑ Touch ID / Face ID
- ☐ True Tone Display
- ☐ Appearance
- ☐ Set Up as New or Restore
- ☐ Apple Pay
- ☐ Screen Time

iOS
- ☐ Transfer Data
- ☐ Set Up Cellular
- ☑ Passcode Lock
- ☐ Move from Android
- ☐ Keep Your Device Up to Date
- ☐ iMessage & FaceTime
- ☐ Apple Watch
- ☑ Home Button
- ☑ Display Zoom
- ☑ New Feature Highlights
- ☑ Welcome

Figure 12-17. *Uncheck the unwanted Setup Assistant prompts*

Click the **Save** button to apply these settings to the ***Sales Team iPads*** device group.

Pro Tip   Optionally, you can also configure Activation Lock settings and enforce a device name standard at this time. I will typically enable Activation Lock and set a device name.

For now, our work in Profile Manager is done. We need to redeem some Apps and assign our new iPads to our MDM in Apple School/Business Manager next. Theoretically, you should have a way to identify your new iPads using their serial numbers. Check the packing slip or invoice and find the serial numbers for the ten new iPads that we will assign using DEP and then head out to the Apple Management Portal. Depending on your circumstances, this would be `http://school.apple.com` or `http://business.apple.com`.

Sign in there and then go to the *Device Assignments* area. Here we are going to enter the serial numbers for each of our ten iPads that will be going to the sales team. Once you have entered each device into the **Serial Numbers** field, assign it to our MDM using the **Perform Action** drop-down and click **Done** to apply as shown in Figure 12-18.

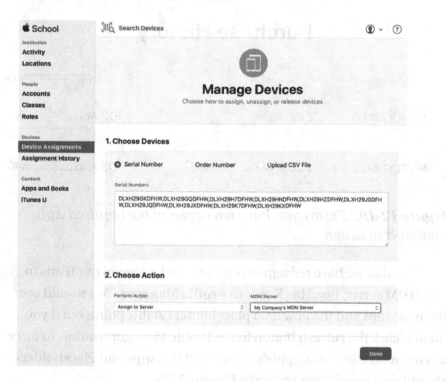

Figure 12-18. *Listing serial numbers separated by commas for all ten of our iPads and assigning them to our MDM server*

Pro Tip   As you have likely already inferred, you can apply all devices from a single order number or upload a *.csv file instead of entering each serial number into the field individually. Since ten is just about the limit as to the number of devices I would like to do manually, I just entered them in by hand.

Once the devices have been assigned successfully, go ahead and jump over to the *Apps and Books* section, and we can redeem the *Zoom* and *Salesforce* Apps. Using the same process that we did in previous chapters with the *Microsoft Office* suite, look up *Salesforce* and *Zoom* and redeem ten copies of each as shown in Figure 12-19.

Purchase History

Order Number	Content Name	Type	Quantity
MV9LY28XLG	Salesforce	iOS App	10
MV9LY28XLG	ZOOM Cloud Meetings	iOS App	10

Figure 12-19. *Ensure you have ten copies of the required Apps available to assign*

Now that we have redeemed our Apps and assigned our iPads to our MDM server, head back over to **Profile Manager**. You should see the new Apps and the new iPad placeholders at this point; but if you do not, click the **refresh** button in the Profile Manager window to force a synchronization with Apple's server, and the Apps and Placeholders should now populate as shown in Figure 12-20.

Figure 12-20. *New placeholder devices are now available courtesy of DEP*

Now that we have our placeholder devices and our App licenses, let's go back to the **Device Groups** area of Profile Manager and click the ***Sales Team iPads*** group to select it. Click the **Apps** tab and then the + button to assign some licenses to this group. Add *Salesforce* and *Zoom* as shown in Figure 12-21 and leave the default **Installation mode** as **Automatic**. Next, click the **OK** button to save these settings and then click **Save** to apply these settings to the device group.

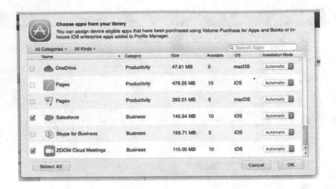

Figure 12-21. *Assigning Apps to our Device Group*

Finally, the last step we need to take is to assign the ten new iPads to the ***Sales Team iPads*** device group. Click the **Members** tab and click the + button in the Members pane and add all ten of the new iPads to this group as shown in Figure 12-22.

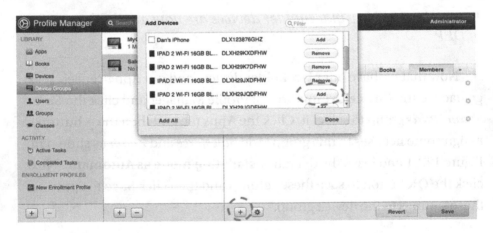

Figure 12-22. *Adding each placeholder iPad to the Device Group*

After you have clicked the **Add** button next to each of the new devices, click the **Done** button and then the **Save** button to apply these changes to the Device Group. At this point, you have added ten placeholder iPads to the *Sales Team iPads* Device Group, configured the settings and restrictions, and assigned the two required Apps. Profile Manager is now configured and ready for these new devices to be deployed to the end users.

You can try this with a test device if you want to add an eleventh iPad to this group. Step through the Setup Assistant on a fresh install of *iPadOS* on a device that is a member of the *Sales Team iPads* group, and you will skip several of the Setup Assistant screens. Now, upon reaching the Home Screen, the Messages, FaceTime, and App Store Apps will be gone, and after a few minutes, the Zoom and Salesforce Apps will appear.

Pro Tip   Because we are enrolling these devices into MDM upon activation during the Setup Assistant, the end user can erase and reset the device as many times as they want to; and once it steps through Setup Assistant again, it will be instantly managed and reconfigured in this exact same way. This effectively allows these remote users to restage their devices on their own as often as needed with minimal assistance from IT.

Summary

In this chapter, we stepped through a couple of scenarios that are common in the day-to-day support of iOS devices in many large- and medium-sized businesses. We put a simple BYOD model into place and developed a process for remotely configuring any number of company-owned iOS devices that can scale from ten devices up to hundreds if needed. Any IT department can follow these basic steps to develop a deployment plan for staging and supporting iOS devices with minimal effort.

CHAPTER 13

Deployment of macOS Clients

Introduction

Throughout this book, we have covered many *macOS* concepts from basic support tools, client utilities, *Profile Manager*, integration with technologies from *Microsoft Corp*, and open source deployment tools like *Munki* and *Munki-Pkg*. In this final chapter, we are going to pull all of these concepts together and step through the process of staging a standard Mac-based office environment.

In this scenario, we are going to deploy ten Macs for a new web design department that our company is hiring for. While the entire department will be using *macOS*-based computers, they will need to interact and share data using the same solutions that the rest of the Windows-based PC users do.

Planning Your Deployment

As we discussed in Chapter 12, it is a good idea to logically plan our deployments before the developing the technology solution that will be put into production. First, we need to understand the systems, infrastructure, and tools available to us. Figure 13-1 provides an updated diagram of our company's network. We have our standard *Windows server*

© Drew Smith 2020
D. Smith, *Apple macOS and iOS System Administration*,
https://doi.org/10.1007/978-1-4842-5820-0_13

and *Active Directory* structure from Chapter 11, our *Munki* environment from Chapter 10, and *Profile Manager* with DEP integration from Chapter 9. Our Mac administrative desktop is running *Apple Remote Desktop* and *MunkiAdmin*. We have all of the required pieces in place to support our department of Mac users.

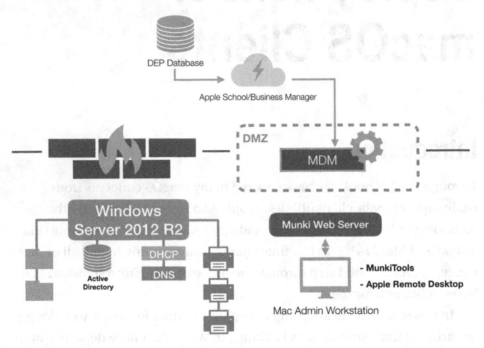

Figure 13-1. *The example company's current network infrastructure*

Next, we can begin our requirements gathering exercise. In discussion with the company leadership, you have heard that while there are ten designers joining the company, this new department is expected to grow exponentially over the next 12–18 months as this new team takes on additional strategic projects for the organization. You also hear that while the size of this new department grows, the IT staffing expense must remain flat. Fortunately, you have the tools necessary to deploy ten or even a hundred new Macs with nearly the same level of effort.

In addition to keeping this a very efficient deployment and support process, we also need to ensure a common user experience with *Windows*. This will minimize support headaches, provide a more consistent office environment, and foster collaboration between users of the diverse platforms. This also has the added benefit of keeping our infrastructure costs in line. Here's a quick hit list of requirements as we build out our Mac deployment project:

- As close to "zero touch" as possible for the IT desktop technicians deploying these systems

- Integration with the company's *Active Directory* and *Office 365* solutions

- Access to Windows-based network shares

- Access to Windows-based network printers

- Desktop security and UI customizations on par with Windows GPO settings

- Suite of required software applications including *Microsoft Office* and *Adobe* products and access to several web browsers for testing

Based on this list, we will need these Macs to be easy for our IT team to set up and deploy, and we can use Device Enrollment Program to point these new machines to our *Profile Manager* environment. We will use *Active Directory* and *Profile Manager* to configure settings and services that closely mirror the company's existing *Windows* PC installation. Finally, we will need to package a couple of *Adobe* installers into *Munki* and deploy *Microsoft Office* via VPP so that the Macs download and install these required applications automatically. Let's get started!

Configuring Active Directory

The very first thing we will do is configure *Active Directory*. As is typical of any new users in my organization, I will need to create a user account for each new hire and add them to the appropriate group. Open **Active Directory Users & Computers** and create ten new user accounts. Name them whatever you would like and set a default password for each. After you have created these accounts, open the **Main Office Group** and add these new hires as members. When completed, the Main Office group should look similar to Figure 13-2.

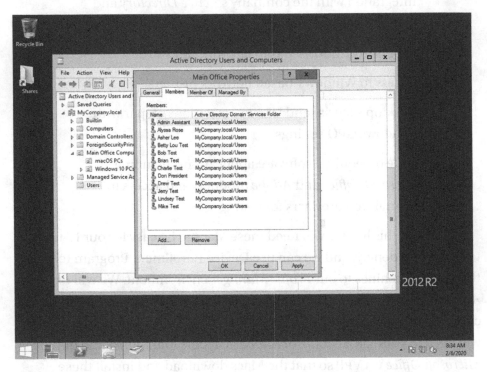

Figure 13-2.   *Create ten new user accounts as members of our Main Office group in Active Directory*

Next, we are going to go to *Main Office Computers* ➤ *macOS PCs OU* and add ten computer records for these new Macs. Go ahead and name these anything you like. I'm going to follow my naming scheme that I used in Chapter 11 for consistency. Once you have created ten new computer records to represent the new Macs we are going to assign to this new web developer team, your *macOS PCs OU* should look like Figure 13-3.

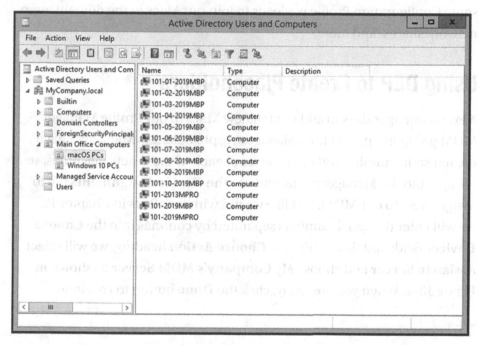

Figure 13-3. *Create ten new computer records in the macOS PCs OU*

At this point, we are done configuring Active Directory.

Configuring Profile Manager

Now that we have our user accounts and computer records created in Active Directory, we are ready to begin configuring *Profile Manager* to enroll our new devices. In this section, we will use DEP to enroll the Macs into our MDM during the *Setup Assistant* and configure Profile Manager to enforce security restrictions using a *Device Group*. We will also create some Configuration Profile payloads to join our Macs to the domain, map network shares, and more.

Using DEP to Create Placeholders

Next on our agenda is to add our ten new Macs to our Profile Manager MDM group in Apple School Manager/Apple Business Manager. I have the ten serial numbers off of the boxes of each of these new machines, so I'll sign into the Manager portal and use the **Device Assignments** tab to assign these to our MDM. Just like we did with the iPads in Chapter 12, we will enter the serial numbers separated by commas into the **Choose Devices** field; and then under the **Choose Action** heading, we will select **Assign to Server** and choose **My Company's MDM Server** as shown in Figure 13-4. When you are ready, click the **Done** button to continue.

Figure 13-4. *Assigning the ten new Macs to our MDM*

When it is done processing the assignments, sign out of the Manager portal. Open **Profile Manager** and go to the **Devices** view. Click the **refresh button** if needed and make sure that all of the new Macs populate into the **Devices** list as shown in Figure 13-5.

Figure 13-5. *After forcing a sync with DEP, the new Macs should appear in our Devices list*

Setting the Device Name

Now that we have all of our *Placeholders* in Profile Manager, we can see they have come in with some basic product information as their default name. We are going to make some changes to the names of these device Placeholders to make it easier to identify them in our list. Using the **Devices** view, click through each device to select it and then click the temporary name in the top-right side of the view to edit the names. **Assign a name** to each of our ten machines that match the names we used when creating new computer records in Active Directory. I have named mine 101-01-2019MBP through 101-10-2019MBP. Next, click the **Settings** tab for each of the devices in this list and check the box next to **Set device named (supervised only),** and it should auto-populate the new name of the Placeholder.

Creating a Device Group

We are going to add all of these Mac Placeholder devices to a *Device Group.* This will allow us to configure the settings at the group level, and each of the Macs in that group will inherit those settings. Click the **Device Groups** button in the left sidebar in Profile Manager. Click the + button in the lower-center column of the page as shown in Figure 13-6, and a new Device Group will appear.

Figure 13-6. Adding a new Device Group

Rename this new group "**Design Team**" and click the **Save** button to apply the name change. The first thing we will do is assign our Placeholder Mac records to this Device Group. Click the **Design Team** Device Group to select it and then click the **Members** tab. Click the + button in the lower-right side of the page and choose **Add Devices**. In the dialog box that appears, click the **Add** button to the right of each of the Mac placeholders as shown in Figure 13-7.

Figure 13-7. *Adding the ten Mac Placeholders into the Design Team Device Group*

Click the **Done** button when you are finished adding devices to the group and then click the **Save** button. We have now successfully created our Device Group.

Configuring MDM Enrollment

We are going to begin by configuring the device enrollment and Setup Assistant settings. We have a few options here that are unique to macOS. In the Device Groups view, click the Design Team group to select it and then click the Settings tab. Scroll down to the Enrollment Settings section where Enrollment during Setup Assistant is listed. Check the box next to Prompt user to enroll device during Setup Assistant. Uncheck the option to require credentials for enrollment and make sure that Do not allow user to skip enrollment step is checked. Your settings should look like Figure 13-8.

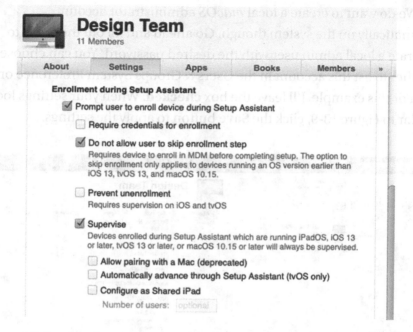

Figure 13-8. *Configuring MDM enrollment during Setup Assistant*

Scroll down further to the **Setup Assistant Options** area. We are only interested in the first two sections and the last section of checkboxes here because these are the only ones that apply to *macOS*. These are the prompts that the computer will ask during the Setup Assistant during the first boot and the subsequent first login by a new end user. We are going to choose to suppress all of these. **Uncheck** every box in this list.

Scroll down further to the **macOS Primary Account Setup** section. Because we are using Active Directory to manage our user accounts, we are not going to create a local Standard user on the machine. If we were not using network user accounts, we could configure this to prompt the user to create their own username/password. For our purposes, we will uncheck the **Prompt user to create an account of type** option.

We do want to create a local *macOS* administrator account automatically on the system though. Go ahead and fill out the fields to generate a local admin user with the desired password. You can choose whether to list this account in the Users & Groups System Preference or not. For this example, I'll leave the box **checked**. When your settings look similar to Figure 13-9, click the **Save** button to apply the settings.

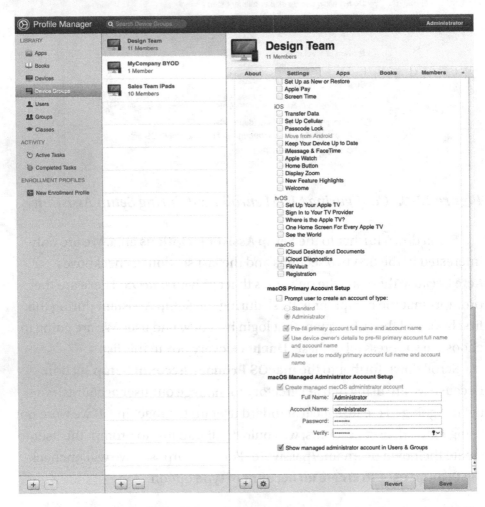

Figure 13-9. *Suppress all Setup Assistant prompts and automatically create a local Administrator account*

Configuration Profile Settings

The last step in Profile Manager is to assign settings to the members of our **Design Team Device Group**. With the Design Team group selected, click the **Settings** tab and then click the **Edit** button under the **Settings for Design Team** heading. This will open our *Configuration Profile* window for assigning restrictions and settings.

We are going to configure a few basic things here to conform to the look and feel of our Windows environment. Start by filling out the **General** payload with the name of the Configuration Profile and description, and set **Security** as **With Authorization** and set a password.

Next, we can configure our **Passcode** payload. Set the passcode requirement to the eight-character minimum passcode length and require complex characters and the delay after login attempts with similar values that we have used several times before in this book.

Next, we are going to set some specific *macOS*-only settings. The first one is the **Directory** payload. Click **Configure** and choose **Active Directory** from the **Directory Type** pop-up menu. We will need to provide the **FQDN** or **IP address** of our Domain Controller as well as username and password for a Domain Admin account. For **Client ID**, I'm using a variable of **%ComputerName%** so that it uses the name we assigned to the machine to match the existing computer record in AD. We will leave the **Organizational Unit** blank because it should join to the correct OU based on the existing record. Your Directory payload should look similar to Figure 13-10.

Figure 13-10. Defining Active Directory settings in the Directory payload

Next, we are going to configure the **Login Items** payload to automatically map the *Main Office Shared* network drive. Click the **Configure** button and, as shown in Figure 13-11, add the SMB share to the Authenticated Network Mounts section.

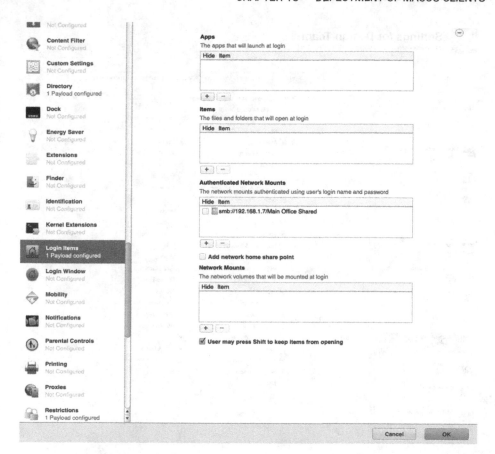

Figure 13-11. *Setting our Main Office Shared drive to mount at login*

Next, we will configure some *restrictions* that are specific to
macOS. Please note that there are two sets of **Restrictions** payloads in this
list. We want to choose the one under the **macOS** heading. Click **Configure**
and start by restricting access to most of the System Preferences. Your
Preferences tab should match Figure 13-12.

547

Figure 13-12. *Identify the System Preferences we want users to be able to interact with and those that we want to restrict*

Pro Tip   Remember that this will restrict access to these System Preferences for all users of the machine. If you want to allow administrators to disable management, be sure to also configure the **Login Window** payload and enable this ability in the **Options** tab.

Finally, we are going to click the **Functionality** tab. Here we will check the box next to **Lock desktop picture** and provide a **Desktop picture path** to the *Color Burst 1.jpg* image as shown in Figure 13-13. This will set our wallpaper to match everyone else in the office and set a consistent user experience between Mac and Windows clients.

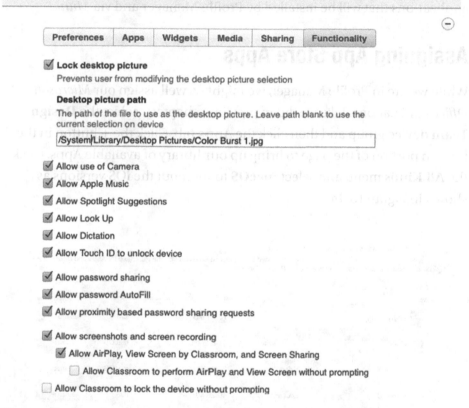

Figure 13-13. Configuring the path to a standard Desktop wallpaper

Pro Tip   In *macOS Catalina*, the path to the Desktop Pictures directory is different than previous versions of the operating system. In older versions it is */Library/Desktop Pictures/,* and in *Catalina* it is */System/Library/Desktop Pictures/*.

Once you have made all of these changes, click the **OK** button to close the Configuration Profile editor and then click the **Save** button.

Configuring Applications

We are nearly ready to deploy these new Macs. The final step is to assign applications that will be installed by Profile Manager and via *Munki*.

Assigning App Store Apps

While we are in Profile Manager, we might as well assign our *Microsoft Office* applications. Like we did in previous chapters, select the **Design Team** device group and then click the **Apps** tab. Click the + button in the bottom portion of the page to bring up our library of available Apps. Click the **All Kinds** menu and select **macOS** to filter out the iOS versions as shown in Figure 13-14.

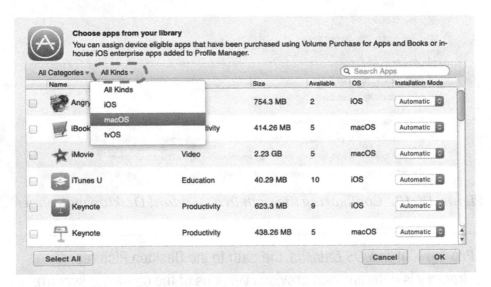

Figure 13-14. *Select macOS to filter out Apps that are not compatible with macOS*

Assign the *macOS* versions of *Microsoft Word, Excel, PowerPoint,* and *Outlook* to our Device Group and leave the default **Installation Mode** as **Automatic**. Click **OK** to assign the applications and then click **Save** to apply them.

Pro Tip   If you see a message about not having enough licenses for these Apps, you can always go back to the Volume Purchase area of the Apple School Manager/Apple Business Manager portal and acquire additional seats.

Importing Munki Packages

I have downloaded the *Adobe Dreamweaver CC* install package and a copy of *Atom*, a developer tool that is commonly used in the industry. Following the same steps that we used in Chapter 10, I will use the `munkiimport` command to get both of these added to our *Munki* environment. I'm going to set them both to install/uninstall unattended, and I'll add them both to the *testing* Catalog.

Pro Tip   If you do not have access to *Adobe Dreamweaver* for this exercise, that is okay. Simply substitute any other application. The purpose is to install a couple of applications that aren't available in the App Store with *Munki. Dreamweaver* was used because it fits in with the scenario.

Once you finish importing the packages, open *MunkiAdmin* and take a look at the list of software packages. Your *MunkiAdmin* window should look similar to Figure 13-15.

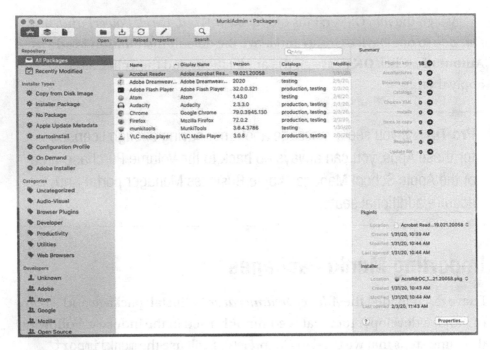

Figure 13-15. *The full list of packages that we have imported up to this point*

Go ahead and test the installation of your new applications on one of your test machines. Once you are satisfied with the results, we can move the new packages into the ***production*** Catalog and add them to the ***site_ default*** Manifest. Using the **Catalog** view as shown in Figure 13-16, **check the boxes** next to *Adobe Dreamweaver CC* and *Atom*. **Save** and **reload** the *MunkiAdmin* console.

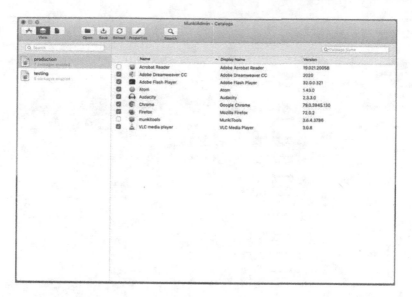

Figure 13-16. *Enable Dreamweaver and Atom in the production Catalog*

Next, click the **Manifest** view and select our ***site_default*** Manifest. **Double-click** to open it. We are going to modify our **Managed Installs** by adding *Atom*. Click the + button and select *Atom*. When complete, your **Managed Installs** tab should look like Figure 13-17.

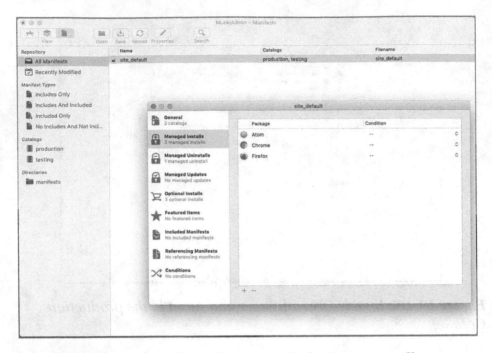

Figure 13-17. *Managed Installs now includes Atom as well as Chrome and Firefox*

Click the **Optional Installs** tab and add *Adobe Dreamweaver CC* to the list. When complete, your **Optional Installs** tab should look like Figure 13-18.

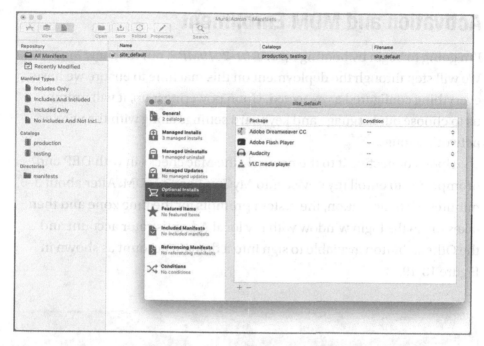

Figure 13-18. *Add Adobe Dreamweaver CC to the Optional Installs list*

Close the ***site_default*** Manifest and click **Save** and **Reload**. When complete, you can close out of the *MunkiAdmin* application. Our applications and settings are now ready to go. Now we need to do a test deployment on one of our new Macs.

Deployment

Our deployment process is going to consist of two stages. The first stage will involve unboxing the hardware, setting it up on the desk, and booting it up. As we step through the *Setup Assistant*, our Mac will connect to Apple's DEP server and then get redirected to enroll in our Profile Manager MDM. Once it is live in Profile Manager, we will use the MDM management commands to enable *Apple Remote Desktop*. The second stage will consist of using ARD to install *Munki,* and then the *Managed Software Center* will finish installing the required applications listed in the Manifest.

Activation and MDM Enrollment

I'm going to begin by booting up *101-01-2019MBP*, our first new Mac.
We will step through the deployment on this machine to ensure we have
everything configured as expected. Upon powering it up, it will prompt
us to choose our language and keyboard settings along with the wireless
network settings.

Upon connecting it to the network, the Mac checks in with DEP and
prompts me to enroll my device into MyCompany's MDM. After about 3–5
minutes of configuration, the system prompts for the time zone and then
takes me to the login window with my local Administrator account and
the Other... button available to sign into a domain account as shown in
Figure 13-19.

Figure 13-19. *After successfully applying our settings, our login
window features the Other... button for signing in as a domain user*

Enabling Apple Remote Desktop

We are not going to sign in yet. First, we need to finish installing *MunkiTools* and our other applications. If I go back to Profile Manager and look at my system, I will see that it is no longer a Placeholder in my Devices list but an actual computer record. Now we can now interact with it using the MDM management tools. In Profile Manager, **click** the **101-01-2019MBP** device to select it and then click the **Action** button to show the Management Tools pop-up menu. Select **Enable Remote Desktop** as shown in Figure 13-20.

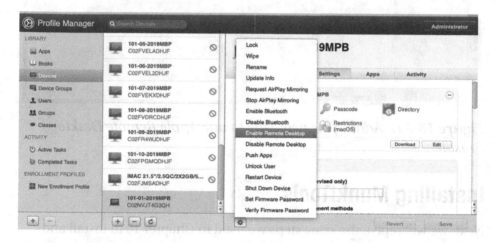

Figure 13-20. *Using Profile Manager to enable Apple Remote Desktop access*

Confirm that you want to enable Remote Desktop. After a few minutes, open *Apple Remote Desktop* and use the **scanner** to search the network. You should find a machine named *101-01-2019MBP* as shown in Figure 13-21. **Drag and drop** the found computer record into the **All Computers** group and authenticate with the local Administrator account that Profile Manager created for us to add the machine to our ARD console.

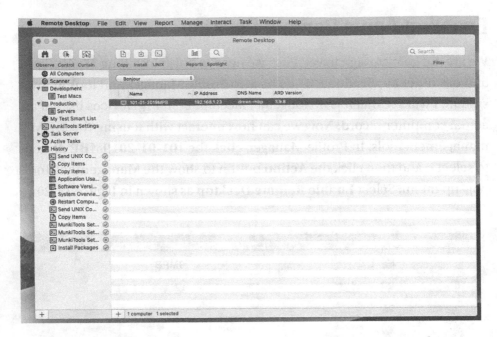

Figure 13-21. *Adding the new Mac to our Apple Remote Desktop console*

Installing MunkiTools

Next, we will repeat the same steps we used in Chapter 10 to install and configure *MunkiTools*. If you saved the **MunkiTools Settings** Unix script, it should be very simple. Install the *MunkiTools.pkg* and run the Unix script on our new computer as shown in Figure 13-22. This will configure it to point to our *munki_repo* and assign it to *the site_default* Manifest.

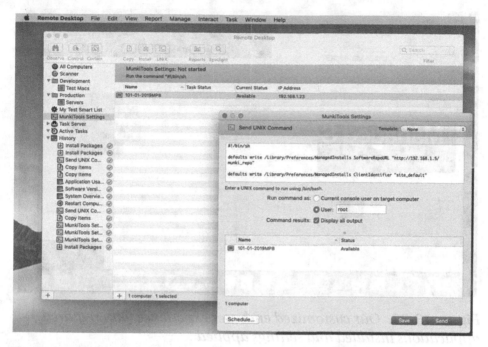

Figure 13-22.   *Install the MunkiTools.pkg package and then run the Unix script to modify the ManagedInstalls.plist to point to our Munki environment*

When complete, restart the computer, and we can sign in as our end user and see that the machine is ready for use.

End-User Sign-In

Using one of the test user accounts that we created for our new hires, sign into the test Mac. As you can see from Figure 13-23, we have all of our applications, settings, and network services ready to go.

Figure 13-23. *Our customized end-user experience with required applications installed and settings applied*

- Logging in as the *Windows* domain user account worked as expected and prompted us to change the default password at first login.

- *Atom* is installed, and *Munki Managed Software Center* is showing available additional applications.

- *Microsoft Word, Excel, PowerPoint*, and *Outlook* are all available in the Applications folder.

- The wallpaper is set to our *Color Burst 1.jpg* selection.

- System Preferences are limited to those we specified.

- The user may browse available Windows printers and add the one they need.

- The *Main Office Shared* network drive is mounted and available in the Finder.

Pro Tip   On *Mojave* and *Catalina*, you may need to browse using the **Network** icon in the Finder for the *Main Office Shared* drive. When selected in the Finder, it should not prompt the user for credentials and instead simply map the drive by passing the AD credentials from the Mac to the Windows server.

If you find something that isn't working as expected, go back into Profile Manager and tweak the settings. Each time you make a change and click Save, it will immediately apply the new settings to the test machine. Once you have confirmed that our deployment works the way we want it to, you are ready to deploy the other nine Macs using the same two-stage process.

Where to Go from Here

In this chapter, we demonstrated how you can use *Munki*, *Profile Manager*, and existing *Microsoft* enterprise solutions to stage new *macOS* clients to be added to an office environment. While this is an effective demo of some of the most important features, there are many more options to explore as you plan out your Macintosh support strategy. I would encourage you to explore, experiment, and get involved in the Apple system administrator community online.

This book has provided you with a solid foundation to build on when it comes to managing a modern deployment of Apple hardware. Apple's platforms continue to change and evolve with each release. I would strongly recommend joining Apple's developer community for no other reason than to get access to preview and beta releases of *macOS* and *iOS* every summer. Every new iteration will bring new challenges and new opportunities, and often you will be forced to keep pace as newer hardware will require the new operating systems.

Index

A

Active Directory (AD), 248

Active Directory integration,
   macOS

   Configuration Profile, 469

   Directory payload, 470

   Domain Admin account, 461, 462

   domain name, 460, 461

   domain payload, 471

   Don President Network
      account, 466, 467

   dsconfigad tool, 472

   login options pane, 460

   Mimic Microsoft Group Policy
      (*see* Microsoft Group Policy)

   mobile account, 467

   101-2019MPRO, 469

   MyCompany domain, 462, 463

   Network user account, 463, 464

   PCs organizational unit,
      458, 459

   record creation, 459

   script, 472–476

   Sharing System Preference, 457

   user account, 466, 468

   user desktop, 464

   Windows domain,
      unreachable, 465

APFS snapshot, 31, 32

Apple Business Manager, (*see*
     Apple School Manager)

Apple Configurator

   Configuration Profiles

     BYOD devices, 165, 168

     iOS and iPadOS payloads,
       157, 159–161

     user installable
       configuration, create,
       166, 167

     VPN settings, 161, 162, 164,
       169, 170

   iOS devices, exploring, 171–173

   iOS devices modify

     Blueprints, 182–190

     device name, 179

     Home Screen Layout,
       180, 181

     wallpaper, 181, 182

   iPads and *iPhones*, 145, 146

   macOS, 146, 147

   organization and supervision
     identity, 150–152

   preparing device, 153–155

   side loading apps, 174–177

   side loading documents, 178

   tools

© Drew Smith 2020

D. Smith, *Apple macOS and iOS System Administration*,
https://doi.org/10.1007/978-1-4842-5820-0

W, X, Y, Z

Printed in the United States
By Bookmasters